D0088189

ENVIRONMENT

00/01

Nineteenth Edition

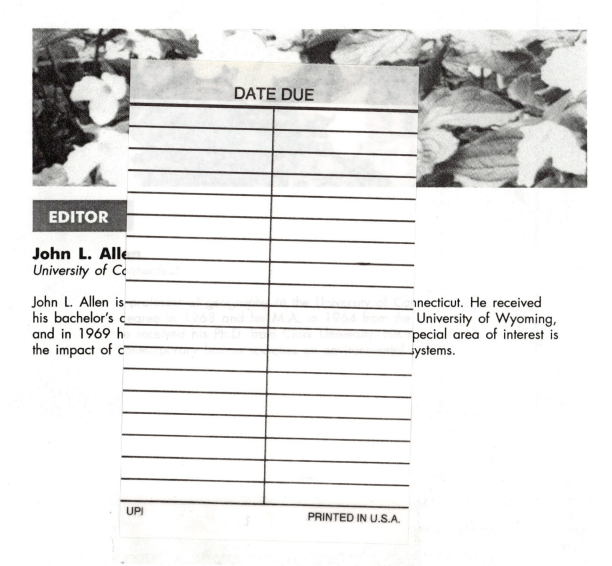

EDITOR

John L. Allen
University of Connecticut

John L. Allen is _____ of geography at the University of Connecticut. He received his bachelor's degree in 1963 and his M.A. in 1964 from the University of Wyoming, and in 1969 he received his Ph.D. from Clark University. His special area of interest is the impact of contemporary human activities on fragile natural systems.

DATE DUE

UPI   PRINTED IN U.S.A.

Dushkin/McGraw-Hill
Sluice Dock, Guilford, Connecticut 06437

Visit us on the Internet
http://www.dushkin.com/annualeditions/

Credits

1. The Global Environment: An Emerging World View
Unit photo—© 2000 by PhotoDisc, Inc.
2. The World's Population: People and Hunger
Unit photo—United Nations photo by J. P. Laffont.
3. Energy: Present and Future Problems
Unit photo—Courtesy of EPA/Documerica.
4. Biosphere: Endangered Species
Unit photo—United Nations photo by M. Gonzalez.
5. Resources: Land, Water, and Air
Unit photo—United Nations photo by Saw Lwin.
6. Pollution: The Hazards of Growth
Unit photo—Courtesy of EPA/Documerica.

Cataloging in Publication Data
Main entry under title: Annual Editions: Environment. 2000/2001.
1. Environment—Periodicals. 2. Ecology—Periodicals. I. Allen, John L., *comp.*
II. Title: Environment.
ISBN 0–07–236549–8   301.31'05   79–644216   ISSN 0272–9008

Nineteenth Edition

Cover image © 2000 Tom Lyon

Printed in the United States of America   1234567890BAHBAH543210   Printed on Recycled Paper

To the Reader

In publishing ANNUAL EDITIONS we recognize the enormous role played by the magazines, newspapers, and journals of the public press in providing current, first-rate educational information in a broad spectrum of interest areas. Many of these articles are appropriate for students, researchers, and professionals seeking accurate, current material to help bridge the gap between principles and theories and the real world. These articles, however, become more useful for study when those of lasting value are carefully collected, organized, indexed, and reproduced in a low-cost format, which provides easy and permanent access when the material is needed. That is the role played by ANNUAL EDITIONS.

New to ANNUAL EDITIONS is the inclusion of related World Wide Web sites. These sites have been selected by our editorial staff to represent some of the best resources found on the World Wide Web today. Through our carefully developed topic guide, we have linked these Web resources to the articles covered in this ANNUAL EDITIONS reader. We think that you will find this volume useful, and we hope that you will take a moment to visit us on the Web at *http://www.dushkin.com* to tell us what you think.

As a new millennium begins, environmental dilemmas long foreseen by natural and social scientists have begun to emerge in a number of guises: population/food imbalances, problems of energy scarcity, acid rain, toxic and hazardous wastes, ozone depletion, water shortages, massive soil erosion, global atmospheric pollution and possible climate change, forest dieback and tropical deforestation, and the highest rates of plant and animal extinction the world has known in 65 million years.

These and other problems have worsened in spite of an increasing amount of national and international attention to environmental issues and increased environmental awareness and legislation. The problems have resulted from centuries of exploitation and unwise use of resources, accelerated recently by the short-sighted public policies that have favored the short-term, expedient approach to problem solving over longer-term economic and ecological good sense. In Africa, for example, the drive to produce enough food to support a growing population has caused the use of increasingly fragile and marginal resources, resulting in the dryland deterioration that brings famine to that troubled continent. Similar social and economic problems have contributed to massive deforestation in Middle and South America and Southeast Asia.

The economic problems generated by resource scarcity have caused the relaxation of environmental quality standards or have contributed to the refusal to enact environmentally sound protective measures that are viewed as too costly. The lack of adequate environmental policy has been particularly apparent in those countries that are striving to become economically developed. But even in the more highly developed nations, economic concerns tend to favor slackening environmental controls. In the interests of maintaining jobs for the timber industry, for example, many of the last areas of old-growth forests in the United States are imperiled, and in the interests of maintaining agricultural productivity at all costs, destructive and toxic chemicals continue to be used on the nation's farmlands. In addition, concerns over energy availability have created the need for foreign policy and military action to protect the developed nations' access to cheap oil and have prompted increasing reliance on technological quick fixes.

There is some reason to hope that, globally, a new environmental consciousness is awakening at the dawning of a new millennium. The dissolution of the Soviet Union lifted the Iron Curtain, and the environmental horror stories that have emerged from Eastern Europe and the newly independent states that made up the former USSR have given new incentives to international cooperation. International conferences have been held on global warming and other environmental issues, and there is some evidence of an increased international desire to do something about environmental quality before it is too late.

The articles contained in *Annual Editions: Environment 00/01* have been selected for the light they shed on these and other problems and issues. The selection process was aimed at including material that will be readily assimilated by the general reader. Additionally, every effort has been made to choose articles that encourage an understanding of the nature of the environmental problems that beset us and how, with wisdom and knowledge and the proper perspective, they can be solved or at least mitigated. Accordingly, the selections in this book have been chosen more for their intellectual content than for their emotional tone. They have been arranged into an order of topics—the global environment, population and food, energy, the biosphere, resources, and pollution—that lends itself to a progressive understanding of the causes and effects of human modifications of Earth's environmental systems. We will not be protected against the ecological consequences of human actions by remaining ignorant of them. Although the knowledge gained through the use of this book may not allow any of us to escape the environmental predicament, it should ensure that we do not continue to act and react in ways that will make that predicament worse.

The *World Wide Web* sites in this edition can be used to further explore the topics. These sites will be cross-referenced by number in the *topic guide*. In addition, this edition contains both a newly refreshed *Environmental Information Retrieval* guide and *glossary*.

Readers can have input into the next edition of *Annual Editions: Environment* by completing and returning the postpaid *article rating form* at the back of the book.

John L. Allen
Editor

Contents

UNIT 1

The Global Environment: An Emerging World View

Four selections provide information on the current state of Earth and the changes we will face.

The concepts in bold italics are developed in the article. For further expansion please refer to the Topic Guide, the Glossary, and the Index.

UNIT 2

The World's Population: People and Hunger

Four selections examine the problems the world will have in feeding its ever-increasing population.

The concepts in bold italics are developed in the article. For further expansion please refer to the Topic Guide, the Glossary, and the Index.

UNIT 3

Energy: Present and Future Problems

Four articles consider the problems
of meeting present and future
energy needs. Alternative energy
sources are also examined.

UNIT 4

Biosphere: Endangered Species

Six articles examine the problems in the world's biosphere. Not only are plants and animals endangered, but many human groups are also disastrously affected by deforestation and primitive agricultural policies.

UNIT 5

Resources: Land, Water, and Air

Seven selections discuss the environmental problems affecting our land, water, and air resources.

The concepts in bold italics are developed in the article. For further expansion please refer to the Topic Guide, the Glossary, and the Index.

ix

The concepts in bold italics are developed in the article. For further expansion please refer to the Topic Guide, the Glossary, and the Index.

UNIT 6

Pollution: The Hazards of Growth

Five selections weigh the
environmental impacts of the
growth of human population.

Topic Guide

This topic guide suggests how the selections and World Wide Web sites found in the next section of this book relate to topics of traditional concern to students and professionals in the field of environmental studies. It is useful for locating interrelated articles and Web sites for reading and research. The guide is arranged alphabetically according to topic.

The relevant Web sites, which are numbered and annotated on pages 4 and 5, are easily identified by the Web icon (◎) under the topic articles. By linking the articles and the Web sites by topic, this ANNUAL EDITIONS reader becomes a powerful learning and research tool.

TOPIC AREA	TREATED IN	TOPIC AREA	TREATED IN
Agricultural Biotechnology	6. The Emperor's New Crops ◎ *11, 12, 13, 14*	**Energy Research**	10. End of Cheap Oil ◎ *15, 16, 17, 18, 19*
Agricultural Chemicals	16. Organic Revolution 29. Lessons from Lake Apopka ◎ *11, 12, 13, 14*	**Energy Resource**	10. End of Cheap Oil ◎ *15, 16, 17, 18, 19*
Agriculture	8. Food Scarcity ◎ *11, 12, 13, 14*	**Environmental Change**	4. Crossing the Threshold ◎ *2, 4, 10, 17, 32*
Air and Water Quality	1. Global Challenge ◎ *5, 6, 7, 25, 28*	**Environmental Cost**	9. King Coal's Weakening Grip on Power ◎ *4, 10, 32*
Animal Populations	18. Ultimate Survivor ◎ *1, 20, 21, 22, 23*	**Environmental Crises**	2. Nemesis Effect 19. Tragedy of the Commons: 30 Years Later ◎ *2, 4, 10, 32*
Atmospheric and Oceanic Systems	1. Global Challenge ◎ *5, 6, 7, 25, 28*	**Environmental Deterioration**	8. Food Scarcity ◎ *2, 4, 10, 17*
Atmospheric Pollution	30. Earth's Last Gasp? ◎ *30, 32*	**Environmental Health**	26. Making Things Last: Reinventing Our Material Culture
Biodiversity	13. Planet of Weeds 15. Alien Invasion ◎ *20, 21, 22, 23*	**Environmental Systems**	2. Nemesis Effect ◎ *2, 4, 10, 32*
Biological Extinction	13. Planet of Weeds ◎ *29, 31*	**Environmental Threshold**	4. Crossing the Threshold ◎ *2, 4, 10, 17, 32*
Biotic Spills	27. Crawling Out of the Pipe ◎ *30, 32*	**Experimental Farm**	20. Lessons from the Land Institute ◎ *1, 3, 7, 21*
Climate Change	24. Great Climate Flip-Flop ◎ *24, 25, 27, 28*	**Fertilizer**	28. Recycling Human Waste ◎ *7, 9, 10*
Conventional Energy Source	11. Sunlight Brightens Our Energy Future ◎ *24, 28*	**Fossil Fuel**	9. King's Coal's Weakening Grip on Power ◎ *4, 10, 32*
Conventional Oil	10. End of Cheap Oil ◎ *15, 17, 19*	**Genetic Engineering**	6. Emperor's New Crops ◎ *1, 3, 29*
Demographic Transition	5. Population Surprise ◎ *11, 12, 13, 14*	**Global Commons**	1. Global Challenge ◎ *6, 7, 8, 24, 25, 28*
Developing Countries	7. Technology of Hope ◎ *9, 10, 11, 12, 13, 14, 16, 29, 32*	**Global Economy**	4. Crossing the Threshold 8. Food Scarcity ◎ *6, 7, 8, 11, 12, 13, 14*
Economic Development	7. Technology of Hope ◎ *16, 32*	**Global Warming**	24. Great Climate Flip-Flop 25. Last Tango in Buenos Aires 30. Earth's Last Gasp? ◎ *2, 6, 7, 8, 20, 24, 27, 28*
Electrical Energy	12. Bull Market in Wind Energy ◎ *15, 17, 18, 19*	**Government Agencies**	18. Ultimate Survivor ◎ *1, 2, 5, 19*
Endangered Species	15. Alien Invasion ◎ *1, 2, 20, 21, 22, 23*	**Greenhouse Effect**	24. Great Climate Flip-Flop ◎ *24*
Energy Cost	9. King's Coal's Weakening Grip on Power ◎ *15, 16, 17, 18, 19*	**Greenhouse Gases**	25. Last Tango in Buenos Aires 30. Earth's Last Gasp? ◎ *24*

● AE: Environment

The following World Wide Web sites have been carefully researched and selected to support the articles found in this reader. If you are interested in learning more about specific topics found in this book, these Web sites are a good place to start. The sites are cross-referenced by number and appear in the topic guide on the previous two pages. Also, you can link to these Web sites through our DUSHKIN ONLINE support site at *http://www.dushkin.com/online/*.

The following sites were available at the time of publication. Visit our Web site—we update DUSHKIN ONLINE regularly to reflect any changes.

General Sources

1. Britannica's Internet Guide
http://www.britannica.com
This site presents extensive links to material on world geography and culture, encompassing material on wildlife, human lifestyles, and the environment.

2. EnviroLink
http://www.envirolink.org
One of the world's largest environmental information clearing houses, EnviroLink is a grassroots nonprofit organization that unites organizations and volunteers around the world and provides up-to-date information and resources.

3. Library of Congress
http://www.loc.gov
Examine this extensive Web site to learn about resource tools, library services/resources, exhibitions, and databases in many different subfields of environmental studies.

4. SocioSite: Sociological Subject Areas
http://www.pscw.uva.nl/sociosite/TOPICS/
This huge sociological site from the University of Amsterdam provides many discussions and references of interest to students of the environment, such as the links to information on ecology and consumerism.

5. U.S. Geological Survey
http://www.usgs.gov
This site and its many links are replete with information and resources in environmental studies, from explanations of El Niño to discussion of concerns about water resources.

The Global Environment: An Emerging World View

6. Earth Science Enterprise
http://www.earth.nasa.gov
This site will direct you to information about NASA's Mission to Planet Earth program and its Science of the Earth System. Surf here to learn about satellites, El Niño, and even "strategic visions" of interest to environmentalists.

7. National Geographic Society
http://www.nationalgeographic.com
This site provides links to National Geographic's huge archive of maps, articles, and other documents. There is a great deal of material related to the atmosphere, the oceans, and other environmental topics.

8. Santa Fe Institute
http://acoma.santafe.edu
This home page of the Santa Fe Institute—a nonprofit, multidisciplinary research and education center—will lead to many interesting links related to its primary goal: to create a new kind of scientific research community, pursuing emerging science. A variety of topics related to the environment are addressed.

9. United Nations
http://www.unsystem.org
Visit this official Web site locator for the United Nations System of Organizations to get a sense of the scope of international environmental inquiry today. Various UN organizations concern themselves with everything from maritime law to habitat protection to agriculture.

10. United Nations Environment Programme
http://www.unep.ch
Consult this home page of UNEP for links to critical topics of concern to environmentalists, including desertification, migratory species, and the impact of trade on the environment. The site will direct you to useful databases and global resource information.

The World's Population: People and Hunger

11. The Hunger Project
http://www.thp.org
Browse through this nonprofit organization's site to explore the ways in which it attempts to achieve its goal: the sustainable end to global hunger through leadership at all levels of society. The Hunger Project contends that the persistence of hunger is at the heart of the major security issues that threaten our planet.

12. Penn Library Resources
http://www.library.upenn.edu/resources/websitest.html
This vast site is rich in links to information about virtually every subject you can think of in environmental studies. Its extensive population and demography resources address such concerns as migration, family planning, and health and nutrition in various world regions.

13. World Health Organization
http://www.who.int
This home page of the World Health Organization will provide links to a wealth of statistical and analytical information about health and the environment in the developing world.

14. WWW Virtual Library: Demography & Population Studies
http://demography.anu.edu.au/VirtualLibrary/
This is a definitive guide to demography and population studies. A multitude of important links to information about global poverty and hunger can be found here.

Energy: Present and Future Problems

15. Alternative Energy Institute, Inc.
http://www.altenergy.org
On this site created by a nonprofit organization, you can learn about the impacts of the use of conventional fuels on the environment. Learn, too, about research work on new forms of energy.

16. Communications for a Sustainable Future
gopher://csf.colorado.edu
This site will lead to information on topics in international environmental sustainability. It pays particular at-

tention to the political economics of protecting the environment.

17. Energy and the Environment: Resources for a Networked World
http://zebu.uoregon.edu/energy.html
This University of Oregon site points you to an extensive array of materials having to do with energy sources—both renewable and nonrenewable—as well as other topics of interest to students of the environment.

18. Institute for Global Communication/EcoNet
http://www.igc.org/igc/issues/energy/
This environmentally friendly site provides links to dozens of governmental, organizational, and commercial sites having to do with energy sources. Resources address energy efficiency, renewable generating sources, global warming, and more.

19. U.S. Department of Energy
http://www.doe.gov
Scrolling through the links provided by this Department of Energy home page will lead you to information about fossil fuels and a variety of sustainable/renewable energy sources.

Biosphere: Endangered Species

20. Friends of the Earth
http://www.foe.co.uk/index.html
Friends of the Earth, a nonprofit organization based in the United Kingdom, pursues a number of campaigns to protect the Earth and its living creatures. This site has links to many important environmental sites, covering such broad topics as ozone depletion, soil erosion, and biodiversity.

21. Smithsonian Institution Web Site
http://www.si.edu
Looking through this site, which will provide access to many of the enormous resources of the Smithsonian, offers a sense of the biological diversity that is threatened by humans' unsound environmental policies and practices.

22. Tennessee Green
http://korrnet.org/tngreen/
Visit this site to find a wealth of information related to sustainability and ways that we can "lighten our load on the environment." It provides links to other environmental sites and guidance to articles and books.

23. World Wildlife Federation
http://www.wwf.org
This home page of the WWF leads to an extensive array of links to information about endangered species, wildlife management and preservation, and more. It provides many suggestions for how to take an active part in protecting the biosphere.

Resources: Land, Water, and Air

24. Global Climate Change
http://www.puc.state.oh.us/consumer/gcc/index.html
PUCO (Public Utilities Commission of Ohio) aims for this site to serve as a clearinghouse of information related to global climate change. Its extensive links provide for explanation of the science and chronology of global climate change, acronyms, definitions, and more.

25. National Oceanic and Atmospheric Administration
http://www.noaa.gov
Through this home page of NOAA, part of the U.S. Department of Commerce, find information about coastal issues, fisheries, climate, and more. The site provides many links to research materials and other Web resources.

26. National Operational Hydrologic Remote Sensing Center
http://www.nohrsc.nws.gov
Flood images are available at this site of the NOHRSC, which works with the U.S. National Weather Service to track weather-related information.

27. Virtual Seminar in Global Political Economy/Global Cities & Social Movements
http://csf.colorado.edu/gpe/gpe95b/resources.html
This site of Internet resources is rich in links to subjects of interest in regional environmental studies, covering topics such as sustainable cities, megacities, and urban planning. Links to many international nongovernmental organizations are included.

28. Websurfers Biweekly Earth Science Review
http://shell.rmi.net/~michaelg/index.html
This is a biweekly compilation of Internet sites devoted to the terrestrial and planetary sciences. It includes a list of hyperlinks to related earth science sites and news items. A great deal of information about climate and the atmosphere can be found here.

Pollution: The Hazards of Growth

29. IISDnet
http://iisd1.iisd.ca
This site of the International Institute for Sustainable Development, a Canadian organization, presents information through links on business and sustainable development, developing ideas, and Hot Topics. Linkages is its multimedia resource for environment and development policymakers.

30. School of Labor and Industrial Relations: Hot Links
http://www.lir.msu.edu/hotlinks/
This Michigan State University SLIR page goes to sites regarding industrial relations throughout the world. It has links to U.S. government statistics, newspapers and libraries, international intergovernmental organizations, and more. With this level of access, it should be possible to research virtually every labor and industrial relations topic of relevance in environmental studies.

31. Space Research Institute
http://arc.iki.rssi.ru/Welcome.html
For a change of pace, browse through this home page of Russia's Space Research Institute for information on its Environment Monitoring Information Systems, the IKI Satellite Situation Center, and its Data Archive.

32. Worldwatch Institute
http://www.worldwatch.org
The Worldwatch Institute is dedicated to fostering the evolution of an environmentally sustainable society in which human needs are met without threatening the health of the natural environment. This site provides access to *World Watch Magazine* and *State of the World 2000*. Click on Alerts and Press Briefings for discussions of current problems.

We highly recommend that you review our Web site for expanded information and our other product lines. We are continually updating and adding links to our Web site in order to offer you the most usable and useful information that will support and expand the value of your Annual Editions. You can reach us at: *http://www.dushkin.com/annualeditions/.*

www.dushkin.com/online/

Unit 1

Key Points to Consider

❖ What are "global commons"? How does management of commonly held resources pose different problems from management of other kinds of resources?

❖ How are environmental systems linked together and how do they tend to converge? Illustrate an example of a synergistic environmental problem such as the link between climate changes and forest fires.

❖ What is meant by the term "scenarios" and how does the use of scenario analysis aid policymakers in coming up with appropriate environmental strategies? How does the concept of sustainability fit into the various scenarios describing the world's future?

❖ What are some social thresholds of environmental problems? How do environmental events like hurricanes increase both public awareness and government and corporate action on environmental issues?

 **Links** | **www.dushkin.com/online/**

These sites are annotated on pages 4 and 5.

More than three decades after the celebration of the first Earth Day in 1970, public apprehension over the environmental future of the planet has reached levels unprecedented even during the late 1960s and early 1970s "Age of Aquarius." No longer are those concerned about the environment dismissed as "ecofreaks" and "tree-huggers." Many serious scientists have joined the rising clamor for environmental protection, as have the more traditional environmentally conscious public interest groups. There are a number of reasons for this increased environmental awareness. Some of these reasons arise from environmental events. But more arise simply from the increase in global information systems and the maturation of concepts about the global nature of environmental processes. For example, the raising of the Iron Curtain has also allowed information and ideas to pass more freely between East and West.

Much of what has been learned through this increased information flow, particularly by Western observers, has been of an environmentally ravaged Eastern Europe and Russia—a chilling forecast of what other industrialized nations will become in the near future unless strict international environmental measures are put in place. For perhaps the first time ever, countries are beginning to recognize that environmental problems have no boundaries and that international cooperation is the only way to solve them.

The subtitle of this first unit, "An Emerging World View," is an optimistic assessment of the future: a future in which less money is spent on defense and more on environmental protection and cleanup. The authors of the Worldwatch Institute's *State of the World* have recently described a new world order in which political influence will be based more upon leadership in environmental and economic issues than upon military might. Perhaps it is far too early to make such optimistic predictions, to name the decade of the 1990s "The Decade of the Environment," or to conclude that the world's nations—developed and underdeveloped—will begin to recognize that Earth's environment is a single unit. Nevertheless, there is growing international realization—aided by the "information superhighway"—that we are all, as environmental activists have been saying for decades, inhabitants of "Spaceship Earth" and will survive or succumb together.

The articles selected for this unit have been chosen to illustrate this increasingly global perspective on environmental problems and the degree to which their solutions must be linked to political, economic, and social problems and solutions. In the lead piece of the unit, "The Global Challenge," author Michael Glantz, program director of the Environmental and Societal Impacts Group of the National Center for Atmospheric Research, discusses the global commons of Earth's atmospheric and oceanic systems. These interlocking systems, he notes, are remarkably resilient, but their resilience is being sorely tested by continuing human demands upon them. Adopting the adages of "what

goes up, must come down" and "what goes around, comes around," Glantz suggests that nearly everything that people do has significance for both the atmosphere and oceans. Our chief problem is in managing a common property resource.

The second selection in the unit is also directed toward the interconnectedness of environmental systems and toward new concepts and ways of thinking about the environment and human impact. In "The Nemesis Effect" Worldwatch Institute research associate Chris Bright describes the manner in which the growing number of overlapping stresses on ecosystems might cause those systems to decline rapidly and unexpectedly. Bright presents "a spreading matrix of trouble" in which he lists 13 of the worst pressures we are inflicting on the planet and on ourselves and shows how these corrosive forces interact. (He suggests that complex systems of policies that are more effective than any of their constituent parts should be developed to deal with systems of environmental problems that are more complex than the problems of any of their discrete parts.)

In "Windows on the Future: Global Scenarios & Sustainability" Gilberto Gallopín and Paul Raskin of the Stockholm Environmental Institute use scenario analysis to clarify views of the future world and to evaluate critical issues for the global environment. They identify three basic visions of the future: Conventional Worlds, in which current trends continue until environmental collapse; Barbarization, in which the world quickly descends into chaos with the onset of major environmental problems; and Great Transitions, in which the world develops sustainable systems that prevent either of the other two scenarios from occurring. Gallopín and Raskin agree that, irrespective of economic development, the destinies of the world's countries are linked, and that "only a truly global solution can achieve a humane and sustainable future."

The prospects of arriving at such a solution, given the global nature of the problem, is the focus of the fourth article in this section. In "Crossing the Threshold: Early Signs of an Environmental Awakening," Lester R. Brown, president of the Worldwatch Institute, notes that in spite of the spate of environmental disruptions capturing headlines (global warming, storms, floods, forest fires), the world may be approaching a social threshold that could profoundly change our way of looking at the environment profoundly. Ecologists speak of thresholds as crucial parameters beyond which ecosystems change dramatically. Brown sees equally dramatic potential changes in social systems on the horizon. Among such changes are breakthroughs in support for alternative energy sources such as wind and solar power, the shifting views on material use and population, and the recognition that resources must be sustainable. What is most important, Brown claims, is that while changes in attitude and perception have, in the past, have taken place among members of the general population, now they are taking place in government agencies and in the corporate boardrooms.

The Global Challenge

M*ICHAEL* H. G*LANTZ*

Circulating freely around the planet, the atmosphere and oceans are shared resources whose resiliency is being tested by ever-growing human demands.

The atmosphere and the oceans are fluids that encircle the globe. Their movements can be described in physical and mathematical terms, or even by some popular adages: "what goes up, must come down" and "what goes around, comes around."

The atmosphere and oceans are two of Earth's truly global commons. In cycles that vary from days to centuries to millions of years, air and water circulate interactively around the globe irrespective of national boundaries and territorial claims.

With regard to the first adage, pollutants emitted into the atmosphere must come down somewhere on Earth's surface—unless, like the chlorofluorocarbons (CFCs), they can escape into the stratosphere until they are broken down by the Sun's rays. Depending on the form of the pollutant (gaseous or particulate), its size, or the height at which it has been ejected into the atmosphere, it can stay airborne for short or long periods. So, pollutants expelled into the air in one country and on one continent may make their way to other countries and continents. The same can be said of the various pollutants that are cast into the ocean. "What goes around, comes around" clearly applies to the global commons.

As human demands on the atmosphere and oceans escalate, the pressures on the commons are clearly increasing. Defining the boundaries between acceptable human impacts and crisis impacts is a demanding and rather subjective task.

The Atmosphere

The atmosphere is owned by no nation, but in a sense it belongs to all nations. Several types of human activity interact with geophysical processes to affect the atmosphere in ways that engender crisis situations. The most obvious example of local effects is urban air pollution resulting from automobile emissions, home heating and cooling, and industrial processes. The Denver "brown cloud" is a case in point, as is the extreme pollution in Mexico City. Such pollution can occur within one political jurisdiction or across state, provincial, or international borders. Air pollution is one of those problems to which almost everyone in the urban area contributes.

Acid rain is an example of pollution of a regional atmospheric commons. Industrial processes release pollutants, which can then interact with the atmosphere and be washed out by rainfall. Acid rain has caused the health of forest ecosystems to deteriorate in such locations as the

northeastern part of North America, central Europe, and Scandinavia. The trajectories of airborne industrial pollutants moving from highly industrialized areas across these regions have been studied. The data tend to support the contention that while acid rain is a regional commons problem, it is also a problem of global interest.

A nation can put any chemical effluents it deems necessary for its well-being into its own airspace. But then the atmosphere's fluid motion can move those effluents across international borders. The purpose of the tall smokestack, for example, was to put effluents higher into the air, so they would be carried away and dispersed farther from their source. The tall stacks, in essence, turned local air pollution problems into regional ones. In many instances, they converted national pollution into an international problem.

Climate as a Global Commons

There is a difference between the atmosphere as a commons and the climate as a commons. Various societies have emitted a wide range of chemicals into the atmosphere, with little understanding of their potential effects on climate. For example, are industrial processes that produce large amounts of carbon dioxide (which contributes to atmospheric warming) or sulfur dioxide (which contributes to atmospheric cooling and acid rain) altering global climate? There seems to be a growing consensus among scientists that these alterations manifest themselves as regional changes in the frequencies, intensities, and even the location of extreme events such as droughts and floods.

Not all pollutants emitted in the air have an impact on the global climate system. But scientists have long known that some gases can affect global climate patterns by interacting with sunlight or the heat radiated from Earth's surface. Emission of such gases, especially CO_2, can result from human activities such as the burning of fossil fuels, tropical deforestation, and food production processes. The amount of CO_2 in the atmosphere has increased considerably since the mid 1700s and is likely to double the preindustrial level by the year 2050. Carbon dioxide is a highly effective greenhouse gas. Other greenhouse gases emitted to the atmosphere as a result of human activities include CFCs (used as refrigerants, foam-blowing agents, and cleansers for electronic components), nitrous oxide (used in fertilizers), and methane (emitted during rice production). Of these trace gases, the CFCs are produced by industrial processes alone; and others are produced by both industrial and natural processes.

The increase in greenhouse gases during the past two centuries has resulted primarily from industrial processes in which fossil fuels are burned. Thus, a large proportion of the greenhouse gases produced by human activity has resulted from economic development in the industrialized countries (a fact that developing countries are not reluctant to mention when discussing the global warming issue).

National leaders around the globe are concerned about the issue of climate change. Mandatory international limits on the emissions of greenhouse gases could substan-tially affect their own energy policies. Today, there are scientific and diplomatic efforts to better understand and deal with the prospects of global atmospheric warming and its possible impacts on society. Many countries have, for a variety of motives, agreed that there are reasons to limit greenhouse gas emissions worldwide. National representatives of the Conference of Parties meet each year to address this concern. In the meantime, few countries, if any, want to forgo economic development to avoid a global environmental problem that is still surrounded by scientific uncertainty.

The Oceans

The oceans represent another truly global commons. Most governments have accepted this as fact by supporting the Law of the Sea Treaty, which notes that the seas, which cover almost 70 percent of Earth's surface, are "the common heritage of mankind." In the early 1940s, Athelstan Spilhaus made a projection map that clearly shows that the world's oceans are really subcomponents of one global ocean.

There are at least three commons-related issues concerning the oceans: pollution, fisheries, and sea level. Problems and possible crises have been identified in each area.

The oceans are the ultimate sink for pollutants. Whether they come from the land or the atmosphere, they are likely to end up in the oceans. But no one really owns the oceans, and coastal countries supervise only bits and pieces of the planet's coastal waters. This becomes a truly global commons problem, as currents carry pollutants from the waters of one country into the waters of others. While there are many rules and regulations governing pollution of the oceans, enforcement is quite difficult. Outside a country's 200-mile exclusive economic zone are the high seas, which are under the jurisdiction of no single country.

In many parts of the world, fisheries represent a common property resource. The oceans provide many countries with protein for domestic food consumption or export. Obtaining the same amount of protein from the land would require that an enormous additional amount of the land's surface be put into agricultural production. Whether under the jurisdiction of one country, several countries, or no country at all, fish populations have often been exploited with incomplete understanding of the causes of variability in their numbers. As a result, most fish stocks that have been commercially sought after have collapsed under the combined pressures of natural variability in the physical environment, population dynamics, and fish catches. This is clearly a serious problem; many perceive it to be a crisis.

Bound Together by Air and Water

- "What goes up must come down" describes the fate of most pollutants ejected into the atmosphere. Taller smokestacks were used to assure that the pollutants did not come down "in my backyard."

- Fish stocks that naturally straddle the boundary between a country's protected zone and the open seas are a global resource requiring international protection measures.

- Sea level in all parts of the world would quickly rise some 8 meters (26 feet) if the vast West Antarctic ice sheet broke away and slid into the sea.

- Scientific controversy still surrounds the notion that human activities can produce enough greenhouse gases to warm the global atmosphere.

In many parts of the world, fisheries represent a common property resource.

For example, an area in the Bering Sea known as the "Donut Hole" had, until recently, also been suffering from overexploitation of pollack stocks. In the midst of the Bering Sea, outside the coastal zones and jurisdictions of the United States and Russia, there is an open-access area that is subject to laws related to the high seas, a truly global commons. Fishermen from Japan and other countries were overexploiting the pollack in this area. But these stocks were part of the same population that also lived in the protected coastal waters of the United States and Russia. In other words, the pollack population was a straddling stock—it straddled the border between the controlled coastal waters and the high seas.

To protect pollack throughout the sea by limiting its exploitation, the two coastal states took responsibility for protecting the commons (namely, the Donut Hole) without having to nationalize it. They did so by threatening to close the Bering Sea to "outsiders," if the outsiders were unable to control their own exploitation of the commonly shared pollack stock. There are several other examples of the overexploitation of straddling stocks, such as the recent collapse of the cod fishery along the Georges Bank in the North Atlantic.

Another commons-related issue is the sea level rise that could result from global warming of the atmosphere. Whereas global warming, if it were to occur, could change rainfall and temperature patterns in yet-unknown ways both locally and regionally, sea level rise will occur everywhere, endangering low-lying coastal areas worldwide. Compounding the problem is the fact that the sea is also an attractor of human populations. For example, about 60 percent of the U.S. population lives within a hundred miles of the coast.

This would truly be a global commons problem because *all* coastal areas and adjoining estuaries would suffer from the consequences of global warming. Concern about sea level rise is highest among the world's small island states, many of which (e.g., the Maldives) are at risk of becoming submerged even with a modest increase in sea level. In sum, there are no winners among coastal states if sea level rises.

Antarctica always appears on the list of global commons. Although it is outside the jurisdiction of any country, some people have questioned its classification as a global commons. It is a fixed piece of territory with no indigenous human population, aside from scientific visitors. It does have a clear link to the oceans as a global commons, however. One key concern about global warming is the possible disintegration of the West Antarctic ice sheet. Unlike Arctic sea ice, which sits in water, the West Antarctic ice sheet would cause sea level to rise an estimated eight meters if it broke away and fell into the Southern Ocean. Viewed from this perspective, the continent clearly belongs on the list of global commons. It is up to the global community to protect it from the adverse influences of human activities occurring elsewhere on the globe.

What's the Problem?

Are the changes in the atmosphere and oceans really problems? And if so, are they serious enough to be considered crises?

The consequences of the greenhouse effect are matters that scien-

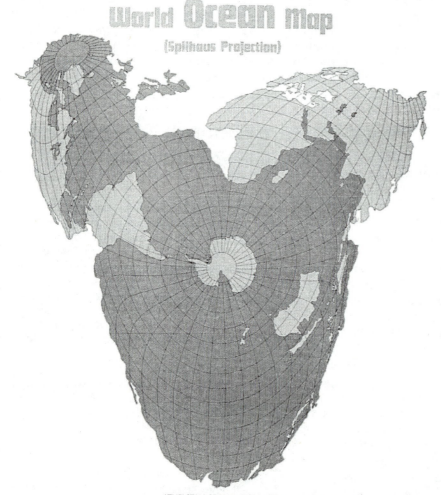

ATHELSTAN SPILHAUS/COURTESY OF CELESTIAL PRODUCTS, PHILMONT, VA.

Our one-ocean world: The oceans are but one body of water, as highlighted by the World Ocean Map developed more than 50 years ago by oceanographer Athelstan Spilhaus.

In 5 or 10 years incremental changes can mount into a major environmental crisis.

tists speculate about. But changes in the environment are taking place *now*. These changes are mostly incremental: low-grade, slow-onset, long-term, but gradually accumulating. They can be referred to as "creeping environmental problems." Daily changes in the environment are not noticed, and today's environment is not much different from yesterday's. In 5 or 10 years, however, those incremental changes can mount into a major environmental crisis [see "Creeping Environmental Problems," THE WORLD & I, June 1994, p. 218].

Just about every environmental change featuring human involvement is of the creeping kind. Examples include air pollution, acid rain, global warming, ozone depletion, tropical deforestation, water pollution, and nuclear waste accumulation. For many such changes, the threshold of irreversible damage is difficult to identify until it has been crossed. It seems that we can recognize the threshold only by the consequences that become manifest after we have crossed it. With regard to increasing amounts of atmospheric carbon dioxide, what is the critical threshold beyond which major changes in the global climate system might be expected? Although scientists regularly refer to a doubling of CO_2 from preindustrial levels, the truth of the matter is that a doubling really has little scientific significance except that it has been selected as some sort of marker or milestone.

Policymakers in industrialized and developing countries alike lack a good process for dealing with creeping environmental changes. As a result, they often delay action on such changes in favor of dealing with issues that seem more pressing. Creeping environmental problems tend to be put on the back burner; that is, they are ignored until they have emerged as full-blown crises. The ways that individuals and societies deal with slow-onset, incremental adverse changes in the environment are at the root of coping effectively with deterioration and destruction of local to global commons.

Societal concerns about human impacts on commonly owned or commonly exploited resources have been recorded for at least 2,500 years. Aristotle, for example, observed "that which is common to the greatest number has the least care bestowed upon it." How to manage a common property resource, whether it is a piece of land, a fish population, a body of water, the atmosphere, or outer space, will likely confound decisionmakers well into the future.

Michael H. Glantz is program director of the Environmental and Societal Impacts Group at the National Center for Atmospheric Research (NCAR) in Boulder, Colorado. NCAR is sponsored by the National Science Foundation.

The Nemesis Effect

Burdened by a growing number of *overlapping* stresses, the world's
ecosystems may grow increasingly susceptible to rapid, unexpected decline.

by Chris Bright

IN 1972, A DAM CALLED THE IRON GATES WAS COMPLETED on a stretch of the Danube River between Romania and what is now Serbia. It was built to generate electricity and to prevent the river from visiting some 26,000 square kilometers of its floodplain. It has done those things, but that's not all it has done.

The Danube is the greatest of the five major rivers that run into the Black Sea. For millennia, these rivers have washed tons of dead vegetation into this nearly landlocked ocean. As it sinks into the sea's stagnant depths, the debris is decomposed by bacteria that consume all the dissolved "free" oxygen (O_2), then continue their work by pulling oxygen out of the sulfate ions (SO_4) that are a normal component of seawater. That process releases hydrogen sulfide gas (H_2S), which is one of the world's most poisonous naturally occurring substances. One deep breath of it would probably kill you. The sea's depths contain the largest reservoir of hydrogen sulfide in the world, and the dissolved gas forces virtually every living thing in the water to cling to the surface or die. The Black Sea is alive only along its coasts, and in an oxygenated surface layer that is just 200 meters thick at most—less than a tenth of the sea's maximum depth.

The Danube contributes 70 percent of the Black Sea's fresh water and about 80 percent of its suspended silicate—essentially, tiny pieces of sand. The silicate is consumed by a group of single-celled algae called diatoms, which use it to encase themselves in glassy coats. The diatoms fuel the sea's food web, but any diatoms that don't get eaten eventually die and sink into the dead zone below, along with any unused silicate. Fresh contributions of silicate are therefore necessary for maintaining the diatom population. But when the Iron Gates closed, most of the Danube's silicate began to settle out in the still waters of the vast lake behind the dam. Black Sea silicate concentrations fell by 60 percent.

The drop in silicate concentrations coincided with an increase in nitrogen and phosphorus pollution from fertilizer runoff and from the sewage of the 160 million people who live in the Black Sea drainage. Nitrogen and phosphorus are plant nutrients—which is why they're in fertilizer. In water, this nutrient pollution promotes explosive algal blooms. The Black Sea diatoms began blooming, but the lack of silicate limited their numbers and prevented them from consuming all the nutrient. That check created an opportunity for other types of algae, formerly suppressed by the diatoms. Some of these were dinoflagellate "red tide" organisms, which produce powerful toxins. Soon after the Iron Gates closed, red tides began to appear along the sea's coasts.

In the early 1980s, a jellyfish native to the Atlantic coast of the Americas was accidentally released into the sea from the ballast tank of a ship. The jellyfish population exploded; it ate virtually all the zooplankton, the tiny animals that feed on the algae. Liberated from their predators, the algae grew even thicker, especially the dinoflagellates. In the late 1980s, during the height of the jellyfish infestation, the dinoflagellates seemed to be summoning the death from below. Their blooms consumed all the oxygen in the shallows and the rotten-egg stench of hydrogen sulfide haunted the streets of Odessa. Carpets of dead fish—asphyxiated or poisoned—bobbed along the shores.

The jellyfish nearly ate the zooplankton into oblivion, then its population collapsed too. But it's still in the Black Sea and there's probably no way to remove it. The red tides have increased six-fold since the early 1970s, and it doesn't look as if antipollution efforts are going to put the dinoflagellates back under the control of the diatoms. The fisheries are in a dismal state—overharvested, starved of zooplankton, periodically suffocated and poisoned. The rest of the ecosystem isn't faring much better. The mollusks, sponges, sea urchins, even the marine worms are disappearing. The shallows, where vast beds of seagrass once breathed life into the waters, are regularly fouled in a fetid algal soup laced with a microbe that thrives in such conditions: cholera.

COULD IT HAVE BEEN PREDICTED THAT THE DAM ON THE DANUBE would end up triggering this spasm of ecological chaos? The engineers who designed the Iron Gates were obviously attempting to make nature more orderly and productive (in a very narrow sense of those terms). Could they have foreseen this form of disorder, which has no obvious relationship to the dam itself? Here is what they would have had to anticipate: that the dam would cause a downstream change in water chemistry which would combine with an increase in a certain type of pollution to produce an effect that neither change would probably have had on its own—and that effect would then be magnified by something that was going to be pumped out of a ship's ballast tank.

It seems absurd even to entertain the idea that such things could be foreseen. Yet this is precisely the kind of foresight that is now required of anyone who is concerned, professionally or otherwise, with the increasingly dysfunctional relationship between our societies and the environment. The forces of ecological corrosion—pollution, overfishing, the invasion of exotic species like that jellyfish—such forces interact in all sorts of ways. Their effects are determined, not just by the activities that initially produced them, but *by each other and by the way ecosystems respond to them.* They are, in other words, parts of an enormously complex system. And unless we can learn to see them *within the system,* we have no hope of anticipating the damage they may do.

A system is a set of interrelated elements in which some sort of change is occurring, and even very simple systems can behave in unpredictable ways. Three elements are enough to do it, as Isaac Newton demonstrated three centuries ago, when he formulated the "N body problem." Is it possible to define the gravitational interaction between three or more moving objects with complete precision? No one has been able to do it thus far. The unpredictable dynamics of system behavior have inspired an entire mathematical science, variously known as complexity or systems theory. (The most famous type of complexity is "chaos.") Systems theory is useful for exploring several other sciences, including ecology. It's also useful for exploring the ways in which we can be surprised.

Suppose, for example, that you were a marine biologist studying Black Sea plankton in the early 1970s. Had you confined your observations solely to the plankton themselves, you would have had no basis for predicting the explosion of red tides that followed the closing of the Iron Gates. Such "nonlinear" events usually come as a surprise, not because they're unusual—they're actually common—but because of a basic mismatch between our ordinary perceptions and system behavior. Most people, most of the time, just aren't looking upriver: we have a strong intuitive tendency to assume that incremental change can be used to predict further incremental change—that the gradual rise or fall of a line on a graph means more of the same. But that's not true. The future of a trend—any trend—depends on the behavior of the system as a whole.

In 1984, the sociologist Charles Perrow published a book, *Normal Accidents: Living with High-Risk Technologies,* in which he explored the highly complex industrial and social systems upon which we've become increasingly dependent. David Ehrenfeld, an ecologist at Rutgers University in New Jersey, has observed that much of what Perrow said of nuclear reactors, air traffic, and so forth could also apply to ecosystems—or more precisely, to the ways in which we interact with them. Here are some of the criteria that Perrow uses to define complex systems:

- many common mode connections between components . . . not in a production sequence [that is, elements may interact in ways that won't fit into a predictable sequence];
- unfamiliar or unintended feedback loops;
- many control parameters with potential interactions [that is, we have many ways to influence the system but we can't be sure what the overall result of our actions will be];
- indirect or inferential information sources [we can't always see what's happening directly];
- limited understanding of some processes.

There's something ominous in Perrow's rather bland, clinical terminology—it's like a needle pointing the wrong way on an instrument panel. "Limited understanding of some processes!" No ecologist could have put it better. Ehrenfeld wrote a paper on Perrow's relevance to ecology; he was fascinated with Perrow's treatment of nuclear accidents. What is it like to be a nuclear plant operator during a Three Mile Island event? You watch the monitors, you try to second-guess your equipment, you make inferences about the state of the core. Perrow says, "You are actually creating a world that is congruent with your interpretation, even though it may be the wrong world. It may be too late before you find that out."

Into the Theaters of Surprise

"NUCLEAR. MORE THAN YOU EVER IMAGINED." THAT'S THE SLOGAN OF the Nuclear Energy Institute, a nuclear power industry association based in Washington, D.C. To me, at least, the phrase isn't very reassuring, and I would bet that it will sound like a joke to most of the people who read this article. My guess, in other words, is that your imagination already operates well beyond the stage settings of nuclear industry PR. But how much farther are you willing to push it?

Throughout most of our species' existence, the bounds of our collective imagination have not been a survival issue in the way that they are today. Either our societies were rather loosely coupled to their environment, so there was more "give" in the system, or when we got into trouble, it was a local or regional predicament rather than a global one. But today, our rapport with the environment is growing increasingly analogous to the task of managing a nuclear power plant. We live within a set of systems that are "tightly coupled," requiring constant attention, not entirely predictable, and capable of various types of meltdown.

Consider, for example, two representative theaters of surprise. See if you find here more than you ever imagined.

1. The Forests of Eastern North America

As far as conservation is concerned, the woodlands of eastern North America might seem about as far as you can get from the highly publicized tropical scenario, with its poorly understood and rapidly disappearing forests, its desperate agrarian poverty and rapacious logging. For this scorched confusion, substitute some of the most thoroughly studied ecosystems in the world, growing over the heads of some of the world's wealthiest, best-educated, and most information-saturated people. These are highly populated woodlands too—138 million people live beneath the trees or within a few hours' drive of them.

Virtually all of the original "old growth" in the eastern United States was cut long ago, but these forests comprise one of the few large regions anywhere in the world that could be thought of as undergoing some sort of ecological renaissance. With the exception of northern New England, the loggers had done their worst to the region a century ago or more, and moved west in search of bigger timber. And over the course of the 19th century, fewer and fewer fields were being tortured by the plow, as the nation's agriculture shifted to the lavish fertility of the midwest. So the eastern second growth has quietly spread and matured, absorbing hundreds of old cutover wood lots and anonymous, abandoned farmsteads. But today these forests are in the throes of a quiet agony—a pathology that is harder to read than tropical deforestation, but which may lead to a form of degradation that is just as profound. The air they are breathing is poisoning them, the water bathes them in acid, the soil is growing toxic, they are gnawed by exotic pests, and the climate to which they are adapted is likely to shift.

A primary cause of this agony involves changes in the "nitrogen cycle." Nitrogen is an essential nutrient of plants and it's the main constituent of the atmosphere: 78 percent of the air is nitrogen gas. But plants can't metabolize this pure, elemental nitrogen directly. The nitrogen must be "fixed" into compounds with hydrogen or oxygen before it can become part of the biological cycle. In nature this process is accomplished by certain types of microbes and by lightning strikes, which fuse atmospheric oxygen and nitrogen into nitrogen oxides.

Humans have radically amplified this process. Farmers boost the nitrogen level of their land through fertilizers and the planting of nitrogen-fixing crops (actually, it's symbiotic microbes that do the fixing). The burning of forests and the draining of wetlands release additional quantities of fixed nitrogen that had been stored in vegetation and organic debris. And fossil-fuel combustion releases still more fixed nitrogen, partly from fuel contaminants, and

partly through the production of nitrogen oxides in the same way that lightning works. Natural processes probably incorporate around 140 million tons of nitrogen into the terrestrial nitrogen cycle every year. (The ocean cycle is largely a mystery.) Thus far, human activity has at least doubled that amount.

As in much of the industrialized world, eastern North America is bathed in the nitrogen oxides pumped into the air from car exhaust and coal-burning power plants. In the presence of sunlight, one of these chemicals, nitric oxide (NO), produces ozone (O_3). Ozone is good in the stratosphere, where it filters out harmful ultraviolet (UV) radiation, but it's very bad in the troposphere, the thick blanket of air at the Earth's surface. Ozone is a primary component of smog. Clean air laws, understandably, aim to cut ozone levels to a point at which they are unlikely to harm people (or at least, healthy people). But the problem for the forests is that leaf tissue is far more sensitive to ozone than human lung tissue. Ozone "bleaches" leaves. According to Charles Little, a seasoned chronicler of North American forests, you might as well be spraying them with Clorox. Ozone also reduces flower, pollen, and seed production, thereby hindering reproduction.

In this region, you can just about name the tree, and ozone is probably injuring it somewhere. Ozone combines with UV radiation to burn and scar the needles of white pine, the region's tallest conifer. Ozone exposure correlates strongly with hickory and oak die-off. Ozone is hard on the tulip tree, a major canopy species especially where white oak has declined. It's injuring native magnolias as well. Nor is it just the obviously smoggy urban areas that suffer. In the Great Smoky Mountains National Park of North Carolina, researchers have found ozone damage to some 90 plant species.

In rural West Virginia, ozone is apparently working a weird, nonlinear form of forest decline: continual ozone exposure can reduce photosynthesis to the point at which the tree can't grow enough roots to support itself. Apparently minor but chronic leaf damage eventually provokes catastrophic failure of the roots, then death. This is one of several mechanisms underlying the syndrome known as the "falling forest." Reasonably healthy-looking trees just keel over and die.

Airborne nitrogen oxides also produce nitric acid, which contributes to acid rain. The other major constituent of acid rain is sulfuric acid, which derives from the sulfur dioxide released by coal-burning power plants and metal smelters. (Sulfur is a common contaminant of coal and metal ores.) Smoke stack "scrubbers" and a growing preference for low-sulfur coal and natural gas have helped reduce sulfur dioxide emissions in the United States, Canada, and Western Europe. U.S. emissions, for example, fell from nearly 30 million tons in 1970 to 16 million in 1995. (The global picture isn't so encouraging: world sulfur dioxide emissions rose from about 115 million tons a year in 1970 to around 140 million tons by 1988 and have remained relatively stable since then.)

Even in the United States, the amount of acid aloft is still substantial by ecological standards. On the fog-drenched slopes of Mount Mitchell, north on the Appalachian spine from the Smoky Mountains, the pH of the dew and ice sometimes drops as low as 2.1, which is more acid than lemon juice. The acid treatment, combined with insect attack and drought, has killed up to 80 percent of mature red spruce and Fraser fir on the most exposed slopes.

But the problem is not just the acid in the air today. Decades of acid rain have begun to leach out the soil's stock of calcium and magnesium, both essential plant nutrients. Replenishing those minerals, a process dependent on the weathering of rock, may take centuries. In the meantime, the legacy of coal is likely to be stunted forests, at least where the leaching is well advanced, as in some areas of New England. Recent studies at the Hubbard Brook Experimental Forest in the mountains of New Hampshire, for instance, have identified minerals leaching as the main reason the vegetation there has shown no overall growth for nearly a decade.

This slowing of the trees' metabolism is not just a matter of gradual, overall decline—there are nonlinear effects here too. Acid rain is making the New England winters lethal to red spruce and balsam fir, two of the region's most important conifers. Like most conifers, these species don't lose their leaves—their "needles"—in winter, so they can't just go dormant when it gets cold. They have to maintain a metabolic rate high enough to keep the needles functioning properly. In cold weather, conifers close the stomata in their needles when light dims, in order to protect the needles from freezing. (The stomata are the microscopic pores in leaf tissue, where gas exchange occurs.) The mineral-starved trees can't readily perform this function, so sometimes the cells in the needles freeze solid. That kills needles; when enough of the needles die, the tree dies. At higher elevations in Vermont's Green Mountains, three-quarters of mature red spruce have frozen to death.

The acid rain hasn't just made the soils less nutritious—it has also made them toxic. In calcium-rich soils, the acid is generally neutralized, since calcium is alkaline. But as the calcium level drops, more and more acid accumulates and that tends to release aluminum from its mineral matrix. Aluminum is a common soil constituent; when it's bonded to other minerals it's biologically inert, but free aluminum is toxic to both plants and animals. In some Appalachian streams, you can find stones covered with a silvery-whitish tinge—that's aluminum released by acid rain. This burden of "mobilized" metal is compounded by the traces of cadmium, lead, and mercury that the air brings in along with the acid and ozone.

The metals poisoning may create a kind of synergistic overlap with ozone pollution. In some dying red spruce stands in Vermont, researchers have found elevated levels of phytochelatins, a class of chemicals that plants produce to bind to toxic metals and render them inert. But to make the phytochelatins, the spruces have to draw down their stocks of another substance, glutathione, which is used to counteract ozone. So exposure to one kind of poison leaves the spruces more vulnerable to another.

There's another big overlap here as well: the trees' ability to fight off stresses is also being weakened by nitrogen pollution. Plants don't have the same kind of immune system that animals do. Instead of killer cells and antibodies, they produce an immense arsenal of chemicals. Some of these, like phytochelatins, neutralize toxins; others kill pathogens or make leaves less palatable to pests. Excess nitrogen tends to clog the cellular machinery that produces these chemicals. Farmers don't have to worry about this problem when they apply fertilizer to crops, because crops are intensively managed for pest control and because they're generally harvested at the end of a single growing season. But trees that are exposed to high nitrogen year after year will inevitably absorb more of the material than they can possibly metabolize. So the nitrogen builds up in their tissues, where it tends to alter the recipes for all those defensive chemicals. As the chemicals lose their punch, toxins aren't effectively neutralized; soil pathogens permeate the roots, and the leaves grow more susceptible to insect attack. It has been estimated that nitrogen pollution in the eastern United States is triple the level that forests can tolerate over the long term. Nitrogen pollution can cause a kind of botanical equivalent of AIDS.

This weakening of the forests' immune system is likely to upset the balance between the trees and their pathogens. Another reason for West Virginia's "falling forests," for example, is a fungal infection called *Armillaria* root rot. *Armillaria* is a widespread type of fungus, common in forest soils all over the world. In healthy stands, it usually satisfies itself with the occasional diseased or very old tree. But in a badly stressed stand, it becomes a subterranean monster—a huge, amorphous disease organism, sprouting rootlike tentacles that probe the soil for victims. It picks away at the stand, gradually killing it, tree by tree.

But it's not just the native pests that are taking advantage of the forests' weakened state. The forests are crawling with a host of exotic insects and diseases as well. The American chestnut and the American elm succumbed to exotic pathogens earlier in the century and are now functionally extinct. (They have not disappeared completely but they are no longer functioning components of their native ecosystems.) Today many other species are in trouble. The Canadian hemlock, for example, is being attacked by an Asian insect, the hemlock wooly adelgid; in parts of New England, the adelgid is wiping out entire stands. Nitrogen pollution puts the adelgid on the insect equivalent of steroids: the excess nitrogen makes the leaves much more nutritious and can boost adelgid densities five-fold. Oaks are the principal victims of the gypsy moth, a European insect whose occasional population explosions defoliate thousands of hectares. In the nitrogen-poisoned stands, the moth droppings produce a weak solution of nitric acid on the forest floor, leaching out soil nutrients as the moth gnaws away at the canopy.

Exotic fungal pathogens are attacking the butter nut, the American beech, and the eastern dogwood. The dogwood has a very broad range, which covers most of the eastern United States, and the fungus that is killing it has spread throughout that range in little more than a decade—a phenomenal rate of spread for a tree pathogen. Acid rain appears to be part of the reason for the dogwood's susceptibility, and the dogwood die-off is liable to reinforce the effects of acid rain on the soil. The dogwood is very efficient at pulling calcium out of the soil and depositing it, through its leaf litter, on the forest floor. That process reduces calcium leaching, so the disappearance of this tree could deal an additional blow to calcium-starved forests.

This is the condition of what is, by world standards, an upper middle-class forest: conifer die-offs of 70 to 80 percent in the southern Appalachians, sugar maple mortality at 35 percent in Vermont; the butternut, eastern dogwood, and red mulberry in widespread decline. The American beech and Canadian hemlock in trouble over large parts of their range. The elm and the chestnut already gone. And besides the pests and pollution, decades of fire suppression have eliminated plant communities dependent on fire for renewing themselves. Other stands are now giving way to asphalt and suburbia. Over all, according to a survey of five eastern states, tree mortality may now stand at three to five times historical levels.

Last year, climate scientists discovered that North American broadleaf forests were probably absorbing far more carbon from the atmosphere than had been previously assumed. The continent's eastern forests, it turns

A Spreading Matrix of Trouble

Below are 13 of the worst pressures that we are inflicting on the planet and ourselves. The lines show a few of the ways in which these corrosive forces interact. See the numbered key for each of the combinations indicated. Note that neither the list of pressures nor the set of interactions is inclusive—if your background is in environmental studies, you will almost certainly be able to extend the matrix. We welcome your thoughts.

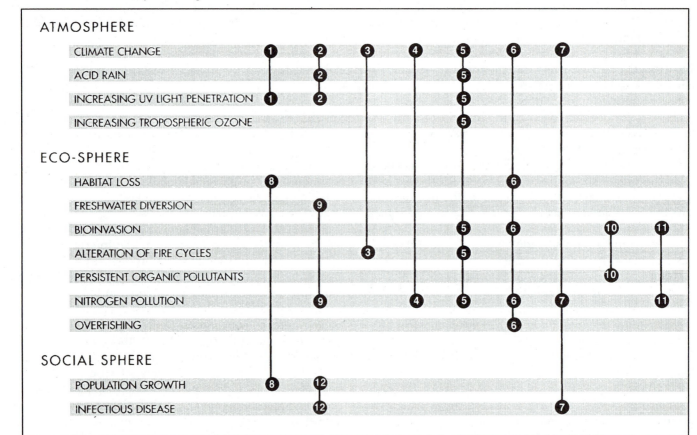

KEY TO THE MATRIX

1 Climate change + UV: Greenhouse-forced warming of the lower atmosphere may cause a *cooling* of the stratosphere, especially over the Arctic. (Major air currents may shift, and block the warmer surface air from moving North and up.) A cooling stratosphere will exacerbate damage to the ozone layer because the colder it is, the more effective CFCs become at breaking down ozone. The ozone layer over the Arctic could grow progressively thinner as warming proceeds.

2 Climate change + acid rain + UV: In eastern Canada, two decades of mild drought and a slight warming trend have

out, are an important part of the "missing carbon sink"—the heretofore unexplained hole in the calculations that attempt to define the global carbon budget. But if these forests continue to sicken, their appetite for carbon will eventually falter. That is likely to speed up the processes of climate change. And climatic instability will add yet another stress to a region that is already exhibiting a kind of paradoxical system effect: it is covered with new growth but many of its forests appear to be dying.

2. Coral Reefs

Coral reefs are perhaps the greatest collective enterprise in nature. Reefs are the massed calcareous skeletons of millions of coral—small, sedentary, worm-like animals that live on the reef surface, filtering the water for edible de-

bris. Reefs form in shallow tropical and subtropical waters, and host huge numbers of plants and animals. The reef biome is small in terms of area—less than 1 percent of the earth's surface—but it's the richest type of ecosystem in the oceans and the second richest on earth, after tropical forests. One-quarter of all ocean species thus far identified are reef-dwellers, including at least 65 percent of marine fish species.

Coral is extremely vulnerable to heat stress and the unusually high sea surface temperatures (SSTs) of the past two decades may have damaged this biome just as badly as the unusual fires have damaged the tropical forests. Much of the ocean warming is related to El Niño the weather pattern that begins with shifting currents and air pressure cells in the tropical Pacific region and ends by

reduced streamflow into many of the region's lakes. The lake water has grown clearer, since the weakened streams are washing in less organic debris. The clearer water allows UV radiation to penetrate more deeply—at a time when more UV light is striking the lakes in the first place, because of the deterioration of the ozone layer. (UV light can injure fish and other aquatic organisms just as it injures humans.) Acid rain, which affects northern lakes in both Canada and Eurasia, causes even more organic matter to precipitate out of the water, further opening the lakes to UV light. In some lakes, the overall effect may be to increase the depth of UV penetration from 20–30 centimeters to over 3 metres.

3 Climate change + alteration of fire cycles: The fire ecology of forests all over the world is in a profound state of flux; we have introduced fire into some tropical rainforests that do not naturally burn at all, while in many temperate forests, where fire is essential for maintaining the native plant community, we have suppressed it. Climate change will probably cause further instability in fire cycles, as some regions become drier and others wetter. The results cannot be predicted, but are unlikely to favor original forest composition. If the overall rate of burning increases, that could create a positive feedback loop in the climate cycle, by releasing ever greater quantities of heat-trapping carbon into the atmosphere.

4 Climate change + N pollution: As a factor in the decline of some temperate-zone forests, nitrogen pollution is probably reducing their capacity to absorb carbon from the atmosphere.

5 Climate change + acid rain + UV + trospheric ozone + bioinvasion + alteration of fire cycles + N pollution: This complex of pressures is pushing eastern North American forests into decline. (See text.)

6 Climate change + habitat loss + bioinvasion + N pollution + overfishing: This set of pressures is pushing the world's coral reefs into decline. (See text.)

7 Climate change + N pollution + infectious disease: Cool weather often limits the ranges of mosquitoes and other insects that carry human pathogens. Even relatively slight increases in minimum temperatures can admit a pest into new

areas. Warm coastal ocean water, especially when it's nitrogen-polluted, creates habitat for cholera.

8 Habitat loss + population growth: Last year, the floodings of China's Yangtze River did $30 billion in damages, displaced 223 million people, and killed another 3,700. The flooding was not wholly a natural event: with 85 percent of its forest cover gone, the Yangtze basin no longer had the capacity to absorb the heavy rains. (Forests are like immense sponges—they hold huge quantities of water.) And the densely settled floodplain guaranteed that the resulting monster flood would find millions of victims. (See "Record Year for Weather-Related Disasters," 27 November 1998, at www.worldwatch.org/alerts/index.)

9 Freshwater diversion + N pollution: Extensive irrigation can turn an arid region into productive cropland, but chemical fertilization is likely to follow and make the fields a source of nitrous oxide.

10 Bioinvasion + POPs: In the Great Lakes, exotic zebra mussels are ingesting dangerous organochlorine pesticides and other persistent organic chemicals that have settled into the loose, lake-bottom muck. Once in the zebra mussels, the chemicals may move elsewhere in the food web. Over the past decade or so, poisoning with such chemicals is also thought to be a factor in the growing susceptibility of marine mammals to the various epidemics that have emerged here and there throughout the world's oceans.

11 Bioinvasion + N pollution: Nitrogen pollution of grassland tends to favor the spread of aggressive exotic weeds. Nitrogen pollution of forests tends to weaken tree defenses against pests, both exotic and native.

12 Population growth + infectious disease. Over the next half-century, the centers of population growth will be the crowded, dirty cities of the developing world. These places are already breeding grounds for most of humanity's deadliest pathogens: cholera, malaria, AIDS, and tuberculosis among them. As the cities become more crowded, rates of infection are likely to grow and "overlapping infections" are likely to increase mortality rates.

rearranging a good deal of the planet's weather. El Niños appear to be growing more frequent and more intense; many climate scientists suspect that this trend is connected with climate change. It's very difficult to sort out the patterns, but there is probably also a general SST warming trend in the background, behind the El Niños. That too is a likely manifestation of climate change.

When SSTs reach the 28–30° C range, the coral polyp may expel the algae that live within its tissues. This action is known as "bleaching" because it turns the coral white. Coral usually recovers from a brief bout of bleaching, but if the syndrome persists it is generally fatal because the coral depends on the algae to help feed it through photosynthesis. Published records of bleaching date back to 1870, but show nothing comparable to what began in the early 1980s, when unusually warm water caused extensive bleaching throughout the Pacific. Coral bleached over thousands of square kilometers. By the end of the decade, mass bleaching was occurring in every coral reef region in the world. The full spectrum of coral species was affected in these events—a phenomenon that had never been observed before.

In the second half of this decade, SSTs set new records over much of the coral's range and the bleaching has become even more intense. Last year saw the most extensive bleaching to date. Over a vast tract of the Indian Ocean, from the African coast to southern India, 70 percent of the coral appears to have died. Some authorities think that a shift from episodic events to chronic levels of bleaching is now under way.

The bleaching has triggered outbreaks of the crown-of-thorns starfish, a coral predator that is chewing its way through reefs in the Red Sea, off South Africa, the Maldives, Indonesia, Australia, and throughout much of the Pacific. The starfish are normally kept at bay by antler-like "branching corals," which have stinging cells and host various aggressive crustaceans. But as the branching corals bleach and die, the more palatable "massive corals" growing among them become ever more vulnerable to starfish attack. Over the course of a year, a single adult crown-of-thorns can consume 13 square meters of coral.

Overfishing is also promoting these outbreaks, by removing the fish that eat starfish. Overfishing also helps another enemy of the reefs: various types of algae that compete with coral. Floating algae can starve corals for light; macro-algae—"seaweeds"—can colonize the reefs themselves and displace the coral directly. Because reefs are shallow-water communities, they generally occur in coastal zones, where they are likely to be exposed to nitrogen-rich agricultural runoff and sewage. Nitrogen pollution is as toxic to reefs as it is to temperate-zone forests, because nitrogen fertilizes algae. Remove the algae-eating fish under these conditions, and you might as well have poisoned the coral directly. This overlap is the main reason Jamaica's reefs never recovered from Hurricane Allen in 1980; 90 percent of the reefs off the island's northwest coast are now just algae-covered humps of limestone.

In the Caribbean, over-fishing seems to have played a role in yet another complication for the reefs: the population collapse of an algae-eating sea urchin, *Diadema antillarum*. This urchin appears to have been the last line of defense against the algae after the progressive elimination of other algae-eating creatures. The first to go may have been the green sea turtle. Now endangered, the turtle once apparently roamed the Caribbean in immense herds, like bison on the Great Plains. Its Caribbean population may have surpassed 600 million. Christopher Columbus's fleet reportedly had to reef sail for a full day to let a migrating herd pass. By the end of the 18th century, the turtles had nearly all been slaughtered for their meat. In the following two centuries, essentially the same operation was repeated with the algae-eating fish.

The removal of its competitors must have given the urchin a great deal of room, and for most of this century it was one of the reefs' most common denizens. But its abundance seems to have set it up for the epidemic that struck during the El Niño of the early 1980s. In roughly a year, a mysterious pathogen virtually eliminated *D. antillarum* from the Caribbean; some 98 percent of the species disappeared over an area of more than 2.5 million square kilometers. Contemporary history offers no precedent for a die-off of that magnitude in a marine animal. The urchin is reportedly back in evidence, at least in some areas of its former range, but until its relationship with the pathogen is better understood, it won't be possible to define its long-term appetite for algae.

With the algae, the pollution, and the warming waters, the Caribbean is becoming an increasingly hostile environment for the organism that has shaped so much of its biological character. And now the coral itself is sickening; the Caribbean has become a caldron of epidemic coral diseases. The first such epidemic, called black-band disease, was detected in 1973 in Belizean waters. Black band is caused by a three-layer complex of "blue-green algae" (actually, cyanobacteria), each layer consisting of a different species. The bottom layer secretes highly toxic sulfides which kill the coral. The complex creeps very slowly over a head of coral in a narrow band, leaving behind only the bare white skeleton.

Black band has since been joined by a whole menagerie of other diseases: white-band, yellow-band, red-band, patchy necrosis, white pox, white plague type I and II, rapid-wasting syndrome, dark spot. The modes of action are as various as the names. White pox, for example, is caused by an unknown pathogen that almost dissolves the living coral tissue. Infected polyps disintegrate into mucous-like strands that trail off into the water, and bare, dead splotches appear on the reefs, giving them a kind of underwater version of the mange. Rapid wasting syndrome probably starts with aggressive biting by spotlight parrotfish; the wounds are then infected by some sort of fungus that spreads out from the wound site. On the reefs off Florida, the number of diseases has increased from five or six to 13 during the past decade. In 1996, nine of the 44 coral species occurring on these reefs were diseased; a year later the number of infected species had climbed to 28. Nor are the Caribbean reefs the only ones under attack; coral epidemics are turning up here and there throughout the Pacific and Indian Oceans, in the Persian Gulf and in the Red Sea.

For most of these diseases, a pathogen has yet to be identified; it's not even clear whether each of those names really refers to a distinct syndrome. But it's not likely that the diseases are "new" in the sense of being caused by pathogens that have recently evolved. It's much more likely that the coral's vulnerability to them is new. Take, for example, the disease that's killing sea-fan coral around the Caribbean. In this case, the pathogen is known: it's *Aspergillus sydowii*, a member of a very common genus of terrestrial fungi. The last time you threw something out of your refrigerator because it was moldy—there's a good chance you were looking at an *Aspergillus* species. In a very bizarre form of invasion, *A. sydowii* breached the land-sea barrier, and found a second home in the ocean. But it evidently took the plunge decades ago and has only been killing sea-fans for some 15 years or so. Why? Part of the answer is probably the higher SSTs: *A. sydowii* likes warmer water. Other coral diseases appear to do especially well in nutrient-laden waters.

Disease lies at one end of the spectrum of threat. Pathogens create a kind of microscopic pressure, but there are macroscopic pressures too: the ecosystems allied in one way or another with the reef biome are also deteriorating. The stretch of shallow, protected water between a reef and the coast often nurtures beds of seagrass. These beds filter out sediment and effluent that would injure the reefs, and the seagrass provides crucial cover for young fish. Seagrass is the major nursery for many fish species that spend their adult lives out on the reefs. Perhaps 70 percent of all commercially important fish spend at least part of their lives in the seagrass. But the tropical seagrass beds are silting up under tons of sediment from development, logging, mining, and the construction of shrimp farms. They are suffocating under algal blooms in nitrogen-polluted waters; they are being poisoned by herbicide runoff. According to one estimate, half of all seagrass beds within about 50 kilometers of a city have disappeared.

If you follow the seagrass-choking sediment back the way it came, you're increasingly likely to find a shoreline denuded of mangroves. In the warmer regions of the world, mangroves knit the land and sea together. These stilt-rooted trees trap sediment that would otherwise leak out to sea and they stabilize coastlines against incoming storms. Like the seagrass beds and the reefs, the mangrove ecosystem is incredibly productive—in the mangroves' case, with both terrestrial and aquatic organisms. (Mangrove roots are important fish nurseries too.)

The mangroves' importance as a sediment filter is perhaps greatest in the center of reef diversity, the Indonesian archipelago and adjoining areas. About 450 coral species are known to grow in the Australasian region; the Caribbean, by comparison, contains just 67 species. Australasia is correspondingly rich in fish too: a quarter of the world's fish species inhabit these waters. It is estimated that half of all the sediments received by oceanic waters are washed from the Indonesian archipelago alone. Nearby areas of Southeast Asia are also major contributors of sediment. But throughout the region, logging and shrimp farming are obliterating the mangroves that once filtered this tremendous burden of silt. Southeast Asia has lost half its mangrove stands over the past half century. A third of the mangrove cover is gone from Indonesian coasts, three-quarters from the Philippines.

About 10 percent of the world's coral reefs may already have been degraded beyond recovery. If we can't find a way to ease the reefs' afflictions, nearly three-quarters of the ocean's richest biome may have disappeared 50 years from now. Such a prospect gives new meaning to the term "natural disaster," but it's also a social disaster in the making. Reef fish make up perhaps 10 percent of the global fish catch; one estimate puts their contribution to the catch of developing countries at 20 to 25 percent.

And there's much more at stake here than just fisheries. The death of the coral would also jeopardize the reef *structures*—leaving them unable to repair storm damage. If the reefs give way, wave erosion of the coasts behind them will increase. The coasts are already facing some unavoidable degree of damage from climate change, as sea-levels rise.

(Warming water expands; that physical effect will combine with runoff from melting glaciers to push sea levels up.) Rising seas, like the crumbling reefs, will allow storm surges to reach farther inland. About one-sixth of the world's coasts are shielded by reefs, and some of these coasts, like the ones in South and Southeast Asia, support some of the densest human populations in the world. The disintegration of the reefs would leave a large portion of humanity hungrier, poorer, and far more vulnerable to the vagaries of a changing climate.

CORAL REEFS AND TEMPERATE-ZONE FORESTS—IN BOTH OF THESE theaters of surprise, the familiar could rapidly become something else. But you can begin to see similar system effects just about anywhere, and emerging from just about any form of environmental pressure:

- Nitrogen pollution has tripled the occurrence of low-oxygen dead zones in coastal ocean waters over the past 30 years. As in the Black Sea, excess nitrogen appears generally to be promoting the emergence of red tide organisms. (Over the past decade, the number of algae species known to be toxic has increased from around 20 to at least 85.)

- Organochlorine pollutants seem to be creating immunodeficiencies in marine mammals, triggering a growing number of viral epidemics. (Exposure to the red-tide toxins may also depress the immune systems of some marine mammals and sea turtles.)
- The hunting of birds and primates in tropical forests may become another form of deforestation, because these creatures are so important in pollinating tree flowers and dispersing seeds.
- Powerful storms, which may grow more common as the climate changes, tend to magnify invasions of exotic plants by dispersing their seeds over huge areas.
- And a whole spectrum of threats appears to underlie the global decline in amphibians: habitat loss, pollution, disease, exotic predators, and higher levels of UV exposure resulting from the disintegration of the ozone layer. (See the table, "A Spreading Matrix of Trouble," for some additional system effects.)

Given the pressures to which the global environment is now subject, the potential for surprise is, for all practical purposes, unlimited. We have stepped into a world in which our assumptions and prejudices are more and more likely to betray us. We are confronting a demon in a hall of mirrors. At this point, a purely reactive approach to our tormentor will lead inevitably to exhaustion and failure.

Towards a Complexity Ethic

OUR PREDICAMENT, ESSENTIALLY, IS THIS: ENVIRONMENTAL PRESSURES ARE converging in ways that are likely to create a growing number of unanticipated crises. Each of these crises will demand some sort of fix, and each fix will demand money, time, and political capital. Yet no matter how many fixes we make, we've no realistic expectation of reducing the potential for additional crises—if "fixing" is all we do. The key to controlling that demon is to do a better job of managing systems in their entirety. And whether the system in question is the global trading network, a national economy, or a single natural area, many of the same operating principles will apply. Here, in my view, are four of the most important ones.

Monoculture technologies are brittle.

Huge, uniform sectors generally exhibit an obvious kind of efficiency because they generate economies of scale. You can see this in fossil fuel-based power grids, car-dominated transit systems, even in the enormous woodpulp plantations that are an increasingly important part of the developing world's forestry sector. But this efficiency is usually superficial because it doesn't account for all sorts of "external" social and environmental costs. Thus, for instance, that apparently cheap fossil-fuel electricity is purchased with the literally incalculable risks of climatic

dislocation, with acid rain and ozone pollution, with mine runoff, and in the countries that rely most heavily on coal—China, for instance, and South Africa—with a heavy burden of respiratory disease.

Yet even when the need for change is obvious and alternative technologies are available, industrial monocultures can be extremely difficult to reform. In energy markets, solar and wind power are already competitive with fossil fuel for many applications, even by a very conventional cost comparison. And when you bring in all those external costs, there's really no comparison at all. But with trillions of dollars already invested in coal and oil, the global energy market is responding to renewables in a very slow and grudging way.

More diverse technologies—in energy and in any other field—will encourage more diverse investment strategies. That will tend to make the system as a whole more adaptable because investors will not all be "betting" on exactly the same future. And a more adaptable system is likely to be more durable over the long term.

Direct opposition to a natural force usually invites failure—or a form of success that is just as bad.

In the "Iron Gates" brand of development, it is sometimes difficult to distinguish success from failure. Less obvious, perhaps, is the fact that even conservation activities can run afoul of natural forces. Take, for example, the categorical approach to forest fire suppression. A no-burn policy may increase a forest's fuel load to the point at which a lightning strike produces a huge crown fire. That's outright failure: a catastrophic "artificial" fire may consume stands that survived centuries of the natural fire cycle. On the other hand, if the moisture regime favors rapid decomposition of dead wood, the policy could eliminate fire entirely. Without burning, the fire-tolerant tree species would probably also begin to disappear, as they are replaced by species better adapted to the absence of fire. That's "success." Either way, you lose the original forest.

Sound policy often tends to be more "oblique" than direct. A vaccine, for instance, turns the power of the pathogen against itself; that's why, when there's a choice, immunization is usually a better tactic for fighting disease than quarantine. Restoration of floodplain ecosystems can be a more effective form of flood control than dams and levees, because wetlands and forests function as immense sponges. (The catastrophic flooding last year in China's Yangtze river basin was largely the result of deforestation.)

An oblique approach might also help reduce demand for especially energy- or materials-intensive goods: if large numbers of people can be convinced to "transfer" their demand from the goods themselves to the services that the goods provide, then it might be possible to encourage consumption patterns that do less environmental damage. For example, joint ownership of cars, especially in cities, could satisfy needs for occasional private transportation, with a little coordination.

Since you can never have just one effect, always plan to have several.

Thinking through the likely systemic effects of a plan will help locate the risks, as well as indirect opportunities. Every day, for example, I ride the car pool lanes into Washington D.C., and my conversations with other commuters have led me to suspect that this environmentally correct ribbon of asphalt could actually *increase* pollution and sprawl, by contributing to a positive feedback loop. Here's how I think it may work: as the car pool lanes extended outward from the city, commute times dropped; that would tend to promote the development of bedroom communities in ever more remote areas. Eventually, the new developments will cause traffic congestion to rebound, and that will create political pressure for another bout of highway widening. A more "system sensitive" policy might have permitted the highway projects only when a county had some realistic plan to limit sprawl. (According to one recent estimate, metropolitan Washington is losing open space faster than any other area in the United States outside of California's central valley.) Car pool lanes might then have become a means of conserving farmland, instead of a possible factor in its demise.

For environmental activists, "system sensitivity" could help locate huge political constituencies. Look, for instance, at the potential politics of nitrogen pollution. Since a great deal of the nitrogen that is threatening coral reefs is likely to be agricultural runoff, and since much of that runoff is likely to be the result of highly mechanized "factory farming," it follows that anyone who cares about reefs should also care about sustainable agriculture. Obviously, the reverse is true as well: if you're trying to encourage organic farming in the Mississippi basin, you're conserving Caribbean reefs. The same kind of political reciprocity could be built around renewable energy and forest conservation.

I don't know the answer and neither do you, but together we can probably find one.

A system can have qualities that exist only *on the system level*—qualities that cannot be attributed directly to any of the components within. No matter how hard you look, for example, at the individual characteristics of oxygen, nitrogen, hydrogen, carbon, and magnesium, you will never find grounds for inferring the amazing activities of chlorophyll—the molecule that powers photosynthesis. There are system properties in political life as well: institutional pluralism can create a public space that no single institution could have created alone. That's one objective of the "balance of powers" aimed at in constitutional government.

It should also be possible to build a "policy system" that is smarter and more effective than any of its component groups of policy makers. Consider, for example, the recent history of the U.S. Forest Service. For decades, environmental activists have accused the service of managing the country's forests almost exclusively for timber production, with virtually no regard for their inherent natural value. Distrust of the service has fueled a widespread, grassroots forest conservation movement, which has grown increasingly sophisticated in its political and legal activities, and now even undertakes its own scientific studies on behalf of the forests. This movement, in turn, has attracted the interest and sympathy of a growing number of officials within the service. Many environmentalists (including this author) would argue that things are nowhere near what they should be inside the service, but it's possible that what we are witnessing here is the creation of a new space for conservation—a space that even a much more ecologically enlightened Forest Service couldn't have created on its own.

It remains to be seen whether this forum will prove powerful enough to the save the forests that inspired it. But in the efforts of the people who are building it, I think I can see, however dimly, a future in which the world's dominant cultures re-experience the shock of living among forests, prairies, and oceans—instead of among "natural resources." After all, the forests and prairies are where we came from and they're where we are going. We are the children of a vast natural complexity that we will never fathom.

Chris Bright is a research associate at the Worldwatch Institute, senior editor of WORLD WATCH, and author of *Life Out of Bounds: Bioinvasion in a Borderless World* (New York: W.W. Norton & Co., 1998).

A FEW KEY SOURCES

Harvard Ayers, Jenny Hager, and Charles E. Little, eds., *An Appalachian Tragedy: Air Pollution and Tree Death in the Eastern Forests of North America* (San Francisco: Sierra Club Books, 1998.

Osha Gray Davidson, *The Enchanted Braid: Coming to Terms with Nature on the Coral Reef* (New York: John Wiley, 1998).

Paul Epstein et al., *Marine Ecosytems: Emerging Diseases as Indicators of Change,* Health Ecological and Economic Dimensions (HEED) of the Global Change Program (Boston: Center for Health and Global Environment, Havard Medical School, December 1998).

Robert Jervis, *System Effects: Complexity in Political and Social Life* (Princeton, NJ: Princeton University Press, 1997).

Charles Perrow, *Normal Accidents: Living with High-Risk Technologies* (New York: Basic Books, 1984).

Windows on the Future:

Global Scenarios & Sustainability

By Gilberto C. Gallopín and Paul Raskin

Of all the environmental policy concepts to emerge in the last 20 years, none is more compelling than that of sustainability. The reason, of course, is the growing recognition that humanity is currently on an unsustainable path, that our activi-

> **By forcing us to clarify alternative world views and challenging the conventional wisdom, scenario analysis offers us a uniquely valuable way to ponder critical issues.**

ties have reached the point where they threaten the very life-support systems of the Earth. The need to preserve those systems was first put on the international policy agenda by the Brundtland Commission more than 10 years ago,

Gilberto C. Gallopín is director of the Systems for Sustainable Development Programme at the Stockholm Environment Institute in Stockholm, Sweden. Paul Raskin is director of the Boston, Massachusetts, center of the Stockholm Environment Institute and president of the Tellus Institute in Boston. The authors may be contacted through Raskin at 11 Arlington Street, Boston, MA 02116-3411 (telephone: 617-266-5400; e-mail: praskin@tellus.org).

which also formulated the classic definition of sustainable development, namely, development that "seeks to meet the needs and aspirations of the present without compromising the ability to meet those of the future."[1] The same goal has guided other international policy endeavors, notably the Earth Summit in 1992 and the recent climate negotiations in Kyoto.

There is no question that the contradiction between the modern world's imperative toward growth and the Earth's finite resources will ultimately be resolved in some way. The only question is how that will come about–whether through enlightened management, economic and environmental catastrophe, or some other means. Unfortunately, no one can predict this with any certainty. Projections that are valid for the short term lose their validity as the time horizon increases from months or years to decades or even generations. This uncertainty stems from our limited understanding of human and ecological systems and the inherent indeterminism of complex dynamic systems. In addition, social futures invariably depend on human choices that have yet to be made.

One way to gain insights into the uncertain future is to construct what are known as scenarios. This technique, in fact, has been used since the 1970s to bring the issue of environment and development to the attention of both scientists and policymakers.[2] This article explores a wide range of long-term scenarios that could unfold from the forces that will drive the world system in the 21st century by considering six contrasting possibilities. The scenarios were

From *Environment*, April 1998, pp. 6-11, 26-31. Reprinted with permission of the Helen Dwight Reid Educational Foundation. Published by Heldref Publications, 1319 Eighteenth St., N.W., Washington, D.C. 20036-1802. © 1998.

developed by an international and interdisciplinary group of 15 development professionals called the Global Scenario Group.[3] This scan of the future illuminates the perils and possibilities before us and, more importantly, helps to clarify the changes in policies and values that will be required for a transition to sustainability during coming decades.

The Scenario Approach

A scenario is essentially a story about the future. It indicates what the future may be like along with the way in which events might unfold. Unlike projections and forecasts, which tend to be more quantitative and more limited in their assumptions, scenarios are logical narratives dealing with possibly far-reaching changes.[4] By forcing us to clarify alternative world views and challenging the conventional wisdom, scenario analysis offers us a uniquely valuable way to ponder critical issues.

Scenarios draw on two sources—science (with its understanding of historical patterns, current conditions, and physical processes) and the imagination. Thus, they reflect the insights of quantitative analysis while giving due weight to key qualitative elements such as culture, values, and institutions. Quantitative modeling lends a certain structure, discipline, and rigor to the analysis of socioeconomic, resource, and environmental conditions; narratives give it texture, richness, and insight.

The major elements of formulating a scenario are represented in Figure 1. First, the *current state* of the system under consideration must be described and quantitatively represented in enough detail to address the key issues. Next, the *driving forces,* that is, those that govern the system and propel it forward, have to be identified and characterized. Along with the driving forces are *attracting* and *repelling forces,* events that can redirect beliefs, behaviors, policies, and institutions away from some visions of the future and toward others;[5] the third step is to ascertain and evaluate these

forces. Finally, one has to consider possible *sideswipes,* major surprises that can alter an otherwise straightforward outcome. Such surprises might include a world war, miracle technologies, an extreme natural disaster, a pandemic, or the breakdown of the climate system.

All scenario exercises must organize the bewildering array of possible futures into an intelligible structure, generally one based on a few stylized scenarios that illuminate the important issues, choices, and uncertainties. In typical policy studies, for instance, a "mid-range" (or most probable) scenario is supplemented by additional scenarios in which key driving forces such as population, economic growth, and technological change are varied across a certain range. In this respect, however, the scenarios that we constructed differ from the standard practice. Rather than reducing the rich diversity of future possibilities to mere variations in quantitative assumptions, we attempted to introduce a framework that would preserve that diversity.

Possible Futures

Our analysis focused on three basic visions of the future, which we call the Conventional Worlds, Barbarization, and Great Transitions scenarios. The Conventional Worlds scenario assumes that current trends will continue without fundamental change in institutions and values. By contrast, both the Barbarization and Great Transitions scenarios assume that there will be a fundamental change from current trends–in one case leading to a negative vision of the future, in the other to a positive vision. Each scenario has two variants, for a total of six possible outcomes. (See Figure 2 for a listing of these variants and their principal characteristics.)

The Reference variant of the Conventional Worlds scenario incorporates mid-range population and development projections. In the absence of major new policy initiatives, technology gradually evolves to promote clean production, efficient resource use, sustainable agriculture, and so forth. The Policy Reform variant adds strong, comprehensive, and coordinated government action to achieve greater social equity and environmental protection. In this variant, society acquires the political will to strengthen management systems and rapidly diffuse environmentally friendly technology. Both variants assume continuity in institutions and values,

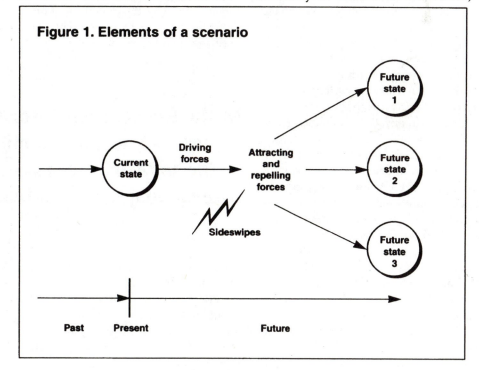

Figure 1. Elements of a scenario

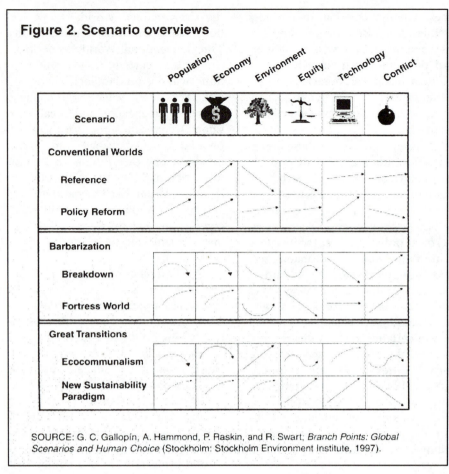

Figure 2. Scenario overviews

SOURCE: G. C. Gallopín, A. Hammond, P. Raskin, and R. Swart; *Branch Points: Global Scenarios and Human Choice* (Stockholm: Stockholm Environment Institute, 1997).

rapid growth in the world economy, and regional convergence toward the norms set by the highly industrialized countries. The principal difference is that in the Reference variant the resolution of the social and environmental problems that arise from global population and economic growth is left to self-regulating competitive markets, whereas in the Policy Reform variant sustainability is a specific policy goal.

The Barbarization scenario envisions the possibility that the social, economic, and moral underpinnings of civilization will deteriorate as emerging problems overwhelm the coping capacity of both markets and policy reforms. The Breakdown variant entails unbridled conflict, institutional disintegration, and economic collapse. The Fortress World variant involves an authoritarian response to the threat of breakdown: Ensconced in protected enclaves, elites safeguard their privileges by managing critical natural resources and controlling the impoverished majority; outside the fortress

there is repression, environmental destruction, and misery.

The Great Transitions scenario postulates visionary solutions to the sustainability challenge, including new socioeconomic arrangements and fundamental changes in values. This scenario contemplates a society that preserves natural systems, that provides high levels of welfare through material sufficiency and equitable distribution, and that enjoys a large degree of social solidarity. Population is stabilized at a moderate level, and the flow of materials through the econ-

omy is radically reduced through less consumerism and the massive use of green technologies. The Ecocommunalism variant incorporates the deep green vision of localism, face-to-face democracy, small technology, and economic autonomy. The New Sustainability Paradigm variant has many of the same goals but pursues them by attempting to build a more humane and equitable global civilization rather than by retreating into localism.

Many other scenarios can be constructed as variations and blends of these pure cases. For instance, more sophisticated scenarios might reflect regional variations and the possibility of discontinuous jumps at critical points in the development trajectory.[6] However, the six possibilities on which we concentrated provide a useful framework for analysis as well as a point of departure for more detailed explorations. At present, most policy discussions focus on some form of a Conventional Worlds scenario. The Barbarization scenario lurks as a danger, however—the punishment that may be imposed on future generations for unwarranted complacency today. The Great Transitions scenario, on the other hand, offers idealistic alternatives, futures that may seem utopian but that are perhaps no less plausible than a transition to sustainability without fundamental social transformation.

In the Conventional Worlds scenario, the values and socioeconomic arrangements of the industrial era continue to evolve without major discontinuities.

The scenarios were designed to represent archetypal social visions that have recurred in various forms in treatises on the relatively distant future. Quantitative representations of scenario variants were made using the PoleStar System, which was designed specifically for this purpose, along with data and assumptions drawn from major sectoral studies.[7]

Conventional Worlds

In the Conventional Worlds scenario, the values and socioeconomic arrangements of the industrial era continue to evolve without major discontinuities. Competitive markets and private investment remain the engines of economic growth and wealth allocation. The globalization of product and labor markets continues apace, catalyzed by free trade agreements, unregulated flows of capital, and advances in information technology. The nation-state remains the dominant unit of governance, while transnational corporations dominate an increasingly borderless economy. Consumerism and possessive individualism endure as the primary motives underlying human behavior; consumer culture permeates all societies via electronic media, eventually reducing diversity, despite fundamentalist, ethnic, and nationalist backlashes. The consumption patterns and production practices of the developing regions converge toward those of the highly industrialized countries.

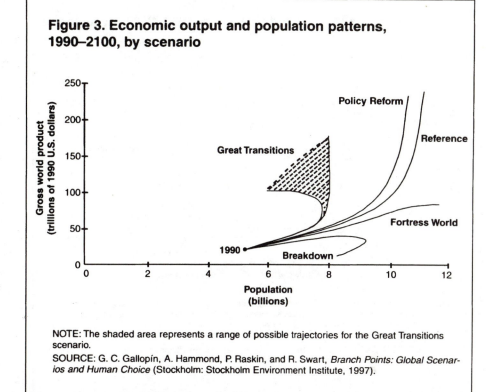

Figure 3. Economic output and population patterns, 1990–2100, by scenario

NOTE: The shaded area represents a range of possible trajectories for the Great Transitions scenario.

SOURCE: G. C. Gallopín, A. Hammond, P. Raskin, and R. Swart, *Branch Points: Global Scenarios and Human Choice* (Stockholm: Stockholm Environment Institute, 1997).

grow more rapidly than those of Organisation for Economic Cooperation and Development (OECD) countries (their average annual growth rates to the year 2050 are approximately 3.6 percent and 2 percent, respectively). Consequently, the OECD countries'

services continues. In particular, the share of materials-intensive industries eventually decreases everywhere, consistent with recent trends in the industrialized countries. The spread of new technology leads to more efficient use of energy and water, growing utilization of renewable energy resources, and cleaner industrial processes. (Figures 3 and 4 present trajectories for population, economic output, and income disparities for the Reference variant and all the other cases considered in this article.)

The Reference variant provides a benchmark for analyzing the constraints and obstacles to business-as-usual development, as well as what would be required to adopt alternative behaviors, institutions, and technologies. Figure 5 shows some of the global demographic, economic, and resource-use patterns for this case. Although energy and water use grow far less rapidly than GDP due to the structural and technological changes described above, pressure on resources and the environment increases as the greater scale of human activity overwhelms these resource efficiency improvements. Several types of destabilizing risks can be

The Reference variant provides a benchmark for analyzing the constraints and obstacles to business-as-usual development.

The Reference variant of this scenario can be represented quantitatively by assuming that current trends and policies are maintained and that development follows a mid-range course (as assumed in many analyses).[8] Population increases from about 6 billion today to about 10 billion by the year 2050, with nearly all the increase in developing regions. The world economy grows from about $20 trillion in 1990 to about $95 trillion in 2050 and continues growing thereafter. The economies of developing countries

share of world output decreases from 80 percent in 1990 to 60 percent in 2050. In one sense, incomes in the two groups of countries gradually converge: The ratio of the average gross domestic product (GDP) per capita in the OECD to that in other regions decreases from 20 in 1990 to 15 in 2050. However, the *absolute* difference increases from an average of $18,000 per capita in 1990 to $55,000 per capita by 2050 as incomes in rich countries soar. The structural shift in economic activity from industry to

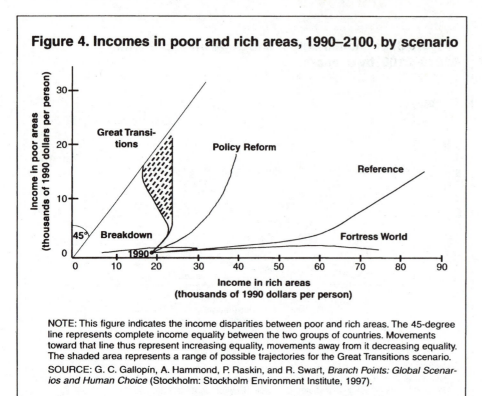

Figure 4. Incomes in poor and rich areas, 1990–2100, by scenario

NOTE: This figure indicates the income disparities between poor and rich areas. The 45-degree line represents complete income equality between the two groups of countries. Movements toward that line thus represent increasing equality, movements away from it decreasing equality. The shaded area represents a range of possible trajectories for the Great Transitions scenario.

SOURCE: G. C. Gallopín, A. Hammond, P. Raskin, and R. Swart, *Branch Points: Global Scenarios and Human Choice* (Stockholm: Stockholm Environment Institute, 1997).

identified. First, the cumulative loads on Earth's biogeochemical cycles and ecosystems could exceed natural assimilative capacities. This is shown by the sharp increase in emissions of carbon dioxide, which radically contradicts the climate stabilization goal of reduced emissions. There are similar problems in such areas as habitat destruction, biodiversity loss, and the accumulation of toxic chemicals in the environment.

Second, heightened pressure on natural resources could lead to economic and social disruptions or even conflicts. Without major unexpected discoveries, oil would become scarce over the next several decades, so that prices would rise and oil would again become a major theme in international affairs. Water pollution and the growing demand for water would increasingly stress renewable water resources, threaten aquatic ecosystems, and generate discord over the allocation of fresh water within and between countries. Agricultural output would need to more than double by 2050 to feed a richer and larger population, which would likely lead to further conversion of forests and wetlands,

more pollution of soils and water systems, and the continued degradation and loss of arable land due to unsustainable farming practices. Unfavorable climate alterations would further complicate matters in many areas.

Third, social and geopolitical stresses would threaten socioeconomic sustainability. The persistence of poverty on a large scale and the continued inequality between and within nations (exacerbated by environmental degradation and resource constraints) would undermine social cohesion, stimulate migration, and put stress on international security systems. Breakdowns in sociopolitical stability could, in turn, provide the necessary conditions for authoritarianism, the flaring of regional, ethnic, and religious conflicts, and the suppression of democratic institutions—that is, for a cataclysmic leap toward Barbarization.

Depending on one's philosophical predisposition, the risks inherent in this variant of the Conventional Worlds scenario will be weighed very differently. Free-market optimists will tend to downgrade the environmental and social concerns, trusting in market adaptations and human ingenuity

o provide timely solutions. Less ideological observers might simply believe that muddling through is less dangerous than well-intentioned but wrong-headed policy activism. Pessimists, distrusting the adequacy of automatic market mechanisms, would fear that business-as-usual would endanger, perhaps catastrophically, the long-range health of social and ecological systems.

Because policy complacency risks serious resource, environmental, and institutional problems, we formulated a Policy Reform variant that assumes strong measures at all levels of government within the context of current values and institutional structures. This variant would require achieving three goals simultaneously: rapid economic growth, greater distributional equity, and serious protection of environmental quality.

The definitive statement of this vision is the report of the Brundtland Commission. This highly influential work offers a comprehensive appraisal of the "interlocking crises" threatening the future, along with an eloquent call for "a new era of economic growth, one that must be based on policies that sustain and expand the environmental resource base."[9] In this formulation, greater social equity is both an ethical imperative and an objective requirement for sustainable development. In support of its various goals, the commission identified a set of policies aimed at reducing poverty, creating better management systems, and hastening the development, transfer, and deployment of environmentally friendly technology.

Do reforms of this nature actually offer a plausible path to sustainability? In practical terms, it would be an immense challenge to marshal the political will for the massive policy interventions required. The scope of that challenge becomes clear when one realizes the improvements in energy efficiency and shifts toward renewable energy sources that would be needed to substantially reduce the risk of climate change (see Figure 6). Even with these changes, the concentration of carbon in the atmosphere would gradually increase over the next century to a level 25 percent greater than today's (which is already about 33 percent greater than the pre-industrial level). In addition to the practical questions, however, there is a major normative consideration: This approach might achieve a sustainable world but not one that is worth living in. That is, the lifestyles and values embodied in the Conventional Worlds scenario could ultimately be deemed undesirable on social, environmental, or ethical grounds. A world that achieves sustainability through comprehensive environmental management, competition, individualism, and global homogenization might not appeal to those who treasure wild places, cooperative communities, and cultural diversity.

Barbarization

Like the Conventional Worlds scenario, the Barbarization scenario is driven by the ascendency of global economic forces, but in this case humanity is unable to manage the resulting change and conventional institutions ultimately unravel. Perhaps the most significant element of this scenario is that the number of people living in poverty increases while the gap between rich and poor grows (both within and among countries). To make matters worse, social concern is radically downgraded as governments gradually lose relevance and power relative to large multinational corporations and global market forces. At the same time, development aid decreases and is increasingly limited to disaster relief.

A number of other consequences follow from the growing disparity in income. Inundated by global media and tourism, millions of people in underdeveloped regions become resentful of the immense differences in lifestyle between rich and poor. The poor become convinced that they have been cheated out of development and that their options have been preempted by the wealthy. This leads to strong social polarization.

With rapid population growth in the poorer regions, a huge international youth culture emerges. Numbering in the billions, teenagers around the world share remarkably similar expectations and attitudes, their consumerist and nihilist tendencies being reinforced by entertainment programs and advertising that reach every corner of the Earth. But these young people ultimately discover that the tantalizing visions of "McWorld" are largely unattainable in their current circumstances.[10] This leads to massive waves of legal and illegal migration to rich countries (and to areas of prosperity within poor countries).

Despite some improvements in the richest countries, environmental conditions continue to worsen. The unfettered expansion of market-based economies leads to increased industrial activity and rising pollution. Rapid urbanization displaces natural ecosystems and places local environments under severe stress. Deepening rural poverty accelerates soil degradation and deforestation. As fresh water becomes increasingly scarce, conflicts over water emerge among countries that share rivers. Already brittle marine fisheries collapse under the additional pressure, depriving a billion people of their primary source of protein. Climate change causes hardship for subsistence farmers in many regions. Famine becomes more frequent and more severe in Africa and elsewhere, while the response capacity of relief agencies declines. Mortality rates increase as a result of the growing environmental degradation, which aids the emergence of new diseases and the resurgence of old ones.[11]

Owing to the growing socioeconomic inequality, increased morbidity, and reduced access to water, grazing land, and other natural resources, social tensions become more widespread and intense. International discord mounts due to widening disparities between regions as well as growing economic competition and the progressive decline in development assistance. People in rich countries increasingly fear that their well-being is being threatened by factors they associate with poor countries, including migration, terrorism, disease, and global environmental degradation. At the same time, a new type of have-not emerges as a significant factor in rich countries, namely, the educated but long-term unemployed.

As such tensions increase, the incidence of violent confrontation rises, sparked by long-standing ethnic and religious differences, politically motivated terrorism, struggles over scarce natural

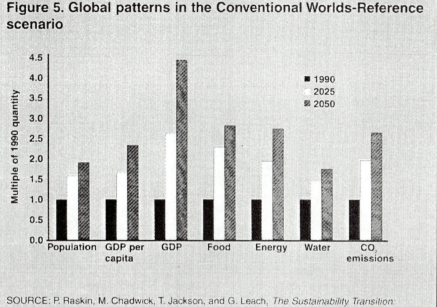

Figure 5. Global patterns in the Conventional Worlds-Reference scenario

SOURCE: P. Raskin, M. Chadwick, T. Jackson, and G. Leach, *The Sustainability Transition: Beyond Conventional Development* (Stockholm: Stockholm Environment Institute, 1996).

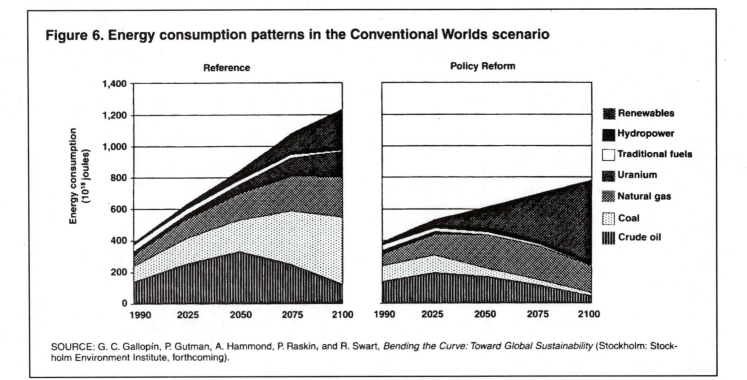

Figure 6. Energy consumption patterns in the Conventional Worlds scenario

SOURCE: G. C. Gallopín, P. Gutman, A. Hammond, P. Raskin, and R. Swart, *Bending the Curve: Toward Global Sustainability* (Stockholm: Stockholm Environment Institute, forthcoming).

resources, competing nationalisms, and commercial conflicts. By and large, however, military actions take the form of multiple small-scale engagements rather than major wars. At the same time, civil order progressively breaks down as a kind of criminal anarchy prevails in many areas.[12] These developments take an increasing toll on economic growth, causing more and more resources to be diverted to security and international investment in troubled regions to plummet. In areas of prolonged conflict, both environmental protection and the maintenance of infrastructure are neglected, reversing decades of progress.

Politically, a jagged pattern of city-states and nebulous regional formations emerges. Some formerly prosperous industrial countries join the ranks of the impoverished. Economic development ceases, technological progress stagnates except for efforts to provide better security for the privileged, and no individual country is able to assume a leadership role.

Like the Conventional Worlds scenario, Barbarization can assume two basic forms. In this case, the two variants differ in the degree to which the prevailing power structure—governments (individually and in alliance with others), transnational corporations, international organizations, and the armed forces—manage to maintain some sense of order. In the Breakdown variant, it is simply impossible to control the tide of violence flowing from disaffected individuals, terrorist organizations, ethno-religious groups, economic factions, and organized criminals. Civil order largely breaks down, ultimately leading to a general collapse of social, cultural, and political institutions along with the market economy. Many regions experience a return to semi-tribal or feudal social structures. Although population continues to grow for some time in the poorer regions (in a vicious cycle of poverty and high birth rates), it eventually decreases everywhere as mortality rates surge in response to the economic decline, infrastructural collapse, and the degradation of the resource base. In a bitter irony, equity increases because everyone is poorer. If such a breakdown were to occur, it could persist for many decades before evolution to a higher level was again possible.

In the Fortress World variant of the Barbarization scenario, powerful regional and international entities manage to impose some form of authoritarian order on the populace at large. In this variant, a well-off elite flourishes in protected enclaves (mostly in the historically rich countries) while the majority remain mired in poverty and denied basic human rights.

To preserve their access to the goods and services provided by the environment, the elite place large areas under protected status and exclude the poor from them. Along the same lines, they put strategic reserves of fossil fuels, minerals, fresh water and germplasm diversity under military control. Pollution is kept low within the fortress by means of increased efficiency, recycling, and external dumping; outside the fortress, environmental conditions deteriorate dramatically.

Although the system embodied in the Fortress World variant would probably contain the seeds of its own destruction, it could last for decades if it were able to control popular unrest. Only an uprising by the outside majority could threaten it, and even then their success would probably hinge on fissures in the alliance of dominant groups.

Great Transitions

Not all alternatives to the Conventional Worlds scenario are gloomy. Indeed, it is possible to conceive of a scenario in which we would transcend the industrial culture of the present without descending into chaos. Like the previous two scenarios, this one has two variants. In the Ecocommunalism variant, a network of largely self-sufficient communities replaces the huge, highly interdependent institutions of the modern world. In this "small is beautiful" and biocentric vision, an ethic of voluntary simplicity and local autonomy comes to dominate. Material consumption levels fall in wealthy areas as a craft economy rises to complement production from small-scale and locally owned facilities and farms while outside economic links are minimal. Population contracts and urban centers gradually give way to town- and village-scale settlements. Proximity to nature becomes highly valued as a spiritual bond that unifies each community. Because it is difficult to imagine a pathway to this variant, this article will focus on the other variant, namely, the New Sustainability Paradigm.

The New Sustainability Paradigm balances the cosmopolitanism of a global outlook with a strong sense of community, egalitarianism, and environmentalism. Most people feel a strong affiliation with a global family as well as with their own regional and local communities. Governance systems, economic relations, and culture reflect this new multilevel perspective. The materialism of the Conventional Worlds scenario gives way to an emphasis on qualitative goals such as education, leisure, the arts, the experience of nature, service, and spiritual pursuits. The flow of energy and materials through the economy is radically reduced in wealthier areas through efficient technologies, lower-input lifestyles, and the widespread use of renewable resources. Poorer regions rapidly converge toward this revised concept of development. Values, institutions, and the very notion of the good life have indeed undergone a great transition.

How might the New Sustainability Paradigm emerge? Most likely it would be through a sequence of events such as the following: During the next few decades, the biosphere is widely perceived to be threatened by cumulative environmental stressors. There is growing evidence that both ecosystems and human health will suffer serious harm as certain related problems reach critical levels (examples include global warming, acidification, disease, and toxification). New insights from the science of complexity lead to greater awareness of the risk of "mega-flips" in the planetary system, that is, of massive, irreversible changes in the climate and life-support systems.[13] At the same time, governments, business, and the general public are increasingly anxious about worsening social polarization and conflict.

A new international polity emerges around these concerns and the widespread feeling that life has lost much of its meaning. The conviction grows that reliance on the profit motive to guide the economy has been environmentally and socially costly and that government has become too weak. Disenchantment with the consumerist lifestyle mushrooms, gradually affecting all groups but particularly the young. The values of simplicity, tranquillity, and community begin to displace those of consumerism, competition, and individualism. Many people opt to work (and earn) less to free up time for study, art, relationships, and myriad hobbies, crafts, sports, and other pastimes.

Almost imperceptibly, these processes slowly coalesce into a worldwide ferment of untold millions searching for new ideals, meaning, and forms of social existence (some turn toward esoteric sects, but they are the minority). Young people around the world discover a collective identity in a new idealism that is directed toward creating a planetary community. The Internet becomes an important forum for this new consciousness, helping to forge a sense of unity. Global meetings and festivals explore the new values of equity, human rights, the environment, and spiritual and aesthetic exploration as a global network of civic groups organizes politically to promote freedom and plurality. Eventually, many communities and some regions opt for alternative lifestyles and economic practices. Some stress high-technology solutions, others prefer frugality, and still others adopt the utopian vision that small is beautiful, emphasizing the protection of the wilderness and a mystical relationship with nature. Gradually, a federation of diverse global constituencies emerges. Initially a reaction against homogenization and manipulation, it leads to a collective discussion about the display of humankind.

At this point, the tension between the forces of conventional development (or barbarization) and the new planetary consciousness has reached the critical moment. Progressive reconstruction then overcomes all resistance. Equity and sustainability, rather than economic growth per se, become the goals of development. Material simplicity becomes the preferred lifestyle, while ostentatious consumption is viewed as primitive and a sign of bad taste. Interestingly, some transnational corporations accept (or even advocate) general limits on growth as part of the new business ethic of ecoefficiency. Others resist change, but under popular pressure governments and corporations begin negotiations for a planetary New Deal. This includes international agreements on the redistribution of wealth in the context of reduced material consumption in the rich countries. Income transfers are tied to developing countries' voluntarily reducing family size and meeting globally agreed upon environmental targets. New technologies for sustainability flourish as public preferences and prices shift.

Complementing the above changes, a *new metropolitan vision* inspires the redesign of urban neighborhoods. Integrated settlement patterns place home, work, shops, and leisure activities in closer proximity. Dependence on the automobile is reduced radically, and a sense of community connectedness is reestablished. The basis for this renaissance of diverse and secure communities is the elimination of the urban underclass, the ubiquitous signal of social distress during the previous era. For many people, the town-within-the-city provides the ideal balance of a human scale and access to cosmopolitan culture.

Small towns also become popular as communication and information technologies increasingly allow for the decentralization of activities. The migration from rural to urban areas begins to reverse as many people opt for the lower stress level and increased contact with nature offered by smaller communities. A new spirit of community is reinforced by more self-reliant production patterns (including decentralized renewable energy systems) and pride in local environments. The mall culture fades as new urban and rural alternatives underscore the sterility, hidden costs, and isolation of suburbia.

In the new economy, markets still play a major role in achieving efficiencies in the production and allocation of goods and services, but the aggregate level of economic activity is constrained by social, cultural, and environmental goals. In addition, the time-horizon for economic decisions is lengthened to decades to take meaningful account of ecological processes. A variety of mechanisms are used to enforce these principles, including a new tax system that discourages environmental "bads" and certain types of consumption as well as regulation that adheres strictly to the polluter-pays principle. Antisocial corporate behavior is further discouraged by thorough public disclosure of key information. Well-designed environmental, economic, and social indicators measure the effectiveness of policies, giving the public an informed basis for seeking change.

Experiments with alternative forms of governance proliferate from local to global scales. Regions and communities have considerable control over their own affairs, being constrained only by the impacts of those decisions on others. Energy offers a good example: Local energy systems vary greatly, but all of them meet per capita greenhouse gas emissions guidelines set by global agreements. Similarly, local water management is compatible with ecosystem goals for the entire watershed from which

water is drawn. Global governance is based on a federation of regions that effectively fosters cooperation, security, and environmental health through a rejuvenated United Nations and a truly global civil service. A fully interactive Internet offers powerful new channels for communication, education, and the democratic process, undercutting any reappearance of authoritarianism. The politics of diversity through global unity has found its natural medium.

Conflicts are resolved by negotiation, collaboration, and consensus. Armies are abolished and defense systems dismantled, and the massive peace dividend is used to speed the transition to sustainability and to eradicate the last vestiges of poverty. Economic development continues indefinitely, but it is mostly concentrated in the low-material-use realm of services, culture, art, sports, and research. A labor-intensive crafts economy rises spontaneously on the platform of the high-technology base, providing a rewarding outlet for creative expression and a dizzying diversity of highly aesthetic and treasured goods. A pervasive exhilaration about pioneering a socially and environmentally superior way of life becomes a powerful attracting force in its own right, a self-fulfilling prophecy that is able to draw the present to itself. Humanity has at last reached the end of its childhood.

Reflections from the Present

Humanity is just beginning to grasp the full meaning of sustainability and what might be required to create a truly sustainable global society. Constructing scenarios can be an important part of the learning process, helping to clarify the scientific, philosophical, and policy dimensions of this great historical challenge. Scenarios aid scientific research by highlighting major conceptual uncertainties and gaps in the data and by providing key parameters for the complex quantitative models of global change. As readily understandable stories about the future, scenarios can also alert the general public to the problems we

face and the choices before us. Finally, scenario analysis can enrich the policy process by identifying emerging risks and required actions.

In constructing scenarios of the future, it will be essential to work from the bottom up as well as from the top down, that is, to consider the local, national, and regional implications of alternative scenarios along with the global implications. The global perspective, of course, is indispensable: It enables us to identify the forces that increasingly shape and constrain development everywhere. But the local, national, and regional perspectives offer important insights of their own. For example, an adequate strategy for sustainable development within the confines of a shared river system requires both a detailed analysis geared to the specific circumstances in the river basin and an appreciation of the ways in which larger forces can influence local environmental, demographic, and economic conditions.

Because most policy discussions currently focus on the Conventional Worlds alternative, it is natural that scenario analysis begin there. But this scenario cannot be taken for granted, any more than significant tilts toward the Barbarization or Great Transitions scenarios can be entirely ruled out. One need not be excessively cynical to observe troubling portents of the Fortress World outcome in the growth of the underclass, the emergence of gated communities, and the mounting social polarization of the present. At the same time, many people throughout the world are increasingly desirous of having a sustainable relationship with nature, of rejecting material profligacy and resurrecting a strong sense of community, and of finding more meaning in their lives. Although such values are at present inchoate and unsystematic, they may herald the appearance of the New Sustainability Paradigm at some point in the future.

The scenarios presented in this article also point to another highly important development, namely, that the destinies of the rich and poor are becoming much more tightly coupled through their sharing of the planet's resources. Social disintegration in poor regions now threatens the security and well-being of the affluent: If they can export nothing else, the poor can export their misery through migration, crime, terrorism, and disease. This coupling of destinies means that there are no separate solutions, one for the South and one for the North. Only a truly global solution can achieve a humane and sustainable future. Policy discussions and planning must rise to the level of humanity as a whole as well as to that of the biosphere. The challenge for current generations is to think and act in ways that reduce social and ecological stresses while keeping future opportunities open.

NOTES

1. World Commission on Environment and Development, *Our Common Future* (Oxford, U.K.: Oxford University Press, 1987), 40.

2. Earlier studies include D. H. Meadows, D. L. Meadows, J. Randers, and W. W. Behrens, *Limits to Growth* (New York: Basic Books, 1972); A. D. Herrera et al., *Catastrophe or New Society?: A Latin American World Model* (Ottawa, Canada: International Development Research Centre, 1976); M. D. Mesarovic and E. Pestel, *Mankind at a Turning Point* (New York: Dutton, 1974); H. Kahn and A. Wiener, *The Year 2000* (New York: MacMillan, 1967); H. Kahn, W. Brown, and L. Martel, *The Next 2000 Years: A Scenario for America and the World* (New York: Morrow, 1976); and G. O. Barney, *The Global 2000 Report to the President of the US: Entering the 21st Century* (Washington, D.C.: U.S. Government Printing Office, 1980). Recent studies include B. Burrows, A. Mayne, and P. Newbury, *Into the 21st Century: A Handbook for a Sustainable Future* (Twickenham, U.K.: Adamantine, 1991); L. W. Milbrath, *Envisioning a Sustainable Society: Learning Our Way Out* (Albany, N.Y.: SUNY Press, 1989); Dutch Central Planning Bureau, *Scanning the Future: A Long-Term Scenario Study of the World Economy, 1990–2015* (The Hague: SDU Publishers, 1992); U. Seven and B. Aniansson, eds., *Surprising Futures:*

Notes from an International Workshop on Long-Term World Development (Stockholm: Swedish Council for Planning and Coordination of Research, 1987); F. I. Toth, E. Hizsnyik, and W. C. Clark, eds., *Scenarios of Socioeconomic Development for Studies of Global Environmental Change: A Critical Review,* RR-89-4 (Laxenburg, Austria: International Institute for Applied Systems Analysis, 1989); United Nations, *Global Outlook 2000: An Economic, Social, and Environmental Perspective* (New York, 1990); and Intergovernmental Panel on Climate Change, *1992 IPCC Supplement* (Geneva: World Meteorological Organization, 1992).

3. The members of the Global Scenario Group all have long experience in scenario and policy analysis at the global and regional levels. This article is based on the group's first report. G. Gallopín, A. Hammond, P. Raskin, and R. Swart, *Branch Points: Global Scenarios and Human Choice* (Stockholm: Stockholm Environment Institute, 1997). A forthcoming report will present the Policy Reform variant in considerable detail. See G. C. Gallopín, P. Gutman, A. Hammond, P. Raskin, and R. Swart, *Bending the Curve: Toward Global Sustainability* (Stockholm: Stockholm Environment Institute, forthcoming). These reports may be accessed on the World Wide Web (www.gsg.org), which also provides information on the participants in and activities of the Global Scenario Group. Primary support for the group's work comes from a grant by the Nippon Foundation.

4. See P. Schwartz, *The Art of the Long View* (New York: Doubleday, 1991); S. Cole, "Methods of Analysis for Long-Term Development Issues," in United Nations Economic, Social, and Cultural Organization, *Methods for Development Planning* (Paris, 1981), 11; I. Miles, "Scenario Analysis: Identifying Ideologies and Issues," ibid., page 31; and M. Godet, *Scenarios and Strategic Management* (London: Butterworths, 1987).

5. See P. Raskin, M. Chadwick, T. Jackson, and G. Leach, *The Sustainability Transition: Beyond Conventional Development* (Stockholm: Stockholm Environment Institute, 1996).

6. The sudden breakup of the Soviet Union is a dramatic example of a developmental discontinuity. More gradual, but no less important, are the transition to settled agriculture and the Industrial Revolution.

7. The PoleStar System is a comprehensive and flexible computer-based framework for organizing data pertinent to sustainability studies and for creating alternative scenarios (visit www.tellus.org/polestar.html for details).

8. These assumptions are summarized in Raskin et al., note 5 above. Details may be found in P. Raskin and R. Margolis, *Global Energy in the 21st Century: Patterns, Projections, and Problems* (Stockholm: Stockholm Environment Institute, 1995); P. Raskin, P. Gleick, P. Kirshen, G. Pontius, and K. Strzepek, *Water Futures: Assessment of Long-Range Patterns and Problems* (Stockholm: Stockholm Environment Institute, 1997); and G. Leach, *Global Land and Food Supply in the 21st Century* (Stockholm: Stockholm Environment Institute, 1995).

9. World Commission on Environment and Development, note 1 above.

10. See B. Barber, *Jihad vs. McWorld* (New York: Random House, 1995).

11. See J. A. Miller, "Diseases for Our Future: Global Ecology and Emerging Viruses," *BioScience* 39, no. 8 (1989): 509.

12. See R. D. Kaplan, "The Coming Anarchy," *The Atlantic Monthly,* February 1994, 44.

13. One possible change of this nature is the disruption of major ocean currents due to global warming. (Warmer sea surface temperatures would lead to more evaporation and increased salinity, thus hampering the downwelling necessary for currents to flow.) This could have drastic implications for humanity. Scientists already have evidence of frequent, large, abrupt (on the order of a few decades), and global cooling episodes during the last glacial period owing to sudden shifts in the operation of ocean currents. See W. S. Broecker, "Thermohaline Circulation, the Achilles Heel of Our Climate System: Will Man-Made CO_2 Upset the Current Balance?," *Science* 278 (1997): 1,582. Other insights from the science of complexity include the discovery of chaotic behavior in deterministic nonlinear systems; the possibility of self-organization in complex systems; and the existence of irreducible unpredictablity in the evolution of complex systems. See G. Nicolis and I. Prigogine, *Exploring Complexity: An Introduction* (New York: W. H. Freeman, 1989); and M. M. Waldrop, *Complexity: The Emerging Science at the Edge of Order and Chaos* (New York: Simon & Schuster, 1992).

Crossing the Threshold

Early Signs of an Environmental Awakening

by Lester R. Brown

At a time when the Earth's average temperature is going off the top of the chart, when storms, floods and tropical forest fires are more damaging than ever before, and when the list of endangered species grows longer by the day, it is difficult to be optimistic about the future. Yet even as these stories of environmental disruption capture the headlines, I see signs that the world may be approaching the threshold of a sweeping change in the way we respond to environmental threats—a social threshold that, once crossed, could change our outlook as profoundly as the one that in 1989 and 1990 led to a political restructuring in Eastern Europe.

If this new threshold is crossed, changes are likely to come at a pace and in ways that we can only begin to anticipate. The overall effect could be the most profound economic transformation since the Industrial Revolution itself. If so, it will affect every facet of human existence, not only reversing the environmental declines with which we now struggle, but also bringing us a better life

Thresholds are encountered in both the natural world and in human society. One of the most familiar natural thresholds, for example, is the freezing point of water. As water temperature falls, the water remains liquid until it reaches the threshold point of 0 degrees Celsius (32 degrees Fahrenheit). Only a modest additional drop produces dramatic change, transforming a liquid into a solid.

The threshold concept is widely used in ecology, in reference to the "sustainable yield threshold" of natural systems such as fisheries or forests. If the harvest from a fishery exceeds that threshold for an extended period, stocks will decline and the fishery may abruptly collapse. When the demands on a forest exceed its sustainable yield and the tree cover begins to shrink, the result can be a cascade of hundreds of changes in the ecosystem. For example, with fewer trees and less leaf litter on the forest floor, the land's water-absorptive capacity diminishes and runoff increases—and that, in turn, may lead to unnaturally destructive flooding lower in the watershed.

In the social world, the thresholds to sudden change are no less real, though they are much more difficult to identify and anticipate. The political revolution in Eastern Europe was so sudden that with no apparent warning the era of the centrally planned economy was over, and those who had formidably defended it for half a century realized it was too late to reverse what had happened. Even the U.S. Central Intelligence Agency failed to foresee the change. And after it happened, the agency had trouble explaining it. But at some point, a critical mass had been reached, where enough people were convinced of the need to change to tip the balance and bring a cascading shift in public perceptions.

In recent months, I have become increasingly curious about such sudden shifts of perception for one compelling reason. If I look at the global environmental trends that we have been tracking since we first launched the Worldwatch Institute 25 years ago, and if I simply extrapolate these trends a few years into the next century, the outlook is alarming to say the least. It is now clear to me that if we are to turn things around in time, we need some kind of *breakthrough*. This is not to discount the many gradual improvements that we have made on the environmental front, such as increased fuel efficiency in cars or better pollution controls on factories. Those are important. But we are not moving fast enough to reverse the trends that are undermining the global economy. What we need now is a rapid shift in consciousness, a dawning awareness in people everywhere that we have to shift quickly to a sustainable economy if we want to avoid damaging our natural support systems beyond repair. The question is whether there is any evidence that we are approaching such a breakthrough.

While shifts of this kind can be shockingly sudden, the underlying causes are not. The conditions for profound social change seem to require a long gestation period. In Eastern Europe, it was fully four decades from the resistance to socialism when it was first imposed until its demise. Roughly 35 years passed between the issuance of

From *World Watch*, March/April 1999, pp. 12-22. © 1999 by the Worldwatch Institute. Reprinted by permission.

New climate data drew intense media interest, as more than 100 reporters gathered for a WORLD WATCH press conference at the release of the January/February issue—and more than 2,000 newspapers carried our followup study on rising storm damages.

the first U.S. Surgeon General's report on smoking and health—and the hundreds of research reports it spawned—and the historic November 1998 $206 billion settlement between the tobacco industry and 46 state governments. (The other four states had already settled for $45 billion.) Thirty-seven years have passed since biologist Rachel Carson published *Silent Spring,* issuing the wake-up call that gave rise to the modern environmental movement.

Not all environmentalists will agree with me, but I believe that there are now some clear signs that the world does seem to be approaching a kind of paradigm shift in environmental consciousness. Across a spectrum of activities, places, and institutions, the atmosphere has changed markedly in just the last few years. Among giant corporations that could once be counted on to mount a monolithic opposition to serious environmental reform, a growing number of high profile CEOs have begun to sound more like spokespersons for Greenpeace than for the bastions of global capitalism of which they are a part. More and more governments are taking revolutionary steps aimed at shoring up the Earth's long-term environmental health. Individuals the world over have established thriving new markets for products that are distinguished by their compatibility with a sustainable economy. What in the world is going on?

Thomas Kuhn, in his classic work *The Structure of Scientific Revolutions,* observes that as scientific understanding in a field advances, reaching a point where existing theory no longer explains reality, theory has to change. Perhaps history's best known example of this process is the shift from the Ptolemaic view of the world, in which people believed the sun revolved around the Earth, to the Copernican view which argued that the Earth

revolved about the sun. Once the Copernican model existed, a lot of things suddenly made sense to those who studied the heavens, leading to an era of steady advances in astronomy.

We are now facing such a situation with the global economy. Although economists have long ignored the Earth's natural systems, evidence that the economy is slowly self-destructing by destroying its natural support systems can be seen on every hand. The Earth's forests are shrinking, fisheries are collapsing, water tables are falling, soils are eroding, coral reefs are dying, atmospheric CO_2 concentrations are increasing, temperatures are rising, floods are becoming more destructive, and the rate of extinction of plant and animal species may be the greatest since the dinosaurs disappeared 65 million years ago.

These ecological trends are driving analysts to a paradigm shift in their view of how the economy will have to work in the future. For years, these trends were marginalized by policymakers and the media as "special interest" topics, but as the trends have come to impinge more and more directly on people's lives, that has begun to change. The findings of these analysts are primary topics now not only for environmentalists, but for governments, corporations, and the media.

Learning From China

If changes in physical conditions are often the driving forces in perceptual shifts, one of the most powerful forces driving the current shift in our understanding of the ecological/economic relationship is the flow of startling information coming from China. Not only the world's most populous country, China since 1980 has been the world's fastest growing economy, raising incomes nearly fourfold. As such, China is in effect telescoping history, showing us what happens when large numbers of people become more affluent.

As incomes have climbed, so has consumption. If the Chinese should reach the point where they eat as much beef as Americans, the production of just that added beef will take an estimated 340 million tons of grain per year, an amount equal to the entire U.S. grain harvest. Similarly, if the Chinese were to consume oil at the American rate, the country would need 80 million barrels of oil a day—more than the entire world's current production of 67 million barrels a day.

What China is dramatizing—to its own scientists and government and to an increasingly worried international community—is that the Western industrial development model will not work for China. And if the fossil-fuel-based, automobile-centered, throwaway economy will not work for it, then it will not work for India, with its billion people, nor for the other two billion in the developing world. And, in an increasingly integrated global economy, it will not work in the long run for the industrial economies either.

Just how powerfully events in China are beginning to sway perceptions was brought home to me at our press lunch for *State of the World 1998* when I was talking with some reporters sitting on the front row before the briefing began. A veteran reporter, rather skeptical as many seasoned reporters are, said that he had never been convinced by our argument that we need to restructure the global economy—but that the section in *State of the World* on rising affluence in China and the associated rising claims on global resources had now convinced him that we have little choice.

Fortunately, we now have a fairly clear picture of how to do that restructuring. When Worldwatch began to pioneer the concept of environmentally sustainable economic development 25 years ago, we were already aware that instead of being based on fossil fuels, the new model would be based on solar energy. Instead of having a sprawling automobile-centered urban transportation system, it would be based on more carefully designed cities, with shorter travel distances and greater reliance on rail, bicycles, and walking. Instead of a throwaway economy, it would be a reuse/recycle economy. And its population would have to be stable.

When we described our model in the early days, it sounded like pie in the sky—as the reporter's skepticism reminded me. Now, with the subsequent advances in solar and wind technologies, gains in recycling, mounting evidence of automobile-exacerbated global warming, and the growing recognition that oil production will decline in the not-too-distant future, it suddenly becomes much more credible, a compelling alternative. Just as early astronomers were limited in how far they could go in understanding the heavens with the Ptolemaic model, so, too, we are limited in how long we can sustain economic progress with the existing economic model. As a result, in each of the four major areas of that model—renewable energy, efficient urban transport, materials recycling, and population stability—I believe public vision is shifting rapidly.

Shifting Views of Energy

A decade ago, there were plenty of avid afficionados of renewable energy, but the subject was of only marginal interest to the global public. That has changed markedly, as escalating climate change has thrust questions about the climate-disrupting effects of burning fossil fuels into the center of public debate. In 1998, not only did the Earth's average temperature literally go off the top of the chart we have been using to track global temperature for many years, but storm-related weather damage that year climbed to a new high of $89 billion. This not only exceeded the previous record set in 1996 by an astonishing 48 percent, but it exceeded the weather-related damage for the entire decade of the 1980s.

When Worldwatch issued a brief report in late 1998 noting the record level of weather-related damage during the year, it was picked up by some 2,000 newspapers worldwide—an indication that energy issues were beginning to hit home, literally. Closely related to the increase in storms and floods was a dramatic rise in the number of people driven from their homes, for days or even months, as a result of more destructive storms and floods. Almost incomprehensibly, 300 million people—a number that exceeds the entire population of North America—were forced out of their homes in 1998.

If the news were only that fossil fuels are implicated in escalating damages, I'm not sure I'd see signs of a paradigm change. But along with the threats of rising damages, there were the data we released in 1998 indicating that the solutions to these threats have been coming on strong. Not only are fossil-fuel-exacerbated damages escalating, but technological alternatives—wind and solar power—are booming. While oil and coal still dominate the world energy economy, the new challengers are expanding at the kind of pace that makes venture capitalists reach for their phones. From 1990 to 1997, coal and oil use increased just over 1 percent per year, while solar cell sales, in contrast, were expanding at roughly 15 percent per year. In 1997 they jumped over 40 percent.

An estimated 500,000 homes, most of them in remote third world villages not linked to an electrical grid, now get their electricity from solar cells. The use of photovoltaic cells to supply electricity has recently gotten a big boost from the new solar roofing tiles developed in Japan. These "solar shingles," which enable the roof of a building to become its own power plant, promise to revolutionize electricity generation worldwide, making it easier to forget fossil fuels.

The growth in wind power has been even more impressive, a striking 26 percent per year since 1990. If you are an energy investor and are interested in growth', it is in wind, not oil. The U.S. Department of Energy's Wind Resource Inventory indicates that three states—North Dakota, South Dakota, and Texas—have enough harnessable wind energy to satisfy national electricity needs. And China could double its current electricity generation with wind alone.

Shifting Views of Urban Transport

In Bangkok, the average motorist last year sat in his car going nowhere for the equivalent of 44 working days. And in London, the average speed of a car today is little better than that of a horse-drawn carriage a century ago. Clearly, the automobiles that once provided much-needed mobility for rural societies cannot do the same for a society that will soon be largely urban. As a result, more and more national and city governments are beginning to confront the inherent conflict between the automobile and the city—a sign that we may be approaching a threshold of revolutionary change in how we view the very nature of urban life.

While the automobile industry still promotes the vision of a world with a car in every garage, some national and many city governments are emphasizing alternatives to the automobile, ones that center on better public rail transport and the bicycle. This movement in Europe is led by the Netherlands and Denmark, where bicycles account for 30 percent and 20 percent respectively of daily trips in cities. In Germany, policies encouraging bicycle use have raised the share of urban trips by bike nationwide from 8 percent in 1972 to 12 percent in 1995.

In Beijing, where air pollution is a health issue and where traffic conditions worsen by the month, the official enthusiasm for the car—dominant model of a few years ago seems to have cooled. A group of eminent scientists in China have directly challenged the government's plans to develop a Western-style, automobile-centered transportation system. They observe that China does not have enough land both to feed its people and to build the roads, highways, and parking lots needed for the automobile. They also argue that the automobile will increase traffic congestion, worsen urban air pollution—already the worst in the world—and force a growing dependence on imported oil.

The Chinese scientists argue that the country should develop "a public transportation network that is convenient, complete, and radiating in all directions." The effort to convince Party leaders to reverse their policy is being led by one of China's most venerated scientists, physicist He Zuoxiu, who worked on the country's first atomic bomb. He says that China "just simply cannot sustain the development of a car economy."

In the United States, scores of cities are beginning to develop more bicycle-friendly transportation systems. More than 300 U.S. cities now have part of their police force on bicycles. Not long ago I found myself standing on a street corner in downtown Washington, D.C., next to a police officer on a bicycle. As we waited for the light to change, I asked him why there were now so many officers on bicycles. He indicated that it was largely a matter of efficiency, since an officer on a bike can respond to some 50 percent more calls in a day than one in a squad car. The fiscal benefits are obvious. He also indicated that the bicycle police make many more arrests, because they are both more mobile and less conspicuous.

Bicycle transport, like solar or wind power, may still seem to many to be a marginal indicator. But I see the

NGO power is growing fast. In Korea, Lester Brown met with Yul Choi of the 50,000-member Korean Federation for Environmental Movement—one of hundreds of such groups taking root around the world.

same kind of signs of quiet, revolutionary change in the bicycle as in the modern wind turbine: the unthinkable consequences of continuing the existing system, combined with recent sales trends. Bicycle use is growing much faster than automobile use, not only because it is more affordable but because it has a range of environmental and social advantages: it uses far less land (a key consideration in a world where the cropland area has shrunk to barely one-half acre per person); it does not contribute to pollution; it helps reduce traffic congestion; it does not contribute to CO_2 emissions; and, for an increasingly desk-bound work-force, it offers much needed exercise. Indeed, during the past three decades, in which annual car sales worldwide increased from 23 million to 37 million, the number of bicycles sold jumped from 25 million to 106 million.

If cars were used in a future world of 10 billion people at the rate they are currently used in the United States (one car for every two people), that would mean a global fleet of 5 billion cars—10 times the existing, already dangerously burdensome, number. That prospect is inconceivable. Although the automobile industry is not abandoning its global dream of a car in every garage, it is *this* dream that now has a distinctly pie-in-the-sky feel.

Shifting Views of Materials Use

There are few areas in which individuals have participated so actively as in the effort to convert the throwaway economy into a reuse/recycle economy. At the individual level, efforts are concentrated on recycling paper, glass, and aluminum. But there are also important shifts coming in basic industries. For example, in the United States, not always a global leader in recycling, 56 percent of the steel produced now comes from scrap. Steel mills built in recent years are no longer located in western Pennsylvania, where coal and iron ore are in close proximity, but are scattered about the country—in North Carolina, Nebraska, or California—feeding on local supplies of scrap. These new electric arc steel furnaces produce steel with much less energy and far less pollution than that produced in the old steel mills from virgin iron ore.

A similar shift has taken place in the recycling of paper. At one time, paper mills were built almost exclusively in heavily forested areas, such as the northwestern United States, western Canada, or Maine, but now they are often built near cities, feeding on the local supply of scrap paper. The shift in *where* these industries are may prefigure a shift in our understanding of *what* they are.

This new economic model can be seen in the densely populated U.S. state of New Jersey where there are now 13 paper mills running only on waste paper. There are also eight steel mini-mills, using electric arc furnaces to manufacture steel largely from scrap. These two industries, with a combined annual output in excess of $1 billion, have developed in a state that has little forest cover and

no iron mines. They operate almost entirely on material already in the system, providing a glimpse of what the reuse/recycle economy of the future looks like.

Shifting Views of Population

No economic system is sustainable with continual population growth, or with continual population declines either. Fortunately, some 32 countries containing 14 percent of the world's people have achieved population stability. All but one (Japan) are in Europe. In another group of some 40 countries, which includes the United States and China, fertility has dropped below two children per

Family planning services—such as the simple expedient of making condoms readily available—are gaining ground in much of the world despite concerted campaigns to suppress them.

woman, which means that these countries are also headed for population stability over the next few decades—assuming, of course, that those fertility trends don't reverse.

Unfortunately, many developing countries are facing huge population increases. Pakistan, Nigeria, and Ethiopia are projected to at least double their populations over the next half-century. India, with a population expected to reach 1 billion this August, is projected to add another 500 million people by 2050. If these countries do not stabilize their populations soon enough by reducing fertility, they will inevitably face a rise in mortality, simply because they will not be able to cope with new threats such as HIV or water and food shortages.

What is new here is that as more people are crowded onto the planet, far more are becoming alarmed about the potentially disastrous consequences of that crowding. In India, for example, the *Hindustan Times,* one of India's leading newspapers, recently commented on the fast-deteriorating water situation, where water tables are falling almost everywhere and wells are going dry by the thousands: "If our population continues to grow as it is now . . . it is certain that a major part of the country would be in the grip of a severe water famine in 10 to 15 years." The article goes on to reflect an emerging sense of desperation: "Only a bitter dose of compulsory family planning can save the coming generation from the fast-approaching Malthusian catastrophe." Among other things, this comment appears to implicitly recognize the emerging conflict between the reproductive rights of the current generation and the survival rights of the next generation.

Corporate Converts

Corporations have been endorsing environmental goals for some three decades, but their efforts have been too often centered in the public relations office, not in corporate planning. Now this is beginning to change, as the better informed, more prescient CEOs recognize that the shift from the old industrial model to the new environmentally sustainable model of economic progress represents the greatest investment opportunity in history. In May 1997, for example, British Petroleum CEO John Browne broke ranks with the other oil companies on the climate issue when he said, "The time to consider the policy dimensions of climate change is not when the link between greenhouse gases and climate change is conclusively proven, but when the possibility cannot be discounted and is taken seriously by the society of which we are a part. We in BP have reached that point."

Browne then went on to announce a $1 billion investment by BP in the development of wind and solar energy. In effect he was saying, "we are no longer an oil company; we are now an energy company." Within a matter of weeks Royal Dutch Shell announced that it was committing $500 million to development of renewable energy sources. And in early 1998, Shell announced that it was leaving the Global Climate Coalition, an industry-supported group in Washington, D.C. that manages a disinformation campaign designed to create public confusion about climate change.

These commitments to renewable energy by BP and Shell are small compared with the continuing investment of vast sums in oil exploration and development, but they are investments in energy sources that cannot be depleted, while those made in oil fields can supply energy only for a relatively short time. In addition, knowing that world oil production likely will peak and begin to decline within the next 5 to 20 years, oil companies are beginning to look at the alternatives. This knowledge, combined with mounting concern about global warming, helps explain why the more forward-looking oil companies are now investing in wind and solar cells, the cornerstones of the new energy economy.

Ken Lay, the head of Enron, a large Texas-based national gas supplier with annual sales of $20 billion that is fast becoming a worldwide energy firm, sees his company, and more broadly the natural gas industry, playing a central role in the conversion from a fossil-fuel-based energy economy to a solar/hydrogen energy economy. As the cost of wind power falls, for example, cheap electricity from wind at wind-rich sites can be used to electrolyze water, producing hydrogen, a convenient means of both storing and transporting wind energy or other renewable energy resources. The pipeline network and storage facilities used for natural gas can also be used for hydrogen. George H.B. Verberg, the managing director of Gasunie in the Netherlands, has publicly outlined a similar role for his organization with its well developed natural gas infrastructure.

In the effort to convert our throwaway economy into a reuse/recycle economy, too, I see signs that new initiatives are coming not just from eco-activists but from industry. In Atlanta, Ray Anderson, the head of Interface, a leading world carpet manufacturer with sales in 106 countries, is starting to shift his firm from the sale of carpets to the sale of carpeting services. With the latter approach, Interface contracts to provide carpeting service to a firm for its offices for say a 10-year period. This service involves installing the carpet, cleaning, repairing and otherwise maintaining the quality of carpeting desired by the client. The advantage of this system is that when the carpet wears out, Interface simply takes it back to one of its plants and recycles it in its entirety into new carpeting. The Interface approach requires no virgin raw material to make carpets, and it leaves nothing for the landfill.

Perhaps one of the most surprising—and significant—signs of impending change came last year from the once notorious MacMillan Bloedel, a giant forest products firm operating in Canada's western-most province of British Columbia. "MacBlo," as it is called, startled the world—and other logging firms—when it announced that it was giving up the standard forest industry practice of clear-cutting. Under the leadership of a new chief executive, Tom Stevens, the company affirmed that clear-cutting will be replaced by selective cutting, leaving trees to check runoff and soil erosion, to provide wildlife habitat, and to help regenerate the forest. In doing so, it acknowledged the growing reach of the environmental movement. MacMillan Bloedel was not only being pressured by local groups, but it also had been the primary target of a Greenpeace campaign to ban clear-cutting everywhere.

Governments Catching On

At the national level, too, there are signs of major changes. Six countries in Europe—Denmark, Finland, the Netherlands, Sweden, Spain, and the United Kingdom—began restructuring their taxes during the 1990s in a process known as tax shifting—reducing income taxes while

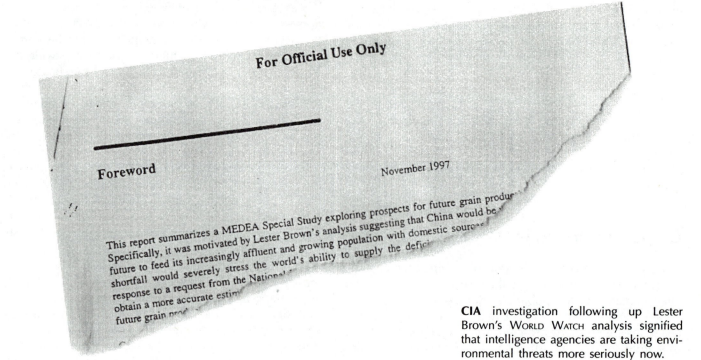

For Official Use Only

Foreword   November 1997

This report summarizes a MEDEA Special Study exploring prospects for future grain produc... Specifically, it was motivated by Lester Brown's analysis suggesting that China would be... future to feed its increasingly affluent and growing population with domestic source... shortfall would severely stress the world's ability to supply the defic... response to a request from the Nation... obtain a more accurate estim... future grain pro...

CIA investigation following up Lester Brown's WORLD WATCH analysis signified that intelligence agencies are taking environmental threats more seriously now.

offsetting these cuts with higher taxes on environmentally destructive activities such as fossil fuel burning, the generation of garbage, the use of pesticides, and the production of toxic wastes. Although the reduction in income taxes does not yet exceed 3 percent in any of these countries, the basic concept is widely accepted. Public opinion polls on both sides of the Atlantic show 70 percent of the public supporting tax shifting.

In mid 1998, the new government taking over in Germany, a coalition of Social Democrats and Greens, announced a massive restructuring of the tax system, one that would simultaneously reduce taxes on wages and raise taxes on CO_2 emissions. This shift, the largest yet contemplated by any government, was taken unilaterally, not bogging down in the politics of the global climate treaty, or contingent on steps taken elsewhere. The framers of the new tax structure argued that this tax restructuring would help strengthen the German economy by creating additional jobs and at the same time reducing air pollution, oil imports, and the rise in atmospheric CO_2—the principal threat to climate stability. With Germany taking this bold initiative unilaterally, other countries may follow.

Over the past generation, the world has relied heavily on regulation to achieve environmental goals, but in most instances using tax policy to restructure the economy is far more likely to be successful because it permits the market to operate, thus taking advantage of its inherent efficiency in linking producers and consumers. Restructuring taxes to achieve environmental goals also minimizes the need for regulation.

In effect, the governments moving toward tax shifting have decided that the emphasis on taxing wages and income from investments discourages both work and saving,

activities that should be encouraged, not discouraged. They believe we should be discouraging environmentally destructive activities by taxing them instead. Since tax shifting does not necessarily change the overall level of taxation, and thus does not materially alter a country's competitive position in the world market, it can be undertaken unilaterally.

Environmental leadership does not always come from large countries. At the December 1997 Kyoto conference on climate, President José Maria Figueres of Costa Rica announced that by the year 2010, his country planned to get all of its electricity from renewable sources. In Copenhagen, the Danish government has banned the construction of coal-fired power plants.

In the U.S. government, no longer a leader on the environmental front, there are signs of a breakthrough in at least some quarters. The Forest Service announced in early 1998 that after several decades of building roads in the national forests to help logging companies remove timber, it was imposing an 18-month moratorium on road building. Restricting this huge public subsidy, which had built some 380,000 miles of roads to facilitate clear-cutting on public lands, signals a fundamental shift in the management of national forests. The new chief of the Forest Service, Michael Dombeck, responding to a major shift in public opinion and no longer intimidated by the "wise-use" movement of the early Clinton years, said the service was focusing on the use of national forests for recreation, for wildlife protection, to supply clean water, and as a means of promoting tourism as well as supplying timber. The shift in opinion seems to reflect a growing public recognition of the environmental consequences of clear-cutting, including more destructive flooding, soil erosion, silting of rivers, and in the Northwest, the destruction of salmon fisheries.

In mid-August 1998, after several weeks of near-record flooding in the Yangtze river basin, Beijing acknowledged for the first time that the flooding was not merely an act of nature, but that it had been greatly exacerbated by the deforestation of the upper reaches of the watershed. Premier Zhu Rongji personally issued orders to not only halt the tree-cutting in the upper reaches of the Yangtze basin and elsewhere in China, but also to convert some state timbering firms into tree-planting firms. The official view in Beijing now is that trees are worth three times as much standing as they are cut, simply because of the water storage and flood retention capacity of forests.

Meanwhile, back in Washington, even the U.S. intelligence community is beginning to realize that environmental trends can adversely affect the global economy on a scale that could lead to political instability. The National Intelligence Council, the organizational umbrella over the CIA, DIA, and other U.S. intelligence agencies, was provoked by the article, "Who Will Feed China?" that I published in WORLD WATCH in 1994. It was concerned that projected losses of cropland and irrigation water in China could lead to soaring grain imports, rising world grain prices and, ultimately, to widespread political instability in third world cities. In response, the Council assembled a team of prominent U.S. scientists to undertake an exhaustive interdisciplinary analysis of China's long-term food prospect.

This analysis, completed in late 1997, showed horrendous water deficits emerging in the water basins of the northern half of China, deficits that could decimate the grain harvest in some regions even as the demand for grain continues to climb. It concluded that China will likely need to import 175 million tons of grain by 2025, an amount that approaches current world grain exports of 200 million tons. When the U.S. intelligence community, which was for half a century fixated on the Communist threat, now raises an alarm about an environmental threat in a Communist country—that is indeed a sign that we are approaching a new threshold.

NGOs as Catalysts

Among the signs that new perceptions are overtaking old institutions is the robust proliferation of nongovernmental organizations (NGOs). The formation of environmental NGOs is a response of civil society to the immobility of existing institutions and specifically to their lack of a timely response to spreading environmental destruction. The new economic model outlined earlier originated not in the halls of academe or in the councils of government but within the research groups among the environmental NGOs. There are hundreds of international and national environmental groups and literally thousands of local single-issue groups.

At the international level, groups like Greenpeace, the International Union for Conservation of Nature, and the Worldwide Fund for Nature have become as influential in shaping environmental policies as national governments. The budgets of some of the individual environmental groups, such as the 1.2 million-member U.S. World Wildlife Fund ($82 million) or Greenpeace International ($60 million), begin to approach the $105 million budget of the United Nations Environment Programme, the U.N. agency responsible for environmental matters. In fact, much of the impetus toward a global consciousness of environmental threats—and much of the hard work of establishing the new mechanisms needed to build an environmentally sustainable economy—have come from NGOs. The research that underpinned the UN-sponsored Earth Summit in Rio de Janeiro in 1992, notably, came largely from organizations like the Wuppertal Institute in Germany and the U.S.-based World Resources Institute and Worldwatch Institute.

Almost every industrialized country now has a number of national environmental groups, many with memberships measured in the hundreds of thousands. Some developing countries, too, now have strong environmental groups. In Korea, for example, the Korean Federation for Environmental Movement, a group with a membership that recently passed 50,000 and a full-time staff of 60, has become a force to be reckoned with by the government.

At the grassroots, thousands of local single-issue groups work on objectives ranging from preventing construction of a nuclear power plant in Japan's Niigata prefecture to protecting the Amazonian rainforest from burning by cattle ranchers so that the forest products can continue to be harvested by local people. The little-heralded work of small groups like this on every continent is quietly helping to move us within reach of a major shift in public awareness.

Approaching the Threshold

One reason more people are aware of the environmental underpinnings of their lives now is that many more have been directly affected by environmental disruptions. And even when events don't impinge directly, media coverage is more likely to expose the damage now than a decade ago. Among the events that are mobilizing public concern, and therefore support for restructuring the economy, are fishery collapses, water shortages, rainforests burning uncontrollably, sudden die-offs of birds, dolphins, and fish, record heat waves, and storms of unprecedented destructiveness.

Weather-related damages are now so extensive that insurance companies can no longer use linear models from the past to calculate risks in the future. When the cost of insuring property rises sharply in the future, as now seems inevitable, millions of people may take notice—including many who have not before.

Are we indeed moving toward a social threshold which, once crossed, will lead to a dizzying rate of environmentally shaped economic change, on a scale that we may not now even imagine? No one knows for sure, but some of the preconditions are clearly here. An effective response to any threat depends on a recognition of that threat, which is broad enough to support the response. There is now a growing worldwide recognition outside the environmental community that the economy we now have cannot take us where we want to go. Three decades ago, it was only environmental activists who were speaking out on the need for change, but the ranks of activists have now broadened to include CEOs of major corporations, government ministers, prominent scientists, and even intelligence agencies.

Getting from here to there quickly is the challenge. But at least we have a clear sense of what has to be done. The key to restructuring the global economy, as noted earlier, is restructuring the tax system. Seven European countries, led by Germany, are advancing on this front.

New institutional initiatives, too, are helping set the stage for the economic restructuring. For example, ecological labeling of consumer products is being implemented as a means of raising awareness—and shifting purchasing priorities—in several industries. Consumers who want to protect forests from irresponsible logging practices now have the option of buying only products that come from those forests that are being managed in a certifiably responsible way. In the United States, even electric power can now be purchased from "green" sources in some areas, if the consumer so chooses. Public awareness of the differences among energy sources is raised significantly, as each power purchaser is confronted with the available options.

Another institutional means for expressing public preferences is government procurement policy. If national or local governments decide to buy only paper that has a high recycled content, for example, they provide market support for economic restructuring. And governments, like individual users, can become "green" consumers by opting for climate-benign sources of electricity.

Trying times require bold responses, and we are beginning to see some, such as the decision by Ted Turner, the founder of Turner Broadcasting and Cable News Network (CNN), now part of the Time Warner complex, to contribute $1 billion to the United Nations to be made available at $100 million per year over the next ten years. Not only is Turner committing a large part of his personal fortune to dealing with some of the world's most pressing population, environmental, and humanitarian problems, but he is also urging other billionaires, of whom there are now more than 600 in the world, not to wait until their deaths to put money in foundations that might work on these issues. He argues, quite rightly, that time is of the essence, that right now we are losing the war to save the future.

In a world where the economy has expanded from $6 trillion in output in 1950 to $39 trillion in 1998, new collisions between the expanding economy as now structured and its environmental support systems are occurring somewhere almost daily. Time is running out. The Aral Sea has died. Its fisheries are gone. The deterioration of Indonesia's rainforests may have reached the point of no return. We may not be able to save the glaciers in Glacier National Park.

The key to quickly gaining acceptance of the new economic model is to accelerate the flow of information about how the old model is now destroying its natural support systems. Some governments are now doing this. For example, beginning in late summer of 1997, the Clinton White House began holding press briefings, regularly reporting new climate findings. On June 8, 1998, Vice President Al Gore held a press conference announcing that for the world 1997 "was the warmest year on record and we've set new temperature records every month since January." He went on to say, "This is a reminder once again that global warming is real and that unless we act, we can expect more extreme weather in the year ahead."

Even China is taking steps toward more open dissemination of information. In early 1998, Beijing became the 39th Chinese city to start issuing weekly air quality reports since the beginning of 1997. These reports, providing data on such indicators as the levels of nitrous oxides from car exhaust and particulate matter from coal burning, reveal that Chinese urban dwellers breathe some of the world's most polluted air. Air pollution is estimated to cause 178,000 pre-mature deaths per year, more than four times the number of automobile fatalities in the United States. "Who Will Feed China?," initially banned in China, is now being promoted on Central Television. This new openness by the government is expected to enhance public support for taking the steps needed to control air pollution, whether it be restricting automobile traffic, closing the most polluting factories, or shifting to clean sources of energy. Information on how the inefficient use of water could lead to food shortages can boost support for water pricing.

Media coverage of environmental trends and events is also increasing, indicating a rising appreciation of their importance. One could cite thousands of examples, but let me mention just two. First is the media coverage given to the 1997/98 El Niño, the periodic rise in the surface temperature of water in the eastern Pacific that affects climate patterns world-wide. This is not a new phenomenon. It has occurred periodically for as far back as climate records exist. But the difference is in the coverage. In 1982/83 there was an El Niño of similar intensity, but it did not become a household word. In 1997/98, it did largely because a more enlightened community of television meteorologists who report daily weather events understood better how El Niño was affecting local climate. Public recognition of the importance of "El Niño" was perhaps most amusingly demonstrated for me last winter, when a large automobile dealer in my area advertised that it was having an "El Niño" sale. It was going to be a big one!

At a more specific level, in the fall of 1997, *Time* magazine produced a special issue of its international edition under the headline "Our Precious Planet:Why Saving the Environment Will be the Next Century's Biggest Challenge." As the title implies, the issue recognized—in a way few major news organizations have in the past—the extraordinary dimensions of the challenge facing humanity as we try to sustain economic progress in the next century.

More and more people in both the corporate and political worlds are now beginning to share a common vision of what an environmentally sustainable economy will look like. If the evidence of a global awakening were limited to one particular indicator, such as growing membership in environmental groups, it might be dubious. But with the evidence of growing momentum now coming from a range of key indicators simultaneously, the prospect that we are approaching the threshold of a major transformation becomes more convincing. The question is, if it does come, whether it will come soon enough to prevent the destruction of natural support systems on a scale that will undermine the economy.

As we prepare to enter the new century, no challenge looms greater than that of transforming the economy into one that is environmentally sustainable. This Environmental Revolution is comparable in scale to the Agricultural Revolution and the Industrial Revolution. The big difference is in the time available. The Agricultural Revolution was spread over thousands of years. The Industrial Revolution has been underway for two centuries.The Environmental Revolution, if it succeeds, will be compressed into a few decades. We study the archeological sites of civilizations that moved onto economic paths that were environmentally destructive and could not make the needed course corrections either because they did not understand what was happening or could not summon the needed political will. We *do* know what is happening. The question for us is whether our global society can cross the threshold that will enable us to restructure the global economy before environmental deterioration leads to economic decline.

Lester Brown is president of Worldwatch Institute.

Unit Selections

Key Points to Consider

❖ What is the role of "fertility rates" in predicting future population growth? Why do fertility rates rise and fall and where have fertility rates dropped below replacement levels?

❖ What is meant by "biotechnology"? Give some examples of biotech in agriculture and explain how some new agricultural methods might pose as many dangers as they offer solutions to food shortages.

❖ Why is it not logical to assume that the world's developing nations will follow exactly the same patterns of resource exploitation and consequent environmental impact as the world's developed nations? What are some of the technological alternatives available to countries like China to reduce the impact of continuing industrialization?

 **Links**

www.dushkin.com/online/

These sites are annotated on pages 4 and 5.

One of the greatest setbacks on the road to the development of more stable and sensible population policies came about as a result of inaccurate population growth projections made in the late 1960s and early 1970s. The world was in for a population explosion, the experts told us back then. But shortly after the publication of the heralded works *The Population Bomb* (Paul Ehrlich, 1975) and *Limits to Growth* (D. H. Meadows et al., 1974), the growth rate of the world's population began to decline slightly. There was no cause and effect relationship at work here. The decline in growth was simply demographic transition at work, a process in which declining population growth tends to accompany increasing levels of economic development. Unfortunately, since the alarming predictions did not come to pass, the world began to relax a little. As a result, two facts still remain—population growth in biological systems must be limited by available resources, and the availability of Earth's resources is finite.

Consider the following: In developing countries, high and growing rural population densities have forced the use of increasingly marginal farmland once considered to be too steep, too dry, too wet, too sterile, or too far from market for efficient agricultural use. Farming this land damages soil and watershed systems, creates deforestation problems, and adds relatively little to total food production. In the more developed world, farmers also have been driven—usually by market forces—to farm more marginal lands and to rely more on environmentally harmful farming methods utilizing high levels of agricultural chemicals (such as pesticides and artificial fertilizers). These chemicals create hazards for all life and rob the soil of its natural ability to renew itself. The increased demand for food production has also created an increase in the use of precious groundwater reserves for irrigation purposes, depleting those reserves beyond their natural capacity to recharge and creating the potential for once-fertile farmland and grazing land to be transformed into desert. The continued demand for higher production levels also contributes to a soil erosion problem that has reached alarming proportions in all agricultural areas of the world, whether high or low on the scale of economic development. The need to increase the food supply and its consequent effects on the agricultural environment are not the only results of continued population growth. For industrialists, the larger market creates an almost irresistible temptation to accelerate production, requiring the use of more marginal resources and resulting in the destruction of more fragile ecological systems, particularly in the tropics. For consumers, the increased demand for products means increased competition for scarce resources, driving up the cost of those resources until only the wealthiest can afford what our grandfathers would have viewed as an adequate standard of living.

The articles selected for this second unit all relate, in one way or another, to the theory and reality of population growth (and its relationship to food supply). In the first selection, "The Population Surprise," Max Singer notes that the pattern of population dynamics in the more developed nations of the world, what we call "the demographic transition," indicates that when population growth begins to slow down—as it has worldwide over the last few decades—the decline in growth does not stop at the replacement rate but often continues beneath that point: in other words, populations begin to decline. Rather than the doubling of the world's population by the middle of the twenty-first century as some believe, Singer expects the global number of people to begin to decline.

The unit's second article moves from a discussion of population dynamics to one of how to feed the world's existing and future people. In "The Emperor's New Crops," Worldwatch Institute staff researcher Brian Halweil claims that the actual performance of biotechnology in producing new crops is far less robust than have been the claims for new agricultural miracles. (More promising, he notes, is the expansion of existing technologies such as organic farming that don't require genetic engineering but simply the application of time-honored methods and common sense.) The third article in this unit continues the argument in favor of using older and more appropriate technology rather than newer and more expensive methods to improve the lot of people in the world's developing nations. In "The Technology of Hope: Tools to Empower the World's Poorest Peoples," educator Rashmi Mayur and journalist Bennett Daviss agree that the hope for the rural poor of developing nations does not lie with large-scale industrialization but with benign technologies whose systemic or cyclic benefits outweigh its drawbacks. (Digging and burning more coal to generate electricity is a malignant technology; energy conservation and the development of alternate technologies such as wind and solar power are not.)

Finally, in the section's concluding piece, Lester Brown claims in "Food Scarcity: An Environmental Wakeup Call" that "the environmental deterioration of the last few decades cannot continue indefinitely without eventually affecting the world economy." It will be the scarcity of food that should, notes Brown, finally provide the "wakeup call" of his title. Brown and the other authors of the selections in this unit make it clear that the global environment is being stressed by population growth and that more people means more pressure and more poverty. (While it should be clear that we can no longer afford to permit the unplanned and unchecked growth of the planet's dominant species, it should also be clear that doomsday predictions of population and food imbalances are less commonplace now than they were just a few years ago.)

The World's Population: People and Hunger

The Population Surprise

The old assumptions about world population trends need to be rethought. One thing is clear: in the next century the world is in for some rapid downsizing

by Max Singer

FIFTY years from now the world's population will be declining, with no end in sight. Unless people's values change greatly, several centuries from now there could be fewer people living in the entire world than live in the United States today. The big surprise of the past twenty years is that in not one country did fertility stop falling when it reached the replacement rate—2.1 children per woman. In Italy, for example, the rate has fallen to 1.2. In Western Europe as a whole and in Japan it is down to 1.5. The evidence now indicates that within fifty years or so world population will peak at about eight billion before starting a fairly rapid decline.

Because in the past two centuries world population has increased from one billion to nearly six billion, many people still fear that it will keep "exploding" until there are too many people for the earth to support. But that is like fearing that your baby will grow to 1,000 pounds because its weight doubles three times in its first seven years. World population was growing by two percent a year in the 1960s; the rate is now down to one percent a year, and if the patterns of the past century don't change radically, it will head into negative numbers. This view is coming to be widely accepted among population experts, even as the public continues to focus on the threat of uncontrolled population growth.

As long ago as September of 1974 *Scientific American* published a special issue on population that described what demographers had begun calling the "demographic transition" from traditional high rates of birth and death to the low ones of modern society. The experts believed that birth and death rates would be more or less equal in the future, as they had been in the past, keeping total population stable after a level of 10–12 billion people was reached during the transition.

Developments over the past twenty years show that the experts were right in thinking that population won't keep going up forever. They were wrong in thinking that after it stops going up, it will stay level. The experts' assumption that population would stabilize because birth rates would stop falling once they matched the new low death rates has not been borne out by experience. Evidence from more than fifty countries demonstrates what should be unsurprising: in a modern society the death rate doesn't determine the birth rate. If in the long run birth rates worldwide do not conveniently match death rates, then population must either rise or fall, depending on whether birth or death rates are higher. Which can we expect?

The rapid increase in population during the past two centuries has been the result of lower death rates, which have produced an increase in worldwide life expectancy from about thirty to about sixty-two. (Since the maximum—if we do not change fundamental human physiology—is about eighty-five, the world has already gone three fifths as far as it can in increasing life expectancy.) For a while the result was a young population with more mothers in each generation, and fewer deaths than births. But even during this population explosion the average number of children born to each woman—the fertility rate—has been falling in modernizing societies. The prediction that world population will soon begin to decline is based on almost universal human behavior. In the United States fertility has been falling for 200 years (except for the blip of the Baby Boom), but partly because of immigration it has stayed only slightly below replacement level for twenty-five years.

Obviously, if for many generations the birth rate averages fewer than 2.1 children per woman, population must eventually stop growing. Recently the United Nations Population Division estimated that 44 percent of the world's people live in countries where the fertility rate has already fallen below the replacement rate, and fertility is falling fast almost everywhere else. In Sweden and Italy fertility has been below replacement level for so long that the population has become old enough to have more deaths than births. Declines in fertility will eventually increase the average age in the world, and will cause a decline in world population forty to fifty years from now.

Because in a modern society the death rate and the fertility rate are

Max Singer was a founder of the Hudson Institute. He is a co-author, with Aaron Wildavsky, of *The Real World Order* (1996).

From *The Atlantic Monthly*, August 1999, pp. 22-25. © 1999 by Max Singer. Reprinted by permission.

largely independent of each other, world population need not be stable. World population can be stable only if fertility rates around the world average out to 2.1 children per woman. But why should they average 2.1, rather than 2.4, or 1.8, or some other number? If there is nothing to keep each country exactly at 2.1, then there is nothing to ensure that the overall average will be exactly 2.1.

The point is that the number of children born depends on families' choices about how many children they want to raise. And when a family is deciding whether to have another child, it is usually thinking about things other than the national or the world population. Who would know or care if world population were to drop from, say, 5.85 billion to 5.81 billion? Population change is too slow and remote for people to feel in their lives—even if the total population were to double or halve in only a century (as a mere 0.7 percent increase or decrease each year would do). Whether world population is increasing or decreasing doesn't necessarily affect the decisions that determine whether it will increase or decrease in the future. As the systems people would say, there is no feedback loop.

WHAT does affect fertility is modernity. In almost every country where people have moved from traditional ways of life to modern ones, they are choosing to have too few children to replace themselves. This is true in Western and in Eastern countries, in Catholic and in secular societies. And it is true in the richest parts of the richest countries. The only exceptions seem to be some small religious communities. We can't be sure what will happen in Muslim countries, because few of them have become modern yet, but so far it looks as if their fertility rates will respond to modernity as others' have.

Nobody can say whether world population will ever dwindle to very low numbers; that depends on what values people hold in the future. After the approaching peak, as long as people continue to prefer saving effort and money by having fewer children, population will continue to decline. (This does not imply that the decision to have fewer children is selfish; it may, for example, be motivated by a desire to do more for each child.)

Some people may have values significantly different from those of the rest of the world, and therefore different fer-

tility rates. If such people live in a particular country or population group, their values can produce marked changes in the size of that country or group, even as world population changes only slowly. For example, the U.S. population, because of immigration and a fertility rate that is only slightly below replacement level, is likely to grow from 4.5 percent of the world today to 10 percent of a smaller world over the next two or three centuries. Much bigger changes in share are possible for smaller groups if they can maintain their difference from the average for a long period of time. (To illustrate: Korea's population could grow from one percent of the world to 10 percent in a single lifetime if it were to increase by two percent a year while the rest of the world population declined by one percent a year.)

World population won't stop declining until human values change. But human values may well change—values, not biological imperatives, are the unfathomable variable in population predictions. It is quite possible that in a century or two or three, when just about the whole world is at least as modern as Western Europe is today, people will start to value children more highly than they do now in modern societies. If they do, and fertility rates start to climb, fertility is no more likely to stop climbing at an average rate of 2.1 children per woman than it was to stop falling at 2.1 on the way down.

In only the past twenty years or so world fertility has dropped by 1.5 births per woman. Such a degree of change, were it to occur again, would be enough to turn a long-term increase in world population of one percent a year into a long-term decrease of one percent a year. Presumably fertility could someday increase just as quickly as it has declined in recent decades, although such a rapid change will be less likely once the world has completed the transition to modernity. If fertility rises only to 2.8, just 33 percent over the replacement rate, world population will eventually grow by one percent a year again—doubling in seventy years and multiplying by twenty in only three centuries.

The decline in fertility that began in some countries, including the United States, in the past century is taking a long time to reduce world population because when it started, fertility was very much higher than replacement level. In addition, because a preference for fewer children is associated with

modern societies, in which high living standards make time valuable and children financially unproductive and expensive to care for and educate, the trend toward lower fertility couldn't spread throughout the world until economic development had spread. But once the whole world has become modern, with fertility everywhere in the neighborhood of replacement level, new social values might spread worldwide in a few decades. Fashions in families might keep changing, so that world fertility bounced above and below replacement rate. If each bounce took only a few decades or generations, world population would stay within a reasonably narrow range—although probably with a long-term trend in one direction or the other.

The values that influence decisions about having children seem, however, to change slowly and to be very widespread. If the average fertility rate were to take a long time to move from well below to well above replacement rate and back again, trends in world population could go a long way before they reversed themselves. The result would be big swings in world population—perhaps down to one or two billion and then up to 20 or 40 billion.

Whether population swings are short and narrow or long and wide, the average level of world population after several cycles will probably have either an upward or a downward trend overall. Just as averaging across the globe need not result in exactly 2.1 children per woman, averaging across the centuries need not result in zero growth rather than a slowly increasing or slowly decreasing world population. But the long-term trend is less important than the effects of the peaks and troughs. The troughs could be so low that human beings become scarcer than they were in ancient times. The peaks might cause harm from some kinds of shortages.

One implication is that not even very large losses from disease or war can affect the world population in the long run nearly as much as changes in human values do. What we have learned from the dramatic changes of the past few centuries is that regardless of the size of the world population at any time, people's personal decisions about how many children they want can make the world population go anywhere—to zero or to 100 billion or more.

THE EMPEROR'S NEW CROPS

*To its proponents, agricultural biotechnology is the way to
reconcile ecological health with the food demand of
the world's 6 billion people—and the billions yet to come.
But it's hard to find that vision in the industry's first products.*

by Brian Halweil

It's June 1998 and Robert Shapiro, CEO of Monsanto Corporation, is delivering a keynote speech at "BIO 98," the annual meeting of the Biotechnology Industry Organization. "Somehow," he says, "we're going to have to figure out how to meet a demand for a doubling of the world's food supply, when it's impossible to conceive of a doubling of the world's acreage under cultivation. And it is impossible, indeed, even to conceive of increases in productivity—using current technologies—that don't produce major issues for the sustainability of agriculture."

Those "major issues" preoccupy a growing number of economists, environmentalists, and other analysts concerned with agriculture. Given the widespread erosion of topsoil, the continued loss of genetic variety in the major crop species, the uncertain effects of long-term agrochemical use, and the chronic hunger that now haunts nearly 1 billion people, it would seem that a major paradigm shift in agriculture is long overdue. Yet Shapiro was anything but gloomy. Noting "the sense of excitement, energy, and confidence" that engulfed the room, he argued

that "biotechnology represents a potentially sustainable solution to the issue of feeding people."

To its proponents, biotech is the key to that new agricultural paradigm. They envision crops genetically engineered to tolerate dry, low-nutrient, or salty soils—allowing some of the world's most degraded farmland to flourish once again. Crops that produce their own pesticides would reduce the need for toxic chemicals, and engineering for better nutrition would help the overfed as well as the hungry. In industry gatherings, biotech appears as some rare hybrid between corporate mega-opportunity and international social program.

The roots of this new paradigm were put down nearly 50 years ago, when James Watson and Francis Crick defined the structure of DNA, the giant molecule that makes up a cell's chromosomes. Once the structure of the genetic code was understood, researchers began looking for ways to isolate little snippets of DNA—particular genes—and manipulate them in various ways. In 1973, scientists managed to paste a gene from one microbe into another microbe of a different spe-

From *World Watch*, July/August 1999, pp. 21-29. © 1999 by the Worldwatch Institute. Reprinted by permission.

cies; the result was the first artificial transfer of genetic information across the species boundary. In the early 1980s, several research teams—including one at Monsanto, then a multinational pesticide company—succeeded in splicing a bacterium gene into a petunia. The first "transgenic" plant was born.

Such plants represented a quantum leap in crop breeding: the fact that a plant could not interbreed with a bacterium was no longer an obstacle to using the microbe's genes in crop design. Theoretically, at least, the world's entire store of genetic wealth became available to plant breeders, and the biotech labs were quick to test the new possibilities. Among the early creations was a tomato armed with a flounder gene to enhance frost resistance and with a rebuilt tomato gene to retard spoilage. A variety of the oilseed crop known as rape or canola was outfitted with a gene from the California Bay tree to alter the composition of its oil. A potato was endowed with bacterial resistance from a chicken gene.

Transgenic crops are no longer just a laboratory phenomenon. Since 1986, 25,000 transgenic field trials have been conducted worldwide—a full 10,000 of these just in the last two years. More than 60 different crops—ranging from corn to strawberries, from apples to potatoes—have been engineered. From 2 million hectares in 1996, the global area planted in transgenics jumped to 27.8 million hectares in 1998. That's nearly a fifteenfold increase in just two years.

In 1992, China planted out a tobacco variety engineered to resist viruses and became the first nation to grow transgenic crops for commercial use. Farmers in the United States sowed their first commercial crop in 1994; their counterparts in Argentina, Australia, Canada, and Mexico followed suit in 1996. By 1998, nine nations were growing transgenics for market and that number is expected to reach 20 to 25 by 2000.

Ag biotech is now a global phenomenon, but it remains powerfully concentrated in several ways:

In terms of where transgenics are planted. Three-quarters of transgenic cropland is in the United States. More than a third of the U.S. soybean crop last year was transgenic, as was nearly one-quarter of the corn and one-fifth of the cotton. The only other countries with a substantial transgenic harvest are Argentina and Canada: over half of the 1998 Argentine soybean crop was transgenic, as was over half of the Canadian canola crop. (See table, "Global Transgenic Area, 1966–98.") These three nations account for 99 percent of global transgenic crop area. (Most countries have been slow to adopt transgenics because of public concern over possible risks to ecological and human health.)

In terms of which crops are in production. While many crops have been engineered, only a very few are cultivated in appreciable quantities. Soybeans account for 52 percent of global transgenic area, corn for another 30 percent. Cotton—almost entirely on U.S. soil—and canola in Canada cover most of the rest.

In terms of which traits are in commercial use. Most of the transgenic harvest has been engineered for "input traits" intended to replace or accommodate the standard chemical "inputs" of large-scale agriculture, especially insecticides and herbicides. Worldwide, nearly 30 percent of transgenic cropland is planted in varieties designed to produce an insect-killing toxin, and almost all of the rest is in crops engineered to resist herbicides. (A crop's inability to tolerate exposure to a particular herbicide will obviously limit the use of that chemical.)

These two types of crops—the insecticidal and the herbicide-resistant varieties—are biotech's first large-scale commercial ventures. They provide the first real opportunity to test the industry's claims to be engineering a new agricultural paradigm.

THE BUGS

The only insecticidal transgenics currently in commercial use are "Bt crops." Grown on nearly 8 million hectares worldwide in 1998, these plants have been equipped with a gene from the soil organism *Bacillus thuringiensis* (Bt), which produces a substance that is deadly to certain insects.

The idea behind Bt crops is to free conventional agriculture from the highly toxic synthetic pesticides that have defined pest control since World War II. Shapiro, for instance, speaks of Monsanto's Bt cotton as a way of substituting "information encoded in a gene in a cotton plant for airplanes flying over cotton fields and spraying toxic chemicals on them." (As with other high technologies, the substitution of information for stuff is a fundamental doctrine of biotech.) At least in the short term, Bt varieties have allowed farmers to cut their spraying of insecticide-intensive crops, like cotton and potato. In 1998, for instance, the typical Bt cotton grower in Mississippi sprayed only once for tobacco budworm and cotton bollworn—the insects targeted by Bt—while non-Bt growers averaged five sprayings.

Farmers are buying into this approach in a big way. Bt crops have had some of the highest adoption rates that the seed industry has ever seen for new varieties. In the United States, just a few years after commercialization, nearly 25 percent of the corn crop and 20 percent of the cotton crop is Bt. In some counties in the southeastern states, the adoption rate of Bt cotton has reached 70 percent. The big draw for farmers is a lowering of production costs from reduced insecticide spraying, although the savings is partly offset by the more expensive seed. Some farmers also report that Bt crops are doing a better job of pest control than conventional spraying, although the crops must still be sprayed for pests that are unaffected by Bt. (Bt is toxic primarily to members of the Lepidoptera, the butterfly and moth family, and the Coleoptera, the beetle family.)

Unfortunately, there is a systemic problem in the background that will almost certainly erode these gains: pes-

Global Transgenic Area, 1996–98

Country	1996	1997	1998	Share of global area, 1998
	(million hectares)			(percent)
United States	1.5	8.1	20.5	74
Argentina	0.1	1.4	4.3	15
Canada	0.1	1.3	2.8	10
Australia	<0.1	0.1	0.1	1
Mexico	<0.1	<0.1	0.1	1
Spain	–	–	<0.1	<1
France	–	–	<0.1	<1
South Africa	–	–	<0.1	<1
TOTAL	1.7	11.0	27.8	100

Note: China is not included because of uncertainty over the extent of area planted, but a rough estimate for 1998 is 1 million hectares.

SOURCE: Clive James, *Global Review of Commercialized Transgenic Crops: 1998* (Ithaca, NY: International Service for the Acquisition of Agri-biotech Applications, 1998).

ticide resistance. Modern pest management tends to be very narrowly focused; the idea, essentially, is that when faced with a problematic pest, you should look for a chemical to kill it. The result has been a continual toughening of the pests, which has rendered successive generations of chemicals useless. After more than 50 years of this evolutionary rivalry, there is abundant evidence that pests of all sorts—insects, weeds, or pathogens—will develop resistance to just about any chemical that humans throw at them. (See graph, "Reported Numbers of Pesticide-Resistant Species, 1908–98.")

The Bt transgenics basically just replace an insecticide that is sprayed on the crop with one that is packaged inside it. The technique may be more sophisticated but the strategy remains the same: aim the chemical at the pest. Some entomologists are predicting that, without comprehensive strategies to prevent it, pest resistance to Bt could appear in the field within three to five years of widespread use, rendering the crops ineffective. Widespread resistance to Bt would affect more than the transgenic crops, since Bt is also commonly used in conventional spraying. Farmers could find one of their most environmentally benign pesticides beginning to slip away.

In one respect, Bt crops are a throwback to the early days of synthetic pesticides, when farmers were encouraged to spray even if their crops didn't appear to need it. The Bt crops show a similar lack of discrimination: they are programmed to churn out toxin during the entire growing season, regardless of the level of infestation. This sort of prophylactic control greatly increases the likelihood of resistance because it tends to maximize exposure to the toxin—it's the plant equivalent of treating antibiotics like vitamins.

Agricultural entomologists now generally agree that Bt crops will have to be managed in a way that discourages

resistance if the effectiveness of Bt is to be maintained. In the United States, the Environmental Protection Agency, which regulates the use of pesticides, now requires producers of Bt crops to develop "resistance management plans." This is a new step for the EPA, which has never required analogous plans from manufacturers of conventional pesticides.

The usual form of resistance management involves the creation of "refugia"—areas planted in a crop variety that isn't armed with the Bt gene. If the refugia are large enough, then a substantial proportion of the target pest population will never encounter the Bt toxin, and will not be under any selection pressure to develop resistance to it. Interbreeding between the refugia insects and the insects in the Bt fields should stall the development of resistance in the population as a whole, assuming the resistance gene is recessive. (See illustration, "BT CROPS: WHAT'S SUPPOSED TO HAPPEN.")

The biotech companies themselves have been recommending that their customers plant refugia, although the recommendations generally fall short of what most resistance experts consider necessary. This is not surprising, of course, since there is an inherent inconsistency between the refugia idea and the inevitable interest on the part of the manufacturer in selling as much product as possible. An even greater obstacle may be the reactions of farmers themselves, since the refugia concept is counter-intuitive: farmers, who spend much of their lives trying to control pests, are being told that the best way to maintain a high yield is to leave substantial portions of their land vulnerable to pests. The impulse to plant smaller refugia—or to count someone else's land as part of one's own refugia—may prove irresistible. And the possibility of enforcing the planting of larger refugia seems remote, especially once Bt crops are deployed to hundreds of millions of small-scale farmers throughout the developing world. (Such a prospect is still remote in most developing countries, but small-scale use of Bt cotton is increasingly common in China.)

But the companies haven't put all their money on the refugia approach. According to Gary Barton, director of ag biotech communications at Monsanto, "products now in the pipeline which rely on different insecticidal toxins or multiple toxins could replace Bt crops in the event of widespread resistance." Every major company in the field is working on potential successors to Bt crops. And as is apparent from Barton's comment, the goal of such research is to engineer not just for toxins that could replace Bt, but for other toxins that kill pests unaffected by Bt. (Multiple-toxin crops are a primary industry objective; a case in point is the rush to develop a form of Bt corn that also resists corn rootworm.)

The result, according to Fred Gould, an entomologist at the University of North Carolina, would be "a crop with a series of silver bullet pest solutions." And each of these solutions, in Gould's view, would be highly vulnerable to pest resistance. This scenario does not differ essentially

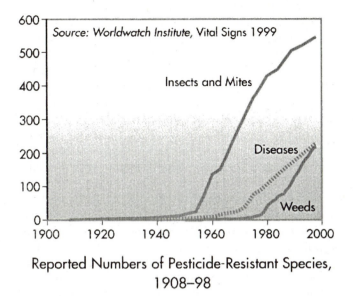

Reported Numbers of Pesticide-Resistant Species, 1908–98

from the current one: in place of a pesticide treadmill, we would substitute a sort of gene treadmill. The arms race between farmers and pests would continue, but would include an additional biochemical dimension. Transgenic plants, designed to secrete increasingly potent combinations of pesticides, would vie with a host of increasingly resistant pests.

THE WEEDS

The global transgenic harvest is currently dominated, not by Bt crops, but by herbicide-resistant crops (HRCs), which occupy 20 million hectares worldwide. HRCs are sold as part of a "technology package" comprised of HRC seed and the herbicide the crop is designed to resist. The two principal product lines are currently Monsanto's "Roundup Ready" crops—so-named because they

tolerate Monsanto's best-selling herbicide, "Roundup" (glyphosate)—and AgrEvo's "Liberty Link" crops, which tolerate that company's "Liberty" herbicide (glufosinate).

It may sound contradictory, but one ostensible objective of HRCs is to reduce herbicide use. By designing crops that tolerate fairly high levels of exposure to a broad-spectrum herbicide (a chemical that is toxic to a wide range of plants), the companies are giving farmers the option of using a heavy, once-in-the-growing-season dousing with that herbicide, instead of the standard practice, which calls for a series of applications of several different compounds. It's not yet clear whether this new herbicide regime actually reduces the amount of material used, but its simplicity is attracting many farmers into the package.

Another potential benefit of HRCs is that they may allow for more "conservation tillage," farming techniques that reduce the need for plowing or even—under "no till" cultivation—eliminate it entirely. A primary reason for plowing is to break up the weeds, but because it exposes bare earth, plowing causes topsoil erosion. Topsoil is the capital upon which agriculture is built, so conserving soil is one of agriculture's primary responsibilities. In the U.S. soybean crop, the area under no-till has been increasing substantially and that increase correlates to some degree with the increasing use of Monsanto's Roundup Ready soybeans. But here too, the data are still vague: it's too early to say how much of the trend is due to the transgenic crop.

The bigger problem is that HRCs, like Bt crops, are really just an extension of the current pesticide paradigm. HRCs may permit a reduction in herbicide use over the short term, but obviously their widespread adoption would encourage herbicide dependency. In many parts of the developing world, where herbicides are not now common, the herbicide habit could mean substantial additional en-

BT CROPS: WHAT'S SUPPOSED TO HAPPEN

❶ A toxin-producing gene from *Bacillus thuringiensis* (Bt), a common soil bacterium, is spliced into the DNA of a crop variety.

❷ Any pests that attempt to eat the Bt crop are poisoned.

Bt is already widely used as a conventional pesticide, especially by small-scale and organic farmers. It's generally considered far less dangerous than synthetic pesticides.

❸ Substantial "refugia"—areas planted in a variety without the Bt gene—insure that much of the pest population won't be exposed to the Bt variety, making it much harder for the pest to evolve resistance to the toxin.

vironmental stresses: herbicides are toxic to many soil organisms, they can pollute groundwater, and they may have long-term effects on both people and wildlife.

And of course, resistance will occur. Bob Hartzler, a weed scientist at Iowa State University, warns that if HRCs encourage reliance on just a few broad-spectrum herbicides, then resistance is likely to develop faster—and agriculture is likely to be more vulnerable to it. Hartzler cites an ad for Roundup Ready cotton, which displays a jug of Roundup and boasts, "The only weed control you need."

In the U.S. Midwest, heavy use of Roundup on Roundup Ready soybeans is already encouraging weed species, like waterhemp, that are naturally resistant to that herbicide. (As Roundup suppresses the susceptible weeds, the resistant ones have more room to grow.) Thus far, the evolution of resistance in weed species that are susceptible to Roundup has been relatively rare, despite decades of use. The first reported case involved wild ryegrass in Australia, in 1995. But with increasing use, more such cases are all but inevitable—especially since Monsanto is on the verge of releasing Roundup Ready corn. Corn and soybeans are the classic crop rotation in the U.S. Midwest—corn is planted in one year, soy in the next. Roundup Ready varieties of both crops could subject vast areas of the U.S. "breadbasket" to an unremitting rain of that herbicide. As with the Bt crops, the early promise of HRCs is liable to be undercut by the very mentality that inspired them: the single-minded chemical pursuit of the pest.

TRANSGENES ON THE LOOSE

In 1997, just one year after its first commercial planting in Canada, a farmer reported—and DNA testing confirmed—that Roundup Ready canola had cross-pollinated with a related weed species growing in the field's margins, and produced an herbicide-tolerant descendant. The gene for herbicide resistance had "escaped."

If a transgenic crop is capable of sexual reproduction (and they generally are), the leaking of "transgenes" is to some degree inevitable, if any close relatives are growing in the vicinity. This type of genetic pollution is not likely to be common in the industrialized countries, where most major crops have relatively few close relatives. But in the developing world—especially in regions where a major crop originated—the picture is very different. Such places are the "hot spots" of agricultural diversity: the cultivation of the ancient, traditional varieties—whether it's corn in Mexico or soybeans in China—often involves a subtle genetic interplay between cultivated forms of a species, wild forms, and related species that aren't cultivated at all. The possibilities for genetic pollution in such contexts are substantial.

Ordinary breeding creates some degree of genetic pollution too. But according to Allison Snow, an Ohio State University plant ecologist who studies transgene flow, biotech could amplify the process considerably because of the far more diverse array of genes it can press into service. Any traits that confer a substantial competitive advantage in the wild could be expected to spread widely. The Bt gene would presumably be an excellent candidate for this process, since its toxin affects so many insect species.

There's no way to predict what would happen if the Bt gene were to escape into a wild flora, but there's good reason to be concerned. John Losey, an entomologist at Cornell University, has been experimenting with Monarch butterflies, by raising their caterpillars on milkweed dusted with Bt-corn pollen. Losey found that nearly half of the insects raised on this fare died and the rest were stunted. (Caterpillars raised on milkweed dusted with ordinarily corn pollen did fine.) According to Losey, "these levels of mortality are comparable to those you find with especially toxic insecticides." If the gene were to work a change that dramatic in a wild plant's toxicity, then it could trigger a cascade of second- and third-order ecological effects. (See illustration, "Some Things that Could Happen.")

The potential for this kind of trouble is likely to grow, since a major interest in biotech product development is "trait-stacking"—combining several engineered genes in a single variety, as with the attempts to develop corn with multiple toxins. Monsanto's "stacked cotton"—Roundup ready and Bt-producing—is already on the market in the United States. Eventually, a single crop could diffuse a wide array of potent genes into the wild.

In the agricultural hot spots, there is an important practical reason to be concerned about any resulting genetic pollution. Plant breeders depend on the genetic wealth of the hot spots to maintain the vigor of the major crops—and there's no realistic possibility of biotech rendering this natural wealth "obsolete." But it certainly is possible that foreign genes could upset the relationships between the local varieties and their wild relatives. How would that affect the entire genetic complex? There's probably no way to know until after the fact.

TOWARD A NEW FEUDALISM

The advent of transgenic crops raises serious social questions as well—beginning with ownership. All transgenic seed is patented, as are most nontransgenic commercial varieties. But beginning in the 1980s, the tendency in industrialized countries and in international law has been to permit increasingly broad agricultural patents—and not just on varieties but even on specific genes. Under the earlier, more limited patents, farmers could buy seed and use it in their own breeding; they could grow it out and save some of the resulting seed for the next year; they could even trade it for other seed. About the only thing they couldn't do was sell it outright. But under the broader patents, all of those activities are illegal; the purchaser is essentially just paying for one-time use of the germplasm.

The right to own genes is a relatively new phenomenon in world history and its effects on agriculture—and life in

SOME THINGS THAT COULD HAPPEN

Farmers may not plant enough of their land in refugia and resistance could develop. The effectiveness of Bt, even as a conventional pesticide, would be compromised.

❶ A more complex scenario could unfold in the tropics, where many crops have wild relatives with which they interbreed. That may allow the Bt gene to "escape" into related species. The wild Bt plants could become much less edible to the insects that normally feed on them and that do not normally feed on the crops. (Such insects, symbolized here by the gray butterfly, would not presumably have acquired resistance to Bt.)

❷ The toxicity of the crop relatives could give them a competitive edge over other plants that grow in the same areas, since the insects would continue to feed on the other plants.

❸ The Bt plants could suppress their competitors and the herbivorous insect population could decline.

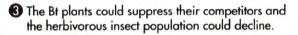

❹ Insect-eating birds could be in trouble. . .

. . . and so could grazers in need of the suppressed plant species.

general—are still very uncertain. The biotech companies argue that ownership is essential for driving their industry: without exclusive rights to a product that costs hundreds of millions of dollars to develop, how will it be possible to attract investors? And some industry advocates see patents as a way of "investing" in biodiversity in general. Val Giddings of the Biotechnology Industry Organization makes this case: "intellectual property rights allow us to harness genetic resources for commercial use, making biodiversity concretely more valuable. One can make economic arguments for the conservation of biodiversity, whereas previously one could only make aesthetic or inherent value arguments."

Patents are clearly an important ingredient in the industry's expansion. Global sales of transgenic crop products grew from $75 million in 1995 to $1.5 billion in 1998—a 20-fold increase. Sales are expected to hit $25 billion by 2010. And as the market has expanded, so has the scramble for patents. Recently, for example, the German agrochemical firm AgrEvo, the maker of "Liberty" herbicide, bought a Dutch biotech company called Plant Genetic Systems (PGS), which owned numerous wheat and corn patents. The patents were so highly valued that AgrEvo was willing to pay $730 million for the acquisition—$700 million more than PGS's annual sales. A recent *Wall Street Journal* article reports that in U.S. patent litigation, only computer software continues to attract more cases than plants.

This patent frenzy is contributing to an intense wave of consolidation within the industry. AgrEvo, for example, is itself a subsidiary of another German chemical company, Hoechst. Hoechst recently merged with one of its French counterparts. Rhône-Poulenc, to form Aventis, which is now the world's largest agrochemical firm and a major player in the biotech industry. On the other side of the Atlantic, Monsanto has spent nearly $8 billion since

1996 to purchase various seed companies. DuPont, a major competitor, has bought the world's largest seed company, Pioneer Hi-Bred. DuPont and Monsanto were minor players in the seed industry just a decade ago, but are now respectively the largest and second-largest seed companies in the world.

Since 1996, the industry has seen $15 billion worth of mergers and acquisitions involving 25 corporations. Of the 56 transgenic products approved for commercial planting in 1998, 33 belonged to just four corporations: Monsanto, Aventis, Novartis, and DuPont. The first three of these companies control the transgenic seed market in the United States, which amounts to three-fourths of the global market. (Monsanto accounted for 88 percent of the U.S. transgenic area in 1998, while Aventis and Novartis split the remainder.)

Even when viewed purely in market terms, these trends may be working a kind of paradox within the young industry: the drive to secure research potential may be leading to less research. According to John Barton, an expert in biotech law at Stanford University Law School, "the incentives for the industry leaders to conduct research are now limited, for these leaders are now in an oligopolistic (and potentially monopolistic) situation." Less competition and innovation and more squabbling over patents—is this the future of ag biotech? One biotech company, Agracetus (recently acquired by Monsanto), has filed a patent that would cover *all* transgenic cotton and soybeans. In the face of such claims, it's not hard to imagine that the focus of industry research may be shifting from the lab to the law library.

But there is far more at stake here than the fortunes of the industry itself: patents and similar legal mechanisms may be giving companies additional control over farmers. As a way of securing their patent rights, biotech companies are requiring farmers to sign "seed contracts" when they purchase transgenic seed—a wholly new phenomenon in agriculture. The contracts may stipulate what brand of pesticides the farmer must use on the crop—a kind of legal cement for those crop-herbicide "technology packages." And the contracts generally forbid the types of activities that had been permitted under the earlier patent regimes.

The most troubling aspect of these contracts is the possible effect on seed saving—the ancient practice of reserving a certain amount of harvested seed for the next planting. In the developing world, some 1.4 billion farmers still rely almost exclusively on seed saving for their planting needs. As a widespread, low-tech form of breeding, seed saving is also critical to the husbandry of crop diversity, since farmers generally save seed from plants that have done best under local conditions. The contracts have little immediate relevance to seed saving in the developing world, since the practice there is employed largely by farmers who could not afford transgenic seed in the first place. But even in industrialized countries, seed savings is still common in certain areas and for certain crops, and

Monsanto has already taken legal action against over 300 farmers for replanting proprietary seeds.

The struggle to enforce those broad patents is unlikely to stop with seed contracts—or to remain a First World concern. A recent invention—officially entitled the "gene protection technology" but popularly dubbed the "terminator technology"—may make the seed contracts a biological reality. The terminator prevents harvested seeds from germinating. Its principal inventor, a U.S. Department of Agriculture molecular biologist named Melvin Oliver, notes that "the technology primarily targets Second and Third World markets"—in effect guaranteeing patent rights even in nations where patent enforcement is weak or nonexistent. The terminator may also encourage the patenting of some major crops, such as rice, wheat, and sorghum, that have generally been ignored by private-sector breeders. Although there has been a great deal of public sector developing of these crops, it has been difficult for private companies to make money on them, because it is relatively easy for farmers to breed stable, productive varieties on their own. The terminator could allow companies to get a better "grip" on such crops.

NGOs focused on agriculture have tended to view the prospect of the terminator with alarm. "The terminator will increase crop uniformity by restricting seed-saving and breeding by farmers," says Neth Daño of the Philippines-based SEARICE, a rural development organization. In that sense, the terminator is just the latest variation on a well-established theme: at least since the 1970s, the developing world's highly diverse farm-saved varieties have been losing ground to a much smaller array of uniform commercial varieties. The substitution of commercial for farm-saved seed has been a primary reason for the loss of genetic diversity in the agricultural hot spots. Hope Shand, research director for the Rural Advancement Foundation International (RAFI), a farmer advocacy group based in Winnipeg, Canada, regards the extension of patents in general as a means of reducing farmers to "bioserfs," who provide little more than land and labor to agribusiness.

Although the terminator is still some five years from commercialization, it has already become a public relations disaster for the entire industry. Monsanto, which had recently acquired exclusive rights to the technology, has announced that it may reconsider its use. But research by RAFI has shown that virtually all the major companies—Monsanto, Novartis, Astra/Zeneca, DuPont, BASF, and Aventis—are working on seed sterility technology. Such technologies, according to Shand are "the Holy Grail of the agricultural biotechnology industry."

The terminator may be the harbinger of technologies that attempt to seal other aspects of farming within the seed. The suicidal terminator genes are activated by dousing the seed with the antibiotic tetracycline. (This external trigger is necessary because it would not otherwise be possible to grow the seeds out for sale.) The development of such trigger mechanisms may ultimately be of far greater consequence than the terminator itself. Novartis was recently awarded a patent for a gene technology that would tie a whole set of plant development processes, including germination, flowering, and fruit ripening, to externally applied chemicals—perhaps even to Novartis' own agrochemicals.

But beyond these control issues, there remains the basic question of biotech's potential for feeding the world's billions. Here too, the current trends are not very encouraging. At present, the industry has funneled its immense pool of investment into a limited range of products for which there are large, secured markets within the capital-intensive production systems of the First World. There is very little connection between the kind of research and the lives of the world's hungry. HRCs, for example, are not helpful to poor farmers who rely on manual labor to pull weeds because they couldn't possibly afford herbicides. (The immediate opportunities for biotech in the developing world are not the subsistence farmers, of course, but the larger operations, which are often producing for export rather than for local consumption.)

Just to get a sense of proportion on this subject, consider this comparison. The entire annual budget of the Consultative Group for International Agricultural Research (CGIAR), a consortium of international research centers that form the world's largest public-sector crop breeding effort, amounts to $400 million. The amount that Monsanto spent to develop Roundup Ready soybeans alone is estimated at $500 million. In such numbers, one can see a kind of financial disconnect. Per Pinstrup-Andersen, director of the International Food Policy Research Institute, the CGIAR's policy arm, puts it flatly: "the private sector will not develop crops to solve poor people's problems, because there is not enough money in it." The very nature of their affliction—poverty—makes hungry people poor customers for expensive technologies.

In addition to the financial obstacle, there is a biological obstacle that may limit the role of biotech as agricultural savior. The crop traits that would be most useful to subsistence farmers tend to be very complex. Miguel Altieri, an entomologist at the University of California at Berkeley, identifies the kind of products that would make sense in a subsistence context: "crop varieties responsive to low levels of soil fertility, crops tolerant of saline or drought conditions and other stresses of marginal lands, improved varieties that are not dependent on agrochemical inputs for increased yields, varieties that are compatible with small, diverse, capital-poor farm settings." In HRCs and Bt crops, the engineering involves the insertion of a single gene. Most of the traits Altieri is talking about are probably governed by many genes, and for the present at least, that kind of complexity is far beyond the technology's reach.

BEYOND THE TECHNO-FIX

In the 1970s, Hans Herren set out to deal with the cassava mealybug, which was decimating harvests of this staple crop throughout Africa. Herren was then an ento-

mologist with the International Centre of Insect Physiology and Ecology, based in Nairobi, and is now the Center's director. He knew that cassava was feeding some of the poorest of Africa's poor, because cassava can be planted on dry, low-nutrient soils where little else will grow. This South American root crop had become an essential part of Africa's food security—a kind of social safety net. But the net had begun to fray rapidly after the arrival of the mealybug, a native predator of cassava in South America. Because the mealybug had arrived in Africa without any of its own natural predators, it was a much more serious pest there than on its native continent. So Herren orchestrated the introduction of a wasp that parasitizes the mealybug in its native range. (The wasp was chosen because of its high degree of prey specificity, minimizing the risk that it would attack anything else.) Seven years after the introduction, the mealybug had been virtually eliminated in most African nations, and remains so today. The latest accounting analysis has put the cost-to-benefit ratio of this "biological control" effort at 1:200—a very modest statement of the benefits, given cassava's role as a crop of last resort.

On a 300-acre farm in Boone, Iowa—the heart of the U.S. corn belt—Dick Thompson rotates corn, soybeans, oats, wheat interplanted with clover, and a hay combination that includes an assortment of grasses and legumes. The pests that plague neighboring farmers—including the corn borer targeted by Bt corn—are generally a minor part of the picture on Thompson's farm. High crop diversity tends to reduce insect populations because insect pests are usually "specialists" on one particular crop. In a very diverse setting, no single pest is likely to be able to get the upper hand. Diversity also tends to shut out weeds, because complex cropping uses resources more efficiently than monocultures, so there's less left over for the weeds to consume. Thompson also keeps the weeds down by grazing a herd of cattle—a rarity on midwestern corn farms. Even without herbicides, Thompson's farm has been on conservation tillage for the last three decades. The cattle, a hog operation, and the nitrogen-fixing legumes provide the soil nutrients that most U.S. farmers buy in a bag. The soil organic matter content—the sentinel indicator of soil health—registers at 6 percent on Thompson's land, which is more than twice that of his neighbors. (Untouched Midwestern prairie registers at 7 percent.) Thompson's soybean and corn yields are well above the county average and even as the U.S. government continues to bail out indebted farmers, Thompson is making money. He profits both from his healthy soil and crops, and from the fact that his "input" costs—for chemical fertilizer, pesticides, and so forth—are almost nil.

In the activities of people like Herren and Thompson it is possible to see a very different kind of agricultural paradigm, which could move farming beyond the techno-fix approach that currently prevails. Known as agroecology, this paradigm recognizes the farm as an ecosystem—an agroecosystem—and employs ecological principles to improve productivity and build stability. The emphasis is on adapting farm design and practice to the ecological processes actually occurring in the fields and in the landscape that surrounds them. Agroecology aims to substitute detailed (and usually local) ecological knowledge for off-the-shelf and off-the-farm "magic bullet" solutions. The point is to treat the disease, rather than just the symptoms. Instead of engineering a corn variety that is toxic to corn rootworm, for example, an agroecologist would ask why there's a rootworm problem in the first place.

Where would biotech fit within such a paradigm? In the industry's current form, at least, it doesn't appear to fit very well at all. Biotech's first agricultural products are "derivative technologies," to use a term favored by Frederick Buttel, a rural sociologist at the University of Wisconsin. Buttel sees those products as "grafted onto an established trajectory, rather than defining or crystallizing a new one."

There is no question that biotech contains some real potential for agriculture, for instance as a supplement to conventional breeding or as a means of studying crop pathogens. But if the industry continues to follow its current trajectory, then biotech's likely contribution will be marginal at best and at worst, given the additional dimensions of ecological and social unpredictability—who knows? In any case, the biggest hope for agriculture is not something biochemists are going to find in a test tube. The biggest opportunities will be found in what farmers already know, or in what they can readily discover on their farms.

Brian Halweil is a staff researcher at the Worldwatch Institute.

The Technology of *Hope*

Tools to Empower the World's Poorest Peoples

By Rashmi Mayur and Bennett Daviss

Yes, there is hope for the rural poor of the emerging nations, but it doesn't lie in large-scale industrialization.

Since the industrial revolution, Western economies have relied on vast supplies of raw material from lesser-developed countries in order to prosper: timber from South America, minerals from Africa, oil from the Middle East. Today, with 20% of the world's population, the Western economies consume more than half of the planet's energy and raw materials. Although industrial production is being globalized swiftly, consumption is not; the same minority of the human species remains the only group able to buy most of the planet's manufactured goods.

The developing countries cannot build their future, as the West did, by consuming more than their proportionate share of the world's resources. The typical resident of Ghana can't outbid the average American for a truck or computer; Nicaragua can't expropriate coal from Germany to fuel its factories. In the new century, the rising economic expectations of the world's poor will have to be met in ways that use resources conservatively and efficiently, not profligately. That necessity forecloses a global economic future rooted in worldwide industrialization.

As we argued in our earlier essay ("How NOT to Develop an Emerging Nation," THE FUTURIST, January-February 1998), the idea that today's emerging economies must pass through a phase of mass industrialization as Western nations did is

UNITED SOLAR SYSTEMS

Mexican mother carries both her child and a solar power kit to her mountain village, where the solar power system will be used to generate electricity.

an antiquated premise, rooted in and suited to a period of social and economic history that has passed. An economy in which strong hands and a time card produced an abundant material life for an individual or for an entire society has yielded to an emerging global economy that drives down industrial wages and places increasing premiums on knowledge, environmental stewardship, decentralization, and the personal touch.

Instead of accepting industrialization as the only way to satisfy the economic aspirations of their people, developing nations can turn to several decentralized, relatively inexpensive, and environmentally compatible tools and techniques—all available now—that can help bring a post-industrial form of prosperity to emerging nations. Together, these technologies can begin to redefine the notion of development, showing that it is possible to balance the demands of people with the needs of the biosphere.

Thanks to these new technologies, it's now possible for countries to develop sound, broad-based economies without industrializing, without draining people from rural areas and concentrating low-paid workers in company towns or urban ghettos, and without degrading and exhausting their land, air, and water.

These technologies will not replace industrial installations around the globe; indeed, many of these benign technologies are produced in manufacturing plants. But they will enable emerging nations to define a future that separates development from industrialization, creating new routes to prosperity.

Benign vs. Malignant Technologies

A "technology" is simply a way to accomplish an objective. A computer is a technology that manipulates data; banking is a technology that allows people to readily store, exchange, and multiply value. But a technology, like any human act, is never free of consequences, often unforeseen, that can render a technology either benign or malignant.

A benign technology is one whose systemic or cyclic benefits outweigh its drawbacks over the life of the technology. The vaccines and inoculation campaigns that eradicated smallpox are an ideal example of a benign technology; so has been the effort, led by Peru's International Potato Center, to genetically engineer a potato containing the basic daily amounts of the amino acids, vitamins, and minerals essential in human nutrition.

A malignant technology is the opposite: one whose drawbacks outweigh its benefits over the life of the technology. There can be no better example than the gasoline engine. Undeniably, its economic benefits have been greater than almost any other invention in human history. But as smog and greenhouse gases accumulate in worrisome amounts and eat away the atmosphere's protective ozone layer, it's clear to most honest observers that the gasoline engine's malignancy is entering a lethal phase. Even automakers themselves are beginning to scramble for alternatives.

A sustainable future can be built only from benign technologies. Fortunately, there is an array of them—simple, relatively inexpensive, and available now—that, taken together, offer a "soft path" to economic development.

Technologies of Energy

Reliable energy supplies are usually a key requirement for emerging nations with poor populations to become self-sufficient. Benign ways to supply electric power underlie all aspects of nonindustrial development and serve as the heart of a prosperous nonindustrial economy.

The industrial-age approach to electrifying an outlying area is to spend hundreds of millions of dollars to build a central generating plant that burns fossil fuels and spews harmful gases—or that dams rivers and disrupts ecosystems—and to run thousands of miles of cable from the plant to all corners of a region. Creating such a system demands that either the national government or a private licensee finance and build the necessary infrastructure. Because emerging nations lack sufficient paying customers to support such an installation, countries typically must finance such projects through foreign debt and repay those loans by exporting hardwoods, oil, and other portions of their natural heritage; usually, these are poor countries' only available assets that fetch the hard currency they must have to repay foreign loans. "Development" then becomes a path to environmental exploitation and depletion, all too often accompanied by resentment and political backlash.

The benign technologies of renewable energy can provide power at far less expense.

Solar technologies are simple enough and inexpensive enough to meet typical household uses in most of the world. Solar ovens use one-way glass with a mirrored inner lid to focus the sun's rays into a black-lined cooking chamber. The devices are the size of a briefcase, require no maintenance, and typically cost no more than $70. A $1,450 solar-powered water pump uses just 200 watts of electricity, as much as three average light bulbs, and can deliver 30 gallons of water—the minimum for health specified by the World Health Organization—for 135 people every day. Cheap solar evaporators can separate clean water from a number of pollutants, making water safe to drink that otherwise would not be potable.

The Washington, D.C.-based Solar Electric Light Fund is equipping village homes in 11 countries with photovoltaic systems to power lights and a television at an installed cost of less than $400 per household. Buyers pay for their systems through a revolving loan fund that

There is no reason to deny millions of people power simply because their nation has not yet built massive fossil-fuel-burning generating plants.

finances other customers and expands solar power's availability.

Energy Conversion Devices in Troy, Michigan, makes paper-thin solar collector sheets that roll up like window shades, can be carried anywhere, and deliver electricity even when shot through with bullets. There is no longer any portion of the world too rugged or remote for effective solar technologies.

Another technology, used by 10 million Chinese farms, is the methane digester power plant. The plants capture natural gas rising from garbage and human or animal dung— "biogas"—and concentrate it in sealed chambers so it can be burned to run pumps, boilers, or small generators. The plants are set into pits as shallow as six feet, can be as small as eight feet in diameter, and can deliver power using the dung from as few as two cows. Farmers themselves can be trained to conduct the needed routine maintenance and to make simple repairs, and the "spent" fuel extracted from the digester can still be used as a rich fertilizer. The installed cost for the smallest biogas plant: less than $150. India's Renewable Energy Development Agency, a project of the national government, is subsidizing installation of the plants in farms and villages. The subsidies' costs are more than offset by the money the government saves—everything from regulatory paperwork to construction—by not bringing energy to rural areas through the traditional centralized, industrial approach.

There is no reason to deny millions of people in the developing world a steady supply of power simply because their nation has not yet built massive, fossil-fuel-burning generating plants and run thou-

SOLAREX

South African villager exults at the new experience of watching television. His TV set is powered by the new solar panel in the background. Such solar technology projects allow rural people to access both information and entertainment

sands of miles of transmission lines. Those technologies are no longer synonymous with electric power. Decentralized approaches can not only spark social and economic progress, but also can enable resource-poor people to stop harvesting dung and vegetation to burn. When they can do so, they can begin to use those resources to renew their soils and ecosystems in ways that will enable the land to support them again.

Technologies of Education And Communication

Until now, outlying areas of emerging nations have been cut off from the world not only physically, but also psychically and socially.

Neither governments nor broadcasters could economically justify building ground-based transmitters that would beam programs to poor areas; people could neither pay for broadcasting services nor buy goods from advertisers. But now in regions lacking cable, poles, and the elabo-

rate infrastructure of conventional communications, wireless communications and decentralized sources of renewable energy are an ideal match that can be installed quickly to fill the need.

For example, the technology now exists to place in every isolated village an "information kiosk"—a booth containing a cellular telephone, radio, television, videocassette recorder, and even a computer linked to the Internet—all powered by solar energy. Satellite broadcasts could bring villagers information ranging from weather alerts to arithmetic lessons to tips on caring for newborns. With a telephone, farmers could monitor market conditions and avoid selling crops when prices are weak, and parents could phone for medical advice when a child is sick. With the strides being made in telemedicine, distance learning, and similar services, the information kiosk could serve as classroom, agricultural extension office, doctor's examination room, and bulletin board—not just as an entertainment center.

The seeds of these rural information networks are already being planted. The Bombay-based International Institute for Sustainable Future is designing prototypes of the kiosks for its two demonstration "ecovillages" in west central India. Meanwhile, in Bangladesh, Mohammad Yunus, founder of the pioneering microlender Grameen Bank, has launched a venture that will place a cellular phone in 65,000 of the nation's villages. An entrepreneur in each village buys the phone, charges customers by the minute, repays the loan from the fees, and makes a small profit on each call. The venture is investing $25 million to cover a third of the country with 50 to 60 relay towers, sharing the cost with companies in New York, Japan, and Norway.

In Africa, Tanzania's Kibadula Farm Institute uses a small ground station to communicate with the world via satellite. The Institute, operated by the Seventh Day Adventist Church to bring education, health care, and improved farming techniques to the remote African villages surrounding it, set up the equipment to communicate with the church's U.S. headquarters. Soon it was using e-mail over the Internet to find expert advice on an array of practical problems, including the assembly of ultralight aircraft. In 1995, the Solar Electric Light Fund provided Africa's Masai people with solar-powered radio-telephones that they use to communicate not only with each other, but also over the country's public telephone system.

These projects provide a small glimpse of a large future. Teledesic, a company formed in 1990 by Microsoft founder Bill Gates and cellu-

lar-phone magnate Craig McCaw, plans to launch as many as 800 low-orbit satellites to bring cellular communications and Internet access to every point on the globe. The company itself will not provide communications services, but rather maintain an open network through which others can offer services. In a key provision, Teledesic has pledged to reserve a number of communications channels specifically for services in poor nations.

This practical, affordable combination of decentralized communications and decentralized energy sources means that no village need remain isolated from knowledge, advice, or opportunity or from their larger societies.

Population Control: A New Opportunity

Unchecked birth rates are a root cause of the spiraling environmental destruction and social desolation rampant in developing nations. Populations that outgrow their water supplies pollute and deplete what sources remain. Burgeoning families strip the countryside for food and fuel, exhausting soils, razing forests, extinguishing wildlife species, and transforming once-productive land into desert. From the sands of Ethiopia to the burning rain forests of Brazil, the global map is dotted with the consequences of overpopulation.

Clearly, most efforts to check population growth in emerging nations have met with mixed results at best. It's not possible to deliver regular supplies of condoms or birth-control pills to remote regions. In some areas, women whose arms bear the marks of having been fitted with sub-skin time-release fertility controls have been stigmatized. And in too many poor countries, adults

still insist that they need flocks of children to help support the family.

The installation of electric lights has been shown to slow birth rates by giving adults new choices of activities after dark, but decentralized energy technologies also enable a new way to achieve the same goal: by changing minds.

The nonprofit, New York-based Population Communications International (PCI) has discovered that one of the most effective routes around the barriers to population control is through an old American invention—the "soap opera," or continuing drama on radio and television.

In Mexico, PCI partnered with sociologists and television producers to create and televise a dramatic series following the struggles of a lower-class Mexican family with two children. The wife has come from a large family that was held in poverty by its sheer size. She aspires to a better life, but her husband's interest in sex is equaled only by his disdain for family planning. After a dramatic crisis, she persuades her husband to go with her to a family-planning clinic. He realizes that they'll have more sex because his wife won't fear the consequences. In the six months following the show, registration at Mexico's family-planning clinics jumped by 33%.

"To change behavior, you have to combine information with culturally tailored emotional content that lets the audience discover the benefits of seeing the world in new ways," says PCI's former executive vice-president, William Ryerson.

The result has been replicated in other countries where PCI works. In Kenya, for example—once considered a hopeless case among family planners—the group helped create a radio serial that reached 85% of the nation's families and was shown to

Solar technologies are simple enough and inexpensive enough to meet typical household uses in most of the world.

be more popular than broadcasts of soccer matches, the national game. The serial probed issues not only of family planning, but of land inheritance—specifically, the problem of dividing the family farm among more and more children, who then would be unable to support their parents in their old age. In the wake of the serial, use of contraceptives in Kenya rose 58%, the desired family size fell from an average of 6.3 children to 4.4, and the birth rate began to fall for the first time in two decades.

But to show poor people these new ways of seeing, one must be able to reach them. Satellite communications coupled to decentralized sources of renewable energy can provide a means by which population growth—the root cause of so many social and environmental ills—can be effectively addressed.

Technologies of Finance

Benign technologies are not only less toxic than their industrial counterparts, but also less expensive per person served. But bringing these technologies to those who need them still will require enormous investment. Under the industrial-age approach to development financing, transglobal institutions such as the World Bank lent money to build power plants, mining ventures, and other large-scale government projects in unindustrialized nations. Now, new technological solutions to poverty require new funding structures to support them.

Although well-intentioned, many of those traditionally funded projects damaged ecosystems and destroyed cultures. For example, the World Bank loaned Brazil money to build a paved highway through the rain-forest state of Rondonia. The road was intended to promote integrated economic development by facilitating the transport of products from ranchers, miners, and farmers. But the road also opened huge areas of the forest to hordes of land-hungry colonists able to support themselves only through slash-and-burn farming. In effect, the World Bank helped to fund global climate change.

In another Brazilian fiasco, the World Bank underwrote the building of two huge dams that drowned vast tracts of the rain forest—homelands of indigenous peoples—to provide electricity for mining operations that, in turn, obliterated even more of the rain forest.

In 1987, the World Bank announced reforms designed to take social and environmental impacts into account in selecting projects for funding, but those reforms have been slow in appearing. As one observer commented, "The World Bank is an elephant that's now facing in the right direction. How fast it's actually moving in that direction is another question."

While large development projects can be justified in a few cases, a decentralized economy that relies on benign technologies requires decentralized funding. There are two models that are showing new directions.

One is being pioneered by the Solar Electric Light Fund (SELF). To bring solar-energy systems to villagers in emerging nations, SELF doesn't rely solely on the charity of international philanthropies. Instead, it often forges partnerships among nonprofit and for-profit groups. Using public and private grants as seed capital, SELF finances local small businesses that sell and service solar-energy equipment in developing countries. Families buy the power systems using low-interest loans from revolving funds that recycle the payments to finance purchases by other families.

In one such joint venture in India, SELF formed a for-profit subsidiary called SELCO India with local partners. Through India's Renewable Energy Development Agency, SELCO tapped World Bank funds set aside specifically for photovoltaic installations. In part, the company used the money to finance rural co-ops' bulk purchase of solar-energy systems for its members, install the systems, train local technicians to continue the work, then repaid the World Bank's loan from funds SELCO collected from the co-ops. In 1997, SELF began working with several nonprofit foundations and the World Bank to evolve an ongoing public-private partnership to fund photovoltaic installations in emerging nations.

SELF's innovative collaborations sketch a new way to fund wide-scale development: pooling funds from several sources and targeting them not only to bring benign, localized technologies to specific areas, but also to develop the support structures and services those technologies need to continue on their own.

The second financial technology that can support nonindustrial economic development is microlending: financial institutions making small loans, usually no more than the equivalent of a few hundred U.S. dollars, to entrepreneurs in emerging nations to launch the kinds of cottage industries that traditional financial institutions would ignore.

The concept is no longer novel; indeed, after having been developed by small institutions such as Bangladesh's Grameen Bank and the Boston-based Accion International, it's become popular. Recent studies have found that more than 98% of microborrowers repay their loans— a higher average rate than commercial borrowers at U.S. banks—and that microlending funds, originally set up to funnel charitable grants to emerging nations, can support themselves just as commercial lenders do.

Technologies of Hope

Together, these benign, inexpensive technologies sketch a vision of economic equity and social stability for hundreds of millions of people throughout the nonurban areas of emerging nations—and even developed ones. It is a vision in which technologies of renewable energy enable people to replenish their soils and ecosystems, allow them to spend less time collecting fuel and water, and give them more abun-

A Better Pump for a Colombian Village Hope

In the middle of the night, sleeping under the stars on a grassy plain in Gaviotas, Colombia, Alonso Gutiérrez suddenly awoke with a start—and with an ingenious idea about pumping water.

Gutiérrez, one of a group of engineering students researching ways to make habitable this most barren savanna of Colombia, had an insight about pumps. He realized that the key to a hydraulic pump—the heavy piston—was also its drawback. It took strength to pump against the piston's own weight as well as the pressure seal it created between the water and the pump sleeve.

Gutiérrez's idea was to raise the sleeve instead of the piston. Not only could a woman or child easily work such a pump, but the well could go down much farther, reaching fresher water than the contaminated liquid near the surface.

The manual sleeve pump eventually provided many settlements with potable water, reducing disease where the pumps—often hooked up to children's see-saws—were used. This pump was just one of many inventions developed in Gaviotas to show the possibilities of home-grown sustainable technology. The story of these inventions and the project that led to them is told in *Gaviotas: A Village to Reinvent the World* by journalist Alan Weisman. Weisman originally told the Gaviotas story for National Public Radio and later for the *Los Angeles Times*.

"To this day, I hear from people . . . who wish they could live in Gaviotas or start their own in the United States," he says.

Distant from the political and criminal problems of Colombia, the new oasis of Gaviotas continues to prosper by using its sustainable technology to help itself. "Its co-generating two-cylinder steam engine, now installed, portends to be so efficient that the diesel plant . . . can finally be junked, making Gaviotas at last self-sufficient in energy. As a result, Gaviotas was awarded the 1997 World Prize in Zero Emissions from ZERI, the United Nations' Zero Emissions Research Initiative."

Source: *Gaviotas: A Village to Reinvent the World* by Alan Weisman. Chelsea Green Publishing Company, 205 Gates-Briggs Building, P.O. Box 428, White River Junction, Vermont 05001. 1998. 232 pages. $22.95.

MICHAEL MIDDLETON/COURTESY OF CHELSEA GREEN PUBLISHING CO.

dant and reliable harvests. Renewable energy also would power lights, radios, and televisions in homes; cellular phones and Internet-linked computers as village utilities—perhaps in the local school; and local health clinics with adequate lighting and refrigerators to store vaccines. Villagers could supplement farm income by using microloans to launch small businesses, also using renewable energy, and market their wares over the Internet.

"These technologies can make nonurban areas of emerging nations a part of twenty-first-century global society that is not homogeneous, that celebrates diversity," says Robert Freling, SELF's executive director. "Indigenous people can maintain their culture and connection to the earth, but also feel part of the global society instead of being cut off from it."

We do not suggest that benign technologies will or should purge industrialization or its products from the earth. However, these technologies can lay the foundation of a new kind of economy—one that enables the people of emerging nations to remain in their villages instead of swelling urban slums, to protect their farmland and resources instead of exhausting them, and to prosper and live with dignity in a human, not a mechanical, context.

There still will be villagers whose personal ambitions lead them to cities. But for those hundreds of millions who wish to live within the heritage of their traditional cultures, these technologies represent a "soft path" to economic development and prosperity. It offers emerging nations a new choice—and that is the point.

About the Authors

Rashmi Mayur is president of the Global Futures Network. He teaches and lectures at several educational institutions, including the University of Pennsylvania, Jersey City State College, and Bombay University. He is a writer, a global traveler, and a consultant to several national governments and United Nations agencies. His address is International Institute for Sustainable Future, 73A Mittal Tower, Nariman Point, Bombay, India, 400-021.

Bennett Daviss is an independent journalist who covers social and technological trends. His articles have appeared in more than 40 magazines on four continents. With Nobel physicist Kenneth Wilson, he is coauthor of *Redesigning Education* (Henry Holt & Co., 1994; paperback by Teachers College Press, 1996.) His address is Walpole Valley Road, Walpole, New Hampshire 03608.

Food Scarcity

An Environmental Wakeup Call

The world's farmers face a steady shrinkage in both per capita cropland and irrigation water. The likely result is higher food prices, leading to economic and social disruptions.

By Lester Brown

The environmental deterioration of the last few decades cannot continue indefinitely without eventually affecting the world economy. Until now, most of the economic effects of environmental damage have been local: the collapse of a fishery here or there from overfishing, the loss of timber exports by a tropical country because of deforestation, or the abandonment of cropland because of soil erosion. But as the scale of environmental damage expands, it threatens to affect the global economy as well.

The consequences of environmental degradation are becoming more clear. We cannot continue to deforest the earth without experiencing more rainfall runoff, accelerated soil erosion, and more destructive flooding. If we continue to discharge excessive amounts of

carbon into the atmosphere, we will eventually face economically disruptive climate change. If we continue to overpump the earth's aquifers, we will one day face acute water scarcity.

If we continue to overfish, still more fisheries will collapse. If overgrazing continues, so, too, will the conversion of rangeland into desert. Continuing soil erosion at the current rate will slowly drain the earth of its productivity. If the loss of plant and animal species continues at the rate of recent decades, we will one day face ecosystem collapse.

Everyone agrees that these trends cannot continue indefinitely, but will they stop because we finally do what we know we should do, or because the economic expansion that is causing environmental decline begins to be disrupted?

Agriculture: The Missing Link

The food system is likely to be the sector through which environmental deterioration eventually translates into economic decline. This should not come as a surprise. Archaeological evidence indicates that agriculture has often been the link between environmental deterioration and economic decline. The decline of the early Mesopotamian civilization was tied to the waterlogging and salting of its irrigated land. Soil erosion converted into desert the fertile wheatlands of North Africa that once supplied the Roman Empire with grain.

Rising grain prices will be the first global economic indicator to tell us that we are on an economic and demographic path that is environmentally unsustainable. Unimpeded

From *The Futurist*, January/February 1998, pp. 34-38. © 1996 by The World Future Society, 7910 Woodmont Ave., Bethesda, MD 20814. http://www.wfs.org/wfs. Reprinted by permission.

environmental damage will seriously impair the capacity of fishers and farmers to keep up with the growth in demand, leading to rising food prices. The social consequences of rising grain prices will become unacceptable to more and more people, leading to political instability. What begins as environmental degradation eventually translates into political instability.

A doubling of grain prices, such as occurred briefly for wheat and corn in early 1996, would not have a major immediate effect on the world's affluent, both because they spend only a small share of their income for food and because their food expenditures are dominated more by processing costs than by commodity prices. But for the 1.3 billion in the world who live on a dollar a day or less, a prolonged period of higher grain prices would quickly become life-threatening.

Heads of households unable to buy enough food to keep their families alive would hold their governments responsible and take to the streets. The resulting bread or rice riots could disrupt economic activity in many countries. If the world could not get inflated food prices back down to traditional levels, this could negatively affect the earnings of multinational corporations, the performance of stock markets, and the stability of the international monetary system. In a world economy more integrated than ever before, the problems of the poor would then become the problems of the rich.

The consequences of environmental abuse that scientists have warned about can be seen everywhere:

• In the European Union, the allowable fish catch has had to be reduced by 20% or more in an effort to avert the collapse of the region's fisheries.

• In Saudi Arabia, overreliance on a fossil aquifer to expand grain production contributed to an abrupt 62% drop in the grain harvest between 1994 and 1996.

• The soil degradation and resulting cropland abandonment that invariably follows the burning off of the Amazon rain forest for agriculture has helped make Brazil the largest grain importer in the Western Hemisphere.

As the number of such situations multiplies, it becomes more and more difficult to feed a world population that is expanding by 80 million people per year. Even without further environmental degradation, we approach the new millennium with 800 million hungry and malnourished people.

These 800 million are hungry because they are too poor to buy enough food to satisfy their basic nutritional needs. If the price of grain were to double, as it already has for some types of seafood, it could impoverish hundreds of millions more almost overnight. In short, a steep rise in grain prices could impoverish more people than any event in history, including the ill-fated Great Leap Forward in China that starved 30 million people to death between 1959 and 1961.

In Search of Land

As the world's population, now approaching 5.8 billion, continues to expand, both the area of cropland and the amount of irrigation water per person are shrinking, threatening to drop below the amount needed to provide minimal levels of food security.

Over time, farmers have used ingenious methods to expand the area used to produce crops. These included irrigation, terracing, drainage, fallowing, and even, for the Dutch, reclaiming land from the sea. Terracing let farmers cultivate steeply sloping land on a sustainable basis, quite literally enabling them to farm the mountains as well as the plains. Drainage of wetlands opened fertile bottomlands for cultivation. Alternate-year fallowing to accumulate moisture helped farmers extend cropping into semiarid regions.

By the middle of this century, the frontiers of agricultural settlement had largely disappeared, contributing to a dramatic slowdown in the growth in area planted to grain. Between 1950 and 1981, the area in grain increased from 587 million to 732 million hectares, a gain of nearly 25%. After reaching a record high in 1981, the area in grain declined, dropping to 683 million hectares in 1993. It has turned upward since then, increasing to 696 million hectares in 1996 as idled cropland was returned to production and as record grain prices in the spring of 1996 led farmers to shift land out of soybeans and other oilseeds.

While the world grain harvested area expanded from 1950 until it peaked in 1981, the growth was quite slow compared with that of population. As a result, the grainland area per person has been declining steadily since mid-century, shrinking from 0.23 hectares in 1950 to 0.12 hectares in 1996. If grainland gains and losses continue to offset each other in the decades ahead, the area will remain stable at roughly 700 million hectares. But with population projected to grow at some 80 million a year over the next few decades, the amount of cropland available to produce grain will continue to decline, shrinking to 0.08 hectares per person in 2030.

In Search of Water

The world's farmers are also facing water scarcity. The expanding demand for water is pushing beyond the sustainable yield of aquifers in many countries and is draining some of the world's major rivers dry before they reach the sea. As the demand for water for irrigation and for industrial and residential uses continues to expand, the competition between countryside and city for available water supplies intensifies. In some parts of the world, meeting growing urban needs is possible only by diverting water from irrigation.

"Evidence that the degradation of the earth is leading to food scarcity has been accumulating for many years."

One of the keys to the near tripling of the world grain harvest from 1950 to 1990 was a 2.5-fold expansion of irrigation, a development that extended agriculture into arid regions with little rainfall, intensified production in low-rainfall areas, and increased dry-season cropping in countries with monsoonal climates. Most of the world's rice and much of its wheat is produced on irrigated land.

A critical irrigation threshold was crossed in 1979. From 1950 until then, irrigation expanded faster than population, increasing the irrigated area per person by nearly one-third. This was closely associated with the worldwide rise in grain production per person of one-third. But since 1979, the growth in irrigation has fallen behind that of population, shrinking the irrigated area per person by some 7%. This trend, now well established, will undoubtedly continue as the demand for water presses ever more tightly against available supplies.

As countries and regions begin to press against the limits of water supplies, the competition between cities and the countryside intensifies. And the cities almost always win. As water is pulled away from agriculture, production often drops, forcing the country to import grain. Importing a ton of grain is, in effect, importing thousands of tons of water. For countries with water shortages, importing grain is the most efficient way to import water. Just as land scarcity has shaped international grain trade patterns historically, water scarcity is now beginning to do the same.

The bottom line is that the world's farmers face a steady shrinkage in both grainland and irrigation water per person. As cropland and irrigation water become ever more scarce, prices of both are likely to rise, pushing grain prices upward.

Aquifer depletion and the future cutbacks in water supplies that will eventually follow may pose a far greater threat to economic progress than most people realize. If aquifer depletion were simply a matter of a few isolated instances, it would be one thing, but it is now in evidence in scores of countries. Among those suffering from extensive aquifer depletion are China, India, and the United States—the three countries that collectively account for about half of the world grain harvest.

The Onset of Food Scarcity

Evidence that the degradation of the earth is leading to food scarcity has been accumulating for many years. The oceanic fish catch, for example, plagued by overfishing and pollution, has grown little after increasing from 19 million tons in 1950 to 89 million tons in 1989. Grainland productivity increased by more than 2% a year from 1950 to 1990, but dropped to scarcely 1% a year from 1990 to 1995—well below the growth in demand.

All the key food-security indicators signal a shift from surplus to scarcity. During the mid-1990s, the United States began using again all the cropland that had been idled under commodity programs in an effort to offset the slower rise in land productivity. Even so, in 1996 world carryover stocks of grain, perhaps the most sensitive indicator of food security, dropped to the lowest level on record—a mere 52 days of consumption. Even with the exceptional

harvest of 1996, stocks were rebuilt to only 57 days of consumption, far below the 70 days needed to provide a minimal buffer against a poor harvest. If grain stocks cannot be rebuilt with an outstanding harvest, when can they be?

During the late spring and early summer of 1996, world wheat and corn prices set record highs under pressure from a 1995 harvest reduced by heat waves in the U.S. Corn Belt and from China's emergence as the world's second-largest grain importer. Wheat traded at over $7 a bushel, more than double the price in early 1995. In mid-July, corn traded at an all-time high of $5.54 a bushel, also double the level of a year earlier.

In the summer of 1996, the government of Jordan, suffering from higher prices for imported wheat and a growing fiscal deficit, was forced to eliminate the bread subsidy. The resulting bread riots lasted several days and threatened to bring down the government.

Food scarcity may provide the environmental wakeup call the world has long needed. Rising food prices may indicate the urgency of reversing the trends of environmental degradation before resulting political instability reaches the point where economic progress is no longer possible.

An Unprecedented Challenge

Making sure that the next generation has enough food is no longer merely an agricultural matter. Achieving an acceptable balance between food and people depends as much on family planners as on farmers. Decisions made in the ministries of energy that will affect future climate stability may have as much effect on the food security of the next generation as those made in agricultural ministries.

The two most difficult components of the effort to secure future food supplies and build an environmentally sustainable economy are stabilizing population and climate.

The former depends on a revolution in human reproductive behavior; the latter, on a restructuring of the global energy economy. Either would thoroughly challenge a single generation, but our generation must attempt both simultaneously. In addition, building an environmentally sustainable economy depends on reversing deforestation, arresting the loss of plant and animal species, and stabilizing fisheries, aquifers, and soils.

In a world where both the seafood catch and the grain harvest per person are declining, it may be time to reassess population policy. For example, some governments, facing a deterioration in their food situation, may have to ask if couples are morally justified in having more than two children, the number needed to replace themselves.

The world has taken one small step in the right direction with the stabilization of population in some 32 countries—all of which, except Japan, are in Europe. These countries, home to some 14% of the world's people, clearly demonstrate that population stabilization is possible.

Stabilizing climate means reducing carbon emissions and, hence, fossil-fuel burning—not an easy undertaking given that 85% of all commercial energy comes from fossil fuels. The outline of a solar/hydrogen economy that is likely to replace the fossil-fuel-based economy of today is beginning to emerge. Both the technology and the economics of harnessing solar and wind energy on a massive scale are beginning to fall into place. Although still small compared with fossil-fuel use, wind-generated electricity is expanding by more than 20% a year, and the use of solar cells is growing almost as fast.

The second major opportunity for reducing carbon emissions is raising the efficiency of energy use. The impressive gains in boosting energy efficiency following the oil price shocks of the 1970s have waned in recent years. Adoption of a carbon tax (offset by a reduction in income taxes) that even partly reflected the costs of air pollution, acid rain, and

"Future food security depends on creating an environmentally sustainable economy."

climate disruption from burning fossil fuels would accelerate investment in solar and wind energy as well as in energy efficiency.

The shift from surplus to scarcity will affect land-use policy. During the last half century, when the world was plagued with farm surpluses and farmers were paid to idle cropland, there seemed little need to worry about the conversion of cropland to nonfarm uses. Cropland was a surplus commodity. But in a world of food scarcity, land use suddenly emerges as a central issue. Already, a group of leading scientists in China has issued a white paper challenging the decision by the Ministry of Heavy Industry to develop an auto-centered transport system, arguing that the country does not have enough land both to provide roads, highways, and parking lots and to feed its people. They argue instead for a state-of-the-art rail passenger system augmented by bicycles.

Perhaps the best model of successful cropland protection is Japan. The determination to protect its riceland with land-use zoning can be seen in the hundreds of small rice fields within the city boundaries of Tokyo. By tenaciously protecting the land needed for rice, Japan remains self-sufficient in staple food.

In addition to protecting cropland from conversion to nonfarm uses, either through zoning or through a stiff tax on conversion, future food security depends on reducing the loss of topsoil from wind and water erosion. In a world facing food scarcity, every ton of topsoil lost from erosion today threatens the food security of the next generation. Here, the United States has emerged as a leader, with its Conservation Reserve Program. Among other things, it promotes the conversion of highly erodible cropland into grass, trans-

forming it to grazing land before it becomes wasteland. This program also denies the benefits of any government programs to farmers with excessive soil erosion on their land if they do not adopt an approved soil conservation management program.

Like land, water is also being diverted to nonfarm uses. With water scarcity now constraining efforts to expand food production in many countries, raising the efficiency of water use is emerging as a key to expanding food production. A shift to water markets, requiring users to pay the full cost of water, would lead to substantial investments in efficiency. The common practice of supplying water either free of charge or at a nominal cost to farmers, industries, and urban dwellers leads to water waste.

Stretching water supplies enough to satisfy future food needs means boosting the efficiency of water use emulating the achievements of Israel—the pacesetter in this field. *Land productivity* has long been part of our vocabulary, an indicator that we measure in yield per hectare. But the term *water productivity* is rarely heard. Until it, too, becomes part of our everyday lexicon, water scarcity will cloud our future.

Feeding the Future

Securing future food supplies will affect every facet of human existence—from land-use policy to water-use policy to how we use leisure time. If food security is the goal, then the dream of some of having a car in every garage, a swimming pool in every backyard, and a golf course in every community may remain simply a dream.

Until recently, the world had three reserves it could call on in the event of a poor harvest—cropland idled under farm programs, surplus stocks of grain in storage, and the one-third of the world grain harvest that is fed to livestock, poultry, and fish. By 1997, the first two of these reserves had largely disappeared. The only one remaining that can be tapped in a world food emergency is the grain used as feed. This is much more difficult to draw on. Higher prices, of course, will encourage the world's affluent to eat less grain-intensive livestock products, but prices high enough to have this effect would also threaten the survival of the world's low-income consumers.

In the event of a world food emergency, one way to restrict the rise in grain prices and restore market stability would be to level a tax on the consumption of livestock products, offsetting it with a reduction in income taxes. Lowering the demand for grain would also lower its price. Unpopular though it would be, such a tax might be acceptable if it were the key to maintaining political stability and sustaining economic progress in low-income countries. Such a step would not solve the food problem, but as a temporary measure it would buy some additional time to stabilize population.

It appears that future food security depends on creating an environmentally sustainable economy. Simply put, if political leaders do manage to secure food supplies for the next generation, it will be because they have moved the world economy off the current path of environmental deterioration and eventual economic disruption and onto an economic and demographic path that is environmentally sustainable.

About the Author

Lester Brown is founder, president, and a senior researcher at the Worldwatch Institute, 1776 Massachusetts Avenue, N.W., Washington, D.C. 20036. Telephone 1-202-452-1999; fax 1-202-296-7365; Web site www.worldwatch.org.

This article is drawn from Worldwatch Paper 136: *The Agricultural Link: How Environmental Deterioration Could Disrupt Economic Progress* by Lester Brown. Worldwatch Institute. 1997. 73 pages. Paperback. $5.

Unit 3

Key Points to Consider

❖ Why is coal such a costly fuel source once all the costs of its use are calculated? Describe some of the costs of coal use in terms of environmental quality, public health, and global climate.

❖ What is the relationship between the supply of and demand for petroleum and how will increasing petroleum costs affect the world's economy? Are current concerns over the supply of oil similar to concerns that have been expressed in the past? If not, how are they different?

❖ What are some of the major benefits of such alternate energy sources as solar power and wind power? Do these energy alternatives really have a chance at competing with fossil fuels for a share of the global energy market?

 **Links**

www.dushkin.com/online/

These sites are annotated on pages 4 and 5.

There has been a tendency, particularly in the developed nations of the world, to view the present high standards of living as exclusively the benefit of a high-technology society. In the "techno-optimism" of post–World War II years, prominent scientists described the technical-industrial civilization of the future as being limited only by a lack of enough trained engineers and scientists to build and maintain it. This euphoria reached its climax in July 1969 when American astronauts walked upon the surface of the Moon, an accomplishment brought about solely by American technology—or so it was supposed. It cannot be denied that technology has been important in raising standards of living and permitting Moon landings. But how much of the growth in living standards and how many outstanding and dramatic feats of space exploration have been the result of technology alone? The answer is few—for in many of humankind's recent successes, the contributions of technology to growth have been no more important than the availability of incredibly cheap energy resources, particularly petroleum and coal.

As the world's supply of recoverable (inexpensive) fossil fuels dwindles and becomes more important as an agency of international diplomacy, it becomes increasingly clear that the energy dilemma is the most serious economic and environmental threat facing the Western world and its high standard of living. With the exception of the population problem, the coming fossil fuel energy scarcity is probably the most serious threat facing the rest of the world as well. The economic dimensions of the energy problem are rooted in the instabilities of monetary systems produced by and dependent upon inexpensive energy. The environmental dimensions of the problem are even more complex, ranging from the hazards posed by the development of such alternative sources as nuclear power to the inability of developing world farmers to purchase necessary fertilizer produced from petroleum, which has suddenly become very costly, and to the enhanced greenhouse effect created by fossil fuel consumption. The only answers to the problems of dwindling and geographically vulnerable inexpensive energy supplies are conservation and sustainable energy technology. Both require a massive readjustment of thinking, away from the exuberant notion that technology can solve any problem. The difficulty with conservation, of course, is a philosophical one that grows out of the still-prevailing optimism about high technology. Conservation is not as exciting as putting a man on the Moon. Its tactical applications—caulking windows and insulating attics—are dog-paddle technologies to people accustomed to the crawl stroke. Does a solution to this problem entail the technological fixes of which many are so enamored? Probably not, as it appears that the accelerating energy demands of the world's developing nations will most likely be first met by increased reliance on the traditional (and still cheap) fossil fuels. Although there is a need to reduce this reliance, there are few ready alternatives available to the poorer, but developing, countries. It would appear that conservation is the only option.

Indeed, it may be that the influence of at least one of the major fossil fuels is on the wane. In the first article in the unit, Seth Dunn of the Worldwatch Institute discusses "King Coal's Weakening Grip on Power." Beginning with a discussion of the recent Chinese decision to attempt to eliminate coal as the fuel of choice in Beijing, Dunn catalogues the social and environmental disadvantages of the world's most available fossil fuel. The benefits of a coal phase-out, Dunn notes, will be enormous. How effective a reduction in coal use can be is problematic in light of the subject of the section's second selection. In "The End of Cheap Oil" Colin Campbell and Jean Laherrère, both petroleum geologists with more than 40 years of experience in the oil industry, predict that the decline in the availability of inexpensive petroleum will begin much sooner than many people think—probably within the next 10 years. Unlike earlier oil crunches that have been politically induced, the coming crunch will be permanent. Part of the problem is that while oil production will be decreasing and the cost of oil rising, there will also be a continuance of the trend toward an increasing demand for the product, largely from the expanding economies of the developing world. The transition to a post–oil economy need not be traumatic if the production of liquid fuel from natural gas and other alternative energy sources could be developed.

The concluding two articles in the section discuss two of the most promising of these relevant new technologies. In "Sunlight Brightens Our Energy Future," science writer Randy Quinn provides an intriguing look at one of the most promising of the new technologies: photovoltaics. And in "Bull Market in Wind Energy" Christopher Flavin, one of the world's foremost energy experts, suggests that the sustainable energy technology of wind power, once the mainstay of the United States' search for energy alternatives, has again surfaced as a powerful global alternative to fossil fuels. Answers to energy questions and issues are as diverse as the world's geography. But all the answers require a reorientation of thought and the action of committed groups of people who have the capacity to change the dominant direction of a culture.

Energy: Present and Future Problems

King Coal's Weakening Grip on Power

*The fuel that ushered in the Industrial
Revolution still burns, but a new era beckons.*

by Seth Dunn

EVOLUTION WAS LITERALLY IN THE AIR ON FEBRUARY 28, 1998, when officials in Beijing and 32 other Chinese cities—under pressure from the national environmental protection agency—began releasing pollution records that had been suppressed for 20 years. The weekly reports—intended to "enable the public to supervise the government's anti-pollution efforts"—revealed that the air outside Beijing's Gate of Heavenly Peace had become hellish. Prolonged exposure to the air posed serious health risks and had increased the city's death rate by 4 percent, according to research from Harvard and Beijing Medical Universities.

The news rocked Beijing, and media reports generated angry outcries from citizens who discovered that the haze hovering over their city—and its related health problems—were almost entirely the result of coal, which supplies 80 percent of the city's energy use for factories, power plants, ovens, and stoves. A few months later, in response to public pressure, city authorities announced a crackdown on coal burning, with the aim of banning it by the end of the century. Beginning with the city's 42-square-mile central limits, the government plans to establish coal-free zones, with local authorities helping residents switch from coal to cleaner-burning natural gas.

Beijing's move to banish what was known as "King Coal" in the nineteenth century in the United States and Europe illustrates how perceptions of this fossilized substance have changed over time. A thousand years ago, China fired coal in blast furnaces to produce the armor and arrowheads that defended its dynasties against outside invaders. But it was in the West that coal was first burned in massive amounts, beginning in the eighteenth century. If the Industrial Revolution was "Prometheus unbound," coal was the fire stolen from the gods that made it possible. With its production paralleling the rise of national powers, this fossil fuel became synonymous with wealth and modernity in the nineteenth century. In his classic 1865 work, *The Coal Question*, economist William Jevons went as far as to predict the collapse of the British Empire as its coal mines approached depletion.

But Prometheus paid dearly for his deed; chained to a mountaintop, he had his liver torn out daily by vultures. Likewise, the reign of King Coal has not been without heavy costs: its use has left a legacy of human and environmental damage that we have only begun to assess. At the close of the twentieth century, coal's smog-choked cityscapes are no longer the symbol of industrial opportunities and wealth that they were 100 years ago. Instead, coal is increasingly recognized as a leading threat to human health, and one of the most environmentally disruptive human activities.

Indeed, the sun may be setting on the empire of coal. Its share of world energy, which peaked at 62 percent in 1910, is now 23 percent and dropping. Although coal's market price has fallen 64 percent in the past 20 years to a historical low of $32 per ton, global use is at its lowest in a decade, having fallen 2.1 percent in 1998. One reason for this decline is that the price of dealing with coal's health and environmental toll—the "hidden cost"—is rising. And now King Coal's remaining colonies find themselves confronted with a concern of the sort that bedeviled

Jevons. This time, however, it is coal dependence—not depletion—that is the potential threat to progress.

Even so, the mirage of coal as a source of cheap energy continues to be a powerful lure, and many countries have gone to great lengths to rationalize their reliance—suppressing information, compartmentalizing problems, or socializing costs. Until now, the problems of coal have been treated with an "emergency room" approach: ecological impacts have been addressed pollutant by pollutant, mine by mine; the health hazards, one urban crisis at a time. This narrow approach has been an expensive one, both economically and environmentally, and has had perverse, unforeseen consequences: each time one of coal's impacts is "mitigated," a more pervasive and chronic problem is created, exacerbating and spreading the fuel's negative effects out over space and time. For example, towering smokestacks, built to alleviate local air pollution, created the problem of acid rain. And efforts to curtail acid rain, in turn, are adding to greenhouse-gas emissions.

Increasingly, human health, ecological, climatic, and socioeconomic concerns are pushing us away from this piecemeal regulation—toward an end to the "end-of-pipe" approach. But for the world to judge whether continued dependence on coal is viable, a more comprehensive examination is in order. After centuries of treating coal like a first-time offender, there is a growing consensus that it is time to assess this fossil fuel in terms of its cumulative offenses and to seriously weigh the benefits of replacing it with cleaner, and ultimately cheaper, alternatives.

Exhibit A: Health Hazard

The solid blackish substance called coal is vegetation that has, over millions of years, accumulated in wetlands and been partially decomposed, suffocated, moisturized, compressed, and baked by the Earth's inner heat underground. During this process, unfathomable quantities of organic matter have been slowly broken down and stored. The act of extracting coal from the Earth's crust and burning it is an experiment without geological precedent, and it is altering the environment in profound, yet poorly understood, ways.

Coal has long been linked to air pollution and ill effects on health. In medieval London, an official proclamation banned coal burning as early as 1306 A.D. in an unsuccessful effort to curb the smog and sulfurous smell hanging over the city. Even today particulate matter (dust, soot, and other solid airborne pollutants) and sulfur are two of the most unhealthy by-products of coal combustion.

Particulates penetrate deep into lungs. Prolonged inhalation causes a range of respiratory and cardiovascular problems, such as emphysema, asthma, bronchitis, lung cancer, and heart disease. It is also linked to higher infant

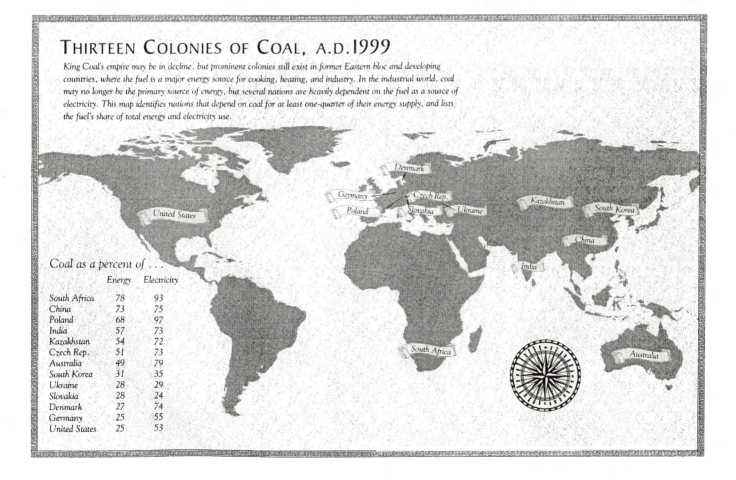

THIRTEEN COLONIES OF COAL, A.D. 1999

King Coal's empire may be in decline, but prominent colonies still exist in former Eastern bloc and developing countries, where the fuel is a major energy source for cooking, heating, and industry. In the industrial world, coal may no longer be the primary source of energy, but several nations are heavily dependent on the fuel as a source of electricity. This map identifies nations that depend on coal for at least one-quarter of their energy supply, and lists the fuel's share of total energy and electricity use.

Coal as a percent of . . .

	Energy	Electricity
South Africa	78	93
China	73	75
Poland	68	97
India	57	73
Kazakhstan	54	72
Czech Rep.	51	73
Australia	49	79
South Korea	31	35
Ukraine	28	29
Slovakia	28	24
Denmark	27	74
Germany	25	55
United States	25	53

mortality rates. The smallest particles can stay in an individual's lungs for a lifetime, potentially increasing the risk of cancer. Sulfur dioxide (SO_2) exposure is associated with increased hospitalization and death from pulmonary and heart disease, particularly among asthmatics and those with existing breathing problems.

These pollutants made up the "coal smogs" that killed 2,200 Londoners in 1880; the "killer fog" that caused 50 deaths in Donora, Pennsylvania in 1948; and the "London fog" that took 4,000 lives in 1952. Today, several coal-dependent cities—including Beijing and Delhi—are approaching the pollution levels of the Donora and London disasters, and the world's ten most air-polluted cities—nine in China, one in India—are all heavy coal users. Worldwide, particulate and SO_2 pollution cause at least 500,000 premature deaths, 4 to 5 million new cases of bronchitis, and millions of other respiratory illnesses per year. Such smogs have become transcontinental travelers: large dust clouds of particulates and sulfur from Asian coal now reach the U.S. West Coast.

Coal burning also releases nitrogen oxides, which react in sunlight to form ground-level ozone. In the United States and Europe, more than 100 cities are exposed to unhealthy ozone levels. Beijing, Calcutta, and Shanghai—all heavily coal dependent—expose millions of children to deadly mixes of particulates, sulfur dioxide, and nitrogen oxides.

Coal smoke contains potent carcinogens, affecting the more than 1 billion rural poor who rely on the fuel for cooking. Rural indoor air pollution from such cooking accounts for 1.8 to 2.7 million global annual deaths from air pollution, with women and children most at risk. In rural China, exposure to coal smoke increases lung cancer risks by a factor of nine or more.

Coal can also contain arsenic, lead, mercury, and fluorine—toxic heavy metals that can impair the development of fetuses and infants and cause open sores and bone decay. In rural China, where 800 million people use coal in their homes for cooking and heating, thousands of cases of arsenic poisoning, and millions of cases of fluorine poisoning have been reported. Millions of rural poor in other developing countries face similar risks.

Coal mining and extraction pose health hazards, as well. Explosions, falls, and hauling accidents injure or kill several thousand coal miners in China, Russia, and Ukraine each year. In China, more than five miners die for every million tons of coal mined. Perhaps the most serious and chronic threat to miners is pneumoconiosis, or "black lung"—a condition caused by continued inhalation of coal dust, which inflames, scars, and discolors lungs, and leads to a debilitating decline in lung function. In the United States, enough was known at the turn of the twentieth century about black lung to have

spurred preventive action to remove or lessen the effects of the disorder, writes Alan Derickson, author of *Black Lung: Anatomy of a Public Health Disaster*. But company doctors misdiagnosed or concealed the illness for more than 50 years, until medical community mavericks and the largest strike in U.S. history forced lawmakers to enact compensatory and preventive measures. By then, the lives of hundreds of thousands of coal miners had been shortened. U.S. taxpayers have since paid more than $30 billion to compensate mining families.

Despite these advances, coal dust continues to plague miners. In Russia and Ukraine, official estimates range from 200 to 500 deaths per year. In China, where 2.5 million coal miners are exposed to dust diseases, the current annual death toll of 2,500 is expected to increase by 10 percent each year. Even in the United States, 1,500 miners died of black lung in 1994, and under-reporting is still prevalent.

Exhibit B: Environmental Damage

The coal smogs in Donora and London sparked public outrage, leading to the enactment of the first major clean-air laws. Setting local air quality standards, these acts prompted industries to install high smokestacks that would spread the pollutants over larger areas and to more distant regions. In parts of the United States, some smokestacks shot up higher than the top floor of the Empire State Building.

But this simple solution for local pollution had an unintended consequence. Carried aloft, nitrogen oxides and sulfur dioxide react in the atmosphere to form acids that fall as rain, snow, or fog or turn to acid on direct con-

World Coal Consumption, 1950–98

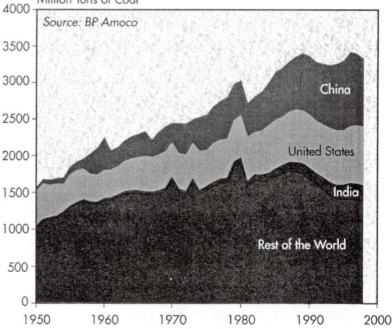

tact—corroding buildings and monuments and damaging vegetation, soils, rivers, lakes, and crops. The problems of acid rain and deposition surfaced first in Norwegian fish kills in the 1960s, and later in the "forest death" of Germany, the "Black Triangle" of dead trees in Central Europe, and the dying lakes and streams of the U.S. Adirondacks—all traced to coal burning hundreds of miles away.

Under pressure from environmental groups, industrial nations have addressed acid rain through an array of agreements focusing on sulfur emissions, which have been significantly reduced. But nitrogen emissions, which initially escaped regulation, have been slower to drop. In fact, in many regions they have risen, offsetting reductions made in sulfur emissions. In Europe, forest decline continues and hundreds of acid-stressed lakes face a long recovery time, as nitrogen persists well above tolerable levels. High-elevation forests in West Virginia, Tennessee, and Southern California are near saturation level for nitrogen, and high-elevation lakes in the Rocky Mountain, Cascade, and Sierra Nevada mountain ranges are on the verge of chronic acidity. In the Adirondacks, many waterways are becoming more acid even as sulfur deposits drop: by 2040, as many as half the region's 2,800 lakes and ponds may be too acid to support much life.

The West's acid deposition debacle is now replicating with potentially greater repercussions in Asia. A haze the size of the United States covers the Indian Ocean in winter, and in summer is blown inland and falls as acid rain, reportedly reducing Indian wheat yields. Acid rain falls on over 40 percent of China, and in 1995 caused $13 billion in damage to its forests and crops. Widening areas of China, India, South Korea, Thailand, Cambodia, and Vietnam are above critical levels of sulfur. Buildings, forests, and farmland close to or downwind from large urban and industrial centers are being hardest hit. Thousand-year-old sculptures from China's Song Dynasty have been corroded. And some scientists believe the Taj Mahal is in similar danger. A fifth of India's farmland faces acidification. China's sulfur emissions may overwhelm fertile soils across China, Japan, and South Korea by 2020.

Other types of ecosystem overload, too, are linked to coal. Nitrogen overfertilizes waterways, causing deadly algal blooms. Ground-level ozone damages forests and crops. Each year, ozone costs the United States between $5 and 10 billion in crop losses alone, and cuts wheat yields in parts of China by 10 percent. The formation and burning of massive slag heaps—piles of cinder left over from combustion—degrades land and emits carbon monoxide. Acidic or highly saline runoff from mines contaminate ground and surface water.

Air pollution regulations have prompted a hunt for low-sulfur coal, with companies turning from underground to surface—also known as strip, or open-pit—mining. In Canada, open-pit mines lie at the foot of Alberta's Jasper National Park, a World Heritage Site; in India's Bihar province, they endanger huge tracts of forest. These mines have uprooted hundreds of thousands of indigenous and poor people—aborigines in Australia, Native Americans in Arizona, villagers in northern Germany, tribals in Raniganj, India—from land they have inhabited for centuries, often with little advance notice or compensation. In West Virginia, huge machines engage in "mountain-top removal"—stripping away dozens of rolling hills, burying streams, and bulldozing mining communities.

As many developing countries follow the path of industrial nations, they too seem unable to steer clear of the pitfalls of a simplistic response to coal pollution. But the folly of focusing solely on coal's air pollutants proves most perverse in the developing world, where the added mining and processing requirements exacerbate severe land and water constraints. Chinese enterprises commonly violate emissions standards and burn high-sulfur coal rather than pay for precious water use to wash coal. In India, citizens' groups criticize the government's coal-washing mandate, arguing that it will waste energy, use up large quantities of scarce water and land, and increase pollution at mines.

Exhibit C: Shifting Climate

The second generation of coal-related pollution laws, motivated by public concern over acid rain, led companies to install another technological quick-fix. This time "clean-coal" technologies were the promised solution, namely flue-gas desulfurization and nitrogen-control equipment. While the equipment lowered emissions of the targeted pollutants, they, like higher smokestacks, had unforeseen side-effects. Clean coal creates added water demands, produces large amounts of sludge and other solid wastes, and decreases energy efficiently, thereby increasing emissions of other compounds—including carbon dioxide (CO_2).

Ranging from less than 20 to more than 98 percent in carbon content, coal is the most carbon-rich fossil fuel. The industrial era's heavy combustion of these fuels is short-circuiting the global carbon cycle, building up atmospheric CO_2 concentrations to their highest point in 420,000 years. The thickening blanket of these and other greenhouse gases has already trapped enough radiative heat to make the planet's surface its warmest in 1,200 years.

Many expected climatic dislocations are appearing: sea level rise; accelerating glacier retreat and ice shelf breakup; migrations and declines of forests, coral reefs, and other temperature-sensitive species; changes in the timing and duration of seasons; greater frequency and intensity of extreme weather events. Climate scenarios for the year 2050 from the Hadley Centre for Climate Prediction and Research show tropical forests turning to desert, adding more carbon to the atmosphere; malaria spreading to currently unaffected populations; an additional 30 million people at risk of hunger; another 66 million in danger of water stress; and 20 million more susceptible to flooding. Heat stress will have increased by 70 to 100 percent by then—adding several thousand deaths each year in large urban areas like New York, New Delhi, and Shanghai, according to Laurence Kalkstein of the University of Delaware.

Carbon emissions are not the only means by which coal changes climate: mining annually releases 25 million tons of methane, equal in warming potential to the United Kingdom's entire carbon output. But CO_2 is the most important contributor to climate change—and coal releases 29 percent more carbon per unit of energy than oil, and 80 percent more than natural gas. The climatic impact of coal burning is disproportionate to its importance as an energy source: with a 26 percent share of world energy, it accounts for 43 percent of annual global carbon emissions—approximately 2.7 billion tons. Climate instability also compounds other coal-related problems: heat stress exacerbates urban air pollution, and higher temperatures make natural systems more vulnerable to acid rain impacts.

Stabilizing atmospheric CO_2 levels at 450 parts per million during the next century, which some scientists believe necessary to avoid far more dangerous disruptions of climate, would constrain coal use to somewhere between 200 and 300 billion tons—less than 7 percent of the total resource base. Burning the entire coal resource, on the other hand, would release 3 trillion tons of carbon into the atmosphere, five times the safe limit. Thus, while energy analysts point to the apparent size of the fuel's reserves, the amount that could be safely used is far smaller. From their perspective of balancing the carbon budget, coal is a highly limited energy source.

Despite studies showing the economic feasibility of switching from coal, several governments and industries are pursuing another end-of-pipe solution: carbon sequestration. Firms and agencies in the United States, Norway, and elsewhere are devoting millions of dollars to test technologies for separating and capturing CO_2 from fossil fuels. The CO_2 would then be locked up by injecting it into oceans, terrestrial ecosystems, and geological formations. But the potential impacts on ocean chemistry and deep-sea ecosystems have not been explored, and injected emissions could be re-released due to geological activity. And if sites subject to slow release are used, carbon management could reduce atmospheric CO_2 concentrations in the near term but increase them in the long term—adding to the climate problem.

Meanwhile, some industrial nations seeking developing-country action on climate change are, contradictorily, redirecting clean coal programs overseas. In a novel form of trade "dumping," clean-coal equipment features prominently in bilateral energy missions, with firms and officials from the United States, Japan, and Australia proselytizing to poor nations that they "need clean-coal technologies." The World Bank and European Commission have aimed clean-coal technology initiatives at developing and former

ADDING UP THE COSTS OF COAL

While the market price for coal was $32 per ton in 1998, when environmental and health disruptions are factored into the equation, coal is not as cheap as it may seem.

	AIR	LAND	WATER	CLIMATE
MINING/ EXTRACTION	• Coal dust causes black lung and other respiratory diseases in miners. • Mining can result in explosions and fires. • Machinery causes dangerous fumes and disruptive noise.	• Mining causes soil degradation, erosion, and subsidence. • Farms and forests are destroyed and communities displaced by strip mining and mountain-top removal.	• Watersheds are degraded and streams filled in by mountain-top removal and strip mining. • Acid mine drainage from tailings as well as wastewater discharge pollute rivers and drinking water sources.	• Mining releases large quantities of methane, a potent greenhouse gas. • Greenhouse gases released by coal combustion play a significant role in destabilizing climate, contributing to sea-level rise, weather extremes, disease outbreaks, shifts in agriculture and water supply, extensive ecosystem damage, loss of species, and other serious disruptions.
TRANSPORTATION	• Coal may be shipped thousands of miles to power plants in open train cars and barges, producing "fugitive dust" that is blown into the air.	• A considerable amount of land has been developed for the rails and roads that transport coal.		• The engines and machines used to transport coal release CO_2, the most prevalent greenhouse gas. • Greenhouse gases released by coal combustion play a significant role in destabilizing climate, contributing to sea-level rise, weather extremes, disease outbreaks, shifts in agriculture and water supply, extensive ecosystem damage, loss of species, and other serious disruptions.
TREATMENT		• Smokestack scrubbers used to filter sulfur out of coal emissions produce large quantities of sludge and other wastes.	• Coal washing, used to strip sulfur from coal before it is burned, requires large quantities of water.	• Technologies used to trap sulfur and nitrogen emissions require more energy, which releases more CO_2. • Greenhouse gases released by coal combustion play a significant role in destabilizing climate, contributing to sea-level rise, weather extremes, disease outbreaks, shifts in agriculture and water supply, extensive ecosystem damage, loss of species, and other serious disruptions.
COMBUSTION/ CONVERSION	• Particulates, sulfur dioxide, ground-level ozone from nitrogen oxides, and toxic metals released by the burning of coal contribute to cancer risks, impair infant development, cause respiratory illness, and increase rates of morbidity and mortality.	• Acid deposition from sulfuric and nitric acid leaches nutrients from soils and damages forests, crops, and buildings. • Ozone impairs plant growth. • Power plants and massive "slag heaps"—piles of ashes from coal burning—take up land and cause degradation.	• Acid deposition and heavy metals poison rivers and lakes. • Nitrogen oxides cause eutrophication, where plant growth cuts off oxygen supplies to other species. • Cooling towers demand and heat up large amounts of water.	• Combustion of coal is the single largest source of CO_2 emissions. • Greenhouse gases released by coal combustion play a significant role in destabilizing climate, contributing to sea-level rise, weather extremes, disease outbreaks, shifts in agriculture and water supply, extensive ecosystem damage, loss of species, and other serious disruptions.

Eastern bloc nations, where the technologies remain unproven. Indeed, clean-coal equipment has failed to demonstrate financial viability in the West (its high capital investment costs make it less attractive than natural-gas-fired combined-cycle turbines), linking its peddling less to economics than to the political clout of the industry.

Exhibit D: Losing Labor

"The story of coal in America," writes Duane Lockard in *Coal: A Memoir and Critique,* "is the story of corporate successes and excesses generally." The same can now be said for the coal industry worldwide. Shrinking profits and growing deficits are leading to drastic cost-cutting practices that translate into lower prices but also major job losses, creating an employment crisis among coal miners round the globe. It is, however, both necessary and possible to reduce reliance on coal while minimizing the displacement of workers that inevitably accompanies the decline of an industry.

Worldwide, only about 10 million coal mining jobs remain, making up one-third of all mining jobs and accounting for one-third of 1 percent of the global workforce. In industrial nations, the coal-mining industry is no longer a major employer, and employment is falling even where production or exports are rising. In developing countries and transitional economies, where employment is still relatively high, pressures to reform the industry and cut costs are causing major job dislocations.

Like other sunset industries, the coal sector is increasingly characterized by bigger and fewer companies, more and larger equipment, and less labor-intensive operations. In the United States, the 10 largest firms account for 60 percent of output, up from 35 percent a decade ago. During coal's peak, in 1924, 705,000 miners toiled in U.S. mines; today there are fewer than 82,000. Thanks mostly to surface mining, employment has declined by two-thirds over the last 20 years and is expected to continue to fall; coal miners now count for less than 0.1 percent of the nation's workforce. Though domestic consumption continues to crawl upward, exports have dropped 25 percent since 1996, and experts agree that they will never return to pre-1998 levels.

The rate of contraction has as much to do with politics as with economic and environmental factors. Coal industries in both the United Kingdom and Germany have been weakened since the 1960s by environmental regulations and the switch to cleaner natural gas, now the fuel of choice for power generation in industrial nations. But while contraction in the United Kingdom has been rapid—only 13,000 union coal miners remain, out of 1.2 million in 1978—the decline in Germany has been more gradual, from 190,000 in 1982 to less than 90,000 today.

Similar struggles lie ahead for other coal-dependent nations. In Australia, 9,000 of the nation's 22,000 coal miners went on strike in 1997 when impending job cuts led

Rio Tinto, the world's largest mining company, to try to deunionize the industry. In South Africa, coal production has risen 65 percent, but employment has fallen over 20 percent, since 1980. In India, where production has doubled since 1980, employment is still declining as a proportion of population. Poland's mines lose nearly $700 million each year. Russia has halted production in 90 mines and intends to have shut 130 of its 200 mines by 2000. Major future losses are expected in these countries as improved productivity and the shift to less energy-intensive service industries make more jobs redundant.

Cost cutting, mine closing, and job losses are greatest in China, where Li Yi, director of the Xishan coal mining bureau, summed up the industry's prevailing philosophy in a 1998 interview: "Our motto is: Cut people, improve efficiency." The world's leading coal producer and consumer, China has lost 870,000 workers over the last five years, and slashed production by 250 million tons in 1998 due to excess capacity and rail transport bottlenecks. (Like India, Australia, and South Africa, China faces a geographic mismatch between coal reserves and energy needs.) The government plans to close down 25,800 coal mines this year—most among the 75,000 mines in township and village areas—and shut off all small, unauthorized mines. In May 1999, the government halted the issuance of permits for new coal mining projects.

The United Kingdom and China highlight both the challenges of and chances for helping workers in the transition to the post-coal era. In both, thousands of laid-off workers have blocked traffic, stopped trains, and stormed official offices. But both governments recognize that coal's heyday is over: they are shifting from coal-reliant industries like steel works to more modern sectors—such as the high-tech and tourism industries—and both are planning solar-cell manufacturing sites in mining areas, to ease the transition for workers.

The Light at the End of the Tunnel

The current, emergency-room approach to coping with coal has proved so expensive, yielded such limited results, and contributed to so many environmental and health problems, that shifting to cleaner alternatives will help solve these problems at a much lower cost. Treating coal's symptoms in isolation has proved insufficient for improving human and planetary health. Fortunately, remedies are available that will allow the world to rapidly reduce the use of coal and accelerate the transition to cleaner energy sources.

Among the keys to cutting coal reliance are blocking mining and power projects through community activism, closing legislative loopholes, and reorienting coal-centric bilateral, multilateral, and multinational investment flows. But two policies are central to the "decoalonization" process: subsidy removal and energy taxation. Without them, the market will continue to deceive us into thinking coal is cheap, abundant, and irreplaceable, just when countries like China are beginning to realize how costly, limited, and unnecessary dependence on this fuel is.

Simply put, removing subsidies cuts coal consumption. Belgium, France, Japan, Spain, and the United Kingdom have collectively halved coal use since slashing or ending supports over the last fifteen years. Russia, India, and China have also made progress: China's coal subsidy rates have been more than halved since 1984, contributing to a slowing—and 5.2 percent drop in 1998—in consumption. Opportunities exist for further reductions. Total world coal subsidies are estimated to be $63 billion, including $30 billion in industrial nations, $27 billion in the former Eastern bloc, and $6 billion in China and India. In Germany, the total is $21 billion—including direct production supports of more than $70,000 per miner.

The experience of Germany highlights the opportunities for—and obstacles to—taxing coal. A European commission study shows that internalizing the external costs of coal from a German power plant would raise the price of power by 50 percent. Yet the government's 1998 ecological tax reform excluded coal due to industry opposition. As Ed Cohen-Rosenthal of Cornell University writes, "The question for coal miners is whether to dig in and fight or use the concern about global warming to negotiate the best deal for current members and retirees as one means of paving the way to a cleaner environment. This is a decision that only they can make and outsiders should respect their feelings. But their leverage for a negotiated outcome will never be higher than it is right now."

Digging in has predominated to date—coal labor groups underwrite skeptical "scientists" and oppose the Kyoto Protocol—though signs of reconciliation exist. In Australia, an Earthworker caucus of trade union and environmental groups is developing a plan for building solar and wind power industries. The AFL-CIO and U.S. environmental groups are crafting "worker-friendly" climate policies, like employing former miners in remediating abandoned mines. But while labor groups stress the need for "just transitions" to aid adversely affected workers, those representing coal miners appear less likely to become advocates of coal subsidy and tax reform, which could help fund such a transition, than to defend these endangered jobs to the bitter end—and at the expense of society at large.

Bold initiatives in coal taxation, meanwhile, can be found in China. The government has introduced a tax on high-sulfur coal to encourage a switch to plentiful natural gas and renewable-energy resources. Like cigarette taxes in the West, the coal levy may spread in the East; as with smoking in public places, coal use might also be banned outright where it is deemed too great a public burden to bear.

Back in Beijing, high-sulfur coal has been banned, 40 "coal-free zones" are planned, and natural-gas pipelines are under discussion. Hundreds of residents in Beijing are mobilizing through citizens' groups, such as the Global Village, to supervise implementation of the policies and raise public consciousness of the problem. The idea is catching on: four more Chinese cities—Shanghai, Lanzhou, Xian, and Shenyang—have followed suit with plans to phase out coal.

The challenge is to turn these local gains into a worldwide movement over the coming century, just as coal's negative consequences have risen from local to global during this one. A global coal phaseout has become as environmentally necessary and economically feasible as it might seem politically radical. Thirty years ago, few could have predicted the nascent anti-smoking effort would ever "go global," but it has. Coal now poses as serious a risk to our collective well-being, if not greater. If China's smoky cities can mobilize to begin eradicating the tobacco of our energy system, it is conceivable that the rest of the world's governments can as well.

Like sustainable development more broadly, achieving independence from King Coal will be no overnight coup, but a lengthy revolution. Yet the social, economic, and environmental rewards of a coal phaseout promise to be enormous. In the third millennium, societies will find themselves—to paraphrase Henry David Thoreau—rich in proportion to the coal they can afford to leave in the ground.

Seth Dunn is a research associate at the Worldwatch Institute.

The End of Cheap Oil

Global production of conventional oil will begin to decline sooner than most people think, probably within 10 years

by Colin J. Campbell and Jean H. Laherrère

In 1973 and 1979 a pair of sudden price increases rudely awakened the industrial world to its dependence on cheap crude oil. Prices first tripled in response to an Arab embargo and then nearly doubled again when Iran dethroned its Shah, sending the major economies sputtering into recession. Many analysts warned that these crises proved that the world would soon run out of oil. Yet they were wrong.

Their dire predictions were emotional and political reactions; even at the time, oil experts knew that they had no scientific basis. Just a few years earlier oil explorers had discovered enormous new oil provinces on the north slope of Alaska and below the North Sea off the coast of Europe. By 1973 the world had consumed, according to many experts' best estimates, only about one eighth of its endowment of readily accessible crude oil (so-called conventional oil). The five Middle Eastern members of the Organization of Petroleum Exporting Countries (OPEC) were able to hike prices not because oil was growing scarce but because they had managed to corner 36 percent of the market. Later, when demand sagged, and the flow of fresh Alaskan and North Sea oil weakened OPEC's economic stranglehold, prices collapsed.

The next oil crunch will not be so temporary. Our analysis of the discovery and production of oil fields around the world suggests that within the next decade, the supply of conventional oil will be unable to keep up with demand. This conclusion contradicts the picture one gets from oil industry reports, which boasted of 1,020 billion barrels of oil (Gbo) in "proved" reserves at the start of 1998. Dividing that figure by the current production rate of about 23.6 Gbo a year might suggest that crude oil could remain plentiful and cheap for 43 more years—probably longer, because official charts show reserves growing.

Unfortunately, this appraisal makes three critical errors. First, it relies on distorted estimates of reserves. A second mistake is to pretend that production will remain constant. Third and most important, conventional wisdom erroneously assumes that the last bucket of oil can be pumped from the ground just as quickly as the barrels of oil gushing from wells today. In fact, the rate at which any well—or any country—can produce oil always rises to a maximum and then, when about half the oil is gone, begins falling gradually back to zero.

From an economic perspective, when the world runs completely out of oil is thus not directly relevant: what matters is when production begins to taper off. Beyond that point, prices will rise unless demand declines commensurately. Using several different techniques to estimate the current reserves of conventional oil and the amount still left to be discovered, we conclude that the decline will begin before 2010.

Digging for the True Numbers

We have spent most of our careers exploring for oil, studying reserve figures and estimating the amount of oil left to discover, first while employed at major oil companies and later as independent consultants. Over the years, we have come to appreciate that the relevant statistics are far more complicated than they first appear.

Consider, for example, three vital numbers needed to project future oil production. The first is the tally of how much oil has been extracted to date, a figure known as cumulative production. The second is an estimate of reserves, the amount that companies can pump out of known oil fields before having to abandon them. Finally, one must have an educated guess at the quantity of conventional oil that remains to be discovered and exploited. Together they add up to ultimate recovery, the total number of barrels that will have been extracted when production ceases many decades from now.

The obvious way to gather these numbers is to look them up in any of several publications. That approach works well enough for cumulative production statistics because companies meter the oil as it flows from their wells. The record of production is not perfect (for example, the two billion barrels of Kuwaiti oil wastefully burned by Iraq in 1991 is usually not included in official statistics), but errors are relatively easy to spot and rectify. Most experts agree that the industry had removed just over 800 Gbo from the earth at the end of 1997.

Getting good estimates of reserves is much harder, however. Almost all the publicly available statistics are taken from surveys conducted by the *Oil and Gas Journal* and *World Oil*. Each year these two trade journals query oil firms and governments around the world. They then publish whatever production and reserve numbers they receive but are not able to verify them.

The results, which are often accepted uncritically, contain systematic errors. For one, many of the reported figures are unrealistic. Estimating reserves is an inexact science to begin with, so petroleum engineers assign a probability to their assessments. For example, if, as geologists estimate, there is a 90 percent chance that the Oseberg field in Norway contains 700 million barrels of recoverable oil but only a 10 percent chance that it will yield 2,500 million more barrels, then the lower figure should be cited as the so-called P90 estimate (P90 for "probability 90 percent") and the higher as the P10 reserves.

In practice, companies and countries are often deliberately vague about the likelihood of the reserves they report, preferring instead to publicize whichever figure, within a P10 to P90 range, best suits them. Exaggerated estimates can, for instance, raise the price of an oil company's stock.

The members of OPEC have faced an even greater temptation to inflate their reports because the higher their reserves, the more oil they are allowed to export. National companies, which have exclusive oil rights in the main OPEC countries, need not (and do not) release detailed statistics on each field that could be used to verify the country's total reserves. There is thus good reason to suspect that when, during the late

FLOW OF OIL starts to fall from any large region when about half the crude is gone. Adding the output of fields of various sizes and ages (*bottom curves at right*) usually yields a bell-shaped production curve for the region as a whole. M. King Hubbert (*left*), a geologist with Shell Oil, exploited this fact in 1956 to predict correctly that oil from the lower 48 American states would peak around 1969.

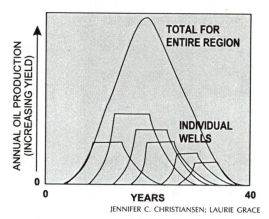

1980s, six of the 11 OPEC nations increased their reserve figures by colossal amounts, ranging from 42 to 197 percent, they did so only to boost their export quotas.

Previous OPEC estimates, inherited from private companies before governments took them over, had probably been conservative, P90 numbers. So some upward revision was warranted. But no major new discoveries or technological breakthroughs justified the addition of a staggering 287 Gbo. That increase is more than all the oil ever discovered in the U.S.—plus 40 percent. Non-OPEC countries, of course, are not above fudging their numbers either: 59 nations stated in 1997 that their reserves were unchanged from 1996. Because reserves naturally drop as old fields are drained and jump when new fields are discovered, perfectly stable numbers year after year are implausible.

Unproved Reserves

Another source of systematic error in the commonly accepted statistics is that the definition of reserves varies widely from region to region. In the U.S., the Securities and Exchange Commission allows companies to call reserves "proved" only if the oil lies near a producing well and there is "reasonable certainty" that it can be recovered profitably at current oil prices, using existing technology. So a proved reserve estimate in the U.S. is roughly equal to a P90 estimate.

Regulators in most other countries do not enforce particular oil-reserve definitions. For many years, the former Soviet countries have routinely released wildly optimistic figures—essentially P10 reserves. Yet analysts have often misinterpreted these as estimates of "proved" reserves. *World Oil* reckoned reserves in the former Soviet Union amounted to 190 Gbo in 1996, whereas the *Oil and Gas Journal* put the number at 57 Gbo. This large discrepancy shows just how elastic these numbers can be.

Using only P90 estimates is not the answer, because adding what is 90 percent likely for each field, as is done in the U.S., does not in fact yield what is 90 percent likely for a country or the entire planet. On the contrary, summing many P90 reserve estimates always understates the amount of proved oil in a region. The only correct way to total up reserve numbers is to add the mean, or average, estimates of oil in each field. In practice, the median estimate, often called "proved and probable," or P50 reserves, is more widely used and is good enough. The P50 value is the number of barrels of oil that are as likely as not to come out of a well during its lifetime, assuming prices remain within a limited range. Errors in P50 estimates tend to cancel one another out.

We were able to work around many of the problems plaguing estimates of conventional reserves by using a large body of statistics maintained by Petroconsultants in Geneva. This information, assembled over 40 years from myriad sources, covers some 18,000 oil fields worldwide. It, too, con-

tains some dubious reports, but we did our best to correct these sporadic errors.

According to our calculations, the world had at the end of 1996 approximately 850 Gbo of conventional oil in P50 reserves—substantially less than the 1,019 Gbo reported in the *Oil and Gas Journal* and the 1,160 Gbo estimated by *World Oil*. The difference is actually greater than it appears because our value represents the amount most likely to come out of known oil fields, whereas the larger number is supposedly a cautious estimate of proved reserves.

For the purposes of calculating when oil production will crest, even more critical than the size of the world's reserves is the size of ultimate recovery—all the cheap oil there is to be had. In order to estimate that, we need to know whether, and how fast, reserves are moving up or down. It is here that the official statistics become dangerously misleading.

Diminishing Returns

According to most accounts, world oil reserves have marched steadily upward over the past 20 years. Extending that apparent trend into the future, one could easily conclude, as the U.S. Energy Information Administration has, that oil production will continue to rise unhindered for decades to come, increasing almost two thirds by 2020.

Such growth is an illusion. About 80 percent of the oil produced today flows

EARTH'S CONVENTIONAL CRUDE OIL is almost half gone. Reserves (defined here as the amount as likely as not to come out of known fields) and future discoveries together will provide little more than what has already been burned.

UNDISCOVERED:
150 BILLION BARRELS

RESERVES:
850 BILLION BARRELS

The End of Cheap Oil

GLOBAL PRODUCTION OF OIL, both conventional and unconventional, recovered after falling in 1973 and 1979. But a more permanent decline is less than 10 years away, according to the authors' model, based in part on multiple Hubbert curves (*thin lines*). U.S. and Canadian oil topped out in 1972; production in the former Soviet Union has fallen 45 percent since 1987. A crest in the oil produced outside the Persian Gulf region now appears imminent.

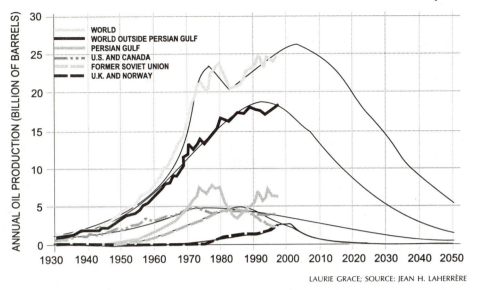

LAURIE GRACE; SOURCE: JEAN H. LAHERRÈRE

from fields that were found before 1973, and the great majority of them are declining. In the 1990s oil companies have discovered an average of seven Gbo a year; last year they drained more than three times as much. Yet official figures indicated that proved reserves did not fall by 16 Gbo, as one would expect—rather they expanded by 11 Gbo. One reason is that several dozen governments opted not to report declines in their reserves, perhaps to enhance their political cachet and their ability to obtain loans. A more important cause of the expansion lies in revisions: oil companies replaced earlier estimates of the reserves left in many fields with higher numbers. For most purposes, such amendments are harmless, but they seriously distort forecasts extrapolated from published reports.

To judge accurately how much oil explorers will uncover in the future, one has to backdate every revision to the year in which the field was first discovered—not to the year in which a company or country corrected an earlier estimate. Doing so reveals that global discovery peaked in the early 1960s and has been falling steadily ever since. By extending the trend to zero, we can make a good guess at how much oil the industry will ultimately find.

We have used other methods to estimate the ultimate recovery of conventional oil for each country [*see box*, "Earth's Conventional Crude Oil"] and we calculate that the oil industry will be able to recover only about another 1,000 billion barrels of conventional oil. This number, though great, is little more than the 800 billion barrels that have already been extracted.

It is important to realize that spending more money on oil exploration will not change this situation. After the price of crude hit all-time highs in the early 1980s,

explorers developed new technology for finding and recovering oil, and they scoured the world for new fields. They found few: the discovery rate continued its decline uninterrupted. There is only so much crude oil in the world, and the industry has found about 90 percent of it.

Predicting the Inevitable

Predicting when oil production will stop rising is relatively straightforward once one has a good estimate of how much oil there is left to produce. We simply apply a refinement of a technique first published in 1956 by M. King Hubbert. Hubbert observed that in any large region, unrestrained extraction of a finite resource rises along a bell-shaped curve that peaks when about half the resource is gone. To demonstrate his theory, Hubbert fitted a bell curve to production statistics and projected that crude oil production in the lower 48 U.S. states would rise for 13 more years, then crest in 1969, give or take a year. He was right: production peaked in 1970 and has continued to follow Hubbert curves with only minor deviations. The flow of oil from several other regions, such as the former Soviet Union and the collection of all oil producers outside the Middle East, also follows Hubbert curves quite faithfully.

The global picture is more complicated, because the Middle East members of OPEC deliberately reined back their oil exports in the 1970s, while other nations continued producing at full capacity. Our analysis reveals that a number of the largest producers, including Norway and the U.K., will reach their peaks around the turn of the millennium unless they sharply curtail production. By 2002 or so the world will rely on Middle East nations, particularly five near the Persian Gulf (Iran, Iraq, Kuwait, Saudi Arabia and the United Arab Emirates), to fill in the gap between dwindling supply and growing demand. But once approximately 900 Gbo have been consumed, production must soon begin to fall. Barring a global recession, it seems most likely that world production of conventional oil will peak during the first decade of the 21st century.

Perhaps surprisingly, that prediction does not shift much even if our estimates are a few hundred billion barrels high or low. Craig Bond Hatfield of the University of Toledo, for example, has conducted his own analysis based on a 1991 estimate by the U.S. Geological Survey of 1,550 Gbo remaining—55 percent higher than our figure. Yet he similarly concludes that the world will hit maximum oil production within the next 15 years. John D. Edwards of the University of Colorado publish-

PRODUCED: 800 BILLION BARRELS

The End of Cheap Oil

How Much Oil Is Left to Find?

We combined several techniques to conclude that about 1,000 billion barrels of conventional oil remain to be produced. First, we extrapolated published production figures for older oil fields that have begun to decline. The Thistle field off the coast of Britain, for example, will yield about 420 million barrels (*a*). Second, we plotted the amount of oil discovered so far in some regions against the cumulative number of exploratory wells drilled there. Because larger fields tend to be found first—they are simply too large to miss—the curve rises rapidly and then flattens, eventually

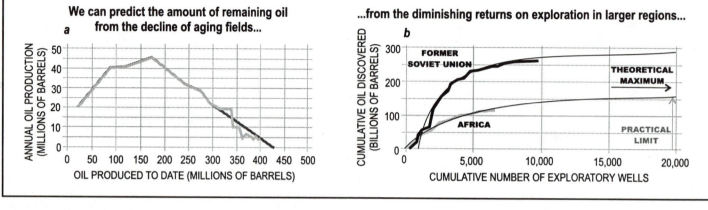

We can predict the amount of remaining oil from the decline of aging fields...

...from the diminishing returns on exploration in larger regions...

ed last August one of the most optimistic recent estimates of oil remaining: 2,036 Gbo. (Edwards concedes that the industry has only a 5 percent chance of attaining that very high goal.) Even so, his calculations suggest that conventional oil will top out in 2020.

Smoothing the Peak

Factors other than major economic changes could speed or delay the point at which oil production begins to decline. Three in particular have often led economists and academic geologists to dismiss concerns about future oil production with naive optimism.

First, some argue, huge deposits of oil may lie undetected in far-off corners of the globe. In fact, that is very unlikely. Exploration has pushed the frontiers back so far that only extremely deep water and polar regions remain to be fully tested, and even their prospects are now reasonably well understood. Theoretical advances in geochemistry and geophysics have made it possible to map productive and prospective fields with impressive accuracy. As a result, large tracts can be condemned as barren. Much of the deepwater realm, for example, has been shown to be absolutely nonprospective for geologic reasons.

What about the much touted Caspian Sea deposits? Our models project that oil production from that region will grow until around 2010. We agree with analysts at the USGS World Oil Assessment program and elsewhere who rank the total resources there as roughly equivalent to those of the North Sea—that is, perhaps 50 Gbo but certainly not several hundreds of billions as sometimes reported in the media.

A second common rejoinder is that new technologies have steadily increased the fraction of oil that can be recovered from fields in a basin—the so-called recovery factor. In the 1960s oil companies assumed as a rule of thumb that only 30 percent of the oil in a field was typically recoverable; now they bank on an average of 40 or 50 percent. That progress will continue and will extend global reserves for many years to come, the argument runs.

Of course, advanced technologies will buy a bit more time before production starts to fall [see "Oil Production in the 21st Century," by Roger N. Anderson*]. But most of the apparent improvement in recovery factors is an artifact of reporting. As oil fields grow old, their owners often deploy newer technology to slow their decline. The falloff also allows engineers to gauge the size of the field more accurately and to correct previous underestimation—in particular P90 estimates that by definition were 90 percent likely to be exceeded.

Another reason not to pin too much hope on better recovery is that oil companies routinely count on technological progress when they compute their reserve estimates. In truth, advanced technologies can offer little help in draining the largest basins of oil, those onshore in the Middle East where the oil needs no assistance to gush from the ground.

Last, economists like to point out that the world contains enormous caches of unconventional oil that can substitute for crude oil as soon as the price rises high enough to make them profitable. There is no question that the resources are ample: the Orinoco oil belt in Venezuela has been assessed to contain a staggering 1.2 trillion barrels of the sludge known as heavy oil. Tar sands and shale deposits in

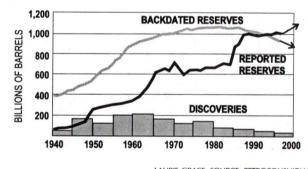

LAURIE GRACE; SOURCE: PETROCONSULTANTS, *OIL AND GAS JOURNAL* AND U.S. GEOLOGICAL SURVEY

GROWTH IN OIL RESERVES since 1980 is an illusion caused by belated corrections to oil-field estimates. Back-dating the revisions to the year in which the fields were discovered reveals that reserves have been falling because of a steady decline in newfound oil (*bottom bars*).

Canada and the former Soviet Union may contain the equivalent of more than 300 billion barrels of oil [see "Mining for Oil," by Richard L. George*]. Theoretically, these unconventional oil reserves could quench the world's thirst for liquid fuels as conventional oil passes its prime. But the industry will be hard-pressed for the time and money needed to ramp up production of unconventional oil quickly enough.

Such substitutes for crude oil might also exact a high environmental price. Tar sands

reaching a theoretical maximum: for Africa, 192 Gbo. But the time and cost of exploration impose a more practical limit of perhaps 165 Gbo (b). Third, we analyzed the distribution of oil-field sizes in the Gulf of Mexico and other provinces. Ranked according to size and then graphed on a logarithmic scale, the fields tend to fall along a parabola that grows predictably over time. (c). (Interestingly, galaxies, urban populations and other natural agglomerations also seem to fall along such parabolas.) Finally, we checked our estimates by matching our projections for oil production in large areas, such as the world outside the Persian Gulf region, to the rise and fall of oil discovery in those places decades earlier (d).

—C.J.C. and J.H.L.

...by extrapolating the size of new fields into the future...

...and by matching production to earlier discovery trends.

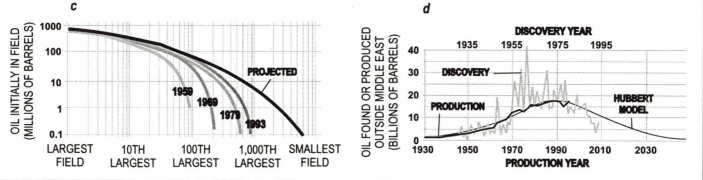

LAURIE GRACE; SOURCE: JEAN H. LAHERRÈRE

typically emerge from strip mines. Extracting oil from these sands and shales creates air pollution. The Orinoco sludge contains heavy metals and sulfur that must be removed. So governments may restrict these industries from growing as fast as they could. In view of these potential obstacles, our skeptical estimate is that only 700 Gbo will be produced from unconventional reserves over the next 60 years.

On the Down Side

Meanwhile global demand for oil is currently rising at more than 2 percent a year. Since 1985, energy use is up about 30 percent in Latin America, 40 percent in Africa and 50 percent in Asia. The Energy Information Administration forecasts that worldwide demand for oil will increase 60 percent (to about 40 Gbo a year) by 2020.

The switch from growth to decline in oil production will thus almost certainly create economic and political tension. Unless alternatives to crude oil quickly prove themselves, the market share of the OPEC states in the Middle East will rise rapidly. Within two years, these nations' share of the global oil business will pass 30 percent, nearing the level reached during the oil-price shocks of the 1970s. By 2010 their share will quite probably hit 50 percent.

The world could thus see radical increases in oil prices. That alone might be sufficient to curb demand, flattening production for perhaps 10 years. (Demand fell more than 10 percent after the 1979 shock and took 17 years to recover.) But by 2010 or so, many Middle Eastern nations will themselves be past the midpoint. World production will then have to fall.

With sufficient preparation, however, the transition to the post-oil economy need not be traumatic. If advanced methods of producing liquid fuels from natural gas can be made profitable and scaled up quickly, gas could become the next source of transportation fuel [see "Liquid Fuels from

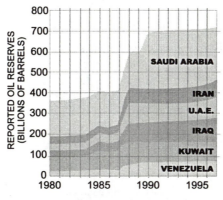

LAURIE GRACE; SOURCE: OIL AND GAS JOURNAL

SUSPICIOUS JUMP in reserves reported by six OPEC members added 300 billion barrels of oil to official reserve tallies yet followed no major discovery of new fields.

Natural Gas," by Safaa A. Fouda*]. Safer nuclear power, cheaper renewable energy, and oil conservation programs could all help postpone the inevitable decline of conventional oil.

Countries should begin planning and investing now. In November a panel of energy experts appointed by President Bill Clinton strongly urged the administration to increase funding for energy research by $1 billion over the next five years. That is a small step in the right direction, one that must be followed by giant leaps from the private sector.

The world is not running out of oil—at least not yet. What our society does face, and soon, is the end of the abundant and cheap oil on which all industrial nations depend.

The Authors

COLIN J. CAMPBELL and JEAN H. LAHERRÈRE have each worked in the oil industry for more than 40 years. After completing his Ph.D. in geology at the University of Oxford, Campbell worked for Texaco as an exploration geologist and then at Amoco as chief geologist for Ecuador. His decade-long study of global oil-production trends has led to two books and numerous papers. Laherrère's early work on seismic refraction surveys contributed to the discovery of Africa's largest oil field. At Total, a French oil company, he supervised exploration techniques worldwide. Both Campbell and Laherrère are currently associated with Petroconsultants in Geneva.

Further Reading

UPDATED HUBBERT CURVES ANALYZE WORLD OIL SUPPLY. L. F. Ivanhoe in *World Oil*, Vol. 217, No. 11, pages 91–94; November 1996.

THE COMING OIL CRISIS. Colin J. Campbell. Multi-Science Publishing and Petroconsultants, Brentwood, England, 1997.

OIL BACK ON THE GLOBAL AGENDA. Craig Bond Hatfield in *Nature*, Vol. 387, page 121; May 8, 1997.

---

*Editor's note: All of the articles mentioned in this article can be found in Scientific American, March 1998.

Sunlight Brightens Our Energy Future

Randy Quinn

New technologies could make solar power a conventional energy source within the next decade.

For nearly 40 years, solar power technology has been the holy grail for those in search of the perfect energy source. Its fuel, sunlight, is certainly plentiful. Estimates show that the sunlight striking the Earth in one second could meet the energy needs of the entire human race for 2,000 years.

Solar power technology is clean. Unlike coal, natural gas, or nuclear power, it emits no air pollutants or greenhouse gases, nor does it leave behind dangerous radioactive waste. And it doesn't require the construction of massive, expensive central power-generating stations or a nation-spanning electrical grid.

Now, with a speed catching many by surprise, our "solar future" may be upon us. Cheaper solar cell production processes; new, less expensive solar cell materials; the energy demands of the developing nations; and First World consumers' desire for clean energy could make solar power competitive with conventional technologies within the next 5 to 10 years.

Betting on photovoltaics

Two basic classes of solar power technology have emerged: photovoltaics (or PV, the technology that powers spacecraft, watches, and calculators), where sunlight is turned directly into electricity; and solar heating technology, where heat from the sun generates usable energy. Of these, PV is rushing to commercialization at a breakneck pace.

According to Steven Johnson, president of the energy consulting firm Sabrina Corporation of Golden, Colorado, "For the first time, PV manufacturers are actually making money." Around the world, countries are turning to PV to meet their electrical needs, and that "market pull" is having its effect. "The U.S. industry saw nearly 30 percent growth last year. We may be approaching a critical mass in the industry."

Experts like Johnson predict a billion-dollar-a-year solar power industry by the year 2000. Ultimately, they see a 9,000 megawatt, $27 billion potential market for PV in the United States alone.

The message is clear: PV isn't just for astronauts, calculators, and watches anymore.

The largest U.S.-owned manufacturer of PV products is Solarex, a business unit of Amoco-Enron Solar. Located in Frederick, Maryland, Solarex produced the PV modules that make up the rooftop array located on the Olympic swimming facility in Atlanta. According to Harvey Forest, CEO and president of Solarex, it's the largest PV rooftop installation in the world.

The $17 million swimming and diving facility houses two pools, seats 15,000 spectators, and contains 40,000 square feet (3,716 square meters) of Solarex photovoltaic modules on its roof. Those modules provide nearly 350 kilowatts of electric power, which offsets the electricity consumed by the building. It's estimated to save 25–30 percent of the building's total electric bill, or about $33,000 per year.

"That particular installation helped put solar power back on the world's radar screen," Forest says.

Business is booming, he confirms. "We have a 4-megawatt project in Hawaii coming on line in 1998, and a project in India for upward of 50 megawatts" to be installed over the next several years. "And that's PV heaven for us," he says.

Siemens Solar, the PV arm of the Siemens Company, is the world's largest manufacturer of photovoltaics. The company recently celebrated producing its 100th megawatt of PV modules. "That's about one-fourth of the total installed base of PV worldwide," says Eric Daniels, director of marketing. And looking into the future, he predicts, "There's room to grow."

"About 83 megawatts were shipped by the entire solar industry in 1996," according to solar industry analyst Tom Jensen of Strategies Unlimited, a market analysis and strategic consulting firm in Mountain View, California. "That's up from 72 in 1995. And the industry is expected to finally surpass 100 megawatts per year in '97."

Two billion waiting to be served

Putting those numbers in perspective, Jensen explains that while conventional coal- or gas-fired power plants might have a generating capacity of 250–500 megawatts and a nuclear plant 1,000 megawatts (1 gigawatt), numbers in the tens of megawatt range are large by PV standards.

"The main reason for the current growth in PV sales," says Jensen, "is the large-scale national rooftop program in Japan. The [Japanese government] subsidizes homeowners for nearly 50 percent of the cost of a rooftop PV array. They've installed 12 megawatts to date since 1994, and they're expected to install between 12 and 15 megawatts in 1997 alone."

Apart from Japan, according to Jensen, "India, the U.S., and Germany are the biggest markets. And the Indonesian and Pacific region

COURTESY OF SOLAREX

Villagers in Oman use electricity from their PV array to run a television. Many common PV applications provide power in remote locations.

markets are emerging, as are those in Central and South America."

As developing countries' need for energy grows, many of them are choosing PV to fill the gap. Although the world market for solar power has grown by an average of 15 percent per year since 1973 to the present installed base of about 400 megawatts, it seems poised to grow even faster now.

Ask any solar industry executive about the worldwide demand for PV and you're likely to hear something like consultant Steven Johnson's answer: "There are two billion people in the world without access to electricity."

According to Johnson, "Much of the world doesn't have grid-based electric power and never will. The economics of building more fossil-fuel, hydroelectric, or nuclear power plants and extending the grid are not there, because the consumers can't pay for it. So it's better to develop other energy sources." Solar power works, and lightweight, rugged PV is the alternative energy source of choice for many.

Once electricity comes to a Third World village, lives change. Bob Gibson, communications manager for the Utility Photovoltaic Group (UPVG), an international association of utilities formed to accelerate PV development, recalls a little village in Guatemala where he saw PV significantly improve the quality of life.

"One woman I met can now run several lights at night so she can feel secure from petty thievery in the village," he recalls. "Her neighbor is able to run her sewing machine and earn extra income from that. PV helped bring those people into the twentieth century."

Electricity from light

While PV may be twenty-first-century technology, its roots lie in an observation made by the German physicist Heinrich Hertz in 1887. In studying the production of sparks between metal electrodes, he noted that ultraviolet light affected the voltage required to produce the sparks. Further studies by several physicists led to the puzzling understanding that light, then thought to be a wave, was triggering the release of electrons (particles discovered in 1895).

Physicists were deeply bothered by the experimentally derived properties of this so-called photoelectric effect until it was explained through a radical proposal by the young Albert Einstein in 1905. What Einstein reasoned was that sunlight—all light, as a matter of fact—is made up of tiny packets of energy. When these packets, called photons, strike an object, some of that energy is handed over to electrons in the material, boosting their energy so high that they escape from the surface of the metal. Applied to PV cells today, the photons of sunlight boost the energy of electrons, so they are unbound from a particular atom and freed to move about in the material.

Einstein won the 1921 Nobel Prize in physics in part for this explanation. But it wasn't until 1954 that scientists at Bell Laboratories developed the first solar cell.

PV cells are made not of metals, which are conductors, but of silicon, a semiconductor, which means that it can conduct electricity only under certain circumstances. Like electrons in any atom, silicon's four outermost electrons exist in only certain orbits, or energy levels, around the atom's nucleus. To move between energy levels, the electrons must absorb or emit the exact amount of energy necessary to jump to another electron orbit in the atom.

In a semiconductor there is, however, an energy level at which electrons enter a "conduction band." That is the orbital where they can leave their parent atom and flow in a current as if they were in a metal. They just have to absorb the right amount of energy to enter that band.

Hence, if the photons in the sunlight striking a silicon PV cell have just the right amount of energy—1.1 electron volts, to be exact—they enable electrons to move into the conduction band and become part of an electric current. The current can then power a toaster or hair dryer, for example.

Photovoltaics first came into use in 1958 when NASA needed a reliable, lightweight power source for its satellites and space probes. Solar technology met both criteria. Since then, NASA space vehicles have soared on solar panel wings.

Solar power works, and lightweight, rugged PV is the alternative energy source of choice for many.

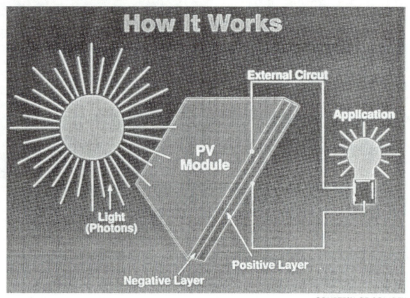

COURTESY OF SOLAREX

PV cells, mounted together to form modules, produce electricity whenever particles of light energy (known as photons) impart the precise energy pulse needed to release electrons to flow from the negative layer through an external circuit to the positive layer.

There's no place like home

A look at the breakdown of demand for photovoltaic power modules in 1995 shows a good global distribution, with the developed countries leading the way. The Pacific Rim region bought 25 percent (16.9 megawatts) of all PV modules sold in 1995, followed by the European continent with 21 percent (14.6 megawatts) and the North American region, including the United States and Canada, with 18 percent (12.5 megawatts). The rest of the world claimed 36 percent (24.5 megawatts).

Most applications so far have been off-grid, beyond the reach of conventional power. In a white paper for the American Solar Energy Society, Donald Osborn, supervisor of the Solar Program for the Sacramento Municipal Utility District (SMUD), discusses some of those ap-

plications. They include vacation cabins, public campgrounds and parks, highway signs and rest stops, public beach facilities, parking lots, cell phone transmission towers, and navigation beacons.

These are instances where the cost of using PV is already comparable to using grid-connected power. Osborn writes that the average cost of extending power lines into nonurban areas ranges from $20,000 to $80,000 per mile, a cost usually borne by the consumer. At that price—and considering the average energy use of a remote, single-family vacation home—"eliminating a power line extension of even one mile could well pay for the PV system."

Now, Osborn says, SMUD is pursuing on-grid applications as well. As of spring 1996, the SMUD Solar Program had placed nearly five megawatts of distributed PV generation on its electrical grid. Much of that is part of SMUD's PV Pioneers Program, which places small- to moderate-sized PV systems on the rooftops of volunteer customers' residences.

What's surprising is that along with providing SMUD the roof area for a system that feeds back into the SMUD electric grid—not their own home—the customers also pay a small "green fee," an additional cost on top of what they would pay for conventional power. Despite the extra cost and the fact that they don't own the rooftop system, about 100 new PV pioneers join the program every year.

"People want PV," says John Bigger, technical director for the UPVG. In marketing studies completed for their member utilities, the association found that from 1 to 3 percent of a utility's customers are willing to pay a premium to help make PV more available.

Why are some customers willing to pay more? "For a cleaner environment," says Bigger, "and to accelerate this technology so more of our country's power is provided by PV."

The cost of being green

But the price of PV has been the prime factor limiting its use in the United States. Usually measured in dollars per watt of power-generating capacity (or thousand dollars per kilowatt), those first solar modules used on 1950s spacecraft cost thousands of dollars per watt of generating capacity. By the early 1970s, PV modules were down to about $30 per watt at the factory, and by 1980 they were down to $10 per watt.

Today, solar modules price out between $4 and $5 per watt at the factory, according to Ken Zweibel, manager of thin-film solar cell research at the National Renewable Energy Laboratory (NREL) in Golden, Colorado. That's still a long way from competing with the average cost of coal, oil, natural gas, or nuclear power generation at from $2 to less than a dollar per watt. "But remember," Zweibel says, "there's a lot of higher-priced electricity in this country and worldwide." Residents of states like California and Hawaii, for example, pay significantly higher rates for conventional electricity, he says, particularly during daytime peak-energy periods when air conditioners work hardest.

If utilities can simply add PV as they need it, rather than extending the electric grid or building a new power plant, PV starts to look attractive.

For grid-connected PV systems, "$3.50 per watt installed is the magic price," says Paul Maycock, president of PV Energy Systems of Warrenton, Virginia, and former head of the Department of Energy's PV effort under President Jimmy Carter. At that cost, he says, PV is fully competitive with conventional power in sunny places like California and Hawaii. And, he predicts, PV prices will be there by the year 2000 if not sooner.

Silicon and beyond

Today's PV technology is, by and large, single-crystal silicon. In 1995, it accounted for 61 percent of all PV shipped, followed by polycrystalline and semicrystalline silicon at 26 percent.

Making single-crystal silicon PV isn't easy. Starting with quartzite grains, the silicon ore is processed into a form that is greater than 99.9999 percent pure silicon. Then it is melted and a seed of pure silicon crystal is introduced to the melt. On contact, the melted silicon adapts to the pattern of the single-crystal seed. The melt cools and solidifies into a cylindrical ingot with the seed's exact crystalline atomic structure.

After the ingot is grown, it is sawed into thin wafers for further processing into PV cells. The sawing step wastes about 20 percent of the silicon as "sawdust." Additional materials called "dopants," like phosphorous and boron, are then embedded separately into different silicon wafers that will have complementary conduction bands.

A typical PV cell consists of several layers that, starting from the top, include a meshlike conducting electrode, an antireflective coating or treated surface layer, a one-micrometer-thick layer of doped silicon, a narrow electric field region that enables a current to be produced, a much thicker silicon base layer doped opposite to the first, and a back-contact electrode. These cells can then be laid out in a rectangle and wired together to form a windowpane-sized PV module. Modules can be connected to form a larger array.

The efficiency of PV modules is usually measured by how much of the sunlight striking the module is converted to electrical energy. For single-crystal silicon modules, that is currently about 12–14 percent. Single-crystal PV modules achieve the highest production efficiency, but manufacturing them is an expensive, time- and materials-consuming process. And experts predict this technology can't bring the price of PV down to conventional-power levels.

As a result, the industry has tried to find cheaper ways of making solar cells. Though they are less efficient at converting sunlight to electricity, semicrystalline and polycrystalline silicon require far less complex manufacturing. And PV modules have also been made by pulling a thin sheet or ribbon of silicon slowly from a molten bath of pure silicon.

Another answer is to use a lens to concentrate more sunlight on a smaller area of silicon. This technology has been pursued by Amonix, of Torrance, California. Its prototype concentrator system focuses 260 times more light on each silicon cell. "You use $1/260$ the amount of silicon," says Amonix operations manager Dave Roubideaux. "So you produce an equal amount of energy using 260 times less silicon." Amonix has installed two test systems with Arizona Public Service's Solar Test and Research (STAR) center in Tempe, Arizona, and is currently installing one in Las Vegas for Nevada Power.

Skating on thin films

After years of diligent research, PV developers believe they have reached a threshold of success with their latest developments, the "thin film" PVs [see "Second-Generation Solar

Cells," THE WORLD & I, May 1988, p. 159]. These include amorphous silicon and cadmium telluride.

Amorphous silicon, made by depositing successive thin layers of silicon directly on a substrate, requires only $\frac{1}{50}$ to $\frac{1}{100}$ the silicon used in other technologies. Solarex is working to complete construction of an amorphous silicon manufacturing facility in James City County, Virginia, capable of producing 10 megawatts of PV panels annually. Industry experts like Maycock believe if Solarex can achieve its production goal and more amorphous silicon plants are built, the price per watt for installed, grid-connected PV systems can meet the "magic price" of $3.50.

And developing innovative products will help, too. United Solar Systems Corp. of Troy, Michigan, for example, recently developed a PV shingle to take the place of standard asphalt roofing shingles. Coated with amorphous PV material on half its surface, the flexible, stainless steel shingles are nailed in place like standard roofing shingles, and the PV "shingle array" is then connected to the house's electrical system.

Incorporating PV directly into a building's roof eliminates the need for any additional PV support structure and reduces the cost of installation, according to Subhendu Guha, executive vice president at United Solar Systems. Plus, "The roof is there, so there's no need for extra real estate to collect sunlight. Now the roof can both shelter and meet the electrical needs of the house." United Solar Systems is currently expanding its manufacturing capacity

with support from one of its parent corporations, Energy Conversion Devices, in Troy. United Solar Systems' other parent, Canon, is establishing a factory in Japan that will use similar processes for producing photovoltaics for a variety of building-integrated Applications.

Promising possibilities

To further reduce the cost of PV, some researchers have suggested using a material other than silicon. Solar cells of gallium arsenide are one possibility. But two other thin-film materials currently hold even greater hope for cheap PV.

The first, cadmium telluride, or CdTe, is closer to realization and currently has a laboratory efficiency of about 16 percent. The second material, copper indium diselenide, or CIS, shows promise of less cost with even greater, world-record efficiency of 17.7 percent. But CIS isn't likely to be ready for a while.

CdTe is developing fast. This past summer, Solar Cells Inc. (SCI), a PV company in Toledo, Ohio, developed a production version of its CdTe module (2 ft. × 4 ft. or 60 cm × 120 cm) with an efficiency of 9.1 percent.

Now, according to company President Mike Cicak, "We're light years ahead of everyone else in solar." But rather than produce the CdTe modules themselves, SCI plans to create the machines that make the PV modules and sell the machines to other companies to do the actual production. Its CdTe machine has a modular design that allows up to five sections with 20-megawatt-per-

year production capabilities to be connected into one 100-megawatt machine. SCI plans to have its first 20-megawatt machine producing panels in the first quarter of 1997.

"I really believe that we're creating a whole new industry with our equipment," says Cicak. He forecasts his machines will be producing 100 megawatts of PV modules per year—the current production capacity of the world—before the year 2000. "And when we're at 100 megawatts, we can compete with nuclear power."

Many watts to megawatts

Predicting who might succeed in bringing down the price of PV to that of conventional power sources, NREL's Zweibel picks SCI with its cadmium telluride technology and Solarex with its amorphous silicon technology. "SCI and Solarex are both aggressive," he says. "They have all the pieces to do it, and they have the resources to carry it out."

Peering into the future, Zweibel sees that "PV may be a multi-gigawatt-per-year industry by 2005. And then we'll see another order of magnitude increase by 2015 of from 10 to 30 gigawatts per year. At that point, you'll see PV up there with nuclear, hydro, and all the rest as part of the national energy mix."

Randy Quinn is a freelance science writer living in Pittsburgh. His last article for The World & I *was "Dancing on the Web," in the April 1996 issue.*

Bull Market in Wind Energy

Many countries may soon find that the cheapest way to produce electricity is to pull it out of the air

By Christopher Flavin

The Spanish city of Pamplona has long been known for its annual running of the bulls. But this mid-sized industrial center, the capital of the state of Navarra in the rugged Pyrenees region, is quickly gaining another distinction: it has the world's fastest growing wind energy industry. Starting from scratch just three years earlier, Navarra was obtaining 23 percent of its electricity from the wind by the end of 1998.

With a population of 180,000, Pamplona has an economy based heavily on manufacturing, including a sizeable car industry. But along with much of the rest of Spain, the city has had a relatively stagnant economy and a high rate of unemployment in recent years. In an effort to deal with that problem—and replace the coal and nuclear energy it imports from other parts of Spain with local power—Navarra recently introduced a set of tax incentives and other inducements for harnessing wind energy using locally manufactured turbines.

These policies paid off well beyond the dreams of the government officials who crafted them. Several wind-energy companies were quickly established in Navarra, most of them joint ventures owned in part by the Danish firms that supplied the technology. And much of the investment is coming from Energia Hidroelectrica de Navarra, the regional electric utility. These firms have provided a strong political base for the region's burgeoning wind power industry. Navarra's wind companies are already looking to expand their horizons to even larger potential markets in areas where Spain has strong historic ties, such as North Africa and South America.

The sudden transformation of Navarra's energy mix may turn out to be foreshadowing something much bigger. During the 1990s, wind power has already become the world's fastest growing energy source. Propelled by supportive new government policies—most of them motivated by environmental concerns—some 2,100 megawatts of new wind generating capacity were added in 1998, according to our preliminary estimate. That's not only a new record, but 35 percent more than the previous record set the year before.

Global wind generating capacity now stands at 9,600 megawatts—a 26 percent increase from a year earlier. (See figure) Wind turbines will generate a projected 21 billion kilowatt-hours of electricity in l999—enough power for 3.5 million suburban homes. And though it now provides less than 1 percent of the world's electricity, these double-digit growth rates could make the wind a major power supplier soon.

Wind power is also one of the world's most rapidly expanding industries. Valued at roughly $2 billion in 1998, the wind industry is creating thousands of jobs at a time when manufacturing employment is falling in many nations. And as a booming new industry, wind energy has become a major investment opportunity—comparable perhaps to some of the internet stocks that are now so hot on Wall Street.

Ancient Ideas, Brand New Markets

Although it has had a recent rebirth, wind power is actually an ancient source of energy. The first windmills for grinding grain appeared in Persia just over 1,000 years ago, and later spread to China, throughout the Mediterranean, and to northern Europe, where the Dutch developed the massive machines for which the country is still known. In the Middle Ages, windmills allowed peasants to grind grain without depending on watermills controlled by feudal lords.

As the fossil-fuel age emerged in the early 20th century, wind power seemed to have become a permanent footnote in the history of energy technology. But in the 1970s, Danish companies invented a machine composed of three propeller-like fiberglass blades that pointed upwind of a steel tower on which they were mounted. The latest versions, which are also manufactured by companies based in Germany, India, Spain, and the United States, have variable pitch blades whose angle of attack varies depending on the wind speed. The blades, which can be as long as 40 meters, will spin in winds of little more than 15 kilometers per hour. They maintain a relatively slow and constant speed, though a new generation of electronic variable-speed drives allow the blade speed to vary, increasing the machines' efficiency. The generator—similar in design to those connected to diesel engines—sits atop the tower, along with the transmission, brakes, and sophisticated microprocessors that coordinate all of the equipment.

The 1998 wind energy boom was led by Germany, which added 790 megawatts, pushing its capacity to 2,875 megawatts, nearly double the total capacity in the United States. Germany's wind industry is only seven years old; it grew out of a 1991 electricity reform law that was motivated in part by the Chernobyl nuclear disaster. But already, wind generators are producing as much power as two of Germany's large coal-fired power plants, or a little more than 1 percent of the country's electricity. In the northern state of Schleswig Holstein, wind now provides 15 percent of the electricity, and is on course to supplant nuclear energy as the state's leading power source. The new German government plans to shut down the nuclear plants that supply 30 percent of the country's electricity—a move that may give wind power another substantial boost.

One of the most notable developments in 1998 was the emergence of Spain as the number-two player in the industry. Spain added an estimated 395 megawatts of wind power last year. That increase pushed the country's total wind capacity up 86 percent, to 850 megawatts. Robust wind energy industries have sprung up not only in Navarra, but also in the northwest state of Galicia, and in the south near Gibraltar. With development in all of these regions accelerating steadily, Spain could soon surpass Germany as the world's leading wind energy producer.

Wind generation also expanded in the United States in 1998. Some 230 megawatts of new capacity were added, to make up the largest increase in wind power that the country has seen since 1986. The new installations are spread across 10 different states, and were spurred by the desire to take advantage of a wind energy tax credit that is currently scheduled to expire in June 1999. They include a 107-megawatt wind farm in Minnesota, a 42-megawatt farm in Wyoming, a 25-megawatt farm in Oregon, and many small projects, ranging from Maine to New Mexico.

In contrast, to the erratic ups and downs of the U.S. industry, Denmark maintained its moderate, steady pace in 1998. The 235 megawatts of capacity added in the last year took Denmark's total wind capacity to 1,350 megawatts. Wind now generates over 8 percent of the country's power. Most notably, Danish wind companies utterly dominate the global export market; more than half the new wind turbines installed worldwide in 1998 were made in Denmark. The Danish companies are also involved in joint-venture manufacturing in India and Spain—an arrangement that has allowed for the rapid transfer of wind technology to the host countries. Altogether, the Danish wind industry had a turnover of just under $1 billion last year. That's roughly equal to the combined sales value of the nation's natural gas and fishing industries—two leading Danish sectors.

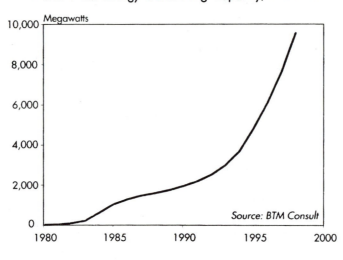

World Wind Energy Generating Capacity, 1980–98

Megawatts

Source: BTM Consult

A Technology That Has Come of Age

The nations that could benefit most from wind power are in the developing world, where power demand is growing rapidly and where most countries lack adequate local supplies of fossil fuels. The developing world's largest wind industry is in India, which has over 900 megawatts of wind power in place. But expansion has slowed there in the last two years, due to a suspension of the generous tax breaks that were in effect in the mid-1990s. Observers expect the new government to restore some of these incentives, which could give the industry a boost in 1999. Although wind power now provides less than 1 percent of India's electricity, its share could one day rise to 20 or 30 percent.

The wind potential of China is even greater. China has not yet established a solid legal basis for wind power, although several companies have installed small projects there in the last few years, with the help of foreign aid. But China could become a wind superpower. It has vast wind resources in several regions, including a huge stretch of Inner Mongolia that by itself could provide most of the power needed in Beijing and the rest of northern China.

China's wind potential is estimated to exceed its total current electricity use. That fact has enormous international implications, since China's coalbased economy exacts a heavy environmental toll. A Chinese wind industry could allow a significant reduction in global greenhouse gas emissions.

The dramatic growth of wind power in the 1990s stems primarily from laws that guarantee access to the grid for wind generators at a fixed price. (The price offered is usually a bit higher than the cost of fossil-fuel power—a recognition that the environmental benefits of renewable energy technologies are worth paying for.) These laws have established a stable market for the new industry, and have overcome resistance from the coal- and nuclear-dependent utilities that monopolize the market today. Some 70 percent of the global wind power market in recent years has been centered in just three countries, Germany, Spain, and Denmark—a distribution that reflects both the success of such laws where they exist, and the failure to adopt them broadly.

Wind energy is also being spurred by steady advances in technology. Larger turbines, more efficient manufacturing, and more careful siting of the machines are among the improvements that have pushed wind power costs down precipitously—from $2,600 per kilowatt in 1981 to $800 in 1998. A typical wind turbine today produces 700 kilowatts of electricity, costs $700,000 (including installation), and provides enough power annually for 200 homes.

State-of-the-art wind turbines are highly automated and reliable; their downtime for maintenance, of less than 5 percent, is less than for fossil fuel plants, and maintenance costs are minimal. The "footprint" of a wind farm is also very small, since wind turbines blend readily with traditional uses of the rural landscape. (Farmers can either install their own wind turbines or lease the land to wind companies. The bulk of the land can still be used for grazing animals or raising crops.)

In many areas, wind power is already less expensive than electricity from coal-fired power plants. And as the technology continues to improve, further cost declines are projected. In many countries, the wind could become the most economical source of power in the next decade.

Over the past few years, wind seems to have achieved the kind of "critical mass" necessary to attract serious corporate interest. In 1996 and 1997, the largest U.S. natural gas company, Enron Corporation, purchased two wind manufacturing companies and is now developing projects around the world. Japanese trading companies have announced plans to build large wind projects, as have the German power giant Siemens and Florida Power and Light, a major U.S. electric utility. Companies in Denmark and the Netherlands are making plans for even larger offshore wind farms in the North Sea.

Continued and perhaps accelerated growth of the wind industry is likely in 1999 and beyond. Spain and the United States are projected to have particularly good years, probably exceeding 500 megawatts of new turbines each. Other countries where growth is likely include Canada, Italy, Japan, Norway, and the United Kingdom. The strongest potential developing-country markets include Argentina, Brazil, Costa Rica, Egypt, Morocco, and Turkey.

Ultimately, wind power could be a major force for transforming the global energy economy. In the United States, the states of North Dakota, South Dakota, and Texas have sufficient wind capacity to provide all U.S. electricity. In windy regions such as Patagonia, the American Great Plains, or the steppes of Central Asia, wind farms could churn out vast amounts of electricity. A study by Danish researchers in 1998 laid out a strategy for providing 10 percent of the world's electricity from the wind within the next few decades. In the longer run, wind power—both onshore and off—could easily exceed hydropower—which now supplies 20 percent of the world's electricity—as an energy source.

Wind power is still considered a laughing matter by many energy industry executives. But soon, such people may look almost as silly as those who once called the airplane an absurd idea. If that happens, Navarra may enter the history books alongside Kitty Hawk, North Carolina as the proving ground for a technology that changed the way the world lives.

Christopher Flavin is senior vice president at Worldwatch Institute, and co-author with Nicholas Lenssen of Power Surge: Guide to the Coming Energy Revolution *(W.W. Norton, 1994).*

Unit 4

Key Points to Consider

❖ What is meant by the term "biodiversity," and how is it related to the concept of ecosystem stability? Are there ways of assessing whether a reduction in biodiversity is the result of human or natural factors?

❖ Contrast the forest protection policies that have recently been developed for the old growth forests in the Pacific Northwest of the United States and the new national park in Honduras. Are there ways in which the relative effectiveness of these policies reflects the political situation in the two countries?

❖ How and why are weedy plants so successful in competing with native species in North America? What advantages to the alien species have that native plants do not?

❖ What is meant by "organic farming"? Are organically produced crops preferable to those grown using pesticides, artificial fertilizers, and other agricultural chemicals? Why or why not?

❖ Describe the nature of the conflict or competition between wildlife and humans for the same set of resources. Are there equitable means of balancing the needs of both people and animals for food and living space?

 **Links**

www.dushkin.com/online/

These sites are annotated on pages 4 and 5.

Tragically, the modern conservation movement began too late to save many species of plants and animals from extinction. In fact, even after concern for the biosphere developed among resource managers, their effectiveness in halting the decline of herds and flocks, packs and schools, or groves and grasslands has been limited by the ruthlessness and efficiency of the competition. Wild plants and animals compete directly with human beings and their domesticated livestock and crop plants for living space and for other resources such as sunlight, air, water, and soil. As the historical record of this competition in North America and other areas attests, since the seventeenth century human settlement has been responsible—either directly or indirectly—for the demise of many plant and wildlife species. It should be noted that extinction is a natural process—part of the evolutionary cycle—and not always created by human activity. But human actions have the capacity to accelerate a natural process that might otherwise take millennia.

In the opening article of this unit, the losses of Earth's plants and animals from human impact are tallied. Author David Quammen makes the point in "Planet of Weeds" that the nature of human impact on the biosphere reduces biodiversity and encourages the dominance of plant and animal species that can be termed "weeds": hardy, resilient, able to live almost anywhere, and capable of choking out native species almost everywhere. Among the weedy species, human beings are paramount and Quammen's pessimistic view of a future world is of humans and a few other survivors "picking through the rubble" of a once-fertile planet.

This theme is continued in the articles of the subsection on plants. The most important component of the biosphere is the primary production of living vegetation, and, in the four articles in the *Plants* subsection, the issue of human impact on vegetation is central. In "Old Growth for Sale," *Audubon* reporter Douglas Gantenbein investigates one of the most hotly debated environmental issues in the United States: the fate of the old-growth forests of the Pacific Northwest. In the next selection, science writer Steven Mirsky examines the role of alien plant species that reduce natural biodiversity by killing off native plants. In "Alien Invasion," Mirsky describes several of the most common alien plant invaders in North America, where they may be found, and what kinds of damage they do to natural systems. Then, in the subsection's concluding selection, a somewhat optimistic tone is struck by Joel Bourne's article on "The Organic Revolution," which focuses on the increasing importance of organic or

chemical-free farming methods in producing both food and fiber crops.

Prospects for the future of wildlife are not appreciably better than they are for many of the world's plant species. Land developers destroy animal habitats as cities encroach upon the countryside. Living space for all wildlife species is destroyed as river valleys are transformed into reservoirs for the generation of hydropower and as forests are removed for construction materials and for paper. Toxic wastes from urban areas work their way into the food chain, annually killing thousands of animals in the United States alone. Rural lands are sprayed with herbicides and pesticides, which also kill bird life and small mammals. Most important, wild animals are placed in jeopardy for the very simple reason that they compete with domestic stock and humans for the same resources. And in any instance in which the protection of wildlife comes at the expense of livestock or humans, the wildlife is going to lose.

One of the clearest and most recent examples of heightened competition between wildlife and animals is currently being played out in the suburbs of America where the expanding fringe of human occupation is impinging on the shrinking area of wildlife habitat. Anthony Brandt, in "Not In My Backyard," tells us that, while many of the more "conservative" species of animals like moose, elk, and grizzlies have generally retreated into areas far beyond the reach of humans, other animals such as deer and coyotes and even black bear and mountain lions are adapting rapidly to the suburban environment. Of all the more adaptive species, perhaps none is quite as adaptive as the coyote and the second article in the section describes the recent success of this "wily creature." In "The Ultimate Survivor," Mike Finkel describes how coyotes, in spite of being killed in increasing numbers by government hunters who shoot and poison these animals, are actually increasing in both numbers and range or geographic area.

PLANET OF WEEDS

Tallying the losses of Earth's animals and plants

By David Quammen

Hope is a duty from which paleontologists are exempt. Their job is to take the long view, the cold and stony view, of triumphs and catastrophes in the history of life. They study the fossil record, that erratic selection of petrified shells, carapaces, bones, teeth, tree trunks, leaves, pollen, and other biological relics, and from it they attempt to discern the lost secrets of time, the big patterns of stasis and change, the trends of innovation and adaptation and refinement and decline that have blown like sea winds among ancient creatures in ancient ecosystems. Although life is their subject, death and burial supply all their data. They're the coroners of biology. This gives to paleontologists a certain distance, a hyperopic perspective beyond the reach of anxiety over outcomes of the struggles they chronicle. If hope is the thing with feathers, as Emily Dickinson said, then it's good to remember that feathers don't generally fossilize well. In lieu of hope and despair, paleontologists have

David Quammen is the author of eight books, including The Song of the Dodo *and, most recently,* Wild Thoughts from Wild Places. *His last article for* Harper's Magazine, *"Brazil's Jungle Blackboard," appeared in the March 1998 issue.*

a highly developed sense of cyclicity. That's why I recently went to Chicago, with a handful of urgently grim questions, and called on a paleontologist named David Jablonski. I wanted answers unvarnished with obligatory hope.

Jablonski is a big-pattern man, a macro-evolutionist, who works fastidiously from the particular to the very broad. He's an expert on the morphology and distribution of marine bivalves and gastropods—or clams and snails, as he calls them when speaking casually. He sifts through the record of those mollusk lineages, preserved in rock and later harvested into museum drawers, to extract ideas about the origin of novelty. His attention roams back through 600 million years of time. His special skill involves framing large, resonant questions that can be answered with small, lithified clamshells. For instance: By what combinations of causal factor and sheer chance have the great evolutionary innovations arisen? How quickly have those innovations taken hold? How long have they abided? He's also interested in extinction, the converse of abidance, the yang to evolution's yin. Why do some species survive for a long time, he wonders, whereas others die out much sooner? And why has the rate of extinction—low throughout most of Earth's history—spiked upward cataclysmically on just a few occasions? How do these cataclysmic episodes, known in the trade as mass extinctions, differ in kind as well as degree from the gradual process of species extinction during the millions of years between? Can what struck in the past strike again?

The concept of mass extinction implies a biological crisis that spanned large parts of the planet and, in a relatively short time, eradicated a sizable number of species from a variety of groups. There's no absolute threshold of magnitude, and dozens of different episodes in geologic history might qualify, but five big ones stand out: Ordovician, Devonian, Permian, Triassic, Cretaceous. The Ordovician extinction, 439 million years ago, entailed the disappearance of roughly 85 percent of marine animal species—and that was before there were any animals *on land*. The Devonian extinction, 367 million years ago, seems to have been almost as severe. About 245 million years ago came the Permian extinction, the worst ever, claiming 95 percent of all known animal species and therefore almost wiping out the animal kingdom altogether. The Triassic, 208 million years ago, was bad again, though not nearly so bad as the Permian. The most recent was the Cretaceous extinction (sometimes called the K-T event because it defines the boundary between two geologic periods, with K for Cretaceous, never mind why, and T for Tertiary), familiar even to schoolchildren because it ended the age of dinosaurs. Less familiarly, the K-T event also brought extinction of the marine reptiles

THE EARTH HAS UNDERGONE FIVE MAJOR EXTINCTION PERIODS, EACH REQUIRING MILLIONS OF YEARS OF RECOVERY

and the ammonites, as well as major losses of species among fish, mammals, amphibians, sea urchins, and other groups, totaling 76 percent of all species. In between these five episodes occurred some lesser mass extinctions, and throughout the intervening lulls extinction continued, too—but at a much slower pace, known as the background rate, claiming only about one species in any major group every million years. At the background rate, extinction is infrequent enough to be counterbalanced by the evolution of new species. Each of the five major episodes, in contrast, represents a drastic net loss of species diversity, a deep trough of biological impoverishment from which Earth only slowly recovered. How slowly? How long is the lag between a nadir of impoverishment and a recovery to ecological fullness? That's another of Jablonski's research interests. His rough estimates run to 5 or 10 million years. What drew me to this man's work, and then to his doorstep, were his special competence on mass extinctions and his willingness to discuss the notion that a sixth one is in progress now.

Some people will tell you that we as a species, *Homo sapiens,* the savvy ape, all 5.9 billion of us in our collective impact, are destroying the world. Me, I won't tell you that, because "the world" is so vague, whereas what we are or aren't destroying is quite specific. Some people will tell you that we are rampaging suicidally toward a degree of global wreckage that will result in our own extinction. I won't tell you that either. Some people say that the environment will be the paramount political and social concern of the twenty-first century, but what they mean by "the environment" is anyone's guess. Polluted air? Polluted water? Acid rain? A frayed skein of ozone over Antarctica? Greenhouse gases emitted by smokestacks and cars? Toxic wastes? None of these concerns is the big one, paleontological in

scope, though some are more closely entangled with it than others. If the world's air is clean for humans to breathe but supports no birds or butterflies, if the world's waters are pure for humans to drink but contain no fish or crustaceans or diatoms, have we solved our environmental problems? Well, I suppose so, at least as environmentalism is commonly construed. That clumsy, confused, and presumptuous formulation "the environment" implies viewing air, water, soil, forests, rivers, swamps, deserts, and oceans as merely a milieu within which something important is set: human life, human history. But what's at issue in fact is not an environment; it's a living world.

Here instead is what I'd like to tell you: The consensus among conscientious biologists is that we're headed into another mass extinction, a vale of biological impoverishment commensurate with the big five. Many experts remain hopeful that we can brake that descent, but my own view is that we're likely to go all the way down. I visited David Jablonski to ask what we might see at the bottom.

On a hot summer morning, Jablonski is busy in his office on the second floor of the Hinds Geophysical Laboratory at the University of Chicago. It's a large open room furnished in tall bookshelves, tables piled high with books, stacks of paper standing knee-high off the floor. The walls are mostly bare, aside from a chart of the geologic time scale, a clipped cartoon of dancing tyrannosaurs in red sneakers, and a poster from a Rodin exhibition, quietly appropriate to the overall theme of eloquent stone. Jablonski is a lean forty-five-year-old man with a dark full beard. Educated at Columbia and Yale, he came to Chicago in 1985 and has helped make its paleontology program perhaps the country's best. Although in not many hours he'll be leaving on a trip to Alaska, he has been cordial about agreeing to this chat. Stepping carefully, we move among the piled journals, reprints, and photocopies. Every pile represents a different research question, he tells me. "I juggle a lot of these things all at once because they feed into one another." That's exactly why I've come: for a little rigorous intellectual synergy.

Let's talk about mass extinctions, I say. When did someone first realize that the concept might apply to current events, not just to the Permian or the Cretaceous?

He begins sorting through memory, back to the early 1970s, when the full scope of the current extinction problem was barely recognized. Before then, some writers warned about "vanishing wildlife" and "endangered species," but generally the warnings were framed around individual species with popular appeal, such as the whooping crane, the tiger, the blue whale, the peregrine falcon. During the 1970s a new form of con-

BIOLOGISTS BELIEVE THAT WE ARE ENTERING ANOTHER MASS EXTINCTION, A VALE OF BIOLOGICAL IMPOVERISHMENT

cern broke forth—call it wholesale concern—from the awareness that unnumbered millions of narrowly endemic (that is, unique and localized) species inhabit the tropical forests and that those forests were quickly being cut. In 1976, a Nairobi-based biologist named Norman Myers published a paper in *Science* on that subject; in passing, he also compared current extinctions with the rate during what he loosely called "the 'great dying' of the dinosaurs." David Jablonski, then a graduate student, read Myers's paper and tucked a copy into his files. This was the first time, as Jablonski recalls, that anyone tried to quantify the rate of present-day extinctions. "Norman was a pretty lonely guy, for a long time, on that," he says. In 1979, Myers published *The Sinking Ark,* explaining the problem and offering some rough projections. Between the years 1600 and 1900, by his tally, humanity had caused the extinction of about 75 known species, almost all of them mammals and birds. Between 1900 and 1979, humans had extinguished about another 75 known species, representing a rate well above the rate of known losses during the Cretaceous extinction. But even more worrisome was the inferable rate of unrecorded extinctions, recent and now impending, among plants and animals still unidentified by science. Myers guessed that 25,000 plant species presently stood jeopardized, and maybe hundreds of thousands of insects. "By the time human communities establish ecologically sound life-styles, the fallout of species could total several million." Rereading that sentence now, I'm struck by the reckless optimism of his assumption that human communities eventually will establish "ecologically sound life-styles."

Although this early stab at quantification helped to galvanize public concern, it also became a target for a handful of critics, who used the inexactitude of the numbers to cast doubt on the reality of the problem. Most conspicuous of the naysayers was Julian Simon, a economist at the University of Maryland, who argued bullishly that human resourcefulness would solve all problems worth solving, of which a decline in diversity of tropical insects wasn't one.

In a 1986 issue of *New Scientist,* Simon rebutted Norman Myers, arguing from his own construal of select data that there was "no obvious recent downward trend in world forests—no obvious 'losses' at all, and certainly no 'near catastrophic' loss." He later co-authored an op-ed piece in the *New York Times* under the headline "Facts, Not Species, Are Periled." Again he went after Myers, asserting a "complete absence of evidence for the claim that the extinction of species is going up rapidly—or even going up at all." Simon's worst disservice to logic in that statement and others was the denial that *inferential* evidence of wholesale extinction counts for anything. Of inferential evidence there was an abundance—for example, from the Centinela Ridge in a cloud-forest zone of western Ecuador, where in 1978 the botanist Alwyn Gentry and a colleague found thirty-eight species of narrowly endemic plants; including several with mysteriously black leaves. Before Gentry could get back, Centinela Ridge had been completely deforested, the native plants replaced by cacao and other crops. As for inferential evidence generally, we might do well to remember what it contributes to our conviction that approximately 105,000 Japanese civilians died in the atomic bombing of Hiroshima. The city's population fell abruptly on August 6, 1945, but there was no one-by-one identification of 105,000 bodies.

Nowadays a few younger writers have taken Simon's line, pooh-poohing the concern over extinction. As for Simon himself, who died earlier this year, perhaps the truest sentence he left behind was, "We must also try to get more reliable information about the number of species that might be lost with various changes in the forests." No one could argue.

But is isn't easy to get such information. Field biologists tend to avoid investing their precious research time in doomed tracts of forest. Beyond that, our culture offers little institutional support for the study of narrowly endemic species in order to register their existence *before* their habitats are destroyed. Despite these obstacles, recent efforts to quantify rates of extinction have supplanted the old warnings. These new estimates use satellite imaging and improved on-the-ground data about deforestation, records of the many human-caused extinctions on islands, and a branch of ecological theory called island biogeography, which connects documented island cases with the mainland problem of forest fragmentation. These efforts differ in particulars, reflecting how much uncertainty is still involved, but their varied tones form a chorus of consensus. I'll mention three of the most credible.

W. V. Reid, of the World Resources Institute, in 1992 gathered numbers on the average annual deforestation in each of sixty-three tropical countries during the 1980s and from them charted three different scenarios (low, middle, high) of presumable forest loss by the year 2040. He chose a standard mathematical model of the relationship between decreasing habitat area and decreasing species diversity, made conservative assumptions about the crucial constant, and ran his various deforestation estimates through the model. Reid's calculations suggest that by the year 2040, between 17 and 35 percent of tropical forest species will be extinct or doomed to be. Either at the high or the low end of this range, it would amount to a bad loss, though not as bad as the K-T event. Then again 2040 won't mark the end of human pressures on biological diversity or landscape.

Robert M. May, an ecologist at Oxford, co-authored a similar effort in 1995. May and his colleagues noted the five causal factors that account for most extinctions: habitat destruction, habitat fragmentation, overkill, invasive species, and secondary effects cascading through an ecosystem from other extinctions. Each of those five is more intricate than it sounds. For instance, habitat fragmentation dooms species by consigning them to small, island-like parcels of habitat surrounded by an ocean of human impact and by then subjecting them to the same jeopardies (small population size, acted upon by environmental fluctuation, catastrophe, inbreeding, bad luck, and cascading effects) that make island species especially vulnerable to extinction. May's team concluded that most extant bird and mammal species can expect average life spans of between 200 and 400 years. That's equivalent to saying that about a third of one percent will go extinct each year until some unimaginable end point is reached. "Much of the diversity we inherited," May and his co-authors wrote, "will be gone before humanity sorts itself out."

The most recent estimate comes from Stuart L. Pimm and Thomas M. Brooks, ecologists at the University of Tennessee. Using a combination of published data on bird species lost from forest fragments and field data gathered themselves, Pimm and Brooks concluded that 50 percent of the

EVEN BY CONSERVATIVE ESTIMATES, HUGE PERCENTAGES OF EARTH'S ANIMALS AND PLANTS WILL SIMPLY DISAPPEAR

IN THE NEXT FIFTY YEARS, DEFORESTATION WILL DOOM ONE HALF OF THE WORLD'S FOREST-BIRD SPECIES

world's forest-bird species will be doomed to extinction by deforestation occurring over the next half century. And birds won't be the sole victims. "How many species will be lost if current trends continue?" the two scientists asked. "Somewhere between one third and two thirds of all species—easily making this event as large as the previous five mass extinctions the planet has experienced."

Jablonski, who started down this line of thought in 1978, offers me a reminder about the conceptual machinery behind such estimates. "All mathematical models," he says cheerily, "are wrong. They are approximations. And the question is: Are they usefully wrong, or are they meaninglessly wrong?" Models projecting present and future species loss are useful, he suggests, if they help people realize that *Homo sapiens* is perturbing Earth's biosphere to a degree it hasn't often been perturbed before. In other words, that this is a drastic experiment in biological drawdown we're engaged in, not a continuation of routine.

Behind the projections of species loss lurk a number of crucial but hard-to-plot variables, among which two are especially weighty: continuing landscape conversion and the growth curve of human population.

Landscape conversion can mean many things: draining wetlands to build roads and airports, turning tallgrass prairies under the plow, fencing savanna and overgrazing it with domestic stock, cutting second-growth forest in Vermont and consigning the land to ski resorts or vacation suburbs, slash-and-burn clearing of Madagascar's rain forest to grow rice on wet hillsides, industrial logging in Borneo to meet Japanese plywood demands. The ecologist John Terborgh and a colleague, Carel P. van Schaik, have described a four-stage process of landscape conversion that they call the land-use cascade. The successive stages are: 1) *wildlands,* encompassing native floral and faunal communities altered little or not at all by human impact; 2) *extensively used areas,* such as natural grasslands lightly grazed, savanna kept open for prey animals by infrequent hu-

man-set fires, or forests sparsely worked by slash-and-burn farmers at low density; 3) *intensively used areas,* meaning crop fields, plantations, village commons, travel corridors, urban and industrial zones; and finally 4) *degraded land,* formerly useful but now abused beyond value to anybody. Madagascar, again, would be a good place to see all four stages, especially the terminal one. Along a thin road that leads inland from a town called Mahajanga, on the west coast, you can gaze out over a vista of degraded land—chalky red hills and gullies, bare of forest, burned too often by graziers wanting a short-term burst of pasturage, sparsely covered in dry grass and scrubby fan palms, eroded starkly, draining red mud into the Betsiboka River, supporting almost no human presence. Another showcase of degraded land—attributable to fuelwood gathering, overgrazing, population density, and decades of apartheid—is the Ciskei homeland in South Africa. Or you might look at overirrigated crop fields left ruinously salinized in the Central Valley of California.

Among all forms of landscape conversion, pushing tropical forest from the *wildlands* category to the *intensively used* category has the greatest impact on biological diversity. You can see it in western India, where a spectacular deciduous ecosystem known as the Gir forest (home to the last surviving population of the Asiatic lion, *Panthera leo persica*) is yielding along its ragged edges to new mango orchards, peanut fields, and lime quarries for cement. You can see it in the central Amazon, where big tracts of rain forest have been felled and burned, in a largely futile attempt (encouraged by misguided government incentives, now revoked) to pasture cattle on sun-hardened clay. According to the United Nations Food and Agriculture Organization, the rate of deforestation in tropical countries has increased (contrary to Julian Simon's claim) since the 1970s, when Myers made his estimates. During the 1980s, as the FAO reported in 1993, that rate reached 15.4 million hectares (a hectare being the metric equivalent of 2.5 acres) annually. South America was losing 6.2 million hectares a year. Southeast Asia was losing less in area but more proportionally: 1.6 percent of its forests yearly. In terms of cumulative loss, as reported by other observers, the Atlantic coastal forest of Brazil is at least 95 percent gone. The Philippines, once nearly covered with rain forest, has lost 92 percent. Costa Rica has continued to lose forest, despite that country's famous concern for its biological resources. The richest of old-growth lowland forests in West Africa, India, the Greater Antilles, Madagascar, and elsewhere have been reduced to less than a tenth of their original areas. By the middle of the next century, if those trends continue, tropical forest will exist virtually nowhere outside of protected ar-

eas—that is, national parks, wildlife refuges, and other official reserves.

How many protected areas will there be? The present worldwide total is about 9,800, encompassing 6.3 percent of the planet's land area. Will those parks and reserves retain their full biological diversity? No. Species with large territorial needs will be unable to maintain viable population levels within small reserves, and as those species die away their absence will affect others. The disappearance of big predators, for instance, can release limits on medium-size predators and scavengers, whose overabundance can drive still other species (such as ground-nesting birds) to extinction. This has already happened in some habitat fragments, such as Panama's Barro Colorado Island, and been well documented in the literature of island biogeography. The lesson of fragmented habitats is Yeatsian: Things fall apart.

Human population growth will make a bad situation worse by putting ever more pressure on all available land.

Population growth rates have declined in many countries within the past several decades, it's true. But world population is still increasing, and even if average fertility suddenly, magically, dropped to 2.0 children per female, population would continue to increase (on the momentum of birth rate exceeding death rate among a generally younger and healthier populace) for some time. The annual increase is now 80 million people, with most of that increment coming in less-developed countries. The latest long-range projections from the Population Division of the United Nations, released earlier this year, are slightly down from previous long-term projections in 1992 but still point toward a problematic future. According to the U.N.'s middle estimate (and most probable? hard to know) among seven fertility scenarios, human population will rise from the present 5.9 billion to 9.4 billion by the year 2050, then to 10.8 billion by 2150, before leveling off there at the end of the twenty-second century. If it happens that way, about 9.7 billion people will inhabit the countries included within Africa, Latin America, the Caribbean, and Asia. The total population of those countries—most of

THE LESSON TO BE LEARNED FROM FRAGMENTED, ISOLATED HABITATS IS YEATSIAN: THINGS FALL APART

WE CONFRONT THE VISION OF A HUMAN POPULATION PRESSING SNUGLY AROUND WHATEVER NATURAL LANDSCAPE REMAINS

which are in the low latitudes, many of which are less developed, and which together encompass a large portion of Earth's remaining tropical forest—will be more than twice what it is today. Those 9.7 billion people, crowded together in hot places, forming the ocean within which tropical nature reserves are insularized, will constitute 90 percent of humanity. Anyone interested in the future of biological diversity needs to think about the pressures these people will face, and the pressures they will exert in return.

We also need to remember that the impact of *Homo sapiens* on the biosphere can't be measured simply in population figures. As the population expert Paul Harrison pointed out in his book *The Third Revolution,* that impact is a product of three variables: population size, consumption level, and technology. Although population growth is highest in less-developed countries, consumption levels are generally far higher in the developed world (for instance, the average American consumes about ten times as much energy as the average Chilean, and about a hundred times as much as the average Angolan), and also higher among the affluent minority in any country than among the rural poor. High consumption exacerbates the impact of a given population, whereas technological developments may either exacerbate it further (think of the automobile, the air conditioner, the chainsaw) or mitigate it (as when a technological innovation improves efficiency for an established function). All three variables play a role in every case, but a directional change in one form of human impact—upon air pollution from fossil-fuel burning, say, or fish harvest from the seas—can be mainly attributable to a change in one variable, with only minor influence from the other two. Sulfur-dioxide emissions in developed countries fell dramatically during the 1970s and '80s, due to technological improvements in papermaking and other industrial processes; those emissions would have fallen still farther if not for increased population (accounting for 25 percent of the upward vector) and increased consumption (accounting for 75 percent). Deforestation, in contrast, is a directional

change that *has* been mostly attributable to population growth.

According to Harrison's calculations, population growth accounted for 79 percent of the deforestation in less-developed countries between 1973 and 1988. Some experts would argue with those calculations, no doubt, and insist on redirecting our concern toward the role that distant consumers, wood-products buyers among slow-growing but affluent populations of the developed nations, play in driving the destruction of Borneo's dipterocarp forests or the hardwoods of West Africa. Still, Harrison's figures point toward an undeniable reality; more total people will need more total land. By his estimate, the minimum land necessary for food growing and other human needs (such as water supply and waste dumping) amounts to one fifth of a hectare per person. Given the U.N.'s projected increase of 4.9 billion souls before the human population finally levels off, that comes to another billion hectares of human-claimed landscape, a billion hectares less forest—even without allowing for any further deforestation by the current human population, or for any further loss of agricultural land to degradation. A billion hectares—in other words, 10 million square kilometers—is, by a conservative estimate, well more than half the remaining forest area in Africa, Latin America, and Asia. This raises the vision of a very exigent human population pressing snugly around whatever patches of natural landscape remain.

Add to that vision the extra, incendiary aggravation of poverty. According to a recent World Bank estimate, about 30 percent of the total population of less-developed countries lives in poverty. Alan Durning, in his 1992 book *How Much Is Enough? The Consumer Society and the Fate of the Earth,* puts it in a broader perspective when he says that the world's human population is divided among three "ecological classes": the consumers, the middle-income, and the poor. His consumer class includes those 1.1 billion fortunate people whose annual income per family member is more than $7,500. At the other extreme, the world's poor also number about 1.1 billion people—all from households with less than $700 annually per member. "They are mostly rural Africans, Indians, and other South Asians," Durning writes. "They eat almost exclusively grains, root crops, beans, and other legumes, and they drink mostly unclean water. They live in huts and shanties, they travel by foot, and most of their possessions are constructed of stone, wood, and other substances available from the local environment." He calls them the "absolute poor." It's only reasonable to assume that another billion people will be added to that class, mostly in what are now the less-developed countries, before population growth stabilizes. How will those additional billion, deprived of education and other advantages, interact with the tropical

landscape? Not likely by entering information-intensive jobs in the service sector of the new global economy. Julian Simon argued that human ingenuity—and by extension, human population itself—is "the ultimate resource" for solving Earth's problems, transcending Earth's limits, and turning scarcity into abundance. But if all the bright ideas generated by a human population of 5.9 billion haven't yet relieved the desperate needfulness of 1.1 billion absolute poor, why should we expect that human ingenuity will do any better for roughly 2 billion poor in the future?

Other writers besides Durning have warned about this deepening class rift. Tom Athanasiou, in *Divided Planet: The Ecology of Rich and Poor,* sees population growth only exacerbating the division, and notes that governments often promote destructive schemes of transmigration and rain-forest colonization as safety valves for the pressures of land hunger and discontent. A young Canadian policy analyst named Thomas F. Homer-Dixon, author of several calm-voiced but frightening articles on the linkage between what he terms "environmental scarcity" and global sociopolitical instability, reports that the amount of cropland available per person is falling in the less-developed countries because of population growth and because millions of hectares "are being lost each year to a combination of problems, including encroachment by cities, erosion, depletion of nutrients, acidification, compacting and salinization and waterlogging from overirrigation." In the cropland pinch and other forms of environmental scarcity, Homer-Dixon foresees potential for "a widening gap" of two sorts—between demands on the state and its ability to deliver, and more basically between rich and poor. In conversation with the journalist Robert D. Kaplan, as quoted in Kaplan's book *The Ends of the Earth,* Homer-Dixon said it more vividly: "Think of a stretch limo in the potholed streets of New York City, where homeless beggars live. Inside the limo are the air-conditioned post-industrial regions of North America, Europe, the emerging Pacific Rim, and a few other isolated places, with their trade summitry and computer information highways. Outside is the rest of mankind, going in a completely different direction."

EVEN NOAH'S ARK ONLY MANAGED TO RESCUE PAIRED ANIMALS, NOT LARGE PARCELS OF HABITAT

MAN'S ACCIDENTAL RELOCATION OF CERTAIN SPECIES HAS LONG CREATED PROFOUND DISLOCATIONS IN NATURE

That direction, necessarily, will be toward ever more desperate exploitation of landscape. When you think of Homer-Dixon's stretch limo on those potholed urban streets, don't assume there will be room inside for tropical forests. Even Noah's ark only managed to rescue paired animals, not large parcels of habitat. The jeopardy of the ecological fragments that we presently cherish as parks, refuges, and reserves is already severe, due to both internal and external forces: internal, because insularity itself leads to ecological unraveling; and external, because those areas are still under siege by needy and covetous people. Projected forward into a future of 10.8 billion humans, of which perhaps 2 billion are starving at the periphery of those areas, while another 2 billion are living in a fool's paradise maintained by unremitting exploitation of whatever resources remain, that jeopardy increases to the point of impossibility. In addition, any form of climate change in the mid-term future, whether caused by greenhouse gases or by a natural flip-flop of climatic forces, is liable to change habitat conditions within a given protected area beyond the tolerance range for many species. If such creatures can't migrate beyond the park or reserve boundaries in order to chase their habitat needs, they may be "protected" from guns and chainsaws within their little island, but they'll still die.

We shouldn't take comfort in assuming that at least Yellowstone National Park will still harbor grizzly bears in the year 2150, that at least Royal Chitwan in Nepal will still harbor tigers, that at least Serengeti in Tanzania and Gir in India will still harbor lions. Those predator populations, and other species down the cascade, are likely to disappear. "Wildness" will be a word applicable only to urban turmoil. Lions, tigers, and bears will exist in zoos, period. Nature won't come to an end, but it will look very different.

The most obvious differences will be those I've already mentioned: tropical forests and other terrestrial ecosystems will be drastically reduced in area, and the fragmented remnants will stand tiny and isolated. Because of those two factors, plus the cascading secondary effects, plus an additional dire factor I'll mention in a moment, much of Earth's biological diversity will be gone. How much? That's impossible to predict confidently, but the careful guesses of Robert May, Stuart Pimm, and other biologists suggest losses reaching half to two thirds of all species. In the oceans, deepwater fish and shellfish populations will be drastically depleted by overharvesting, if not to the point of extinction then at least enough to cause more cascading consequences. Coral reefs and other shallow-water ecosystems will be badly stressed, if not devastated, by erosion and chemical runoff from the land. The additional dire factor is invasive species, fifth of the five factors contributing to our current experiment in mass extinction.

That factor, even more than habitat destruction and fragmentation, is a symptom of modernity. Maybe you haven't heard much about invasive species, but in coming years you will. The ecologist Daniel Simberloff takes it so seriously that he recently committed himself to founding an institute on invasive biology at the University of Tennessee, and Interior Secretary Bruce Babbitt sounded the alarm last April in a speech to a weed-management symposium in Denver. The spectacle of a cabinet secretary denouncing an alien plant called purple loosestrife struck some observers as droll, but it wasn't as silly as it seemed. Forty years ago, the British ecologist Charles Elton warned prophetically in a little book titled *The Ecology of Invasions by Animals and Plants* that "we are living in a period of the world's history when the mingling of thousands of kinds of organisms from different parts of the world is setting up terrific dislocations in nature." Elton's word "dislocations" was nicely chosen to ring with a double meaning: species are being moved from one location to another, and as a result ecosystems are being thrown into disorder.

The problem dates back to when people began using ingenious new modes of conveyance (the horse, the camel, the canoe) to travel quickly across mountains, deserts, and oceans, bringing with them rats, lice, disease microbes, burrs, dogs, pigs, goats, cats, cows, and other forms of parasitic, commensal, or domesticated creature. One immediate result of those travels was a wave of island-bird extinctions, claiming more than a thousand species, that followed oceangoing canoes across the Pacific and elsewhere. Having evolved in insular ecosystems free of predators, many of those species were flightless, unequipped to defend themselves or their eggs against ravenous mammals. *Raphus cucullatus,* a giant cousin of the pigeon lineage, endemic to Mauritius in the Indian Ocean and better known as the dodo, was only the most easily caricatured representative of this much larger pattern. Dutch sailors killed and ate dodos during the seventeenth century, but probably what guaranteed the extinction of *Raphus cucullatus* is that the European ships put ashore rats, pigs, and *Macaca fascicularis,* an opportunistic species of Asian monkey. Although commonly known as the crab-eating macaque, *M. fascicularis* will eat almost anything. The monkeys are still pestilential on Mauritius, hungry and daring and always ready to grab what they can, including raw eggs. But the dodo hasn't been seen since 1662.

The European age of discovery and conquest was also the great age of biogeography—that is, the study of what creatures live where, a branch of biology practiced by attentive travelers such as Carolus Linnaeus, Alexander von Humboldt, Charles Darwin, and Alfred Russel Wallace. Darwin and Wallace even made biogeography the basis of their discovery that species, rather than being created and plopped onto Earth by divine magic, evolve in particular locales by the process of natural selection. Ironically, the same trend of far-flung human travel that gave biogeographers their data also began to muddle and nullify those data, by transplanting the most ready and roguish species to new places and thereby delivering misery unto death for many other species. Rats and cats went everywhere, causing havoc in what for millions of years had been sheltered, less competitive ecosystems. The Asiatic chestnut blight and the European starling came to America; the American muskrat and the Chinese mitten crab got to Europe. Sometimes these human-mediated transfers were unintentional, sometimes merely shortsighted. Nostalgic sportsmen in New Zealand imported British red deer; European brown trout and Coastal rainbows were planted in disregard of the native cutthroats of Rocky Mountain rivers. Prickly-pear cactus, rabbits, and cane toads were inadvisedly welcomed to Australia. Goats went wild in the Galapagos. The bacterium that causes bubonic plague journeyed from China to California by way of a flea, a rat, and a ship. The Atlantic sea lamprey found its own way up into Lake Erie, but only after the Welland Canal gave it a bypass around Niagara Falls. Un-

THE SPECIES THAT SURVIVE WILL BE LIKE WEEDS, REPRODUCING QUICKLY AND SURVIVING ALMOST ANYWHERE

WILDLIFE WILL CONSIST OF PIGEONS, COYOTES, RATS, ROACHES, HOUSE SPARROWS, CROWS, AND FERAL DOGS

intentional or otherwise, all these transfers had unforeseen consequences, which in many cases included the extinction of less competitive, less opportunistic native species. The rosy wolfsnail, a small creature introduced onto Oahu for the purpose of controlling a larger and more obviously noxious species of snail, which was itself invasive, proved to be medicine worse than the disease; it became a fearsome predator upon native snails, of which twenty species are now gone. The Nile perch, a big predatory fish introduced into Lake Victoria in 1962 because it promised good eating, seems to have exterminated at least eighty species of smaller cichlid fishes that were native to the lake's Mwanza Gulf.

The problem is vastly amplified by modern shipping and air transport, which are quick and capacious enough to allow many more kinds of organisms to get themselves transplanted into zones of habitat they never could have reached on their own. The brown tree snake, having hitchhiked aboard military planes from the New Guinea region near the end of World War II, has eaten most of the native forest birds of Guam. Hanta virus, first identified in Korea, burbles quietly in the deer mice of Arizona. Ebola will next appear who knows where. Apart from the frightening epidemiological possibilities, agricultural damages are the most conspicuous form of impact. One study, by the congressional Office of Technology Assessment, reports that in the United States 4,500 nonnative species have established free-living populations, of which about 15 percent cause severe harm; looking at just 79 of those species, the OTA documented $97 billion in damages. The lost value in Hawaiian snail species or cichlid diversity is harder to measure. But another report, from the U.N. Environmental Program, declares that almost 20 percent of the world's endangered vertebrates suffer from pressures (competition, predation, habitat transformation) created by exotic interlopers. Michael Soulé, a biologist much respected for his work on landscape conversion and extinction, has said that invasive species may soon surpass habitat loss and fragmentation as the major cause of

"ecological disintegration." Having exterminated Guam's avifauna, the brown tree snake has lately been spotted in Hawaii.

Is there a larger pattern to these invasions? What do fire ants, zebra mussels, Asian gypsy mothers, tamarisk trees, maleleuca trees, kudzu, Mediterranean fruit flies, boll weevils, and water hyacinths have in common with crab-eating macaques or Nile perch? Answers: They're *weedy* species, in the sense that animals as well as plants can be weedy. What that implies is a constellation of characteristics: They reproduce quickly, disperse widely when given a chance, tolerate a fairly broad range of habitat conditions, take hold in strange places, succeed especially in disturbed ecosystems, and resist eradication once they're established. They are scrappers, generalists, opportunists. They tend to thrive in human-dominated terrain because in crucial ways they resemble *Homo sapiens:* aggressive, versatile, prolific, and ready to travel. The city pigeon, a cosmopolitan creature derived from wild ancestry as a Eurasian rock dove (*Columba livia*) by way of centuries of pigeon fanciers whose coop-bred birds occasionally went AWOL, is a weed. So are those species that, benefiting from human impacts upon landscape, have increased grossly in abundance or expanded their geographical scope without having to cross an ocean by plane or by boat—for instance, the coyote in New York, the raccoon in Montana, the while-tailed deer in northern Wisconsin or western Connecticut. The brown-headed cowbird, also weedy, has enlarged its range from the Eastern United States into the agricultural Midwest at the expense of migratory songbirds. In gardening usage the word "weed" may be utterly subjective, indicating any plant you don't happen to like, but in ecological usage it has these firmer meanings. Biologists frequently talk of weedy species, meaning animals as well as plants.

Paleontologists, too, embrace the idea and even the term. Jablonski himself, in a 1991 paper published in *Science,* extrapolated from past mass extinctions to our current one and suggested that human activities are likely to take their heaviest toll on narrowly endemic species, while causing fewer extinctions among those species that are broadly adapted and broadly distributed. "In the face of ongoing habitat alteration and fragmentation," he wrote, "this implies a biota increasingly enriched in widespread, weedy species—rats, ragweed, and cockroaches—relative to the large number of species that are more vulnerable and potentially more useful to humans as food, medicines, and genetic resources." Now, as we sit in his office, he repeats: "It's just a question of how much the world becomes enriched in these weedy species." Both in print and in talk he uses "enriched" somewhat caustically, knowing that the actual direction of the trend is toward impoverishment.

Regarding impoverishment, let's note another dark, interesting irony: that the two converse trends I've described—partitioning the world's landscape by habitat fragmentation, and unifying the world's landscape by global transport for weedy species—produce not converse results but one redoubled result, the further loss of biological diversity. Immersing myself in the literature of extinctions, and making dilettantish excursions across India, Madagascar, New Guinea, Indonesia, Brazil, Guam, Australia, New Zealand, Wyoming, the hills of Burbank, and other semi-wild places over the past decade, I've seen those redoubling trends everywhere, portending a near-term future in which Earth's landscape is threadbare, leached of diversity, heavy with humans, and "enriched" in weedy species. That's an ugly vision, but I find it vivid. Wildlife will consist of the pigeons and the coyotes and the white-tails, the black rats (*Rattus rattus*) and the brown rats (*Rattus norvegicus*) and a few other species of worldly rodent, the crab-eating macaques and the cockroaches (though, as with the rats, not *every* species—some are narrowly endemic, like the giant Madagascar hissing cockroach) and the mongooses, the house sparrows and the house geckos and the houseflies and the barn cats and the skinny brown feral dogs and a short list of additional species that play by our rules. Forests will be tiny insular patches existing on bare sufferance, much of their biological diversity (the big predators, the migratory birds, the shy creatures that can't tolerate edges, and many other species linked inextricably with those) long since decayed away. They'll essentially be tall woody gardens, not forests in the richer sense. Elsewhere the landscape will have its strips and swatches of green, but except on much-poisoned lawns and golf courses the foliage will be infested with cheat-grass and European buckthorn and spotted knapweed and Russian thistle and leafy spurge and salt meadow cordgrass and Bruce Babbitt's purple loosestrife. Having recently passed the great age of biogeography, we will have entered the age *after* biogeography, in that virtually everything will live virtually everywhere, though the list of species that constitute "everything" will be small. I see this world

HOMO SAPIENS— REMARKABLY WIDESPREAD, PROLIFIC, AND ADAPTABLE—IS THE CONSUMMATE WEED

implicitly foretold in the U.N. population projections, the FAO reports on deforestation, the northward advance into Texas of Africanized honeybees, the rhesus monkeys that haunt the parapets of public buildings in New Delhi, and every fat gray squirrel on a bird feeder in England. Earth will be a different sort of place—soon, in just five or six human generations. My label for that place, that time, that apparently unavoidable prospect, is the Planet of Weeds. Its main consoling felicity, as far as I can imagine, is that there will be no shortage of crows.

Now we come to the question of human survival, a matter of some interest to many. We come to a certain fretful leap of logic that otherwise thoughtful observers seem willing, even eager, to make: that the ultimate consequence will be the extinction of us. By seizing such a huge share of Earth's landscape, by imposing so wantonly on its providence and presuming so recklessly on its forgiveness, by killing off so many species, they say, we will doom our own species to extinction. My quibbles with the idea are that it seems ecologically improbable and too optimistic. But it bears examining, because it's frequently offered as the ultimate argument against proceeding as we are.

Jablonski also has his doubts. Do you see *Homo sapiens* as a likely survivor, I ask him, or as a casualty? "Oh, we've got to be one of the most bomb-proof species on the planet," he says "We're geographically widespread, we have a pretty remarkable reproductive rate, we're incredibly good at co-opting and monopolizing resources. I think it would take really serious, concerted effort to wipe out the human species." The point he's making is one that has probably already dawned on you: *Homo sapiens* itself is the consummate weed. Why shouldn't we survive, then, on the Planet of Weeds? But there's a wide range of possible circumstances, Jablonski reminds me, between the extinction of our species and the continued growth of human population, consumptions, and comfort. "I think we'll be one of the survivors," he says, "sort of picking through the rubble." Besides losing all the pharmaceutical and generic resources that lay hidden within those extinguished species, and all the spiritual and aesthetic values they offered, he foresees unpredictable levels of loss in many physical and biochemical functions that ordinarily come as benefits from diverse, robust ecosystems—functions such as cleaning and recirculating air and water, mitigating droughts and floods, decomposing wastes, controlling erosion, creating new soil, pollinating crops, capturing and transporting nutrients, damping short-term temperature extremes and longer-term fluctuations of climate, restraining outbreaks of pestiferous species, and shielding Earth's

WHAT WILL HAPPEN AFTER THIS MASS EXTINCTION, AFTER WE DESTROY TWO THIRDS OF ALL LIVING SPECIES?

surface from the full brunt of ultraviolet radiation. Strip away the ecosystems that perform those services, Jablonski says, and you can expect grievous detriment to the reality we inhabit. "A lot of things are going to happen that will make this a crummier place to live—a more stressful place to live, a more difficult place to live, a less resilient place to live—before the human species is at any risk at all." And maybe some of the new difficulties, he adds, will serve as incentive for major changes in the trajectory along which we pursue our aggregate self-interests. Maybe we'll pull back before our current episode matches the Triassic extinction or the K-T event. Maybe it will turn out to be no worse than the Eocene extinction, with a 35 percent loss of species.

"Are you hopeful?" I ask.

Given that hope is a duty from which paleontologists are exempt, I'm surprised when he answers, "Yes, I am."

I'm not. My own guess about the mid-term future, excused by no exemption, is that our Planet of Weeds will indeed be a crummier place, a lonelier and uglier place, and a particularly wretched place for the 2 billion people comprising Alan Durning's absolute poor. What will increase most dramatically as time proceeds, I suspect won't be generalized misery or futuristic modes of consumption but the gulf between two global classes experiencing those extremes. Progressive failure of ecosystem functions? Yes, but human resourcefulness of the sort Julian Simon so admired will probably find stopgap technological remedies, to be available for a price. So the world's privileged class—that's your class and my class—will probably still manage to maintain themselves inside Homer-Dixon's stretch limo, drinking bottled water and breathing bottled air and eating reasonably healthy food that has become incredibly precious, while the potholes on the road outside grow ever deeper. Eventually the limo will look more like a lunar rover. Ragtag mobs of desperate souls will cling to its bumpers, like groupies on Elvis's final Cadillac. The absolute poor will suffer

their lack of ecological privilege in the form of lowered life expectancy, bad health, absence of education, corrosive want, and anger. Maybe in time they'll find ways to gather themselves in localized revolt against the affluent class. Not likely, though, as long as affluence buys guns. In any case, well before that they will have burned the last stick of Bornean dipterocarp for firewood and roasted the last lemur, the last grizzly bear, the last elephant left unprotected outside a zoo.

Jablonski has a hundred things to do before leaving for Alaska, so after two hours I clear out. The heat on the sidewalk is fierce, though not nearly as fierce as this summer's heat in New Delhi or Dallas, where people are dying. Since my flight doesn't leave until early evening, I cab downtown and take refuge in a nouveau-Cajun restaurant near the river. Over a beer and jambalaya, I glance again at Jablonski's 1991 *Science* paper, titled "Extinctions: A Paleontological Perspective." I also play back the tape of our conversation, pressing my ear against the little recorder to hear it over the lunch-crowd noise.

Among the last questions I asked Jablonski was, What will happen *after* this mass extinction, assuming it proceeds to a worst-case scenario? If we destroy half or two thirds of all living species, how long will it take for evolution to fill the planet back up? "I don't know the answer to that," he said. "I'd rather not bottom out and see what happens next." In the journal paper he had hazarded that, based on fossil evidence in rock laid down atop the K-T event and others, the time required for full recovery might be 5 or 10 million years. From a paleontological perspective, that's fast. "Biotic recoveries after mass extinctions are geologically rapid but immensely prolonged on human time scales," he wrote. There was also the proviso, cited from another expert, that recovery might not begin until *after* the extinction-causing circumstances have disappeared. But in this case, of course, the circumstances won't likely disappear until *we* do.

Still, evolution never rests. It's happening right now, in weed patches all over the planet. I'm not presuming to alert you to the end of the world, the end of evolution, or the end of nature. What I've tried to describe here is not an absolute end but a very deep dip, a repeat point within a long, violent cycle. Species die, species arise. The relative pace of those two processes is what matters. Even rats and cockroaches are capable—given the requisite conditions, namely, habitat diversity and time—of speciation. And speciation brings new diversity. So we might reasonably imagine an Earth upon which, 10 million years after the extinction (or, alternatively, the drastic transformation) of *Homo sapiens,* wondrous forests are again filled with wondrous beasts. That's the good news.

Old Growth for Sale

Five years ago, environmentalists pinned their hopes of saving old-growth forests on the Northwest Forest Plan. Today they're in an uproar because thousands of trees, some as old as 400 years, continue to be logged.

By Douglas Gantenbein

KEMP HYATT, a pilot for the Lighthawk "environmental air force," which exposes abuses on public lands, sharply banks the twin-engine Britten-Norman Islander. Some 1,000 feet below, a fresh coat of late-February snow highlights a gash as big as a football field in the canopy of Washington's Gifford Pinchot National Forest. Eight Douglas fir trees are all that remain of the old-growth forest that grew there until last year, most of its trees at least 150 years old. "The Forest Service says, 'Oh, we're not doing clearcuts anymore,'" says David Jennings, conservation cochair of Washington's Black Hills Audubon Society, who is aboard the plane. "But to us this seems like the same old thing."

In February, 21 local and national environmental groups joined forces to sound the alarm about recent sales of timber on federal lands. The ForestWater Alliance—a coalition of groups in Oregon, Washington, and California (including several chapters of the National Audubon Society)—issued a scathing 15-page report stating that "the federal agencies charged with protecting the public's national forests continue to clear-cut the Northwest's ancient forests at an alarming rate."

This isn't what anyone had in mind. In 1993, with great fanfare, President Bill Clinton flew to Portland, Oregon, for a "timber summit," which produced the much-touted

---

Doug Gantenbein is the Northwest correspondent for The Economist, *for which he has written about northwestern forests and political and regional issues since 1987.*

Northwest Forest Plan. It aimed to bring a new day to forestry practices, slashing logging levels by 85 percent on 24.5 million acres of national forest. The forests would be managed less for timber than for wildlife, fish, and recreation.

Yet the gap between the plan's goals and reality has widened since its inception. The ForestWater Alliance accuses the Forest Service of exploiting loopholes in the plan and even rewriting portions of it to allow extensive logging of the nation's last 5 percent of old-growth forests, many of which are in important watersheds and/or roadless areas and provide critical wildlife habitat. "There's lots of discretion in the forest plan," says Bonnie Phillips, coordinator of the ForestWater Alliance. "And the abuse of that discretion is enormous."

> **Douglas firs, which are among the world's oldest trees, can reach 330 feet in height and 16 feet in diameter.**

To prove that the Forest Service—and to a lesser extent the Bureau of Land Management (BLM)—is violating both the spirit and the letter of the forest plan, in 1997 the alliance's members took a "snapshot" of logging activity on land managed by the two agencies. They visited scores of national-forest and BLM offices to examine the agencies' own numbers.

They found that during 1997 the Forest Service and the Bureau of Land Management had sold timber from 22,496 acres of old-growth forest and from more than 10,000 acres of forests that border either critical salmon habitat or city water supplies. The timber that has been sold will be cut within three years of the sale. Among the most egregious cases:

- The Skeeter timber sale in the Gifford Pinchot forest—200 acres, including 400-year-old trees, that are home to many threatened species, including spotted owls, bald eagles, northern goshawks, peregrine falcons, and gray wolves.

- The Little River sale in Oregon's Umpqua National Forest—160 acres of centuries-old trees along several

streams. In some places there will be no streamside buffers left.

- The Beegum Corral-Regan timber sale in California's Shasta-Trinity National Forest—880 acres of trees as old as 300 years. Less-valuable, 80-year-old trees will be spared.

Not surprisingly, the report has drawn a sharp reaction from Forest Service and BLM administrators. They maintain that the Northwest Forest Plan's objective is to slow, not stop, logging and that they are safeguarding watersheds, and other natural resources. They also insist that they have launched the most aggressive, far-reaching effort to revamp forest practices since the national forests were established more than a century ago. "The change is comparable to when we went from cut-and-run [before private timber companies were regulated] to sustainable forestry at the turn of the century," says Tom Tuchmann, who helped organize the 1993 summit and helped implement the plan. He calls it "the only ecosystem plan of its size that has made the tough decisions by taking land out of timber production."

Environmentalists were not completely satisfied with the Northwest Forest Plan back in 1993. They objected to the continued logging of old growth and to restrictions on legal challenges. Still, they agreed to give the plan a try. "Most of us decided that the Northwest Forest Plan was all we had," recalls Phillips, a member of the Pilchuck Audubon Society and a major figure in the spotted owl wars of the early 1990s. "We were going to try to make it work—and hold the Forest Service accountable to it."

But the plan began to crumble in 1995, with the passage of the "salvage rider" by Congress. That legislation, which expired at the end of 1996, was part of a wider budget-cutting package that suspended all environmental laws as they pertained to salvage logging. The rider permitted more than just the cutting of dead or dying trees. It allowed the logging of "associated trees," those considered in imminent danger of mortality or infection—thus opening to the chainsaw vast tracts of healthy forest, some of which had been declared off-limits by the forest plan. The rider infuriated environmentalists, some of whom engaged in civil disobedience by blocking access to logging sites and tying themselves to trees. As part of their long-term political strategy, some environmentalists formed the ForestWater Alliance.

Phillips says a backlash to the forest plan was inevitable. But the rider "made us realize that the protections we thought we had could be taken away just like that," she says. "And with or without the rider, the Forest Service is simply not

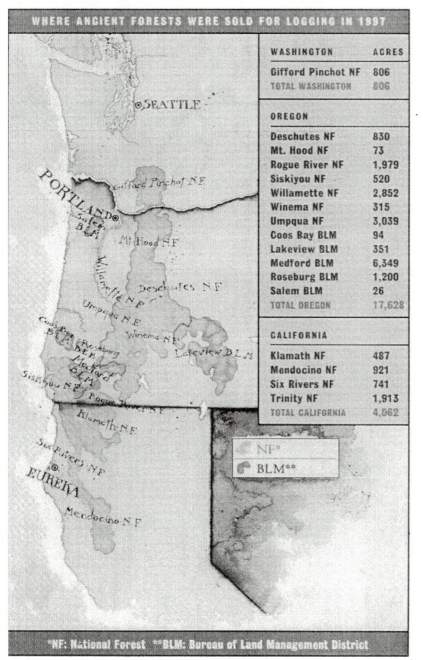

WHERE ANCIENT FORESTS WERE SOLD FOR LOGGING IN 1997	
WASHINGTON	**ACRES**
Gifford Pinchot NF	806
TOTAL WASHINGTON	806
OREGON	
Deschutes NF	830
Mt. Hood NF	73
Rogue River NF	1,979
Siskiyou NF	520
Willamette NF	2,852
Winema NF	315
Umpqua NF	3,039
Coos Bay BLM	94
Lakeview BLM	351
Medford BLM	6,349
Roseburg BLM	1,200
Salem BLM	26
TOTAL OREGON	17,628
CALIFORNIA	
Klamath NF	487
Mendocino NF	921
Six Rivers NF	741
Trinity NF	1,913
TOTAL CALIFORNIA	4,062

*NF: National Forest **BLM: Bureau of Land Management District

> "Our goal was to come up with a sound, scientific plan for managing Northwest forests, and I think we succeeded."

implementing the plan properly." She cites practices such as "near clearcuts," which leave a few trees standing instead of taking every one. The goal is to provide more nesting habitat for birds and more variation in canopy height as trees mature. But as Phillips says, such techniques compact soil, dump sediment into streams, and disturb wildlife habitat. Furthermore, Phillips says, the plan's annual goal of 1.1 billion board feet of timber has become increasingly unrealistic as new inventories of woodlands have shown just how few big trees are still left. "The law does not require the Forest Service to cut that much," she says, "but it does require it to follow practices that don't damage the forests."

Forest Service officials don't dispute the precise numbers in the alliance report, but they take exception to its conclusions. They say the timber sales have all conformed to the plan's strict guidelines for logging—except for those governed by the salvage rider. "Our goal was to come up with a sound, scientific plan for managing Northwest forests, and I think we succeeded," says James Lyons, the undersecretary of agriculture who oversees the Forest Service. "The plan was never intended to completely halt logging of old-growth trees."

Tom Tuchmann, who is now the agriculture department's western director, faults the ForestWater Alliance for exaggerating the effects of logging. For example, the report claims that a sale in Oregon's Willamette National Forest will cause erosion, threatening water supplies in the nearby city of Salem. But Tuchmann says, "We put together an interdisciplinary team, including the Environmental Protection Agency, to take a look at that sale. They gave it a clean bill of health."

Jerry Franklin, a noted forestry professor at the University of Washington and a scientist whose work influenced the plan, believes the Forest Service deserves credit for its transition from timber production to the protection of wildlife and other natural resources. "There really has been a big change in the approach people in the Forest Service are taking to the forest," he says. "The people managing the Northwest forests are determined to make this approach work."

No matter how earnest their reform efforts, however, Forest Service administrators must answer to the powerful politicians who wrote the salvage rider and who have the final say in the agency's funding. Just days before Lyons talked with *Audubon,* the Forest Service had received a letter from Senator Frank Murkowski (R-AK) and other prologging members of Congress threatening to slash the agency's budget unless logging levels increased. That's "the old timber agenda," Lyons shoots back. "We've turned a corner in the Forest Service. Now is the time when our expertise should be used to restore watersheds and restore forest health."

Ultimately, many environmentalists want to slash logging levels even further than stipulated in the Northwest Forest Plan. In fact, a measure now pending in the House of Representatives would ban logging on all federal lands. It has 14 cosponsors, including the influential chair of the Banking Committee, Jim Leach (R-IA). But it's so controversial that it may take years for it to pass. Environmentalists also hope to pressure the Clinton administration to ban road building in the Pacific Northwest. But in February, when the administration announced the suspension of road building on 33 million acres of federal land, the politically contentious region was exempted.

The Lighthawk craft hovers over the Limbo area of the Gifford Pinchot, site of a proposed timber sale. Hundreds of acres of old growth and maturing forest straddle a rugged ridge. The Limbo, a largely roadless area that drains into several key salmon streams is typical of the tracts that members of the ForestWater Alliance believe should be saved. "It's sad to be here in 1998," says Jennings, looking at the trees below, "still fighting over the scraps of mature forest we have left."

ALIEN INVASION

They are quiet, patient, deadly, and insatiable. Alien weeds are stealing our land and killing our native plants.　**BY STEVE MIRSKY**

THEY'RE OUT THERE. They have traveled far to do their damage. Some are quite beautiful, which only adds to their threat. Preposterous though it may be to think of plants as a pestilence, several hundred species truly are. These interlopers have already swept through millions of acres across the United States. Fortunately, we're fighting back.

Often simply called weeds, invasive plants are destructive species alien to an area. Aliens serve as staples of science fiction, and one movie's vegetative invading force comes to mind when thinking of true alien plants: the plant-people of *Invasion of the Body Snatchers,* who grow in pods and wipe out the human population. In the real-life incursion now under way, the invaders snatch land. Finally free of whatever ate them back in the old country, these killer plants reduce biodiversity, destroy wet-

---

Steve Mirsky has written numerous articles for such magazines as *Wildlife Conservation* and *National Wildlife.* He is also a contributing editor at *Scientific American,* where he pens the Anti Gravity column, a look at the lighter side of science.

All illustrations by Jason Holley

lands and streams, and decrease forage for animals. In other words, they're bad.

Historically, alien plants have invaded in various and devious ways. Some showed up in grain shipments or ship ballast. Others were purposefully brought here to prettify lawns or to control erosion. Between 3,500 and 4,000 species have made themselves at home; of these, at least 400 are considered truly dangerous. In fact, alien plants threaten two-thirds of all endangered native plants. Animals that depend on specific plants for food and shelter suffer, too. Last year the extent of the damage led Secretary of the Interior Bruce Babbitt to call the spread "an explosion in slow motion." He summed up the problem thus: "The invasion of noxious alien species wreaks a level of havoc on America's environment and economy that is matched only by the damage caused by floods, earthquakes, mud slides, hurricanes, and wildfire."

Randy "Weeds Have Been My Life For 20 Years" Westbrooks, the invasive-plant specialist who serves as a liaison between the U.S. departments of Agriculture and the Interior, believes that "about 5 percent of the 700 million acres of public land are seriously infested." In 1985 the Bureau of Land Management (BLM) did a survey of public lands in western states and found aliens on about 2.5 million acres. In 1995 that amount had increased to 8 million acres.

Fortunately, some folks in Washington, D.C., occupied themselves with activities other than making Al Gore president before 2001. This past February President Clinton signed an executive order that commits the United States to fighting the scourge of invading species, both animals and plants. The order sets in motion federal efforts to intercept fresh troops of invaders at the border and to snuff out any infestations that are already here.

Visit the Alien Plant working Group's web site to learn more <.nps.gov/ plants/ alien>. Being aware of non-native species can make anyone an eco-hero: If you spot an outbreak, snip a cutting and call the cooperative-extension service of your county, the weed specialist of your state's department of agriculture, or Westbrooks (910–648–6762).

On the following pages are indepth looks at a few of the worst offenders among alien weeds. Think of them as MOST WANTED posters.

From *Audubon,* May/June 1999, pp. 71-77. © 1999 by Steve Mirsky. Reprinted by permission.

LEAFY SPURGE

aka: *Euphorbia esula*
Last seen: Primarily on ranches and farmlands in the northern Great Plains, but outbreaks are known in most regions of the continental United States.
Infiltration: Hitched a ride from Eurasia to Massachusetts with a seed delivery in about 1827.

IT'S THE WORST of the worst of wildland weeds," says Jerry Asher, the invasive-nonnative-plant outreach leader for the BLM. Leafy spurge crowds out forage grasses and pasture plants of rangelands. Cattle steer clear of land that is only 10 to 20 percent covered with leafy spurge; the stuff irritates their mouth, eyes, and digestive tract, an effect it has on many animals. And it kills property values. The owners of a 1,360-acre Oregon ranch that had become infested with spurge just up and walked away one day. Their land was auctioned in the 1980s for 17 percent of what it had been worth without the weed.

About three feet tall, leafy spurge keeps its true strength hidden: an extensive root system that gropes through the ground for 10 to 15 feet below the surface. "You can plow it, burn it, pull it," Asher laments, "and it just keeps sprouting."

This weed war is a never-ending fight. In 1986 employees at the Ashley National Forest, in Utah, spotted a 75-by 100-foot patch of leafy spurge, probably from seeds brought in accidentally by woodcutters. (See "Killer Weeds," Incite, March–April 1997). An herbicide has been battling the spurge scourge for the past 13 years; some plants are still growing. Herbicides, though anathema to many environmentalists, are the lesser of two evils when it comes to aliens: Herbicides don't multiply.

Another way to fight spurge is with biocontrol—insects that will eat the weed in question and nothing else. (Researchers look for an insect that feasts on the plant back home but has no taste for any other vegetation it might encounter here.) Some 13 insect species, notably a few root-eating beetles, have been let loose in the northern Great Plains and are happily munching away at the spurge. Goats and sheep also tolerate the weed. Their dining fails to wipe out a given infestation, but it helps stop the spread.

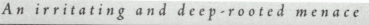

An irritating and deep-rooted menace

SALTCEDAR

aka: Tamarisk, including *Tamarix chinensis, T. parviflora, T. ramosissima*
Last seen: Most serious in the Southwest, but present elsewhere in the West.
Infiltration: Eight species, originating in Asia, were planted here in the early 1800s as windbreaks, for shade, and to control erosion.

BAD GUYS" sums up saltcedars, says John Randall, The Nature Conservancy's invasive-weed specialist. The weed's modus operandi is to take over areas near springs or streams and push out the native species, mostly willows and cottonwoods. Once established, it sucks up so much water it may leave the place high and dry. Water is life in the Southwest, and saltcedar trees swig some 5 million acre-feet of it every year. Some estimates have the plant using 10 to 20 times more water than the native species it displaces. "That's a major change," says Randall. "You go from an area with open water and mammals coming to drink to one where that's gone."

A small spring on the San Carlos Apache Indian Reservation, in Arizona, considered sacred waters, dried up after a tamarisk invasion. Environmentalists considered the water sacred too, accommodating as it did a population of the endangered Gila top-minnow. Other springs are drying up; an invasion in White Sands National Monument, in New Mexico, is threatening the White Sands pupfish.

Saltcedars are not content to merely steal land and water. They have their name for a reason: Like a ruthless army bent on destruction, these vicious invaders literally salt the earth. "Tamarisks accumulate a great deal of salt in their leaves," Asher points out. "Where they fall, there's a big accumulation of salt in the soil. Over not-too-many years, the soil isn't fit for native plants anymore."

Insects like the taste of saltcedar less than the natural vegetation, so they stay away. Fewer insects means less food for birds.

Burning, sawing, and "chaining" are the desperate measures for these desperate times. "You get two bulldozers with a chain between them," Randall explains, "and drive them parallel to one another. The chain snaps off the trunks. Pretty brutal." Ridding an area of saltcedar may free its hostage. "Frequently, when you remove tamarisks," Asher notes, "the water flows again."

A tree with a drinking problem

KUDZU

aka: *Pueraria montana var. lobata*
Last seen: Throughout the South, but also as far north as Massachusetts.
Infiltration: Displayed at the Philadelphia Centennial Exposition in 1876 by the Japanese. Americans subsequently raised it.

PERHAPS THE MOST familiar of the invading plants, kudzu is a southern staple, renowned for its incredible growth spurts. The vine can grow as much as a foot a day.

In the first part of this century, kudzu had a good reputation. Clubs like the 20,000-member Kudzu Club of America crowned "kudzu queens." The federal government paid farmers to grow the stuff. It was the "miracle vine" that could play the roles of ornamental, forage crop, and antierosion agent. "Kudzu cuttings were planted in the tens of millions," Randall explains. "But its roots don't bind the soil as well as a grass."

Those roots, however, are hearty enough to make it through the winter frosts that kill the visible parts of the vine. So kudzu explodes each spring. "It can engulf trees, abandoned homes, cars," Randall notes. "I've seen areas of 10 or more acres where the surface layer is only kudzu."

Kudzu patiently and relentlessly attacks forests. It grows over the first row or two of trees at the forest's edge; within a few years those trees die. "You can get a wave of faltering trees, and the kudzu is able to move in a little bit," says Randall. "Yesterday's inner layer of trees becomes tomorrow's edge."

Mowing and herbicides can help stop an invasion. Researchers are looking at root-eating insects in China and are investigating the deployment of a military force: armyworms. Really caterpillars, armyworms chow down on kudzu. The key to the plan is that the army must be sterile, so it disappears after it finishes off the kudzu but before it starts munching soybeans, another favorite.

Kudzu may have another surprise in store. All the known infestations came about vegetatively, through cuttings. The plants are basically all clones, having the same strengths and weaknesses. In the past year, however, Randall has heard of kudzu setting seed in North Carolina and Illinois. With seed comes the potential for genetic recombination—which could mean different kinds of kudzu, with different characteristics. "We may get types that are even worse," he warns.

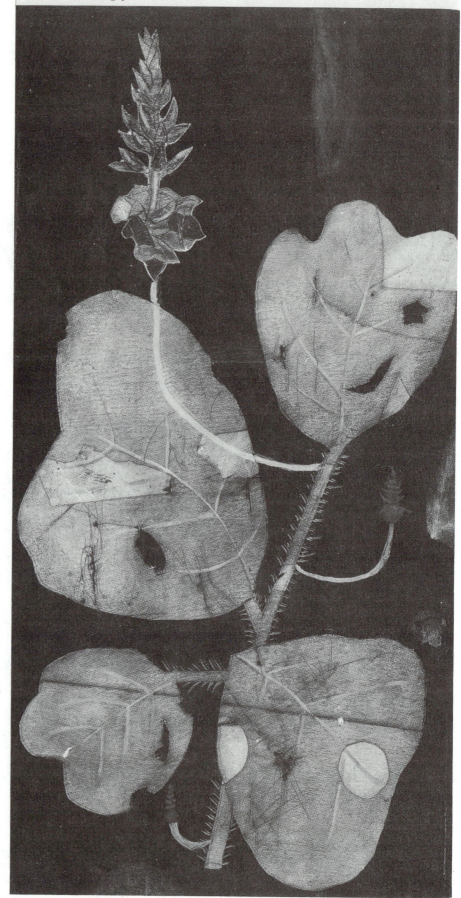

The creepy vine that ate the South

OLD WORLD CLIMBING FERN

aka: *Lygodium microphyllum*
Last seen: South Florida
Infiltration: Unclear—best bet is Africa or Asia. May have been introduced by Florida nurseries. First found in the wild in the 1950s.

Old World climbing fern hit the radar screens only recently. "But already we're terrified of what's happening in the wild," says Dan Austin, a biologist at Florida Atlantic University, in Boca Raton.

Since its discovery, the vine has galloped across the peninsula, making its way from east to west. "It is climbing over other plants in much the same way kudzu does," Austin explains. Although it has done its greatest damage so far by covering and killing trees such as cypresses, bays, and willows, perhaps its most frightening flaw is its ability to shade out sawgrass marshes. That nefarious bent gives the fern the potential to devastate the entire Everglades, in which sawgrass is a crucial species. In fact, it is already taking over the Arthur R. Marshall Loxahatchee National Wildlife Refuge, a northern remnant of the Everglades ecosystem.

As the weed continues to spread, so does anxiety. "We're rather markedly concerned about it," Austin understates.

Burning and pulling the feisty fern causes its spores to parachute into the air, spreading the pest once again. Herbicides can have some success; spot spraying of specific plants is the preferred means in the fragile Florida ecosystem. Nevertheless, when an infestation was found creeping toward the National Audubon Society's Corkscrew Swamp Sanctuary, the fear was great enough to warrant an aerial herbicide attack last January. "The patch was several acres," says Ed Carlson, Corkscrews manager, "and that made doing hand treatment impractical."

Bob Pemberton, an entomologist with the U.S. Department of Agriculture in Fort Lauderdale, is surveying foreign countries for insects in the hope of bringing them here for a big fern feast. As this issue of *Audubon* was going to press, a first-of-its-kind meeting was taking places in West Palm Beach to share the fragmented information dug up about the vine in the past few years. "If we don't work on it now," warns Carlson, "we could have a situation that's out of control."

A Florida fiend and Everglades enemy

PURPLE LOOSESTRIFE

aka: *Lythrum salicaria*
Last seen: Big problem in New England, near the Great Lakes, and in the mid-Atlantic states, but most states have some.
Infiltration: Stowaway in ship ballast from Europe in early 1800s. Later imported as an ornamental plant and medicinal herb.

PURPLE LOOSESTRIFE is true to its name: It lets loose strife upon wetlands. And it's purple. Growing as tall as eight feet, this plant's beautiful flowers have enticed humans to throw it around like pocket change. Some state-beautification projects have actually planted it along roads. The help was unnecessary, as a single plant can produce 2 million seeds annually.

Unfortunately, purple loosestrife's loveliness belies its character. An incursion can overgrow marshy areas, which denies marsh birds their habitat. Particularly affected are species of concern like the least bittern, the American bittern, the least grebe, and the black tern, says Bernd Blossey, director of Cornell University's Biological Control of Nonindigenous Plant Species Program.

Large stands of loosestrife also knock off native plants such as sedges and cattails. In Massachusetts, loosestrife is a direct threat to the endangered bulrush; in New York, it's trouble for the endangered dwarf spike rush.

Amazingly, this purple plague is still sold in many areas, with only about 15 states having outlawed its sale. Asher tells this horror story: "A county weed supervisor I know had a local florist send flowers to his mother. The next day he visited and found a bouquet of purple loosestrife on her breakfast table."

Uprooting the plants can stop a fresh infestation, but loosestrife's watery environment presents special problems for herbicides. Insect control is the most promising approach against big outbreaks. Blossey has come up with four species of insects that are helping halt the loosestrife lifestyle. These four Europeans chew loosestrife and eschew even closely related species. They divide up the work: one eats roots, one favors flowers, and two feed on leaves. "Over the past few years," he says, "we have sent off something like 3 million insects to more than 32 states and Canada. And they're doing extremely well. We have at least five sites where they have reduced purple loosestrife by more than 95 percent."

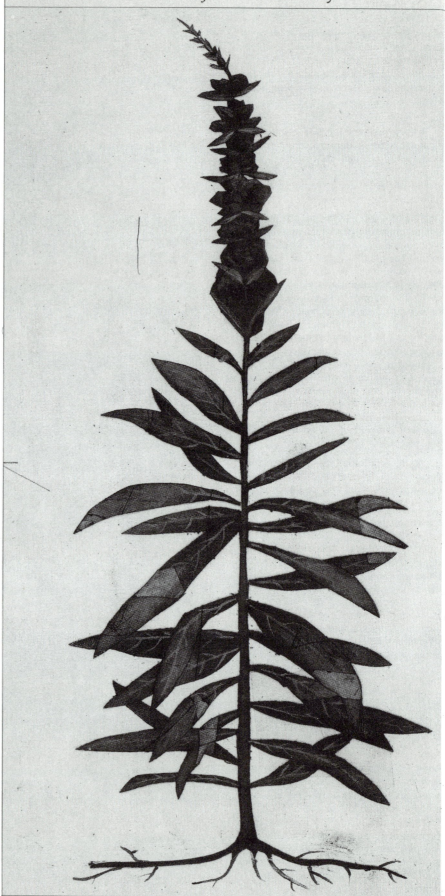

A bad seed—beautiful but deadly

The illegal water tapper

SPOTTED KNAPWEED

aka: *Centaurea biebersteinii, C. maculosa*
Last seen: Western rangelands, but has set up camp in most states coast to coast.
Infiltration: Snuck in with alfalfa and clover seed from Eurasia in the 1800s.

SPOTTED KNAPWEED does its dirty work in the dirt. It stands about three feet tall, but the secret to its success is its deep taproot—a single long extension that hunts for water far below the surface. "It's displacing native-range perennial grasses such as blue bunchweed grass and Idaho fescue," says Harold Stepper, the Noxious Weed Trust Fund coordinator with the Montana Department of Agriculture. "Livestock and wildlife can't use the range as they once did. Most foraging animals are being hurt." Elk can lose as much as 80 percent of their winter forage because of knapweed encroachment. Smaller creatures, such as squirrels and prairie dogs, count on native grasses for food as well.

Spotted knapweed also hurts the soil. The native plants it displaces grow a network of fibrous roots that help stabilize dirt. Taprooted plants—with their single root—leave a lot more loose topsoil. Furthermore, the spotted knapweed keeps drinking in the summer, when water is sparse. "It can tap a deeper reservoir of water, and that gives it a greater competitive advantage," Asher notes.

A study in Montana compared the effect of rainfall on land with spotted knapweed versus rainfall on land with native bunchgrasses: Sediment runoff was almost two times greater from knapweed-infested land. The eroded soil finds its way into waterways. Salmon habitat in the Selway-Bitterroot Wilderness of Idaho, for example, is threatened because of sedimentation caused by banks full of spotted knapweed. The problem hits the East too. "A couple of sites along eastern Lake Ontario are just thick with spotted knapweed," relates Randall.

Combatting knapweed requires the whole weed-management toolbox, including herbicides. Other ways to cap knapweed include hand-pulling, plowing, and control by insects such as root-feeding weevils. Asher's advice: "Find it early. And snuff it."

Science writer and weed warrior Steve Mirsky lives in New York City.

THE ORGANIC REVOLUTION

For the past 50 years, pesticides have been poisoning our soil and our wildlife— even our children. Will organic farming be able to reverse this toxic trend?

BY JOEL BOURNE

IF YOU WALK THROUGH THE produce section of many supermarkets today you will see, next to one pile of perfect red tomatoes, another pile of perfect red tomatoes. The more expensive pile is labeled "organic." Before you choose the cheaper tomatoes, consider how they were grown.

Many conventional tomatoes begin life in a greenhouse with a starter solution of synthetic fertilizer, then are transplanted to a field that has been treated with 400 to 600 pounds per acre of 10-20-20 fertilizer. (The numbers represent the percentages of nitrogen, phosphorous, and potassium.) The field has been fumigated with methyl bromide gas—an ozone-depleting chemical that is so toxic it is scheduled to be banned in 2005. The gas kills weed seeds and virtually everything else in the soil, but just in case, some growers use preemergence herbicides or paraquat, another highly toxic chemical, to destroy any

---

Joel Bourne lives on a farm that's been in his family for more than 60 years. "Right now we grow cotton, tobacco— all the big nasties," he says. But Bourne says that writing about organic agriculture has introduced him to methods that he could employ to help his farm operate in a less environmentally damaging way. His most recent contribution to *Audubon* was "The End of the Roads?" (July-August 1998).

weeds that do emerge. Many tomato crops are sprayed every week or two with fungicides such as chlorothalonil or mancozeb (chemicals highly toxic to fish) to control diseases. These chemicals are often mixed with insecticides such as endosulfan or methomyl—pesticides that have caused die-offs in birds.

> **"WHEN YOU BUY ORGANIC PRODUCE, YOU BUY THE WHOLE PACKAGE. YOU ARE BUYING THE CONCEPT THAT THE FARMING SYSTEM IS GOOD FOR THE ENVIRONMENT."**

If all this sounds a little too unappetizing, consider those sweet, vine-ripened organic tomatoes, grown by someone like Stefan Hartmann and his wife, Carmen Buechel-Hartmann. At their Black River Organic Farm, in eastern North Carolina, the Hartmanns grow more than a dozen vegetables, from eggplant to winter squash. Every year their tomatoes win the taste-testing contest at Raleigh's trendy Wellspring Grocery.

The Hartmanns' growing process sounds downright bucolic. In the fall Stefan plants a cover crop of rye and vetch on his fields to provide nutrients and organic matter to the soil. He then chooses a tomato variety based on its resistance to disease and nematodes. The young plants are raised in a greenhouse using a home-brewed mixture of compost, peat moss, fish emulsion, and seaweed extract. The Hartmanns collect ladybugs and release them in the greenhouse to feed on the aphids that often appear. Instead of using chemical fertilizer, Stefan makes his own, using composted chicken litter, limestone, and potash. After planting, he covers the beds with wheat-straw mulch to control weeds.

MELANIE ACEVEDO; ILLUSTRATION BY ALLISON SEIFFER

THIS YEAR FARMERS WILL PLANT 70 PERCENT OF THE NATION'S FIELDS IN JUST FOUR CROPS—CORN, WHEAT, SOYBEANS, AND COTTON—AND WILL LOSE TOPSOIL AT 10 TIMES ITS RATE OF REPLENISHMENT.

"Basically, at that point I stand back and let them go," Hartmann says. Tomato fruitworms are his biggest concern. At the first sign of them, he sprays a biopesticide containing *Bacillus thuringiensis* (Bt), a naturally occurring insect pathogen that controls lepidopterous insects but has no adverse impact on the environment. Last year, when the larvae were particularly bad, he sprayed only twice, a total of half a gallon on a half-acre plot. He never grows tomatoes in the same field until five years have passed; that keeps soil diseases and nematodes in check.

"When you buy organic produce, you buy the whole package," Hartmann says. "You are buying the concept that the farming system is good for the environment. This is what we're constantly telling consumers, and we as farmers have to constantly make sure that's so. Organic farmers are held accountable. Conventional farmers are not."

THE DIFFERENCE BETWEEN ORGANIC and conventional farming is the subject of a growing debate on the future of U.S. agriculture. The health of the nation's soil, waterways, wildlife, and even citizens hangs in the balance. Few human endeavors have more impact on our environment than the process by which we grow food. From the clearing of the eastern forests to the plowing of the Great Plains to the damming of western rivers for irrigation, agriculture has been a driving force in altering our landscape. As you read this, U.S. farmers are gearing up for another growing season. They will plant 70 percent of the nation's fields in just four crops—corn, wheat, soybeans, and cotton—and will lose precious topsoil at an average of 10 times its rate of replenishment. They will apply 24 million tons of fertilizer and nearly 1 billion pounds of pesticides on their land. Some of these chemicals will invariably wind up in our groundwater, rivers, and estuaries. Some will also wind up in our food, our body fat, even the breast milk we feed our babies. An estimated 300,000 farmworkers will be poisoned by exposure to pesticides.

Researchers at Cornell University estimate that at least 67 million birds die each year from pesticides sprayed on U.S. fields; the annual number of fish killed is conservatively estimated at 6 to 14 million. Pesticides have also been implicated in numerous cases of wildlife deformities, including the shrunken reproductive organs of alligators in Florida and grotesque abnormalities of the eyes and limbs of frogs around the country. DDT, one of the greatest bird killers of all time, was banned in the United States in 1972, but it is still manufactured and exported overseas, particularly to Latin America, where many U.S. birds overwinter. Between 1992 and 1996 the U.S. Geological Survey sampled thousands of wells and streams around the nation and discovered that half the wells and nearly all the streams contained at least one pesticide.

What makes these figures even more dramatic is the fact that chemical-intensive agriculture is a fairly recent phenomenon. Many modern pesticides are the descendants of chemical weapons developed in World War II and were not widely used until the 1950s. Some in-

MELANIE ACEVEDO

"WE'RE GETTING YIELDS THAT MEET OR EXCEED CONVENTIONAL YIELDS, AND WE EMPLOY 100 PEOPLE IN THE AREA. WE'RE NOT WEIRD. WE'RE GOOD BUSINESSPEOPLE."

secticides used today act exactly like VX or sarin nerve gas: They inhibit the production of cholinesterase, causing the nervous system to backfire. Birds feeding in treated fields may exhibit quivering facial muscles and excessive tearing and salivation. At high doses their respiratory muscles begin to contract, and they die of asphyxiation.

Most farmers, however, saw pesticides as silver bullets, providing relatively cheap, extremely effective control of their worst problems. Even the professors at land grant universities seemed to give up on alternatives to chemical pest control—especially since chemical companies and the U.S. Department of Agriculture were shelling out millions of dollars for pesticide research. The trend continues: Of 30,000 research projects supported by the USDA in 1995 and 1996, only 34 focused on organic production, according to the Organic Farming Research Foundation, in Santa Cruz, California.

"The majority of farmers really want to do the right thing for the environment," says Fred Kirschenmann, a leader in the organic movement. "But they don't know how. They don't know where to get the information, and the companies they buy their chemicals from are certainly not helping them."

THERE ARE ALTERNATIVES. IN 1940, J. I. Rodale, the Pennsylvania agriculturist and publisher, was the first in the United States to use the word *organic* to describe a method of farming that enhanced the health of consumers, the soil, and the planet. Rodale's method, promoted in his *Organic Gardening* and *Prevention* magazines, involves intense composting. At the other end of the spectrum, biodynamic gardening, developed in Germany by Rudolph Steiner in the 1920s, was based on more cosmic concepts: Planting and harvesting were timed to coincide with phases of the moon and the planets. Other methods of organic farming evolved in the 1970s, focusing on production as well as philosophy. John Jeavons, a California master gardener, and John Seymour, an Irish self-sufficiency guru, both developed small-scale, high-yielding organic-gardening techniques that use deep beds of fertile, well-aerated soil. Their philosophies stress self-sufficiency as well as a lifestyle in harmony with nature. In Japan, Masanobu Fukuoka, a plant pathologist turned farmer, developed a technique for growing rice, vegetables, and oranges without chemicals, tillage, or fertilizer, while minimizing human effort. The most recent branch of organic agriculture is known as permaculture. Developed by Tasmanian ecologist Bill Mollison, it integrates every aspect of life, including water, energy, and waste.

Though methods vary, the tenets of each philosophy remain the same. Organic farmers eschew synthetic fertilizers in favor of compost and green manure crops, such as ryegrass and clovers, that enrich the soil. In lieu of pesticides, they control insects and weeds with techniques that have been around for eons: rotating crops to break soil-disease and nematode life cycles; mulching with straws that suppress weed-seed germination; and promoting insects such as ladybugs and lacewings, which prey on aphids and other pests. Some organic growers do use biopesticides derived from plants or bacteria, as well as soaps and various metals and minerals deemed natural. Some of these materials—such as rotenone from cubé roots and pyrethrum from chrysanthemums—can be as toxic as synthetic pesticides, so farmers use them as a last resort.

Most distributors and buyers of organic food demand some form of certification. Currently, 15 state agencies and dozens of private groups police the or-

ganic-food market in more than 40 states by certifying foods according to varying standards. The Department of Agriculture is now hammering out the final draft of national standards that would bring organic labeling under federal law.

It hasn't been easy. The USDA created a firestorm within the organic community in December 1997 with its first draft proposal, which left open the possibility of using irradiation, sewage sludge, and genetic engineering to produce "organic" foods. These processes and materials, rarely if ever used by organic growers, have strong supporters in the food industry. Irradiation involves bombarding food with gamma rays, which kills most bacteria, but because of public concerns over safety and radioactive waste, it hasn't become widespread. Though human waste is used as fertilizer in other countries, sewage sludge in the United States is often contaminated with toxic heavy metals and hundreds of synthetic chemicals. Even major conventional food processors such as Del Monte and Heinz have refused to allow sludge on their crops.

Genetic engineering—the high-tech shuffling of genes between species—in theory has great potential, such as using a tropical-fish gene to help wheat survive in warmer climates. In practice, it sometimes does little more than help sell more pesticides. Over the past few years the chemical giant Monsanto has introduced genetically engineered soybean and cotton varieties called Roundup Ready, which are allegedly impervious to the popular herbicide Roundup, also made by Monsanto. Other companies have introduced transgenic varieties implanted with Bt—which many organic growers and environmentalists contend will only increase pest resistance to the valuable bacterium, disabling an effective and relatively benign biopesticide.

After the release of its draft proposal, the USDA was deluged by more than 280,000 public comments, causing Secretary of Agriculture Dan Glickman to drop the controversial methods from the proposed standards. "Honest to God, we thought they just didn't get it," says Robert Anderson, chairman of the National Organic Standards Board (NOSB), an advisory group appointed by Glickman that recommended strict standards for organic food. "I don't think any secretary of agriculture would

"IN THE INDUSTRIAL MODEL, WE'VE BEEN CLEARING NATURE OUT OF THE WAY. WHAT WE DIDN'T RECOGNIZE IS THAT FARMS AREN'T FACTORIES. THEY ARE ECOSYSTEMS."

have poked anybody in the eye that intentionally."

Some experts, however, are starting to come around. A few years ago Anderson took experts from Pennsylvania State University's agricultural college on a tour of his 600-acre organic farm, near Penns Creek, Pennsylvania. Anderson was extremely nervous. But the scientists soon jumped off the wagon and began to grab handfuls of rich soil. One entomologist found insects he hadn't seen in years, not to mention pheasants, grosbeaks, finches, phoebes, and wrens living in the area. Last year one of the school's strongest proponents of chemical agriculture finally admitted to Anderson that it was time to start looking at alternatives. When Glickman invited Anderson and other NOSB members to his office to discuss organic standards, the enthusiastic farmer took it as a sign that organic agriculture had finally come of age.

"We've gone from the lunatic fringe to one of the leading edges," Anderson says with a laugh. "We're getting yields that meet or exceed conventional yields, and we employ 100 people in the area. We're not weird. We're good businesspeople."

Anderson is one of an estimated 10,000 certified organic farmers in the United States. They tend less than 1 percent of its farmland, but their impact is growing like the proverbial weed. Organic food is the fastest-growing segment of retail food sales, having increased more than 20 percent a year since 1989. Upscale natural-foods grocery stores such as Whole Foods and Wild Oats can now be found in almost every major metropolitan area. In 1996 American shoppers spent an estimated $3.5 billion on organic foods. Though this represents less than 1 percent of the U.S. food market, a recent survey showed that 60 percent of consumers were interested in buying organic prod-

ucts because they felt those were better for their health and for the environment.

"The emergence and growth of organic agriculture is very important," says Margaret Mellon, director of agriculture and biotechnology for the Union of Concerned Scientists, a Boston—based research and lobbying group. "It is the vanguard of the transition in agriculture toward sustainability. It can't

be overemphasized how courageous the folks who started organic agriculture really were. The conventional wisdom was that in order to have abundant, reasonably priced agricultural products, you had to depend on the pesticide inputs of industrial agriculture. These folks said no."

CAN ORGANIC FARMING REVERSE some of the ills wrought in the past 50 years? Does it produce healthier food? Will it ever be an economically viable alternative to conventional farming?

At the 1996 meeting of the United Nations Environment Programme's Convention on Biological Diversity, held in Buenos Aires, representatives from 148 countries and the European Union agreed on this statement: "Inappropriate reliance on monoculture, overmechanization, and misuse of agri-

A Softer Side for *COTTON*

The organic revolution has now reached well beyond the fruit and vegetable aisle: You can buy an organic version of just about anything, from steak to shampoo. The word *organic*, in such cases, refers to a growing or manufacturing process that is chemical free. In this issue of *Audubon* we focus on produce, which, from soil to supermarket, affects the health of both habitat and humans.

The crop that may have the greatest impact on wildlife habitat, however, is cotton. The plant has been cultivated for thousands of years, but in the past half-century many cotton fields have become virtual pesticide sinks. Cotton farmers use 25 percent of all insecticides sprayed worldwide—even though the crop is grown on only 5 percent of the world's agricultural land. Numerous studies have linked the chemicals used in growing cotton to soil and ground-

water contamination: After heavy rains in 1995, runoff of endosulfan killed 240,000 fish in Alabama.

"Of all our fibers, conventionally grown cotton is probably the worst," says Yvon Chouinard, founder of the sportswear company Patagonia. In 1996, after touring several cotton farms in California, Chouinard began using only organically grown cotton in his products. "I was so appalled at what I saw, I didn't want to be in business if I had to use this fiber," Chouinard said. "It would be like making land mines."

Patagonia's move gave a boost to the fledgling organic-cotton indus- try, which currently cultivates about 10,000 acres, less than 1 percent of the domestic cotton crop. Patagonia is the only major label to go fully organic, though more than 100 smaller companies are manufacturing and selling organic-cotton products.   —J. B.

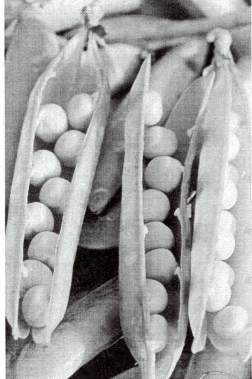

MELANIE ACEVEDO

cultural chemicals diminishes the diversity of fauna, flora, and microorganisms, including beneficial organisms. Those practices normally lead to a simplification of the components of the environment and to unstable production systems."

Numerous studies have shown that organic farming, on the other hand, increases biodiversity and benefits soil microorganisms that break down organic matter, earthworms that build soil structure, and soil arthropods that prey on insect pests. It may take 10 to 15 years for microorganisms to return to equilibrium after a conversion from conventional to organic farming. Small creatures are not the only ones to benefit. A recent study in England showed significantly higher populations of birds on organic

farms than on neighboring conventional farms. One farm that converted to organic methods had a 10 percent increase in bird species. The increase was attributed to larger hedgerows, the types of crops grown, and in-crop diversity (planting two or more crops in the same field).

The benefits to humans are less clear. A recent study by *Consumer Reports* found that nutritional value and flavor were roughly the same, no matter how a product had been grown. But organic products consistently had much lower toxic pesticide residues than conventionally grown food. Organic doesn't always mean pesticide-free, however. Traces of pesticides were found on 25 percent of the organic samples—compared with 77 percent of the conventional samples. It wasn't known whether the pesticides were intentionally sprayed on the organic produce or whether it was contaminated in other ways, such as by drift from nearby fields. Nonetheless, the magazine concluded, eating organic foods ensures the least amount of pesticide residues in the diet, while also supporting an agricultural system that is much less harmful to the environment.

Organic foods still cost an average of 57 percent more than their conventional counterparts, though seasonal, locally grown produce is often more competitively priced. "People wonder why organic food costs so much," says Peter Martinelli of Fresh Run Farms, an organic farm in Bolinas, California. "Instead, they should ask why other food is so cheap. You pay for the other stuff in other ways"—including, he says, through soil erosion, water pollution, health care, and subsidies to conventional farmers.

Critics of organic agriculture also maintain that yields are lower, production costs are higher, and it can't be

done in all parts of the country. Many large-scale organic farms look much the same as conventional farms, they point out, merely replacing chemical inputs with approved organic substitutes. Perhaps the most common criticism is the one voiced by the American Farm Bureau and other proponents of conventional agriculture: It will never feed the world.

"High-yield agriculture is already saving 10 million square miles per year of global wildlands," claims Dennis Avery, a senior fellow at the pro-technology Hudson Institute, in Indianapolis, and author of *Saving the Planet With Pesticides and Plastics*. "Current cropping levels are estimated to be 5.8 million square miles. Based on 1950s production levels, before the widespread use of pesticides, we would need 15 to 16 million square miles of land to meet present-day global food requirements. . . . The unfortunate implication of organic agriculture is that we would be clearing more natural areas around the world to feed the planet."

Organic growers like Kirschenmann disagree. He says, "The industrial-agriculture folks are trying to gain the moral high ground by saying if we don't continue increasing production, we can't feed the world. There are more than 800 million malnourished people on this planet today, and grain surpluses in many countries. Production is not the problem. Access and the tools for these people to feed themselves—that's the cause of hunger."

Lower yields may also be a thing of the past. In the nation's longest-running study of conventional and organic systems, researchers at Pennsylvania's Rodale Institute have found that over the past 13 years, yields of organic corn and soybeans have consistently equaled those of conventionally grown crops and have been substantially higher in dry years. More important, the study suggested

"THERE ARE MORE THAN 800 MILLION MALNOURISHED PEOPLE ON THIS PLANET TODAY, AND GRAIN SURPLUSES IN MANY COUNTRIES. PRODUCTION IS NOT THE PROBLEM. ACCESS AND THE TOOLS FOR THESE PEOPLE TO FEED THEMSELVES—THAT'S THE CAUSE OF HUNGER."

that increased organic matter in composted fields could play an important role in reducing atmospheric carbon, a major constituent of greenhouse gases.

On his own land, Kirschenmann has proven that diversified organic agriculture can be practiced on a large scale year after year. Since 1980 he and his family have produced beef and at least 10 different organic grains on 3,100 acres near Windsor, North Dakota. The prairie potholes that dot the farm provide habitat for white pelicans and plovers, whooping cranes and sandhill cranes, even the occasional moose. For Kirschenmann, the shift from industrial agriculture to a system based on land-scape ecology is critical to restoring the biodiversity lost over the past 50 years.

"In the industrial model, we've been clearing nature out of the way," Kirschenmann says. "Thoughtful scientists now know that's a dead end. What we didn't recognize is that farms aren't factories. They are ecosystems."

AT BLACK RIVER ORGANIC FARM last fall, the vegetables were harvested, the cover crop had been planted, and Stefan and Carmen Hartmann sat at their kitchen table talking about the year they'd had. While conventional farmers may have groused about which pesticides might be banned or the perennially low price of corn, wheat, or hogs, the Hartmanns spoke enthusiastically of expanding local markets and of tasty varieties of tomatoes and sweet corn.

"This is how we wanted to farm," says Stefan, who moved from Germany to take over his grandparents' small farm in 1984. "I couldn't imagine using all those chemicals. How could you sell something you wouldn't eat yourself?"

Joel Bourne, who has a degree in agronomy, grew up on a conventional farm.

NOT IN MY BACKYARD

Wildlife is rapidly encroaching on America's suburbs—and vice versa.
How are we to tolerate the hometown proliferation of predators and prey?

BY ANTHONY BRANDT

The village of North Haven occupies a 2.5-square-mile peninsula that lies some 200 yards across the water from Sag Harbor, where I live, and is connected to the South Fork of Long Island, New York, by a spit of sand. Except for that spit of sand, North Haven is an island. It used to be called Hog Neck, but *haven* is an appropriate name for it. The place is quiet and serene. It has no downtown, and the houses of its 733 full-time residents are scattered about a lovely landscape of meadows and fields and small ponds and the oak forests that seem to thrive on glacial moraines. Everywhere there are water views. If you drive through quickly—and you could; it's only three miles from the bridge to the end of Ferry Road—you might never see a deer. You might never know that this is the hottest of spots in what is rapidly becoming the war of the suburbs, the war between humans and the wildlife they love and fear.

The deer are definitely here. Drive through slowly, on the back roads and side streets, as I did early one evening in June, and you will see white-tailed deer in abundance, walking through the woods, feeding in meadows and fields and people's yards. In an hour and a half I counted 30 deer. They do not startle at the sound of a car; sometimes they don't even look up. "There were deer here when I was a kid, but you didn't see them much," says

From his home on eastern Long Island, Anthony Brandt has watched deer populations become larger and more troublesome. For now, his own garden has escaped the hungry deer, but he says, "they are down the street—literally." He currently writes the book-review column for Men's Journal.

Bob Ratcliffe, the mayor. "I spent a lot of time in the woods, and there was a lot of wildlife on an old stock farm—pheasants, foxes, ducks. We thought it was a thrill to see deer. North Haven was rural back then, a gorgeous place."

It's still pretty, but in the woods the understory has disappeared. Nothing grows below five feet off the ground. Small mammals and ground-nesting birds have vanished, their habitat destroyed. Nobody sees pheasants in North Haven anymore; the foxes are gone, too. The woods cannot replenish themselves because the deer eat all the saplings. North Haven's ecosystem could handle a herd of about 60 deer, Ratcliffe believes. In the fall of 1996 the number stood at more than 600.

The costs are not only to the environment. Deer carry deer ticks, *Ixodes scapularis*, which in turn carry a spirochete called *Borrelia burgdorferi*, which causes Lyme disease. The symptoms include nausea, fever, night sweats, and arthritis-like pain in the joints; if not treated early, with heavy doses of antibiotics, it can cause damage to the central nervous system. A survey taken by graduate students at Southampton College in January 1997 indicated that 65 percent of the families in North Haven had Lyme disease; 29 percent of the households reported three or more cases. This level of infection can only be described as a plague. Miriam Ungerer, who moved to North Haven in 1981 with her husband, writer Wilfrid Sheed, has had Lyme disease three times. "We were looking for peace and quiet and privacy," says Ungerer. "North Haven had a hunting season then. It stopped in 1987, when somebody managed to pass a law that no firearms could be discharged in the village. That's when the deer started to increase." She no longer tries to grow ornamentals around her house: "All my perennial borders are gone. The huge bed of Montauk daisies I had is completely eaten. I'm sure the damage comes to ten thousand dollars." Three-fourths of the residents of North Haven have had damage to their ornamental plantings; the other fourth have built fences around their property. A fence must be eight feet high to keep out deer. "I don't have thousands of dollars to build a fence around my property," says Ungerer. "We do not have the use of our yard. We can't let any visiting small children go out there."

Deer can have as many as 300 ticks *on each ear*—not to mention the ticks on its body, says Paul Curtis, a wildlife biologist and deer specialist at Cornell University's Department of Natural Resources. About 25 to 50 percent of deer ticks carry the Lyme disease spirochete.

The deer issue has divided North Haven violently in two. Rival political parties were formed wholly around the issue. Meetings of the Village Board became screaming matches; the police had to be called to maintain order. Pro-deer types phoned Bob Ratcliffe's house anonymously and told his daughter, "If a deer dies in North Haven, one of your family will die." The village has been sued repeatedly to stop proposed hunts. The uproar was big enough to attract the attention of *The New York Times*. "We've been told we should try to live with the wildlife," says Ratcliffe, "but we're being pushed out. If you had a manageable herd you could live with it, but not with this population—not when it's as big as it is."

For four years the Village Board was divided, three to two, between Ratcliffe's North Haven Party, which advocated controlled hunting, and the Preservation Party, which favors an experimental program of immunocontraception and opposes hunting. In 1996 the North Haven Party candidates won in a close vote. Ratcliffe then pushed through a bow-and-arrow hunting program, governed by nuisance-deer permits that individual property owners have to apply for. Opponents of the hunt tried to disrupt it when the hunters showed up, following them to their stands, banging pot lids, and blowing horns to frighten the deer away. Last winter the hunting hours were extended. Eventually some 250 deer were killed; another 50 were killed in car accidents. In the most recent election, in June, Ratcliffe's party took all five seats on the board by wide margins.

But nobody thinks the problem is solved. Five of the 30 deer I saw on my tour were fawns. Some people in North Haven feed the deer. Ratcliffe would like to see a roundup, in which the state would come in and haul the deer someplace else. But where? The entire Northeast is jammed with deer. The United States has somewhere between 14 and 20 million deer—more now, according to some wildlife biologists, than there were in 1492. Deer are thriving in suburbs all across the country. The problem is intractable, and it is quite literally growing. It is also, again quite literally, bringing home to us our own enduring ambivalence toward the natural world and its creatures. For this issue is not about spotted owls in remote untouched wilderness areas or the endangered cheetahs of the Serengeti, in far-off Africa. This is about local wildlife bringing disease, damage, and even danger to our very own backyard.

It's not just deer, either. For a host of reasons—including population growth, changing hunting laws, a dearth of natural predators, and changing attitudes toward nature—the spread of wildlife into human habitats and vice versa is generating more and more problems, more frequent collisions, particularly with mountain lions, moose, bears, and coyotes. "The animal populations are recovering strongly, and the suburbs are spreading into what was animal habitat," says Cornell wildlife researcher Jody Enck. "It's likely to continue into the future." For their part, the animals are spreading into what is nearly ideal habitat: plenty of food and virtually no natural enemies. In this habitat, the only mortal threat is a moving automobile.

None of the wildlife specialists I talked to was quite ready to use the word *crisis* for this burgeoning conflict in the suburbs, but add it up: Lyme disease cases now run to more than 16,000 a year nationwide. In New York State alone, the tab for beaver damage runs to $6 million annually. There are 1 million car-deer collisions in the United States every year, causing some $1.1 billion in damage and more than 200 human fatalities. "The management of wildlife in urban environments is one of the few growth areas in wildlife management," says Scott Craven of the Department of Wildlife Ecology at the University of Wisconsin-Madison. "This is an exciting time for wildlife managers." It may not be a crisis yet, but in many areas, with certain species of wildlife, it looks to become one.

Mountain lions are appearing with increasing frequency in the suburbs of Los Angeles and other California cities, with domestic pets becoming a sometime source of food. In 1995 a lion wandered into a shopping center in Montclair, a suburb of Los Angeles; another killed two dogs in La Crescenta, another Los Angeles suburb. Lion tracks have been found in school playgrounds. A mountain lion was spotted last October in Plymouth, Minnesota, near Minneapolis. The animals may even be returning to the Northeast; sightings have been reported as far south as Connecticut.

> # How should we deal with animals that have become inconvenient?

Moose also are expanding their range from northern New England south. In June a moose found its way into downtown Agawam, Massachusetts, near Springfield; last fall one appeared in the Delaware Water Gap, on the Pennsylvania–New Jersey line. Moose can be major road hazards. Cars do not intimidate them, and they stand their ground. When your car strikes a moose, it sweeps the legs out from under the animal, resulting in 1,000 pounds or so of meat and bone coming through the windshield into your lap. In northern New England the human-fatality rate in car-moose collisions is one in 75. That's 65 times higher than the car-deer collision rate.

A black bear made the front page of *The New York Times* last May, when it moved through several of New York's Westchester County suburbs and into Yonkers. It was cornered on a golf course near White Plains, shot with tranquilizing darts, and taken upstate to be released. Three weeks later a second bear was spotted in northern Westchester County. In New Jersey a black bear turned up recently in Mountainside, just 12 miles southwest of Newark and some 25 miles from New York City. In 1971 there were perhaps 20 to 30 bears in New Jersey; now the number is estimated at 550. Jon Rosenberg, a bear specialist with the New Jersey Division of Fish, Game, and Wildlife, says the state's bear population began to explode in the late 1970s, when Pennsylvania halted bear hunting and the resulting bear surplus began to migrate into New Jersey. Bears come into the state from southern New York as well. The hunting of bears has been banned in New Jersey since 1971, but the state is now considering a hunt to bring the numbers down.

The problems that come with bear proliferation are not confined to New Jersey and New York. A black bear attacked a 14-year-old girl in her backyard in Monroe, Washington, in 1995. Last year in Wisconsin, wildlife agents handled 1,200 calls complaining about black bears. Bears have been sighted inside the city limits of Chattanooga and Pittsburgh, captured in the suburbs of Knoxville, Tennessee, discovered on the outskirts of Orlando, Florida. In a town in western Massachusetts a black bear came through a screen door, grabbed a bag of Milky Ways off the kitchen table, and fled.

It is the coyote, however, that constitutes the most widespread, if not the most dangerous, challenge to our ideas of where wildlife should live. When colonists first came to North America the coyote was largely confined to the prairies of the Midwest and beyond; there were fewer coyotes in the East. One reason may be that coyote and wolf populations do not seem to tolerate each other (although coyotes and wolves will interbreed on a one-to-one basis), and the woods of the East were full of

> The real test comes when wildlife affects you and your property.

wolves. But those wolves were wiped out by the end of the 19th century, and the coyote's range began to expand. Now coyotes roam in every one of the 48 contiguous states, and they have spread into Central America and Alaska as well. They are by no means confined to rural areas. They have been seen in resort communities on barrier islands off the Atlantic Coast. They are howling in the suburbs of New York City and living in Van Cortlandt Park, in the Bronx. The cities of the Southwest are full of them. In the early 1970s the coyote population of Indiana numbered fewer than 500. Now it runs to more than 20,000. Coyotes even managed to colonize Newfoundland, which is 65 miles across the ocean from Nova Scotia.

No predatory mammal is as adaptable, as successful, as the coyote. Notes Marc Bekoff, a professor of biology at the University of Colorado, "It's a generalist that eats any and all types of food." That's putting it mildly. Here's what's been found in coyote stomachs, according to Charles Cadieux's fascinating book *Coyotes: Predators and Survivors:* mice and other small rodents, rabbits, small birds, large birds, eggs, snakes both venomous and nonvenomous, bats, iguanas and other lizards, watermelon, tomatoes, sheep large and small, goats large and small, belt buckles and their belts, carrion, fish, frogs, grasshoppers, bear scat, the scat of other coyotes, crickets, berries, potatoes both cooked and raw, grass, and deer. What they eat depends on where they are. In farming areas their diet may be composed largely of mice. In the Adirondacks, 50 to 80 percent of their diet consists of deer, according to Robert Chambers, a retired professor of wildlife biology at the State University of New York's College of Environmental Science and Forestry, who studied coyotes in New York State for 20 years. In the suburbs, increasingly, coyotes are eating human garbage; the dumpster is one of their favorite sources. They also eat pets. Coyotes killed 50 cats in a year in Benbrook, a suburb of Fort Worth, Texas; 40 cats in a few months in Rancho Murieta, outside Sacramento, California; and some 11 dogs and a great many more cats in Westminster, a suburb of Denver.

Coyotes are common in the suburbs of Chicago; they have been spotted in nearly every suburb of St. Louis. They sun themselves on the runways of the airport in Toronto, creating a hazard to air traffic. A coyote den was found on the median strip of Route 128, which circles Boston. The animals were living off roadkill.

Coyotes are very hard to control. In the West, outright eradication has been tried without much success. Bounties, poisoning, hunting—nothing has worked. Chambers says, "Our own limited information shows that some of the young animals in their first year will disperse up to a hundred and fifty miles." And not always on foot: There's evidence that coyotes rode freight cars and canal boats into the Chicago area. Chambers rates their intelligence as "extremely high. They're very educable. They're very intelligent." They're also difficult to trap, and more so the older and wilier they become. In Burbank, where traps were steam-cleaned to remove the odor of humans, trapping was still successful only one time in 10. Coyotes have been known to attack small children: In 1980 one killed a three-year-old girl in Los Angeles. In 1995 another three-year-old was attacked, in the Los Angeles suburb of Fullerton.

Not every collision between humans and wildlife these days is a matter of mortal danger. Canada geese, which defecate as frequently as every eight minutes, are fouling golf courses, municipal parks, and suburban lawns all over the East and Midwest. Beavers are flooding roads and basements and crops in New York, Minnesota, and New England; they cause an estimated $22 million in damage annually to forests in six Southeastern states. Raccoons spread rabies, and they love urban and suburban living.

All wild animals bring their particular behaviors with them wherever they go. When their numbers are small, these habits seem picturesque, exotic, appealing. But when the numbers grow large, as with the deer of North Haven, they become A Problem.

There are no obvious solutions, perhaps no solutions at all. Nobody seriously wants to eradicate deer or moose or geese or bears. (And we evidently could not eradicate coyotes even if we all wanted to.) In any case, they are protected, one way or another, by laws and regulations.

Few of us are easy in our conscience about this situation. We humans are proliferating and expanding our habitat at an alarming, truly dangerous rate, even as we profess to love the animals whose territory we steal. Are we not morally obligated to deal fairly with them, to learn to live with them? And who does not admire the fleetness and grace of the deer? The street smarts of the coyote? Attempts to manage the populations of any "nuisance" animal frequently generate protests, if not lawsuits, from animal-rights activists. If our relationship to the natural world is one of stewardship, how should we deal with animals that have become inconvenient? What are the precedents for dealing with these situations?

Most of the big environmental battles have been fought over remote wilderness areas or exotic (and beautiful) wildlife species. These battles fit a conceptual pattern that assumes nature is Out There, at a distance from us; it fits the town-country dichotomy in our mind, the idea that nature and its creatures constitute a refuge that we can visit from our urban or suburban life. How fortunate we feel, how privileged, how thrilled to see a cougar in its natural habitat! I saw one once in California's Ventana Wilderness, east of Big Sur. I shivered down to my soul; I felt as if I had met my totem animal. A black bear crossed my wife's path on Leadbetter Point in the

Willapa National Wildlife Refuge, in Washington. She loves to tell the tale.

But a black bear in our garbage can? Coyotes feeding on our beloved dog, Jack? That's a different story, and it would be dishonest not to acknowledge that we don't like it. Wild animals are supposed to be wild; they're supposed to keep their distance. They don't belong in our backyard. The idea violates our ideas about the order of things, about the divisions and the boundaries between the domestic and the wild. In West Milford, New Jersey, a man named Tom Sheridan maintains an 80-acre woodlot for local wildlife, but when a large black bear came out of those woods in the spring of 1996, chased down a ewe, and killed her while Sheridan watched helplessly, he wanted to shoot the bear. "They tell you there's never been a bear attack on a person, and yada, yada, yada," he told a writer for the *New Jersey Reporter*. "No one's got to tell me what that bear had in mind." It's one thing to watch acts of predation on the Discovery Channel. It's something else to see them up close and personal, only yards from your house.

The suburban-wildlife problem confronts us with our attitudes toward the natural world in a uniquely compelling fashion. Wildlife-management professionals, recognizing that fact, have begun to survey urban and suburban residents on these issues. For the most part the surveys have not been very revealing. Michael Conover, director of the Berryman Institute at Utah State University, conducted a survey that was published in the *Wildlife Society Bulletin*. He found that people generally like deer, rabbits, ducks, hummingbirds, blue jays, Canada geese, woodpeckers, robins, and cardinals. They don't like moles, raccoons, bats, skunks, squirrels, house sparrows, and snakes. But his was a random sample of people in 10 metropolitan regions around the country—areas where deer, for example, may not create the problems they do in North Haven. The votes for Bob Ratcliffe's pro-hunting political party are a more realistic test of how people feel about deer that chew up their perennials or drop thousands of ticks on their lawns. A 1988 study in upstate New York showed that public acceptance of beavers was inversely related to the amount of damage they did to the respondents' property.

The real test, in other words, comes when wildlife affects you and your property. And the answer is usually, Not in My Backyard. People think beavers are wonderful mammals with cute tails—until they have to spend several thousand dollars bailing out the basement. Beavers were once close to extinction in New York State. Now the population numbers nearly 100,000. The animal's major natural predator, the wolf, is extinct in New York. Beavers are trapped for their pelts, but the price is market driven and fluctuates wildly; right now it stands at about $24 per pelt. Trapping is a hard business. Says Bob Gotie, a senior wildlife biologist with the New York Department of Environmental Conservation, "It's a lot of work. It's lugging and hauling. The traps are large. Beavers can weigh more than fifty pounds." Trappers, he says, spend 12 hours for each beaver trapped. "That's not much return. And our population demands that we take thirty thousand beaver a year." Any less, and the population growth would increase by as much as 15 percent a year.

If that were 30,000 deer, the uproar would almost certainly be heard all the way to the White House. Deer create the most widespread problems of any wildlife species—three-fourths of the states report problems with urban and suburban deer—but they also arouse the most intense feelings. Public preferences for managing deer are the direct opposite of those of state wildlife agencies. A recent survey by Terry Messmer of the Berryman Institute found that among state wildlife biologists, the most acceptable method is a controlled hunt and the least acceptable method is immunocontraception. With the general public, especially animal-rights activists, the preferences are exactly reversed. When the deer problem became acute in North Haven, the community did consider immunocontraception, but the costs proved prohibitive. "The contraceptive is a vaccine derived from pig ovaries, and it must be administered by dart gun," explains biologist Curtis of Cornell. "Each free-ranging deer must be tagged as a warning, to prevent human consumption of the vaccine. Just to capture and mark the animal is two hundred dollars per deer. Two doses of the vaccine per deer per year are necessary. Vaccinating each deer twice a year is an expensive proposition." In North Haven, the cost would have been $120,000 per year.

No one has any easy answers. The Berryman Institute's Conover asks, "How can we create a world that has the wildlife we all love and cherish, yet solve these problems with deer and geese and other animals?" Conover is trying to find specific solutions to specific problems without resorting to large-scale slaughter. You can put up fences against the deer—if you have the money. Orchard owners have had some success with hanging soap bars all over their trees; there have even been studies of which

soap is the most effective. You can spray Canada goose repellent on golf courses, or harass the geese with noise-makers, or change the design and plantings of the landscape to discourage them. An entrepreneur in Northbrook, Illinois, rents out swans to local landowners; swans, being highly territorial, attack geese in their vicinity. In Glen Ellyn, Illinois, residents are hoping to frighten Canada geese away by leaving "dead goose" decoys in the lakes. "It's much better to solve the problem by changing the animals' behavior," says Conover. "If you kill an animal you've changed its behavior, but it's a crude way to do so."

Yes, it is. But what do you do with 600 deer in 2.5 square miles? And how much money is the public willing to spend on wildlife problems? Nobody knows; the problem is too new. "We've had this huge investment in studying deer and geese and other animals from the extractive perspective," says John Hadidian, who directs the Urban Wildlife Protection Program of the Humane Society of the United States. "Now we need a whole new science to understand what the problems are in the suburbs and to figure out what to do." In the meantime, he says, we need to become more tolerant of local wildlife. Curtis agrees but adds, "Increased tolerance isn't going to reduce the incidence of Lyme disease." If you've had Lyme disease, as I have, it will almost certainly change your attitude toward deer.

The science of ecology teaches us that the world is a vast web of relationships, climate to species, species to other species. And we appear to be the chief spider. By moving into their habitat, by eliminating their predators, we have caused the explosion of deer and geese and beavers and moose and coyotes on what we persist in thinking is our property. We are the stewards of the world; we hold it in sacred trust. But the world isn't "out there" any longer, somewhere in Montana or the rainforest of the Amazon basin. The world is staring at us with big soulful brown eyes, right where our azaleas used to be.

THE ULTIMATE SURVIVOR

Every year 400,000 coyotes are exterminated in the United States, yet the wily creature continues to flourish.   BY MIKE FINKEL

I HOPE YOU KILL A LOT OF COYOTES." THE LOCAL GAME warden pronounces the word *kai-oats*, the way it's said in most of the West. "I don't care how you kill 'em. Blow 'em up with dynamite. Run 'em over. Punt 'em like footballs. Whatever." This elicits a good deal of laughter from the 100 or so people I've joined in the small hunting lodge at the Circle G Shooting Park, just south of Gillette, Wyoming.

It is the evening of December 4, 1998, a few minutes before the sixth annual Campbell County Predator Calling Contest is scheduled to begin. The competitors sit shoulder-to-shoulder at long tables, eating steak and baked potatoes. All but two of the participants are men, most of them dressed top-to-bottom in camouflage. Mustaches hang like awnings over upper lips. There are bellies. One wall is decorated with a poster of the cartoon character Wile E. Coyote, overlaid with crosshairs.

The game warden is reviewing the contest rules. Over the next 40 hours, the two-person team that kills the most coyotes will win a $200 cash prize. When the warden is finished and the dinner is over, the competitors hurry out of the lodge, climb into pickup trucks, and head onto the back roads of Campbell County, ready to hunt.

Central Wyoming is sere and wind ravaged and sagey—too harsh for cultivating—but it is prime sheep-ranching country. These days, however, ranching is in trouble. Profit margins are thin. Coyotes, say sheep

---

When Mike Finkel discovered that a coyote-killing contest was taking place near his Montana home, he figured the best way to learn more was to attend a hunt. "It certainly wasn't an ordinary day at the office," he says. Not that many of his days are; the self-described "ski bum who writes" will have a collection of his itinerant adventures on the slopes, *Alpine Circus*, published by Lyons Press this fall. His articles have appeared in *the Atlantic Monthly*, *The New York Times*, and *Sports Illustrated*.

ANTONIN KRATOCHVIL FOR *AUDUBON*

Despite the killing, **coyotes are spreading** not just in ranching country, but in Los Angeles and New York City.

ranchers, are a significant part of the problem. Coyotes eat lambs and sheep, and they eat a lot of them—as many as 250,000 head a year, according to the National Agricultural Statistical Service, costing the wool industry tens of millions of dollars. While in Campbell County, I spend an afternoon on the Iberlin Ranch, where John Iberlin runs 7,000 sheep on 50,000 acres. "Some years I lose 20 or 25 percent of my lambs to coyotes," he tells me. "All my profits are killed off. It doesn't take many coyotes to put you out of business."

In response, some ranchers kill as many coyotes as they can. They organize contests like the one in Campbell

ANTONIN KRATOCHVIL FOR *AUDUBON*

"If we simply **stopped killing coyotes,** it might actually reduce the population."

County, dozens of them every year. There is the Coyote Derby in Montana, the Predator Hunt Spectacular in Arizona, the San Juan Coyote Hunt in New Mexico, and on the East Coast, the Pennsylvania Coyote Hunt. The contests are advertised in sporting-goods stores, gun clubs, and *Varmint Masters* magazine. It is all perfectly legal.

Contests, though, are not the primary means of exterminating coyotes. One of the largest killers of coyotes is the U.S. government, which has been destroying them on a regular basis since 1931. The program is conducted by a division of the U.S. Department of Agriculture known as Wildlife Services. (The agency changed its name from Animal Damage Control last summer in an attempt to soften its image.) In 1996 Wildlife Services agents killed a total of 82,261 coyotes, almost all of them in the 17 states that constitute the American West, where both coyote and sheep populations are concentrated. Twenty-eight thousand of those coyotes were shot from helicopters or airplanes, under Wildlife Services' extensive aerial-gunning program. Twenty-two thousand were poisoned by devices known as M-44s—baited traps that spray sodium cyanide into the mouths and noses of animals that tug on the bait. Eight thousand were captured using steel-jaw leghold traps. One thousand six hundred were killed in their dens, either by digging them out and shooting them or by gassing them. Each year, approximately $20 million in taxpayer money is used to fund these activities.

Between killing contests, Wildlife Services actions, and state, local, and private agencies, it is estimated that 400,000 coyotes are killed each year. That is more than

1,000 coyotes a day—almost a coyote a minute. Coyotes are the most maligned mammal in the United States. "It is impossible to exaggerate the intensity of loathing a coyote engenders in some westerners," Hope Ryden writes in her book *God's Dog: The North American Coyote.*

When killing a certain species becomes a matter of human policy and concerted effort, the fight is almost always one-sided. Passenger pigeons, grizzly bears, gray wolves, blue whales—all have been brought to extinction, or to the brink of extinction, with ease. Coyotes pose a different challenge altogether. Despite almost a century of uninterrupted killing, despite increasingly sophisticated hunting methods, despite hundreds of millions of government dollars devoted to coyote removal, today more coyotes are living in more places than ever before. And coyotes are spreading not just in ranching country but in metropolises nationwide, from the suburbs of Los Angeles to the streets of New York City.

A FEW DAYS AFTER THE CAMPBELL COUNTY CONTEST, in another part of Wyoming, Bob Crabtree and I are standing behind spotting scopes in the Lamar Valley of Yellowstone National Park, observing a pack of coyotes feeding on an elk carcass. Crabtree, 40, has been studying coyotes for 15 years, the past 9 in Yellowstone. He is the founder and research director of Yellowstone Ecosystem Studies, a nonprofit foundation that conducts long-term research projects in the Yellowstone area. Crabtree is a tall man who seems continually surprised by his tallness. He possesses the type of boundless energy that can exhaust everyone around him; he claims to require only four hours of sleep per night. When something inspires him, which is often, he can furnish long, almost professorial disquisitions— except that every seventh word is an expletive better suited for a men's room wall.

The coyotes tugging and digging at the carcass are from the Bison Peak pack. The elk was killed by gray wolves, which fed first, stuffed themselves, and bedded down. Now it is the coyotes' turn. Coyotes, found only in North America, look much like domesticated dogs— say, small German shepherds. Adults weigh about 35 pounds. They are often described as occupying a niche halfway between foxes and wolves, and they have close genetic ties to both.

Most coyotes have burnished silver or reddish gray coats, with black detailing along the saddle area, and with ears, snouts, and legs the color of a bad sunburn. Their tails are great feather dusters of fur, often with a tip that appears to have been dipped into an inkwell. They move across the land with feline precision, stealthy and alert. They can accelerate to speeds of 35 miles per hour.

Coyotes are primarily pack animals, though loners do exist, especially in populations that have been heavily hunted. Relationships within a pack, which can consist of as many as seven adults and a litter of pups, are complex and hierarchical. I watch through the scope as the Bison Peak pack's alpha female strides up to the elk carcass. The beta male promptly steps back, giving her access to the choicest meat. Two low-ranking yearlings remain a short distance from the elk, waiting for their opportunity to feed. The alpha male, having already eaten, trots up a small rise and assumes sentry duties, scanning the horizon. Crabtree points out a loner coyote, a quarter-mile away, that is hiding in the sagebrush and waiting for the pack to finish their meal. Skirmishes between coyotes are common, but unlike wolves, coyotes never kill one another.

When choosing a mate, coyotes tend to be finicky. Courtship involves much licking and vocalizing, and occasionally, generous food offerings. Once coyotes form a pair, they sometimes bond for life.

In a pack, the alpha female usually bears the young, but other adults help with the pup-rearing. Lower-ranking coyotes play with newborns, aid with food gathering, and frequently guard the den. If the parents are killed, these surrogate parents will raise the pups to adulthood. Coyotes can live as long as 10 years, but they often don't survive past their third year, due to predation.

Coyotes can subsist on virtually any type of food. Their preference is rodents—voles, gophers, mice. In some places, though, they have become insectivores, feeding on grasshoppers, beetles, and grubs. They also eat snakes and lizards and frogs. In cities they dine on rats and house cats. In rural areas a pack will work together to bring down an elk. There has been at least one documented coyote-killed bison. Coyotes enjoy porcupines and turtles and cactus fruit. They can make a buffet out of a city landfill. In 1940 biologist Adolph Murie conducted a detailed study of coyote scat and enumerated 100 different food items. In the Southeast, coyotes have become so enamored of watermelon that many fruit growers have taken to shooting them.

CRABTREE AND I OBSERVE THE SMALL DRAMA TAKING place around the elk carcass until it is nearly sunset. Then, as we are walking back to our cars, the song begins. The Bison Peak pack starts to vocalize: high-pitched yips intermingled with long, plaintive howls—a richly harmonized cry wavering with crescendos and diminuendos. It is the natural music of the American West, majestic and mesmerizing, cherished even by some people who spend their days trying to silence it.

For coyotes, the vocalizations appear to be used primarily to stake out their territory and to communicate with their pack. Ryden, in *God's Dog*, chronicles her observations of an adult coyote that seemed to be teaching her pups how to howl—the adult singing at a certain octave, the pups trying to mimic, the lesson being repeated

ANTONIN KRATOCHVIL FOR *AUDUBON*

over and over. At least 11 different kinds of vocalization have been documented, including woofs, barks, yips, growls, yelps, lone howls, group howls, greeting songs, and group yip-howls.

After the Bison Peak pack sings, other coyotes join in a group yip-howl. The Druid pack takes up the melody, then the Jasper pack, then the Amethyst pack, the song working its way down the Lamar Valley, echoing off the hillsides.

Crabtree is conducting a coyote study with his wife, Jennifer Sheldon, a biologist with Yellowstone Ecosystem Studies and the author of *Wild Dogs: Natural History of the Non-Domestic Canidae*. This is an unprecedented time to observe coyote behavior in Yellowstone. For the first six years of the study, coyotes had few natural predators in the Lamar Valley. Then, in 1995, the federal government reintroduced gray wolves to the park. Wolves kill a lot of coyotes, primarily loner adults but also incautious pack members. Crabtree and Sheldon have been documenting the social, behavioral, and dietary changes among coyotes since the reintroduction. Their findings have helped explain how the coyote population, in the face of unrelenting persecution, has proven so extraordinarily resilient.

During the past four years the Yellowstone wolves have reduced the coyote population by about 30 percent. The coyotes have had to rearrange their territorial boundaries, alter their hunting habits, and cope with the continual disruption of their pack structures. Still, the animals are not going to be wiped out in the area. Having evolved in conjunction with wolves—the two species have shared the same turf for millennia—coyotes have adapted to being hunted animals. Humans are merely another, less effective predator. (Unlike wolves, humans do not hunt all year, all the time.) Bears, like wolves, prey on coyotes and evolved as top animals in the food chain. "Before the invention of guns and traps, top-level carnivores like bears and wolves had virtually no predators," says Daniel Harrison, a professor of wildlife ecology at the University of Maine. "They don't show a lot of inherent fear." As a result, bears and wolves did not develop the survival skills they needed to thrive. These species are now endangered primarily because they are so easy to kill.

Coyotes, on the other hand, have an uncanny ability to adapt to almost any situation. A hundred years ago they lived only in the West. Now, as wolves and bears have been killed off, coyotes have been spotted in 49 states (all except Hawaii) and every Canadian province. Biologists believe there are twice as many coyotes now as in 1850, though even a rough estimate of the coyote population is impossible to calculate. Coyotes have been seen near Mexico City and outside Atlanta. Recently two coyotes were photographed in the Bronx, New York, running between taxicabs. These urban coyotes, which can

Evidence exists that hunting (opposite) increases the chances of coyote pups' surviving to adulthood, although it shortens the lives of the adults.

GARY CRANDALL/ENVISION

kill pets, are usually rounded up by local authorities and destroyed.

Crabtree and Sheldon's study indicates that coyotes may have a paradoxical survival mechanism. When they are being hunted—by either wolves or humans—the number of pups that survive to adulthood is increased significantly. In an unexploited population, only one or two pups in a six-pup litter will live beyond a few months. But in populations that are subject to predation or trapping, most pups survive to adulthood, according to Crabtree and Sheldon. This seems to occur because a decrease in the number of adult coyotes from predation leaves more food for the pups, ensuring a higher survival rate.

Coyotes are naturally wary creatures: When the animals have pups, they dig multiple dens, and with any sign that a den has been spotted, a pack—under cover of night—will move all the pups to a new den. Unless coyotes

are hunted day and night all year long, their population may well continue to expand.

"The more coyotes are attacked by humans, the more they become entrenched," Crabtree says. "It is easy to view nature as strictly linear—coyotes kill sheep, so we kill coyotes—but the truth is that nature is extraordinarily dynamic. If we simply stopped killing coyotes, it might actually reduce the coyote population and decrease the kills of sheep." Crabtree adds that if the money and effort used to kill coyotes were redirected toward nonlethal predator-control methods—guard dogs, guard llamas, and better fencing practices—sheep losses would be even lower.

"What Bob is doing in Yellowstone is absolutely seminal," says Marc Bekoff, a biology professor at the University of Colorado who has been studying coyotes for 29 years. "If Wildlife Services would pay attention, instead of being married to killing animals, they might

ANTONIN KRATOCHVIL FOR *AUDUBON*

change their policies, and coyotes would be more manageable. Coyotes are too elusive to be controlled using the government's methods. They can live alone or in pairs or in packs. They can exploit an incredibly wide variety of foods. Of course, these findings are really nothing new. Native Americans have known for centuries about the coyote's adaptability. Why do you think they called coyotes Trickster?"

CRABTREE'S CRITICS—AND THEY ARE MANY, PRIMARily those employed by Wildlife Services—and even some of his supporters point to the fact that very little of Crabtree and Sheldon's data has been made public, preventing scientific scrutiny. Crabtree and Sheldon say they intend to publish their studies over the next two years. "It's difficult to put a lot of faith into what Bob Crabtree says—his words and his data may not agree," says Frederick Knowlton, a research biologist with the National Wildlife Research Center, in Logan, Utah. (The center is affiliated with Wildlife Services.) Knowlton, who has been studying coyote behavior since 1960, argues that it is necessary to kill coyotes to protect livestock even if the coyotes return. "I've been mowing my

DANIEL J. COX/NATURAL EXPOSURES

grass for 30 years, and it still grows back," he says. "That doesn't mean I'm not doing it right."

A powerful minority of Americans wants coyotes dead, and so **the slaughter will continue.**

Crabtree admits that even if government-sponsored killing of coyotes were halted, the animals' innate form of self-regulation would not happen immediately—he expects that it would require several years for the coyote population to revert to a more natural level. During these years, there would probably be even higher losses of sheep. The livestock industry is a powerful lobby; policy change that would result in greater woes for wool growers, even if only short-term, is not likely to occur.

In all probability, nothing will change. We will continue to kill 400,000 coyotes a year and cause the population to increase when it is entirely possible that, given patience, we wouldn't have to kill any coyotes and the population would shrink. One irony is that if we had not already killed so many wolves and bears, there would be no need to try to reduce the number of coyotes. "Why can't we let wolves control population?" Harrison asks.

Another irony is that if humans could kill coyotes more efficiently, the impact might have unexpected consequences throughout the food chain. "If you removed all the coyotes, the rodent population would expand unchecked," says David Gaillard, a researcher with the Predator Project, an environmental organization that opposes coyote hunting. "Voles and gophers would do more damage, in terms of monetary losses, to rangelands—damaging forage, digging up fields—than coyotes cost the livestock industry." So then we would have to start killing voles and gophers. That, of course, could lead to even more species to control.

An all-too-human hubris keeps us from admitting that we have met our match in coyotes, that they have outsmarted us for 100 years and will continue to do so. A powerful minority of Americans wants them dead, and so we keep killing them. The government-funded slaughter and the killing contests will continue. But coyotes—ever faster, ever stronger, still yipping and howling at the moon—will prevail. "Coyotes," Crabtree says, "are the ultimate icon of success and defiance of humans who think they can control nature."

Mike Finkel is the author of Alpine Circus, *which was published Nobember 1999 by Lyons Press. His last article for* Audubon, *a profile of tree-canopy researcher Nalini Nadkarni, appeared in the September–October issue.*

Unit Selections

Key Points to Consider

❖ Explain the analogy of the "commons" to describe global resources available to everyone. Is the concept a helpful one in assessing the future of resource management?

❖ What lessons can be learned from the ecosystem of the tall-grass prairie that will benefit crop agriculture? Is it possible to develop economically viable agricultural systems that can be as self-sustaining as natural systems, such as a prairie?

❖ How does livestock grazing have an impact on the riparian or waterside environment? How can advocates for wise use of public lands and livestock growers interested in maintaining large herds at minimum costs reach common ground in riparian land management?

❖ How is irrigation agriculture contributing to a decrease in the world's groundwater supply? Are there solutions to the problem of increasing food demand that rely on irrigation techniques that will be less demanding of the groundwater resource?

❖ Why and how has overfishing contributed to a decline in the food supply from the oceans? Has oceanic pollution contributed to this decline?

❖ What are some of the uncertainties about the future impact of global temperature increase on human social and economic systems? What reasons are there to modify existing international agreements to control greenhouse gas emissions, beyond the obvious concerns over global climate change?

 **Links** **www.dushkin.com/online/**

These sites are annotated on pages 4 and 5.

The worldwide situations regarding reduction of biodiversity, scarce energy resources, and environmental pollution have received the greatest amount of attention among members of the environmentalist community. But there are a number of other resource issues that demonstrate the interrelated nature of all human activities and the environments in which they occur. One such issue is that of declining agricultural land. In the developing world, excessive rural populations have forced the overuse of lands and sparked a shift into marginal areas, and the total availability of new farmland is decreasing at an alarming rate of 2 percent per year. In the developed world, intensive mechanized agriculture has resulted in such a loss of topsoil that some agricultural experts are predicting a decline in food production. Other natural resources, such as minerals and timber, are declining in quantity and quality as well. The overuse of groundwater reserves has resulted in potential shortages beside which the energy crisis pales in significance. And the very productivity of Earth's environmental systems—their ability to support human and other life—is being threatened by processes that derive at least in part from energy overuse and inefficiency and from pollution.

Uppermost in the minds of many who think of the environment in terms of an integrated whole, as evidenced by many of the selections in this unit, is the concept of the threshold or critical limit of human interference with natural systems of land, water, and air. This concept suggests that the environmental systems we occupy have been pushed to the brink of tolerance in terms of stability and that destabilization of environmental systems has consequences that can only be hinted at.

Many of these ideas are brought together in the lead article of this unit. Research scholars Joanna Burger and Michael Gochfeld revisit one of the most important of all environmental essays in "The Tragedy of the Commons: 30 Years Later." In the original essay, Garrett Hardin invoked the argument of common resources in support of his argument that as human population increased the global environment would eventually begin to suffer. Burger and Gochfeld note that Hardin's article was seminal in defining the problem of environmental impact in a way that resource managers could deal with and, as a consequence, management of the global commons (fisheries, forests, wildlife, the atmosphere) has received more attention. Whether the commons have received enough attention is for the future to determine.

In the *Land* subsection of this unit, both of the articles deal less with the impacts of marginality and exploitation and more with recent efforts to reduce them. In the first article, "Lessons from the Land Institute," Scott Russell Sanders describes the ultimate in potentially sustainable agriculture, the natural prairie grassland. Experimental farms based on the natural ecosystem of the tall-grass prairie are attempting to develop agricultural systems that will

reduce both exploitation and marginality. Similarly, in the second article in the *Land* subsection, Perri Knize describes the changes that are taking place in one of the world's more marginal agricultural activities: livestock grazing. In "Winning the War for the West" Knize points to increasing cooperation between livestock growers and public land advocates in the American West, long a battleground between the two groups. The ultimate winner is the public land environment.

The second subsection of the unit, *Water,* contains articles concerning water management on two quite different levels: groundwater and the boundless ocean. In each article, the concept of marginality is relevant. In the first selection, "When the World's Wells Runs Dry," Worldwatch researcher Sandra Postel addresses the problem of the world's dwindling groundwater resources as a result of enhanced irrigation technology. Virtually by definition, irrigation agriculture is marginal agriculture and the potential consequences of groundwater withdrawal at rates in excess of recharge are of major concern. The second selection in this subsection also deals with limits to wise use, in this instance, use of the resources of the world's oceans. In "The Deep Green Sea," Edward Carr describes how the world's oceans, once viewed as infinite in their bounty, are now suffering from overfishing and pollution. Where immensity and fecundity once seemed to be defining characteristics of the sea, now it is just another threatened environment.

In *Air*, the final subsection in this unit, the articles deal with the most critical and controversial of the problems that characterize the global atmosphere: the continuing accumulation of "greenhouse gases," the continuing deterioration of the ozone layer, and the global politics of atmospheric management. In the first article, "The Great Climate Flip-Flop," William Calvin introduces a concept that, while well known to atmospheric and oceanic scientists, is relatively new to the public: global warming could, paradoxically, lead to drastic and rapid cooling. The mechanism for such cooling is an ocean current, the North Atlantic Current, which regulates heat energy flows throughout the Atlantic. The last selection in this subsection deals with still another atmospheric problem, that of politics. Christopher Flavin of the Worldwatch Institute, in "Last Tango in Buenos Aires," provides a candid assessment of the potential for the Kyoto Protocol to limit carbon dioxide emissions. Flavin's view is that continued progress on the issue of global warming is stalled in politics while the consequences of atmospheric change are beginning to be felt in new and unexpected ways.

There are two possible solutions to all these problems posed by the use of increasingly marginal and scarce resources and by continuing global atmosphere pollution. One is to halt increasing population and consumption. The other is to provide incentives and techniques for the conservation of existing resources.

The Tragedy of the Commons:

by Joanna Burger and Michael Gochfeld

How do we manage resources that seem to belong to everyone? Fish swimming in lakes, game mammals wandering the open plains, and birds migrating overhead belong to everyone and yet are protected by no one. For the sturgeon and bison this lack of protection spelled disaster, for the passenger pigeon, extinction. Today, protecting such common-pool resources has become a challenge, not only on the local scale but on national and global ones as well.

Thirty years ago this December, ecologist Garrett Hardin invoked the analogy of a "commons" in support of his thesis that as human populations increased, there would be increasing pressure on finite resources at both the local and particularly the global levels, with the inevitable result of overexploitation and ruin. He termed this phenomenon the "tragedy of the commons."[1] More specifically, this phrase means that an increase in human population creates an increased strain on limited resources, which jeopardizes sustainability. Hardin argued that common resources could be exploited by anyone who could assert their rights to do so. He painted a bleak picture, emphasizing that the solutions were social rather than technical, and called for privatization or exclusion and for rigorous and even coercive regulation of human population.[2] Recently, he reaffirmed this position.[3]

This article looks at both the positive and negative management of common resources and the legal and ecological progress that has been made since Hardin's original article was written. (See the box, "Hardin's Tragedy of the Commons Thesis.")

Birth of a Discipline

Hardin's original paper was widely cited and stimulated many examples showing that increasing populations did lead to overexploitation, habitat degradation, and species extinctions.[4] Even those ecologists who found Hardin's reliance on coercion distasteful emphasized the consequences of the imbalance between population and resources.[5] Hardin's paper also stimulated many social scientists to alter their perspectives in relation to commons issues, with the result that many examples of both successful and unsuccessful maintenance of common resources have now been published.

The concept of commons is a useful model for understanding environmental management and sustainability. While Hardin believed that ruin was inevitable without coercive population control—an option at odds with our cherished democratic beliefs—recent works by a range of interdisciplinary scientists have identified systems and institutions that do not inevitably lead to overexploitation but that in some cases result in the sustainable use of selected resources, at least on local scales.[6]

While 30 years of research has shown that Hardin's initial thesis emphasizing inevitability and ruin was perhaps too bleak on the local scale, it has been enormously helpful in generating thought-provoking analyses across a wide range of disciplines. His work was widely cited, first by natural scientists and later by social scientists, yet unlike most scientific papers the rate of citation is increasing even 30 years later (see Figure 1). Perhaps its most useful role has been in illustrating the importance of integrating social and political theory with biological data. The traditional theory regarding resource users as unbridled appropriators is being replaced by the recognition that users can communicate and cooperate when it is in their interest to do so and when the resources at their disposal and the sociopolitical context permits it.[7]

What are Commons and Common-Pool Resources?

Common-pool resources (sometimes designated "common property") such as land, fish, and water can be identified and quantified, while the commons is a broader concept that includes the context in which common-pool resources exist and the property system embracing them. Indeed, the switch from discussing the commons to analyzing common-pool resources and property rights illustrates the disagreement many biological and social scientists have with Hardin's original thesis.

In the broad sense, a commons includes the resources held in common by a group of people, all of whom have access and who derive benefit with increasing access. Access may be equal or unequal, and control may be democratic or not. There is some disagreement as to what constitutes a common-pool resource. The term is often restricted to land, grass, wildlife, fish, for-

From *Environment*, December 1998, pp. 4-13, 26-27. Reprinted with permission of the Helen Dwight Reid Educational Foundation. Published by Heldref Publications, 1319 Eighteenth St., NW, Washington, DC 20036-1802. © 1998.

ests, and water. The concept can also be applied to non-natural resources such as national treasuries, medical care, and the Internet,[8] but the focus of this article will be on the more traditional commons issues of fisheries, recreational areas, public land, and air quality (although atmosphere has been a highly disputed commons with unique qualities to be discussed later). Once these resources could be held in common by small tribes or villages, communities could limit both access to the resources and the amount extracted. Limitation often involved aggression against would-be usurpers.

In many places, this system still exists. In the dry desert lands of northern Namibia and southern Angola, tribal councils control large blocks of land and tribe members are free to build their houses and farm wherever they choose. The councils can mediate disputes, limit intruders, and impose sanctions. While the primary resource held in common is land for farming and grazing, another very important resource in these arid lands is water for people and livestock. Thus, even where overall population density is low, land is not equally desirable and people congregate near the rivers and marshes, potentially leading to overexploitation of these lands and depletion and fouling of water.

Categories of Commons and Property Rights

Current reexamination of the applicability of common-pool resource management is fitting because the use of many resources has become truly globalized, requiring new and more global solutions. International attention has now focused on various aspects of sustainability. Global economies, multinational corporations, international trade agreements, and international commissions have created an institutional framework in which resource sustainability is one prevailing theme among a virtual cacophony of others.[9] As Elinor Ostrom, professor of political theory and policy analysis at Indiana University, points out, it is unclear whether existing international cooperative efforts are adequate to protect essential resources.[10] Rates of population growth and resource consumption vary among regions. The gap in who has access to resources is not narrowing, and there is rapid emergence of new technologies that allow even more efficient exploitation of resources. At the same time, improved communication has heightened expectations of a higher standard of living, even in remote re-

HARDIN'S TRAGEDY OF THE COMMONS THESIS

Hardin based his thesis of the tragedy of the commons on earlier studies written during the late 18th and early 19th centuries. In 1798, Thomas Robert Malthus wrote that human population could grow exponentially, unmatched by resource growth.[1] Charles Darwin's theory of evolution predicted that the characteristics of people who produced more children than others would increase over time. These observations are even more true today given medical care and social systems to protect the children of those who cannot support them. For most of human history, the world seemed like an infinite space with unlimited resources (forests, oceans, wildlife) available for the taking because in nearly every part of the globe there were sufficient resources for the existing, low-density populations. In the past century, however, human population has increased almost everywhere, demonstrating that demand can more than match even very abundant resources.[2]

In 1968, Hardin predicted that with increasing population the eventual fate of all common resources was overexploitation and degradation.[3] His credo, "Freedom in a Commons brings ruin to all," became a universal cry. Others made the same point, although with less flare and consequently less effect. Hardin's concerns focused people's attention on the relationship between individual behavior and resource sustainability.[4] The underlying tenet of his thesis, however, was that populations were increasing beyond the ability of the Earth's resources to support them at a sufficiently high standard of living.

Hardin used William Foster Lloyd's example of herdsmen sharing village lands to graze cattle.[5] Each herdsman derives full benefit from each cow he adds to his herd, while the depletion of grass attributable to that cow is shared among all users. Thus, at each decision point, Hardin argued, each herdsman would choose to add a cow rather than maintain status quo. This leads to each herdsman increasing his herd without limit and to ultimate and inevitable ruin for all. Hardin made several assumptions, including that the world and its resources are finite, human populations will continue to increase, and every person will want to use an increasing share of the resources. Hardin's solution was to have government controls to limit access to the commons or to privatize common-pool resources and, above all, to limit population, even through coercion. Recently Hardin has reaffirmed his predictions, noting that expanding cities must control traffic and parking, nations seek to limit air pollution, and the freedom of the seas is being constrained.[6]

1. T. R. Malthus, *Population: The First Essay* (Ann Arbor, Mich.; University of Michigan Press, 1959).

2. J. Cohen, *How Many People Can the Earth Support?* (New York: W. W. Norton, 1995).

3. G. Hardin, "The Tragedy of the Commons," *Science*, 13 December 1968, 1,243–48.

4. G. Hardin and J. Baden, eds., *Managing the Commons* (New York; W. H. Freeman, 1977).

5. W. F. Lloyd, "Population," "Value," "Poor-laws," and "Rent," in *Reprints of Economic Classics* (New York: Kelley, 1968).

6. G. Hardin, "Extensions of 'The Tragedy of the Commons'," *Science*, 1 May 1998, 682–83.

gions of developing nations. The rate of these changes is also accelerating.

The following examples of commons challenges are drawn from fisheries, public land use, and air quality. Each of these represent similar themes but different scales and solutions. Ostrom identifies four properties of these resources that facilitate cooperative management: the resource has not already been depleted beyond hope of recovery; there are reliable indicators of resource condition; the resource is sufficiently predictable; and the distribution of the resource is sufficiently localized to be studied and controlled by the political entity.

There are also four general categories of property rights: open or uncon-

trolled access, communal, state, and private[11] (see Table 1). Access refers to who controls access or who has access to the resources under what conditions or for what time period (while subtractability refers to the ability of one user to subtract from the welfare of the others).[12] These categories are not discrete but intergrade, and some common-pool resources can be managed under more than one category.[13] For some fisheries, such as shellfish, the government enforces regulations on seasons, size limits, and overall take, but the local shell-fishermen may claim traditional rights or ownership of particular clam beds that they seed with young shellfish, waiting for them to mature to a marketable size. Infringement of these beds can often lead to violence, as has happened in Maine when interlopers tried to fish for lobster in a territory claimed by someone else.[14]

Different modes of property rights may compete—for example federal versus local government or privatization versus community control. Even where a community or state maintains ownership, restricted access for exploitation of certain resources may be granted by concession. There may be a dissociation between resources: One may own land and trees privately whereas wildlife is communal property, or individuals may own rights to certain trees on communal land.

Basically, there is the question of how access can be controlled or managed, and who wins and who loses. Access can be managed by agreed-upon rights and rules, which are uniformly adhered to or enforced.[15] For example, in a small fishing community without outsiders, fishermen can agree to fish only in certain zones or only at certain times, catching a prescribed amount of fish. As long as everyone follows the rules, and the community governs wisely, the fishermen's extraction would not exceed the carrying capacity or regeneration rate of the fish stocks, the resource would not be depleted, and the situation would be considered sustainable. The failure of someone to follow the agreed-upon rules necessitates sanctions, which must also be agreed upon by the users or commoners.

One difficulty in protecting common-pool resources is that there is often an incongruence between the distribution of the resource and property regimes. Fisheries provide many examples of such disparities; many commercial fish are migratory, making property rights, even those as broad as the 200-mile exclusive economic zones, effective for only part of the year.

Local to Global: The Commons Comes of Age

The greatest changes that have come about since Hardin proposed the tragedy of the commons have been an increase in human populations worldwide, shrinking resources, and the globalization of economies. The focus on commons management as a discrete area of social and economic challenge overlaps broadly with the focus on sustainability of resources. Indeed, those concerned with the sustainability of resources should examine whether a commons represents an appropriate avenue for developing sustainable management, and if so, at what spatial scale.

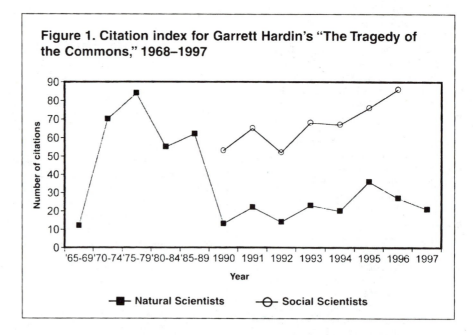

Figure 1. Citation index for Garrett Hardin's "The Tragedy of the Commons," 1968–1997

Temporal scales are important as well, for there are intergenerational aspects that need consideration.[16] The wise or unwise use of resources today directly affects the health and well-being of the next generation. We are borrowing from the next generation at a time when our resources are not only decreasing but population, and thus resource needs, is increasing.

Understanding the use of common-pool resources has been greatly enhanced by two developments: a new economic theory of cooperation that suggests cooperation could lead to the wise and sustained use of common-pool resources; and very detailed empirical work on commons issues that were well founded in theory.[17] Both were essential for the field to move forward. The traditional model of examining commons assumed that each person acted only in his or her own immediate best interest. More recently, economic theory suggests that by cooperating with others (even if there is an initial cost), common users can not only protect the resource but keep it sustainable as well. By examining case studies, researchers found that cooperation can lead to sustainable use and economic viability at least on small regional and short temporal scales.

There are many examples of both failed and successful attempts to manage common resources on local levels. Bonnie McCay, professor of human ecology at Rutgers University, and Fikret Berkes, professor at the Natural Resources Institute at the University of Manitoba, have been instrumental in providing examples where fishermen, hunters, and foresters have established norms, rules, and institutions to successfully extract resources without overexploitation.[18] They argue persuasively that although the tragedy of the commons has been accorded the status of a scientific law, much more detailed study of common-property resource management is needed. There are good examples of self-regulation, including Maine lobstermen and New Jersey fisherman who maintain yields and thus stable or even raise prices.

Three major categories of environmental problems that are useful in understanding methods of dealing with common-pool resources are fisheries, public lands, and air pollution. They are interesting because they illustrate the two main abuses of the commons: resource depletion and capacity depletion (due to pollution). Fish are a traditional, depletable common-pool resource, public land can fall under either category, and air pollution is a more global issue that affects the world at large. Traditional approaches to air pollution are being complemented by viewing the atmosphere's capacity to absorb pollutants as a commons issue. Although at first air seems markedly different from renewable resources such as fish, firewood, and lumber, viewing the atmosphere in terms of limited capacity means that everyone who introduces pollutants, even though he or she does not consume air, subtracts from its use by others.

Fisheries and Water-Related Issues

Fisheries offer classic examples of commons issues that can be local (a stream or lake), regional (North Atlantic), or global, depending upon the fishery. Fisheries also provide examples of the best and worst management schemes concerning common resources. They are instructive because there are examples of local and institutional control that have effectively protected a resource and a livelihood in a sustainable manner, as well as examples of massive overexploitation that threaten not only the commercial but the biological viability of some species.[19]

Although the major fisheries challenges involve oceanic species and a system of uncontrolled, open access on the high seas, shrimp farming along the tropical coastlines is one important example of a land-margin commons issue where a combination of private, state, and communal property rights prevail. Increasing market demand for shrimp provides an incentive for the conversion of otherwise valuable mangrove habitats—where many fish species spawn—to shrimp farms, often at the expense rather than enrichment of fishing communities. The shrimp farms are often owned by corporations with the capital for transforming the habitat rather than being managed by local cooperatives. These farms are economically viable for only a few years, after which they are often abandoned.

In the United States, inshore marine resources are managed by state governments as a trust for all citizens. However, even within this government-regulated system fishermen can cooperate locally to preserve a common-pool resource. Lobster, for example, are a common-pool resource that can be easily overexploited if everyone has a right to harvest and if there are no limits on the number of lobster each fisherman takes. Additionally, if fishermen can come in from outside the region the problem increases. In Maine, the state government does not limit the number of licenses, but the lobstermen practice exclusion through a system of traditional fishing rights. Acceptance into the lobster fishing community is essential before someone can fish, and thereafter one can extract lobsters only in the territory held by that community. The end result has been a sustainable harvest and higher catches of larger, commercially valuable lobsters by fishermen in the exclusion communities.[20]

McCay and colleagues have also shown that in a trawl fishery in the New York Bight, the fishermen belong to a co-operative that has maintained relatively high prices and sustainability by limiting entry into the local fishery and establishing catch quotas among members. In this case, self-regulation is both flexible and effective.[21] The trawl fishery illus-trates another critical point about commons resources: It is not only important to have sufficient fish to catch and fish populations that are stable but the price must be maintained or the industry will not be viable for the users.

In both of these examples, success has been achieved by local management of a local fishery. The fishermen were effective in excluding outsiders and in limiting the fishing rights of insiders so that fish stocks were sustainable, prices were maintained, and the fishery was viable. Management of fisheries on a regional or global scale is far more problematic because of the difficulty of exclusion or of monitoring catches.

At the opposite end of the spatial spectrum are cases where fisheries management has been ineffective, with declines in the fish stocks so serious that both the fishery and the fish are threatened with extinction.[22] Many of the examples where fish stocks have declined precipitously involve marine fish with wide geographical ranges. Swordfish and bluefin tuna are classic illustrations of Hardin's thesis. They are a common-pool resource that have suffered overexploitation because of the difficulty of exclusion and the pressure from fishermen of many countries who, stimulated by high market value, push for the maximum catch possible.

Carl Safina, conservation writer and director of the Living Oceans Program of the National Audubon Society, has highlighted the plight of bluefin tuna, one of the largest, fastest, and most wide-ranging fish in the ocean.[23] Its west Atlantic breeding population has declined by 90 percent since 1975 (see Figure 2).[24] The International Commission for the Conservation of Atlantic Tunas, responsible for stewardship of these tuna, is made up of members from 20 countries, many of whom are major tuna users. Although the commission's scientific advisory committees repeatedly presented them with data showing drastic declines, the commission continued to allow catches that exceeded the maximum sustainable yield. In this case, the problem has multiple facets: Some countries that catch tuna are not members of the commission and are thus not regulated; some countries that belong to the commission fish under flags from non-commission countries so they elude the regulations; the fishery is pelagic and global, making enforcement of regulation difficult if not impossible; and last-ditch efforts to place the species on Convention on International Trade in Endangered Species of Wild Flora and Fauna (CITES) lists, which would limit fishing, have so far failed due to pressure from user nations. Even aggressive efforts by the conservation community have been unable to prevent the continued destruction of bluefin tuna.

On a national scale, the United States successfully excluded foreign fishing fleets from its exclusive economic zone and dominated these waters. Even where outsiders have been excluded, however, the commons problem remains because without institutional controls, insiders are free to exploit resources. As Safina pointed out, excluding outsiders did not prevent U.S. fishermen from overexploiting fish resources despite the establishment of agencies and commissions nominally charged with protecting these resources. The problem partly lies with the membership on such commissions; many members represent fishermen who want to get their share (or more) rather than people who are charged with protecting the fish stocks regardless of the economic pressures.

Although successful management of common-pool resources for sustainability is desirable, there are other approaches that do not incorporate sustainability. Some marine fisheries exemplify an alternative approach involving overcapitalization of fleets, rapid sequential elimination of one common-pool fishery resource after another, and shifting to new resources.[25] This allows the industry to perpetuate itself in the short term with little attention to sustainability of a specific resource. When local resources are exhausted, fishermen must exploit more distant sources or sell their fleets and make other investments.

Moreover, understanding of traditional common-pool resources in fisheries has been expanded to include other coastal resources. Two examples illustrate this point: the serious reduction in horseshoe crabs and shorebirds; and personal watercraft users versus fishermen and other water users.

Horseshoe Crabs and Shorebirds

Since 1990, a directed fishery for horseshoe crabs has developed along the East Coast of North America to fulfill the demand for bait for eels, conch, and other fish. This had led to overexploitation and the reduction in the number of horseshoe crabs spawning in many regions. While this problem may once have been considered a fisheries issue only, it is compounded by the fact that several species of migratory shorebirds are threatened by the massive reduction in horseshoe crab eggs, their major food source on Delaware Bay and other stopover places during their northward migration.[26] Although the animals themselves are transitory, the phenomenon

Table 1. Types of property rights regimes

Type	Description	Example
Open Access	Absence of any well-defined property rights; completely open access to resources that are free to everyone	Recreational fishing in open ocean. Bison and passenger pigeon overharvested leading to decline and even extinction
Common Property	Resource held by community of users who may apportion or regulate access by members and may exclude non-members	Small fishing village that regulates fishing rights among users
State Property	The resource is held by government, which may regulate or exploit the resource or grant public access; government can enforce, sanction, or subsidize the use by some people	Public lands such as national forests or parks where grazing, lumber, or recreational rights are granted by government
Private Property	Individual owns property and has the right to exclude others from use as well as sell or rent the property rights	Private ownership of a woods where owner can sell or rent the land, cut or sell the trees.

occurs annually and predictably on the same beaches.

Apart from the fishermen, several local communities depend on the tourist income generated by the attraction of huge concentrations of migratory shorebirds and breeding horseshoe crabs. Having large populations of both species available for viewing is a commons resource. The fishermen's direct extraction of crabs and the indirect extraction of birds reduces the resource attractive to the tourists, decreasing their pleasure and ultimately their visits. Although less conspicuous from an ecotourism viewpoint, other species, such as green sea turtles, also depend on horseshoe crabs for food, while a medical industry relies on horseshoe crabs for the production of an important laboratory reagent. Thus, a traditional commons fisheries problem has now emerged as a multispecies conservation problem involving other vertebrates as well as economic issues that affect not only the conservation community but fishing, industry, and tourism. A further complication is that the demand for the eels (for which ground up female horseshoe crab is the only bait) emanates from around the globe. Japan, having depleted its own eel populations and those of nearby Asian countries, now offers extremely high prices for American eels, rendering both eel trapping and horseshoe crabbing economically lucrative. Rapid extraction and rapid financial remuneration is the apparent priority rather than sustainability of the resource. While the Atlantic Coastal Marine Fisheries Commission is responsible for maintaining sustainable horseshoe crab populations, the protection of the shorebirds falls under the U.S. Fish and Wildlife Service, which has a conflicting prerogative.

Personal Watercraft versus Fishermen

Recreational use of public land and waterways, one of the commons resources that Hardin mentioned in his classic paper, has received little attention or rigorous analysis. In this example, the massive increase in the use of personal watercraft (often called "jet skis") threatens a number of common-pool resources: the safe nesting of estuarine birds and other animals, the quality of aquatic vegetation so essential to the production of fish and shellfish, the peace and quiet of residents in shore communities, the physical safety of others using aquatic environments, and the undisturbed fishing of both recreational and commercial fishermen.[27] Fast, noisy, and numerous, these craft speed through habitats inaccessible to boats and are not yet regulated in most areas. However, the U.S. National Park Service is in the process of restricting or eliminating their use.

In many estuaries, commercial fishermen are already reporting decreases in catch because of the physical disturbance caused by personal watercraft, while other users report a serious reduction in aesthetic values such as "peace and quiet." This problem is not limited to coastal environments but threatens inland waterways as well. At issue is the freedom of personal watercraft users to take over aquatic environments where their open access subtracts ecological, aesthetic, and commercial benefits long sought by others.[28] Regulation of their use is in its infancy. Ultimately it may be the fatalities they cause, rather than aesthetic or economic impacts on the commons, that leads to further regulation and exclusion.

Public Land

One commons resource currently under discussion in the United States is the huge tracts of public land used for nuclear weapons production by the U.S. Department of Energy during the Cold War.[29] These are now being considered for transfer back to regional, local, or even private ownership, with the inherent problems of determining access and subtractability. For 50 years the federal government excluded all other users from these lands, which in the future could become commons for recreational, industrial, or agricultural use. Which option will be chosen remains undetermined and is likely to vary from site to site.

The Department of Energy's Savannah River Site in South Carolina is a good example. The site is composed of 800 square kilometers of land alongside the river. It includes habitat for a number of endangered species, such as the red-cockaded woodpecker, the wood stork, and the bald eagle, as well as some of the only remaining pristine Carolina Bay habitats. It also offers excellent hunting, fishing, and forestry opportunities. Only a small portion of the area contains industrial facilities and converting these to alternative industrial applications could be accomplished without detracting from the recreational and other uses of the site. Deciding how these lands will be used is a commons issue because the use by one group of people (expanded industrial development, agriculture, or forestry) could detract from the use of others. There are many users with conflicting ideas and stakes in how these public lands should be used, and the question of winners and losers is not only one of human values but of ecological values as well.

Air Quality as a Common-Pool Concern

Traditional approaches to the commons have usually not dealt with air quality or air pollution. Although the atmosphere is a common-pool resource, it is in its use for waste disposal—where unequal access is very difficult to control—that the resource suffers degradation. Studies of global atmospheric transport reveal that air pollutants travel around the globe, to be deposited thousands of miles away from the source. (See "Atmosphere as a Global Commons" in the March 1998 issue of *Environment* for more on transboundary air pollution problems.)

Air pollution from power plants has long been of concern to downwind receptors. While the downwind states and provinces in northeastern North America were encouraging more stringent air pollution standards to control emissions of acid gases and toxic air pollutants, a serious countervailing force arose in the form of energy deregulation. By requiring states to allow the importation of electric power from any producer, the production of cheaper electricity from more polluting plants might actually be increased through demand from users within the downwind states (who will both provide the incentive for and suffer the consequences of increased energy production). Current legislation in the 12 states that have already deregulated electricity includes a variety of incentives for producers (both in-state and out-of-state) to reduce emissions, including disclosure portfolios that would allow consumers to know the emission characteristics of their vendors. In this example, there is no community of producers or consumers of electricity, but there is a clear community of users of air quality, who may have little prerogative for controlling the quality of their air. The states, which would normally be responsible for protecting their residents' health, are clearly not sufficient, and even the regional or multistate consortiums that have formed may be inadequate to protect this common environment. Moreover, the prerogative of the responsible federal agency, the U.S. Environmental Protection Agency, is in jeopardy unless the final deregulation legislation empowers that agency to improve air pollution standards nationwide (even if the lowered cost of electricity is compromised).

Common-Pool Resources and Conflict Resolution

Our understanding of both common-pool resources and the institutions governing their use comes from a number of case studies of resource management in a variety of cultures. Some of the most enlightening case studies deal with the use of public lands, fisheries, agriculture and irrigation systems, groundwater, and contamination of the air. Conflicts inevitably arise and are resolved differently under different property access systems. By examining what systems have worked as well as which ones have allowed or even accelerated resource depletion and habitat degradation, it is possible to begin to understand the rights, rules, and institutions that govern the wise and sustainable use of common-pool resources. This is the legacy of Hardin's initial article, and the responsibility falls on a wide range of disciplines to accomplish it.

The management of common-pool resources is in various stages of development. Recreational and agricultural lands and forests remain as commons in some regions of the world but are privately or governmentally owned in others. Other common-pool resources, such as clean air and water, are clearly regional or global concerns requiring cooperation among widely dispersed people and governments. In many cases, existing national governments are not presently able to manage them effectively at the national, much less at the global, scale.

The oceans may be in transition from being nationally managed to being regionally or globally controlled, as reflected in the increasing reliance on international treaties to establish exclusive economic zones and international commissions to set quotas, close certain fisheries, and maintain catch statistics. Likewise, there are attempts through international conventions to protect major regional airsheds and even the global atmosphere and ultimately global climate. The Montreal protocol offers an example of a partially successful attempt to retard ozone depletion on a global scale by limiting the use of chlorofluorocarbons.

Social Policy Meets Ecology

Our understanding of common-pool resources is entering a new era of more global influence over resource use and pollution abatement coupled with local institutions managing the resources within their own domains. Ostrom argues that international treaty practices are in a position to take commons management actions on a global scale. But this will require hard decisions and long-term considerations on the part of user nations. Such decisions are often difficult to make in light of short-term domestic economic constraints influenced by the multinational nature of corporations wielding power and the potential for blackmail by user nations.[30]

The United Nations is the logical forum for developing commons approaches, but its potential is yet to be realized and it seems to be dismissed or ignored in most discussions. Nonetheless, under its aegis a number of attempts are being made. These include the Kyoto protocol on climate change and the Convention on Long-Range Transboundary Air Pollution, which together call for at least a 50 percent reduction in metal emissions and cover basic obligations, cooperative research, reporting, monitoring, compliance, and dispute resolution.[31]

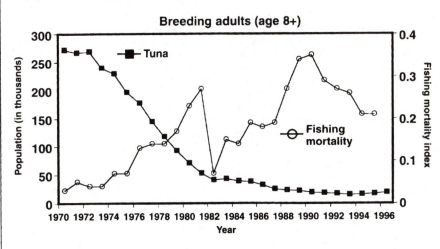

Figure 2. Population size and harvest figures for Western Atlantic bluefin tuna

It has become increasingly clear that there are great differences among individuals' access and use of resources, both locally and globally. We will not find one set of rights, rules, and regulations that will fit all common-pool resources. It is also apparent that the social institutions of an ethnically homogeneous, interrelated tribe cooperatively managing a local fishery or plot of land are not a complete model for cooperation among diverse nations managing a global resource.

Social scientists have established a framework for evaluating characteristics of the user. Commons management is more likely to succeed when the users depend on the resource and share a common understanding of it; when there are grounds for trust; when the users can form an autonomous controlling body; and when they have prior experience with successful management.[32]

Increasing our understanding of how to make the Earth sustainable will require more detailed knowledge about the biology of resources, the social and cultural systems that depend upon these resources, and the economic pressures that govern them. Discussions of sustainability must be based on an understanding of common-pool resource management. The reliance of Western civilization on technological solutions will not solve many of the issues raised by common-pool resources.[33] This is particularly true given the globalization of resource extraction, where the parties that benefit and those that incur the costs are separated geographically and economically and where the benefits are derived by one generation but the costs are incurred by future generations.

Conclusions

Hardin's thesis was seminal in defining the problem of the management of commons and common-pool resources. It met with immediate support by many resource managers who noted that a variety of species had declined dramatically because of overexploitation. Thereafter, social scientists began to note exceptions to his tragedy scenarios, arguing that his thesis was oversimplified and providing examples where institutions allowed people to manage resources sustainably.

Theoretical and empirical studies of common-pool resources have centered on two areas: depletable resources (such as fish, trees, and grasslands) and the depletable waste capacity of resources (such as air and water). While concepts of the commons are equally applicable to both types and remarkable

headway has been made in the study of depletable resources, understanding the use of air and water as waste sinks still lags behind. This difference may reflect the more global nature of air and water resources, where the benefits are accrued in one place and the costs are borne by users many thousands of miles away.

The major research thrusts for the future will be in understanding the management of common-pool resources on different temporal and spatial scales, with a view to applying the lessons learned and expanding their applicability. Many of the examples of wise management of common-pool resources have been managed effectively, such as the successful recovery of striped bass along the Atlantic Coast, which required a combination of governmental intervention and user cooperation. The management of global commons resources, particularly fisheries, forests, and wildlife has received considerable attention over the last 10 years and will be an important global issue for many years to come. Although we are making some headway with international treaties to manage global resources (the Montreal protocol and CITES are good examples), other attempts have been disastrous (for example, bluefin tuna). Yet institutions must be developed to deal with these resources or the species are doomed, along with their fisheries.

The difficulty of managing global resources is partly one of attempting to create global treaties and other institutions where there is no global government and few global sanctions. Privatization or long-term governmental stewardship offer alternatives to communal management at the local and regional level, but international conservation will require cooperation across nations where principles of the commons can be invoked to take advantage of common self-interest in protecting a resource. The management of common-pool resources seems to function best where there are sanctions that everyone agrees to and that can be enforced and where the benefits of management are widely recognized.

Joanna Burger is a distinguished research professor of biology at Rutgers University. Michael Gochfeld is clinical professor of environmental and community medicine at the University of Medicine and Dentistry of New Jersey's Robert Wood Johnson Medical School. The authors can be reached at the Environmental and Occupational Health Sciences Institute, Piscataway, NJ 08854

(Burger's telephone: (732) 445-4318, e-mail: burger@biology.rutgers.edu; Gochfeld's telephone: (732) 445-0123, ext. 627, e-mail: gochfeld@ eohsi.rutgers.edu).

The authors would like to thank several people for comments on the manuscript, including C. Safina, B. McCay, C. Powers, and B. Goldstein. Alana Darnell extracted data from citation abstracts and Robert Ramos prepared the illustrations. Some of the research discussed herein was funded by the New Jersey Department of Environmental Protection, the U.S. Environmental Protection Agency, the Trust for Public Lands, the Department of Energy (cooperative agreement with the Consortium for Risk Evaluation with Stakeholder Participation, DE-FC01-95EW55084) and the National Institute for Environmental Health Sciences (ES05022).

Notes

1. G. Hardin, "The Tragedy of the Commons," *Science*, 13 December 1968, 1,243–48.

2. Ibid.

3. G. Hardin, "Extensions of 'The Tragedy of the Commons'," Science, 1 May 1998, 682–83.

4. P. Ehrlich and J. P. Holdren, "Impact of Population Growth," *Science*, March 1971, 1,212–17.

5. B. Commoner, *The Closing Circle* (New York: A. Knopf, 1971); and G. C. Daily and P. R. Ehrlich, "Population, Sustainability, and Earth's Carrying Capacity," *BioScience* 42 (1992): 761–71.

6. D. Feeny, F. Berkes, B. J. McCay, and J. M. Acheson, "The Tragedy of the Commons: Twenty-Two Years Later," *Human Ecology* 18 (1990): 1–19; and F. Berkes, ed., *Common Property Resources: Ecology and Community-Based Sustainable Development* (London; Belhaven Press, 1989).

7. E. Ostrom, "Self-Governance of Common-Pool Resources," in P. Newman, ed., *The New Palgrave Dictionary of Economics and the Law* (London: MacMillan, in press).

8. C. Hess, "Untangling the Web: The Internet as a Commons" (unpublished manuscript presented at the workshop Reinventing the Commons, Transnational Institute, Bonn, Germany, 4–5 November 1995).

9. M. McGinnis and E. Ostrom, "Design Principles for Local and Global Commons," in O. R. Young et al, eds., *International Political Economy and International Institutions* 11 (Cheltenham, U.K.: Edward Elgar Publications, 1996).

10. Ostrom, note 7 above.

11. S. Hanna and M. Monasinghe, eds., *Property Rights and the Environment:*

Social and Ecological Issues (Washington, D.C.: The Beijer Institute of Ecological Economics and the World Bank, 1995); and National Research Council, *Proceedings of the Conference on Common Property Resource Management* (Washington, D.C.: National Academy Press, 1986).

12. F. Berkes, D. Feeny, B. J. McCay, and J. M. Acheson, "The Benefits of the Commons," *Nature,* July 1989, 91–93.

13. Feeny et al., note 6 above.

14. J. M. Acheson, *The Lobster Gangs of Maine* (Hanover, N.H.: University Press of New England, 1988).

15. E. Ostrom, *Governing the Commons: The Evolution of Institutions for Collective Action* (New York: Cambridge University Press, 1990).

16. R. B. Norgaard, "Intergenerational Commons, Globalization, Economism, and Unsustainable Development," *Advances in Human Ecology* 4 (1995): 141–71.

17. Ostrom, note 7 above.

18. B. J. McCay, "Muddling through the Clam Beds: Cooperative Management of New Jersey's Hard Clam Spawner Sanctuaries," *Journal of Shellfish Research* 7 (1988): 327–40; and B. J. McCay and J. M. Acheson, eds., *The Question of the Commons: The Culture and Ecology of Communal Resources* (Tucson, Ariz.: University of Arizona Press, 1987).

19. C. Safina, *Song for the Blue Ocean* (New York: Henry Holt & Co., 1997).

20. Ostrom, note 15 above.

21. Norgaard, note 16 above.

22. C. Safina, "Where Have All the Fishes Gone?," *Issues in Science and Technology* 10 (1994): 37–43.

23. C. Safina, "Bluefin Tuna in the West Atlantic: Negligent Management and the Making of an Endangered Species," *Conservation Biology* 7 (1993): 229–34.

24. International Commission for the Conservation of Atlantic Tunas, *Report of the Standing Committee on Research and Statistics* (Genoa, Italy, 1996).

25. Safina, note 19 above.

26. J. Burger, *A. Naturalist along the Jersey Shore* (New Brunswick, N.J.: Rutgers University Press, 1996).

27. J. Burger, "Effects of Motorboats and Personal Watercraft on Flight Behavior over a Colony of Common Terns," *Condor* 105 (1998): 528–34.

28. J. Burger, "Attitudes about Recreation, Environmental Problems, and Estuarine Health along the New Jersey Shore, U.S.A." *Environmental Management* 22 (1998): 889–96.

29. Commission on Risk Assessment and Risk Management, *Report of the Commission on Risk Assessment and Risk Management* (Washington, D.C.: U.S. Congress, 1997); Department of Energy, *Charting the Course: the Future Use Report,* DOE/EM-0283 (Washington, D.C., 1996); and J. Burger, J. Sanchez, J. W. Gibbons, and M. Gochfeld, "Risk Perception, Federal Spending, and the Savannah River Site: Attitudes of Hunters and Fishermen," *Risk Analysis* 17 (1997): 313–20.

30. Safina, note 22 above.

31. H. E. Ott, "The Kyoto Protocol; Unfinished Business," *Environment,* July/August 1998, 17; Economic and Social Council, "Convention on the Long-Range Transboundary Air Pollution of Heavy Metals" (Aarhus, Denmark: United Nations, 1998).

32. Ostrom, note 7 above.

33. Hardin, note 1 above.

LESSONS FROM THE
LAND INSTITUTE

Could the prairie, which runs on sunlight and rain, be a model
for the perfect farm? Wes Jackson thinks so.

BY SCOTT RUSSELL SANDERS

REVOLUTION IN SALINA, KANSAS, FIRST thing in the morning on the last day of October, not much is stirring except pickup trucks and rain. Pumpkins on porch railings gleam in the streetlights. Scarecrows and skeletons loom outside low frame houses. Tonight the children of Salina will troop from door to door in costumes, begging candy. But this morning, only a few of their grandparents cruise the wet streets, in search of breakfast.

In the diner where I come to rest, the talk is mainly about family and politics and prices. Beef sells for less than the cost of raising it. There's a glut of wheat. More local farmers have gone bankrupt. An older woman bustles in from the street, tugs a scarf from her helmet of white curls, and demands gaily, "Who says it can't rain in Kansas?" Another woman answers, "Oh, it rains every once in a while—and when it does, look out!"

Here in the heart of Kansas, where tallgrass prairie gives way to mid-grass, about 29 inches of water fall every year, enough to keep the pastures thick and lure farmers into planting row crops. Like farmers elsewhere, they spray pesticides and herbicides, spread artificial fertilizer, and irrigate in dry weather. They plow and plant and harvest with machinery that runs on petroleum. They do everything the land grant colleges

and agribusinesses tell them to do, and still many of them go broke. And every year, from every plowed acre in Kansas, an average of two to eight tons of topsoil wash away. The streams near Salina carry rich dirt and troubling chemicals into the Missouri River, then to the Mississippi, and eventually to the Gulf of Mexico.

Industrial agriculture puts food on our tables and those of much of the rest of the world. But the land and the farmers pay a terrible price, and so do all the species that depend on the land, including us.

I've come to Salina to speak with a man who's seeking a radical remedy for all of that—literally radical, as in going back to the roots, both of plants and of agriculture. Wes Jackson and his then-wife, Dana, founded the Land Institute in 1976 to seek ways of providing food, shelter, and energy without degrading the planet. Wes won a MacArthur fellowship in 1992 for his efforts, and he has begun to win support in the scientific community for a revolutionary approach to farming that he calls perennial polyculture—crops intermingled in a field that is never plowed, because the plants grow back on their own every year. The goal of his grand experiment: a form of agriculture that, like a prairie, runs entirely on sunlight and rain.

To reach the Land Institute, I drive past grain silos bound side to side like the columns of a great cathedral, past filling stations where gas sells for 85

cents a gallon, then onto a gravel road. The windshield wipers can't keep up with the rain. After the road crosses the Smoky Hill River, it leaves the flat bottomland, where bright-green shoots of alfalfa and winter wheat sprout from dirt the color of bittersweet chocolate, and climbs up onto a rolling prairie, where the Land Institute occupies 370 acres. Wes Jackson meets me in the yellow-brick house that serves as an office. It's easy to believe he played football at Kansas Wesleyan, because he's a burly man, with a broad, outdoor face leathered by sun and a full head of steel-gray hair. Although he'll soon be able to collect Social Security, he looks a decade younger. He holds a Ph.D. in genetics, and in the middle of a conversation he'll draw genomes and cells on whatever's handy—a notepad, a napkin, or thin air. For a man who thinks we've been farming the wrong way for about 10,000 years, he laughs often and delights in much. He also talks readily and well, with a prairie drawl acquired while growing up on a farm in the Kansas River valley, over near Topeka.

Where our ancestors went wrong, he believes, was in choosing to cultivate annual crops, which have to be planted each year in newly turned soil. The choice is understandable, since annual plants take hold more quickly and bear more abundantly than perennials do, and since our ancestors had no way of measuring the long-term consequences of all that digging and tilling.

But what's the alternative? Jackson takes me outside to look at the radically different model for agriculture that he's been studying for 22 years: the native prairie. Because the rain hasn't let up, we drive a short distance along the road to his battered Toyota pickup, then pass through a gate and go jouncing onto an

adapted to local conditions. "The earth is an ecological mosaic," Jackson says. "We're only beginning to recognize the powers inherent in local adaptation."

If you wish to draw on that natural wisdom in agriculture, he tells me as we drive toward the greenhouse, then here in Kansas you need to mimic the struc-

ture—as opposed to the annual monoculture of traditional farming—by experimenting with mixtures of wild plants. Recently they've focused on Illinois bundleflower, a nitrogen-fixing legume whose seed is about 38 percent protein; *Leymus*, a mammoth wild rye; eastern gamagrass, a bunchgrass that's related to

THE UNITED STATES LOSES 2 BILLION TONS OF TOPSOIL A YEAR TO EROSION, SAYS THE USDA, COSTING THE NATION $40 BILLION.

80-acre stretch of prairie that's never been plowed. The rusty, swaying stalks of big bluestem wave higher than the windshield. The shorter stalks of little bluestem, Indian grass, and switchgrass brush against the fenders. We stop on the highest ridge and roll down the windows so rain blows on our faces, and we gaze across a rippling, sensuous landscape, all rounded flanks and shadowy crevices.

The grasses are like a luxurious covering of fur, tinted copper and silver and gold. In spring or summer this place would be fiercely green and spangled with flowers, vibrant with butterflies and songbirds. Now, in the fall, it's thick with pheasant, quail, and wild turkey, Jackson reports. He and his colleagues don't harvest seeds here, but they do burn the prairie once every two or three years and let Texas longhorns graze it. Eventually they'll replace the cattle with bison, a species better adapted to these grasslands. From the pickup, we can see a few bison browsing on a neighbor's land, their shaggy coats dark with rain.

I N EVERY SEASON, THE PRAIRIE IS lovely beyond words. It supports a wealth of wildlife, resists diseases and pests, holds water, recycles, fixes nitrogen, and builds soil. And it achieves all of that while using only sunlight, air, snow, and rain. If we hope to achieve as much in our agriculture, Jackson argues, then we'd better study how the prairie works: by combining four basic types of perennial plants—warm-season grasses, cool-season grasses, legumes, and sunflowers—all growing year after year from the same roots. The soil is never laid bare. The prairie survives droughts and floods and insects and pathogens because the long winnowing process of evolution has created plant communities

ture of the prairie. It is all the more crucial a model, he figures, because at least 70 percent of the calories that humans eat come directly or indirectly from grains, and all our grains started as wild grasses. For nearly a quarter-century, Jackson and his colleagues have been working to develop perennial polycul-

corn but is three times as rich in protein; and Maximilian sunflower, a plentiful source of oil.

In the sweet-smelling greenhouse, we find seeds from these and other plants drying in paper bags clipped to lines with clothespins. The bags are marked so as to identify the plots where the

Illustration by Allison Seiffer

Tradition meets technology at the Land Institute. Longhorns graze the unplowed prairie; sorghum hybrids get a dose of water.

seeds were gathered; each plot represents a distinct ecological community. Over the years, researchers at the Land Institute have experimented with hundreds of combinations, seeking to answer four fundamental questions, which Jackson recites for me in a near shout as rain hammers down on the greenhouse roof: Can perennial grains, which invest so much in roots, also produce high seed yields? Can perennial species yield more when planted in combination with other species, as on the prairie, than when planted alone? Can a perennial polyculture meet its own need for nitrogen? Can it adequately manage weeds and insects and disease?

So far, Jackson believes, the researchers can offer a tentative yes to all those questions. For example, his daughter Laura, now a professor of biology at the University of Northern Iowa, identified a mutant strain of eastern gamagrass whose seed production is four times greater than normal—without any corresponding loss of root mass or vigor. "Prior to this work, researchers believed that perennial plants had to yield less than annuals," says Stephen Jones, a plant geneticist at Washington State University. "But that was only because there had been so little effort at breeding perennials." Jones is now working to develop perennial forms of wheat suited to the dry soils of eastern Washington. He has already achieved yields up to 70 percent as large as those of the annual varieties.

Recent experiments at the Land Institute suggest that mixtures of wild plants not only rival monocultures in productivity but also inhibit weeds, resist pathogens, and build fertility. Stuart Pimm, a conservation biologist at the University of Tennessee who reported those results in *Nature,* sees clear promise in a design-with-nature approach—although he concedes that "perennial, mixed-species agriculture will probably not replace all conventional monocultures."

But Wes Jackson argues that on highly erodible soil, it makes sense to replace the current farming practice with the one he's working toward. The United States loses 2 billion tons of topsoil a year to erosion, and the cost—in lost productivity, silting of reservoirs, pollution of waterways—is $40 billion, according to the U.S. Department of Agriculture. Jackson estimates that only 50 million of the 400 million tillable acres in the United States are flatland, and

even those are susceptible to erosion. The remaining 350 million acres—seven-eighths of the total—range from mildly to highly erodible, and they are thus prime territory for perennial polyculture.

More and more scientists are now testing this approach. Andrew Paterson, director of the plant-biotechnology program at the University of Georgia, is experimenting with perennial grains, and he draws encouragement from the work of the Land Institute. "They are among the few U.S. research institutions I am aware of that have a serious interest in this possibility," he says. Outside the United States, scientists at the International Rice Research Institute in the Philippines are working to develop perennial strains of rice.

John Reganold, a professor of soil science and a colleague of Jones's at Washington State, predicts that with natural-systems agriculture, "soil quality will significantly improve—better struc-

ture, more organic matter, increased biological activity, and thicker topsoil." Jones himself admits that the effort needed to bring perennial polyculture to the marketplace will be huge. "But remember," he points out, "the amount of research going into conventional agriculture is equally huge."

Transforming perennial polyculture from a research program into a feasible alternative for the working farmer will require many more years of painstaking effort. Researchers must breed high-yielding varieties of perennial grains and discover combinations of species that rival the productivity of the wild prairie. Engineers must design machinery for harvesting mixed grains. Farmers must be persuaded to try the new seeds and new practices, and consumers must be persuaded to eat unfamiliar foods.

The training of farmers is especially close to Jackson's heart. "The children in rural schools are one day going to be in charge of the 400 million acres of till-

Rivers like the Smoky Hill carry topsoil to the sea, but Wes Jackson (opposite) says Indian grass and big bluestem will hold it in place.

able land in this country," he says. "They'll have the greatest ecological impact of any group." To help inform those schools—and help resettle the small towns in which many of those children will grow up—the Land Institute has created a Rural Community Studies Center in Matfield Green, a tiny settlement in the Flint Hills about 100 miles southeast of Salina. "We want to bring the message of ecology to bear on the curriculum of rural schools," Jackson says. "I want those young people to go to Kansas State, Ohio State, all the ag schools, and ask questions that push beyond the existing paradigm."

One question is how well annual monoculture would perform if it weren't subsidized by inputs of petroleum and groundwater, and if it weren't able to write off the ecological costs of pesticides and herbicides and erosion. To answer that question, the Land Institute has devoted 150 acres to the Sunshine Farm, a 10-year project for growing livestock and conventional crops with-

what you see on Amish farms. And that tells me we're on the right track."

ACK IN THE YELLOW-BRICK OFFICE, Jackson unrolls onto a table what he calls the Big Chart, which lays out a 25-year research plan. The boxes on the chart frame problems to be solved, and the arrows all point toward the vision of a sustainable agriculture that will overturn the mistaken practices of the past 10 millennia. It's a bold scheme, and Jackson calculates that it will cost $5 million to $7 million a year—up from the Land Institute's current annual budget of $850,000. To secure that level of funding, Jackson will need backing from the U.S. Department of Agriculture and even from agribusiness firms. "So far," he admits, "we've hit a brick wall at USDA." He realizes how difficult it will be to pry money from institutions whose philosophy of farming he so squarely opposes, but he relishes the challenge.

"In America," he tells me, "we've got mostly two kinds of scientists—the ones

ling population? "We don't know how this is all going to turn out," he admits. "But the risky thing is to do nothing, to

"WE DON'T KNOW HOW THIS IS GOING TO TURN OUT," ADMITS JACKSON. "THE RISKY THING IS TO KEEP GOING THE WAY WE'VE BEEN GOING."

out fossil fuels, chemicals, or irrigation. The Sunshine Farm is where we go next, and the arrival of our truck wakes three dappled-gray Percheron draft horses from their rainy drowse in a paddock beside the barn. There's also a tractor, for the heaviest work; it runs on biodiesel fuel made from soybeans and sunflower seeds. The farmhouse is heated with wood, and all the buildings are lit by batteries charged by a bank of photovoltaic cells.

Six years into the study, data from the Sunshine Farm are providing a truer measure of how much conventional farming costs. Marty Bender, who manages the farm, explains, "We look at the energy content of all the crops and livestock that we produce, and we look at the inputs—fuels, feeds, stock, seeds, tools, labor. If you divide our outputs by our inputs, the ratio is comparable to

who get us in trouble, and the ones who tell us what the troubles are—but very few who are looking for solutions. Here at the Land Institute, we're looking for solutions."

Before I go, I can't help asking him to explain how a Kansas farm boy grew up to be a visionary who's trying to revolutionize farming. He can't say for sure. His family's been in Kansas since 1854 (the year that *Walden* was published); his grandchildren are the sixth generation to live here. So he feels committed to this place for the long haul, and he wants it to be a beautiful and fertile place well after he's gone. "It seems like, no matter what else I tried, I just kept thinking about the source— soil, water, photosynthesis, the things that sustain us." Is he hopeful that a sustainable form of agriculture will be found in time to feed the earth's swel-

keep going the way we've been going. No matter how dark the times, it's still worthwhile to do good work."

The next morning, as I drive east toward my home in Indiana, the radio carries reports of brimming rivers and flooded roads across Kansas. The plowed fields I pass are gouged by rivulets, and the roadside ditches run black with dirt. But where grass covers the land, there's no sign of runoff, for the prairie keeps doing what it's learned how to do over thousands of years: Holding water, building soil, waiting for spring.

Scott Russell Sanders is the author of numerous books, most recently Hunting for Hope, *published last fall by Beacon Press. He lived and worked on farms as a boy in Ohio.*

Winning the War for the West

After fiercely battling each other over the best use of public lands, some ranchers and environmentalists are beginning to agree: letting livestock graze can benefit the environment

by PERRI KNIZE

I N June of last year, while ranchers in Natrona County, Wyoming, waited out three days of rain to finish branding their calves, vandals calling themselves "Islamic Jihad Ecoterrorists" cut the barbed-wire fences separating Bureau of Land Management public range from private land, allowing the unbranded cattle of seven neighbors to mix. More than 150 cuts were made, resulting in about $100,000 in damage. At least two perpetrators left notes under rocks and nailed to posts on county roads reading, "No more welfare for cowboys" and "Just in time for the welfare cowboys' convention."

It was only one of the more extreme offensives in an ongoing regional battle over who owns the West. Ranchers today are up against a world that no longer views cowboys with nostalgia. The epithet "welfare cowboys" has become common in the national media, along with calls for an end to subsidized grazing on public lands. At the forefront of the grazing controversy are environmental groups, from the National Wildlife Federation and the Natural Resources Defense Council to grassroots organizations like the Southwest Center for Biological Diversity and the Oregon Natural Resources Council. The time has come, they say, to make rich and politically powerful "corporate" ranchers—an elite that has dominated the affairs of the West for more than a century—pay the full cost of the range program and manage their herds to environmentally correct standards. Better yet, some groups say, run them off the range, and use the land only for wildlife and recreation.

According to critics, domestic livestock that spend some time on the public range—88 percent of western sheep and roughly half of western cattle—are defecating in trout streams, trampling stream banks, and denuding the ground of forage and protective cover needed by wildlife, wreaking havoc on fragile ecosystems. Even worse, the public is paying for this devastation: federal outlays for the management of public grazing lands exceed permit fees from ranchers.

This call to arms is based on half-truths, skewed facts, and outright fallacies. The typical public-lands rancher is not a wealthy cattle baron. Though his ranch may be registered as a family corporation, he is barely making a living. His permit fees are not a form of subsidy—he has already paid full market value for the right to graze public lands. Overall the federal range is in better condition than it has been in more than a century. Furthermore, many scientists who study what happens to land where cattle graze admit that no definitive case can be made for or against livestock grazing.

It would be comforting to believe, for the sake of the West's future, that the Islamic Jihad Ecoterrorists terrorized the Wyoming ranchers only because they do not realize how debilitating any extra burden can be for a

---

Perri Knize is a freelance writer who lives in Montana. Her articles on environmental policy and on travel have appeared in *Audubon*, *Sports Illustrated*, and *Condé Nast Traveler*.

struggling ranch family. But then, few people in our technological age can comprehend the backbreaking physical labor during every daylight hour—with no vacations and little financial reward—that a western livestock operation requires.

Even worse for these families, cattle prices are about the lowest they have been in twenty years—and operating costs and land values have skyrocketed as new residents inundate the region. This means that the pickup truck a rancher could buy in the 1950s with the proceeds from selling eight steers now costs more than forty steers. On average, ranchers make only a two percent return on their operations, and many don't do that well. They would be better off liquidating their assets and putting them in a passbook savings account. Instead they turn down big offers from real-estate developers, put up with "ecoterrorists," and hang on by taking temporary jobs in town when the cattle market bottoms out. Ranching, it would seem, is a profession for romantic idealists, not profiteers. Those who hew to it do so for only one reason—they love the land and their way of life.

Caught in the Crossfire

DEAN Welborn, a lifelong cattle rancher, was sixty-three, suffering from bursitis, and looking for a way that his son and daughter-in-law and their four children could continue to ranch without him. Welborn figured he'd have to sell the Lima Peaks outfit in southwest Montana that he has owned for thirty years and buy a smaller, more manageable place. But before he could buy the nearby Briggs ranch, he needed to know if federal managers would let him run enough cattle on the ranch's attached 25,000-acre grazing allotment on public lands, known as the Muddy Creek allotment, to make the operation pay.

It looked promising. The Bureau of Land Management's file on the allotment—habitat for elk, mule deer, nesting waterfowl, and a pure strain of West Slope cutthroat trout—reported that it was showing continual improvement from the years when the land had been severely overgrazed by domestic sheep and cattle. BLM managers had recommended the Muddy Creek permit holders for a Stewardship Award in 1989, and had granted a 15 percent increase in cattle numbers for 1990. Welborn bought the ranch in the spring of 1992, believing that the BLM's glowing review made it safe to assume that stock allocations would remain the same.

Aggressive programs are now in place to help the banks of streams and lakes recover from overgrazing.

But 1992 was a bad year for safe assumptions in the cattle business. Anti-grazing sentiment was running high in the environmental movement and in Washington, D.C.: the cry was "Cattle-free in '93." After the election of Bill Clinton the Department of the Interior—parent agency of the BLM—came out in force against grazing. The new Secretary of the Interior, Bruce Babbitt, proposed a series of "range reforms," including doubling grazing fees, setting national land-management standards, and changing the agency's objectives from cattle and grass production to ecosystem health.

In response to these pressures the U.S. Forest Service—the other manager of the federal range—and the BLM set new standards and guidelines for grazing permits. The region where Welborn ranches became a demonstration area for what some characterize as a "cookbook" grazing prescription: throw the cows off the stream banks when animal tracks exceed a certain number, and throw the cows off the grass when stubble height is down to a certain number of inches. The goal was an easily applied standard that would help riparian zones, along the banks of streams and lakes, and uplands, above the stream banks, recover from more than a century of destructive overgrazing.

The Muddy Creek allotment was one of two areas chosen for aggressive implementation of the Beaverhead Riparian Guidelines, named for the Forest Service office that drafted them. After the BLM transferred the allotment to Welborn, managers reduced his allowable herd by 72 percent. This not only left Welborn financially hamstrung (he has since used up his family's savings trying to keep the ranch afloat) but also ended up threatening the trout fishery it was intended to protect. With his cattle sometimes thrown off Muddy Creek after only three days of grazing, Welborn has no choice but to graze them on his own deeded land—the location, ironically, of most of the prime West Slope cutthroat-trout habitat.

Being forced to degrade fisheries habitat does not sit well with Dean Welborn. He hardly fits the profile of the environmentally rapacious cattle rancher: he and fellow members of the Snowline Grazing Association, a ranching collaborative, have fenced off riparian areas for neotropical birds; pulled noxious weeds so that they don't go to seed; and put in water troughs to lure cows away from riparian zones. "We've gone out of our way to be good stewards of the soil," he says.

Ecosystems are far more complex and chaotic than anyone fully understands, and the Beaverhead guidelines, critics say, don't allow for that complexity. With cows moved off his allotment after very short use, Welborn claims, the upland grass is not being grazed enough to attract wildlife. Elk, deer, wild sheep, and antelope prefer the younger, more palatable shoots that are stimulated by the pruning of cattle grazing—a function that bison once provided in the same region. So the wild animals, instead of grazing the uplands, make camp in the riparian areas, where the vegetation is tender and lush. Hundreds of elk pound the stream banks and pollute the water with their droppings, just as cattle do. But the BLM doesn't manage wildlife.

In 1994 Welborn persuaded the BLM to reconsider the Beaverhead Riparian Guidelines. A new BLM area manager who was sympathetic to Welborn's predicament and understood the threat to the trout drafted a remedial management plan, but it was quickly appealed by a local environmentalist. After three years of waiting for a hearing in federal court, the BLM finally withdrew the remedial plan and at press time was drafting another allotment-management plan. In the meantime, Welborn has had to abide by the standards and guidelines in the 1993 grazing plan. He says he hopes that the new plan will allow him to run enough cattle to make his ranch viable while enhancing the natural-resource value of the land. Otherwise, he says, he will have to put his ranch up for sale, and the grazing restrictions will oblige any new owner to subdivide it.

> The capacity of cattle to revegetate has proved useful for reclaiming mining sites that resisted other methods.

The Ranching "Subsidy"

IN fiscal year 1998 the Bureau of Land Management and the U.S. Forest Service together spent at least $75 million on the federal grazing program, and took in only about $20 million in grazing fees. This deficit does not mean, however, that ranchers underpay. Setting aside for the moment the questions of whether ranchers should bear the full cost of the range program and whether taxpayers benefit from it, the fact is that 90 percent of ranchers with grazing allotments have paid full value for their leases, though the money didn't go to the federal government.

The value of a ranch is based on the number of cows it can support, so a grazing allotment attached to a ranch adds significant value to the deeded land. The buyer of a ranch has no choice but to pay for this added market value. Although courts have ruled that grazing permits are not private commodities to be traded, federal agencies customarily transfer them to the buyers of private land to which they are attached. Banks recognize them as a commodity by financing their purchase, and the government recognizes their private-property value by taxing it.

Only the approximately 10 percent of public-lands ranchers who are still on their families' original homesteads are receiving a subsidy, in that they did not have to pay for their ranches or their allotments. These subsidies were legislated because grazing on the public range was a necessity if the West was to be settled. The Homestead Act granted pioneers only 160 acres in country where that much land might support just one or two cows; the land's aridity and ruggedness make it useless for most other forms of agriculture. Both the allotments and the homesteads were given as incentives to build communities in the West, and fees were set low to encourage private investment to improve these public lands.

Such incentives are of course obsolete today, when the West is growing faster than any other part of the country. But when all the costs of private and public forage are compared, it becomes clear that in many cases ranchers pay more for public range than they do for private. On average, according to some economic studies, it is a wash.

Even so, many ranchers say they would pay more for their permits before they would give up ranching—if their banks would let them. They've invested money and sometimes the effort of generations in their allotments, and consider these to be part of their ranches. Ranchers say they will pay more if need be even though they are subsidized far less than the average citizen: agricultural landowners get back only twenty-one cents' worth of local public services for every tax dollar they spend, whereas people living in low-density residential areas get a return of $1.36, according to a 1990 study by the U.S. Department of Agriculture.

When confronted with these facts, many of ranching's harshest critics say that their central concern is not federal spending but the impact of grazing on biodiversity. In their view, all grazing is environmentally destructive, and it is impossible to manage livestock responsibly on the West's fragile, arid public lands. George Wuerthner, an ardent and well-known anti-grazing activist, claims, "Livestock grazing is the single most ecologically damaging activity we engage in."

Yet it is the rancher who monitors land and wildlife conditions that would otherwise be neglected by short-staffed agencies. It is the rancher who enters into agreements with state fish-and-game departments to allow the public to hunt and fish on his ranch, because that is where most of the wildlife is. And it is the rancher who through the winter feeds much of the wildlife the public enjoys watching.

Both ranchers and wildlife would suffer if cattle were entirely removed from the public range. BLM and Forest

Service lands together support about four million cattle. If those cattle had to be sold quickly because there was no place to put them, prices would plunge, and the cost of private forage in the West would rise by about 10 percent, destabilizing even ranchers not dependent on grazing allotments. Those public-lands ranchers who did survive would have to graze their private land intensively, regardless of the impact on wildlife. After failed ranches had been sold and divvied up into suburban-style lots with tract houses, dogs, fences, and noxious weeds, it would be difficult at best for wildlife to find what was left of their winter range. When ranchers are forced to sell, we lose precisely what environmentalists say they are fighting for—wildlife habitat.

> **T**he appeal for many is restoring the West to its natural condition. But what does "natural" mean?

What Is a "Natural" Landscape?

IN 1990 the Bureau of Land Management reported that the public range was in the best condition yet this century, and improving. The Forest Service has said the same thing. But a report issued by the Natural Resources Defense Council and the National Wildlife Federation at about the same time declared that the condition of the public range was "unsatisfactory."

Both views may be correct, and both may be wrong. According to the National Research Council, a division of the National Academy of Sciences, we have no consistent field data that can be used to test theories or make general statements about the health of grasslands. The agencies' and the environmental groups' reports used the same data, according to a follow-up study by the General Accounting Office. The GAO, for its part, found that 29 percent of BLM rangelands are in excellent to good condition, 43 percent are in fair to poor condition, and 28 percent have not yet been classified. The BLM points out that it does not define these terms as we might in common parlance: "fair" or "poor" conditions might include high-quality forage, cover for wildlife, watershed protection, and an aesthetically pleasing landscape—but not conditions that fulfill some management objectives, such as the presence of plants like those found by the first settlers.

What almost everyone does agree on is that from about 1880 to 1930 livestock grazing did terrible harm to the public range, and the range is slow to recover. But conditions have vastly improved since the passage of the Taylor Grazing Act, in 1934, which for the first time restricted grazing and imposed fees on what are now BLM

lands. The number of western livestock sank drastically, from 28.6 million in 1934 to 10.3 million in 1994. Additional protective legislation was passed in the 1970s. And grazing management has improved. Rangeland acreage rated good or excellent has more than doubled since the 1930s, according to the BLM, and acreage rated poor has been halved. Wildlife populations have been rebounding; more wildlife is on these lands today than at any other time in this century.

Although it is generally acknowledged that riparian zones are still suffering, until a decade or two ago no one understood their importance, and riparian recovery efforts are just beginning. Aggressive restoration programs are now in place, using methods such as installing water tanks to divert cattle from streams, selective exclosure fencing to keep cattle off stream banks, and rotational grazing systems that change the timing and the duration of grazing. The GAO has found these efforts to be very successful, calling the improvements "dramatic." When we see degraded rangeland today, for the most part we are seeing the sins of ranchers' grandfathers and great-grandfathers. Today's progressive ranchers have no plans to return to those methods; they have found that ecosystem management is ultimately more economical, producing healthier cattle and better forage.

Yet environmentalists would have us believe that cattle grazing is an ecological evil on a par with clear-cut logging and open-pit mining. There is no justification for this claim. Modern livestock grazing has comparatively little environmental impact. Nevertheless, many environmentalists simply want all ranchers off the public lands. Some two dozen U.S. environmental groups have signed on to the Wildlands Project, a plan to create a reserve stretching from Central America to the Arctic Circle, in order to protect biodiversity. Dave Foreman, a founder of Earth First! and now chairman of the Wildlands Project, describes it as a vision of "extensive areas of native vegetation . . . off-limits to human exploitation. Vast landscapes without roads, dams, motorized vehicles, powerlines, overflights, or other artifacts of civilization."

The appeal for many is the idea of restoring the West to its natural condition. But what is "natural"? Researchers call it an unscientific and unrealistic standard. We do not know what "natural" looks like, and even if we did, it is probably no longer achievable, in view of the changes that have occurred on the land during the past century, including the introduction of exotic species—especially noxious weeds.

Although it might seem logical to say that because domestic livestock were introduced, they are inherently undesirable, longtime observers of range ecology have discovered otherwise. In recent years wildlife biologists at the Montana Department of Fish, Wildlife, and Parks have returned cattle to wildlife management areas as part of a cooperative arrangement with local ranchers. They have observed that when cattle remove rank vegetation, in the fall, they enhance spring fodder for geese, elk, and antelope. Cattle are also used in these areas as a reseeding tool; they knock the seeds from mature seed heads to the ground and plant them with their trampling. The capacity of cattle to revegetate has proved useful, too, for reclaiming mining sites in Arizona that have resisted reclamation by other means.

Efforts to remove all cattle from wildlife areas have proved in some instances to be misguided. Managers at the Hart Mountain National Antelope Refuge, in Oregon, are perplexed by a drop in antelope numbers only seven years after livestock were banished from the refuge so that the land could "recover." The managers theorize that the problem is a rising number of coyotes, which prey on antelope fawns. But local ranchers say that the managers have it wrong: numbers are dropping because pronghorn antelope depend on cattle to clear away older grasses and make available younger, more palatable shoots.

"Whatever you do to change habitat will benefit some species and negatively impact others," Jack Ward Thomas, a wildlife biologist and a former chief of the U.S. Forest Service, says. "It's not as simple as getting the cows on or off."

It is likely that ungrazed grasslands will burn far more frequently than grazed ones; if cows are removed, wildlife populations will change, as palatable forage for elk, antelope, and deer decreases and annual plants and the animal species that prefer them also decline. There will be fewer rodents, which will mean less food for raptors, coyotes, and other predators.

"The question is, How do you make changes that will improve range conditions in a reasonable time frame and also not negatively affect people's ability to make a living?" says Donald J. Bedunah, a plant ecophysiologist at the University of Montana. "I don't believe rapid change is necessary. We don't have to persecute ranchers to accomplish what is needed."

Who Owns the West?

A FORCE akin to persecution has been gathering momentum. Environmentalists from the desert Southwest to the Great Basin to the Rocky Mountain Front have been mounting a barrage of lawsuits calculated to shut down or cripple commodity uses of public lands and further incapacitate land-management agencies that are already suffering from congressional budget cuts and layoffs.

In 1994 the National Wildlife Federation sued the Forest Service for not complying with the Beaverhead Riparian Guidelines and demanded that all grazing allotments not in compliance be suspended. The same group later scored a court victory in Utah that forced the BLM to remove all cows from the canyons of the Comb Wash grazing allotment. The Oregon Natural Desert Association sued the BLM for violations of the Wild and Scenic Rivers Act, ultimately seeking a permanent ban on grazing. Gila Watch, a local watchdog group, appealed the 230-square-mile Diamond Bar allotment, in southern New Mexico. In Idaho a campaign by activists forced the Forest Service to remove two thirds of the cattle grazed on the Stanley Basin allotment, in the Sawtooth National Recreation Area. And in the Southwest a zealous assortment of biologists, land planners, and other activists, known as the Southwest Center for Biological Diversity, has created a legal "train wreck" with more than a hundred lawsuits against federal agencies, hindering range and timber management until forest plans are amended.

It's no accident that these clashes are escalating at a time of new westward migration. The population of the West has increased by 14 percent since 1990, and the nation's five fastest-growing states are in the West—Nevada, Arizona, Idaho, Utah, and Colorado. These are also among the states where ranchers are the most dependent on public-lands grazing. Since 1982 urban growth in the West has consumed more than two million acres of land. In Montana alone, where the land rush is slower than in other western states, about three million acres of agricultural land have been subdivided since 1985.

Rarely do New West migrants blend seamlessly into Old West culture. KEEP OUT signs now bar country lanes that once were open to the community. Drugs and gangs are overtaking some small-town secondary schools. Traffic jams and road rage are becoming more common than tractors on the highways. Off-road, mountain bikes roam the range. For good or ill, the last remnants of the Old West are dying.

What we lose with the cowboy is far more than some antiquated and romantic notion of the West. When we lose the family ranch, we lose much that we need as human beings, and much of what brought migrants like me to the inland West in the first place: a daily, personal relationship with nature; a social contract that works; a sense of connection with others; a sense of fully inhabiting a place for the long haul. Ranching communities are ruled by ethics that knit neighbors tightly and securely together—the antithesis of the alienated urban culture in which 75 percent of Americans now live.

If ranches are to work as businesses and as a way of life, says Aaron Harp, a rural sociologist at the University of Idaho, ranchers need to rely on social relations established over years, even generations—such as buying feed from the same local retailer their grandfathers bought feed from, even though it might be cheaper to send to Billings. Newcomers want a small-town feeling, but they don't recognize that their insistence on changing how things are done displaces exactly what they say they came for. "You have to interact—pitch in and sandbag the creek when it floods," Harp says. "When the neighbor's cows get into your garden, you have to round them up for him and not complain—then maybe he'll plough out your driveway for you in the winter."

Social issues are never explicitly addressed as a significant component of the grazing debate. Instead it is framed as a controversy over public-land use. When environmentalists and agency managers promote tourism and recreation as alternatives to the prevailing agricultural economy, they don't stop to ask whether tourism will force established communities to give up their traditional livelihoods, because hikers don't like cow pies. Meanwhile, bankruptcy by bankruptcy, family ranching is vanishing. "It comes down to who will live and who will die," Harp says. "Who gets to stay? What people? What wildlife?"

The irony is that most ranchers share most environmentalists' objectives: clean water, flourishing wildlife, and healthy ecosystems. Unlike the farmer, who must break the soil, the progressive rancher adapts to the land he grazes. His understanding of the ecosystems on his land is built on years of daily observation and interaction. This is an untapped reservoir of knowledge that could be of great value to federal land managers, who rarely have the luxury of getting to know one landscape well. Ranchers want to leave the range in better condition than they found it, and they have made a multigenerational commitment to that ethic. There should be common cause between ranchers and environmentalists, not divisiveness.

Working Together

DAN Dagget is an unlikely defender of the cowboy. While living in southeastern Ohio in the early 1970s as part of a back-to-the-land community, Dagget fought a company that wanted to re-open a major coal strip mine adjacent to his farm. He became a relentless environmental advocate, organizing demonstrations for Earth First! and similar groups. The Sierra Club declared him one of the most effective grassroots activists in America. He entered the range wars when he worked to dismantle a state predator-control program and supported the reintroduction of the endangered Mexican gray wolf. It was as a wolf advocate in Arizona that he first encountered ranchers.

"I was convinced there was nothing for an enviro like me to talk to ranchers about," he says. But more-moderate wolf advocates, concerned that extremists like Dagget would make things so hot with the ranchers that the wolf would never be reintroduced, invited him and five other radical environmentalists to meet with six archconservative ranchers. They were asked to try to find common ground with the help of a facilitator.

The ranchers and the environmentalists found they wanted the same things: a relationship with the land that would sustain them and future generations ecologically, economically, and spiritually—that would, above all, leave a healthy environment as a legacy. The six ranchers took the six environmentalists to visit their grazing allotments and showed them their efforts to restore the ecosystem. To Dagget's amazement, he says, "I saw the ranchers were achieving my goals better than I was."

The "Six-Six Group" began working together to adopt environmental-restoration goals and implement practical solutions. They also began to visit and exchange ideas with similar coalitions around the Southwest. And Dagget experienced a conversion: as relentlessly as he had once fought ranchers he became vociferous in their defense, promoting cattle grazing as a tool for range rehabilitation. In his book, *Beyond the Rangeland Conflict*, he tells the stories of ten ranches where livestock grazing is compatible with healthy range and wildlife habitat. He says that he chose these ten from many around the West that are meeting environmental goals.

The grazing methods advocated by the Six-Six Group are revitalizing the ecosystem, Dagget claims. Whether it and similar groups will prevail and save the land for both people and wildlife may depend on whether they can win policymakers' attention away from the extremists on both sides of the debate.

These coalitions are beginning to get the recognition they deserve. In June of last year a MacArthur grant was awarded to William McDonald, a rancher and a director of the nonprofit Malpai Borderlands Group, at the juncture of Mexico, New Mexico, and Arizona. The group's mission statement declares a commitment to restoring and maintaining "the natural processes that create and protect a healthy, unfragmented landscape to support a diverse, flourishing community of human, plant, and animal life in our Borderlands Region." The Malpai Group, which is managing a million-acre ecosystem divided almost equally between public and private lands, consists of about twenty ranchers, the Nature Conservancy, the U.S. Forest Service, the BLM, and a team of conservation biologists and other scientists from all over the country. So far it has preserved a threatened population of Chiricahua leopard frogs during a drought, by hauling 1,000 gallons of water a week to stock ponds; funded brush removal and native range reseeding programs; and begun to study the character and causes of rangeland vegetation shifts—a source of heated debate about the effects of cattle grazing.

The group is also working to preserve the endangered rancher. One of its innovations is the Grassbank. If a neighbor needs to rest his pasture, because of drought or other environmental concerns, he can graze his herd on a neighboring ranch without paying the usual leasing fees. In return for use of the Grassbank, the rancher places a conservation easement, held by the Malpai Group, on his own ranch, barring subdivision and forfeiting his development rights.

Conservation easements are among the most powerful tools available for saving family ranches and protecting wildlife habitat. State governments, nonprofit agencies, and private coalitions buy the development rights to ecologically valuable private ranchland; the family retains ownership of the land itself, and the right to continue using it in the traditional agricultural way. Such an agreement reduces the land's market value, generates cash for the family, and thereby reduces or pays for estate taxes when the time comes to pass the ranch on to the next generation. Ranchers can stay on the land, wildlife winter range is protected, and the public continues to enjoy undeveloped scenic vistas.

Near the town of Brothers, Oregon, Doc and Connie Hatfield, the owners of the High Desert Ranch, have helped to organize the Trout Creek Mountain Working Group, one of the first and most successful efforts to bring ranchers, environmentalists, and agency managers together to solve rangeland problems. They are marketing hormone- and antibiotic-free beef through a cooperative that includes other area ranchers. The Hatfield ranch is open to the public, to demonstrate how sound ranching practices can improve the environment.

In 1996 Jack Ward Thomas, then the chief of the Forest Service, and Mike Dombeck, then the acting director of the BLM, initiated the National Riparian Service Team. The project sends a team to assist local cooperatives in improving their watersheds. It also offers public demonstrations of good management practices and helps conflict-ridden regions to forge collaborative partnerships and find local solutions to riparian problems.

More and more environmentalists are recognizing the stake that all westerners have in the preservation of private ranchlands—and the inevitable consequences of inflaming the range wars. COWS NOT CONDOS is a bumper sticker seen around Montana's more liberal communities lately. It's the concept behind the Montana Land Reliance, a conservation group that is helping ranchers find tools—such as conservation easements—to save family ranches from subdivision and thereby keep ecosystems intact. The Sonoran Institute, in Tucson, Arizona, is another conservation group dedicated to finding collaborative solutions to the grazing controversy, and the Nature Conservancy is also a major player in ecosystem ranching—from the famous Gray Ranch, in New Mexico's bootheel, to Utah's Canyonlands region, where it recently spent $4.6 million to save a working ranch from real-estate developers. The Conservancy will continue to run the 5,167 acres of deeded land plus 250,000 acres of public grazing allotments as a model of sustainable ranching. The previous owners of the ranch want to preserve its fragile desert, wildlife, and archaeological sites, including forty-two miles of riparian areas, and will continue to manage it for the Conservancy.

Despite these models of how ranchers and environmentalists can together achieve their goals, some ranchers will go down defending the way they've always done things, and some environmentalists will never veer far from regarding ranchers with an attitude that approaches a form of racism. "I have rancher friends, too," say many environmentalists who nevertheless advocate the wholesale removal of ranches from the range. "But ranchers are obsolete anyway—why waste our time and money on them?"

Those ranchers who have survived until now have made it because they are as tough and as adaptable as coyotes. Given half a chance, they will survive the new westward migration as well. The real question is whether the people at either extreme—who want public land used only as they see fit—will get what they wish for. If they do, they may ultimately regret it.

When the World's Wells Run Dry

It may seem to defy the logic of a closed planetary system, but the supply of water available for irrigation is indeed diminishing—at an alarming rate

by Sandra Postel

In 1970, farmers in rural Deaf Smith County in the Texas panhandle encountered a small but definite sign that local agriculture was seriously out of balance. An irrigation well that had been drilled in 1936 went dry. After more than 30 years of heavy pumping, the water table had dropped 24 meters. Soon other wells began to dry up too.

Water tables were falling across a wide area of the Texas High Plains, and when energy prices shot up in the 1970s, farmers were forced to close down thousands of wells because they could not longer afford to pump from such depths.

During the last three decades, the depletion of underground water reserves, known as aquifers, has spread from isolated pockets of the agricultural landscape to large portions of the world's irrigated land. Many farmers are now pumping groundwater faster than nature is replenishing it, causing a steady drop in water tables. Just as a bank account dwindles if withdrawals routinely exceed deposits, so will an underground water reserve decline if pumping exceeds recharge. Groundwater overdrafting is now widespread in the crop-producing regions of central and northern China, northwest and southern India, parts of Pakistan, much of the western United States, North Africa, the Middle East, and the Arabian Peninsula.

Many cities are overexploiting groundwater as well. Portions of Bangkok and Mexico City are actually sinking as geologic formations compact after the water is removed. Albuquerque, Phoenix, and Tucson are among the larger U.S. cities that are overdrafting their aquifers.

Globally, however, it is in agriculture where the greatest social risks lie. Irrigated land is disproportionately important to world food production. Some 40 percent of the global harvest comes from the 17 percent of cropland that is irrigated. Because of limited opportunities for expanding rainfed production, we are betting on that share to increase markedly in the decades ahead, in order to feed the world's growing population. As irrigation goes deeper and deeper into hydrologic debt, the possibilities for serious disruption grow ever greater. Should energy prices rise again, for example, farmers in many parts of the world could find it too expensive to irrigate. Groundwater overpumping may now be the single biggest threat to food production.

Our irrigation base is remarkably young: 60 percent of it is less than 50 years old. Yet a number of threats to its continued productivity are already apparent. Along with groundwater depletion, there is the buildup of salts in the soil, the silting up of reservoirs and canals, mounting competition for water between cities and farms and between countries sharing rivers, rapid population growth in regions that are already water-stressed—and on top of all that, the uncertainties of climate change. Any one of these threats could seriously compromise agriculture's productivity. But these stresses are evolving simultaneously—making it increasingly likely that cracks will appear in our agricultural foundation.

Few governments are taking adequate steps to address any of these threats and, hidden below the surface, groundwater depletion often gets the least attention of all. Yet this hydrologic equivalent of deficit financing cannot continue indefinitely. Groundwater withdrawals will eventually come back into balance with replenishment—the only question is whether they do so in a planned and coordinated way that maintains food supplies, or in a chaotic and unexpected way that reduces food production, worsens poverty, and disrupts regional economies.

From *World Watch*, September/October 1999, pp. 30-38. © 1999 by the Worldwatch Institute. Reprinted by permission.

It is true that there are enormous inefficiencies elsewhere in the agricultural sector—and tackling these could take some of the pressure off aquifers. A shift in diets, for example, could conserve large amounts of irrigation water. The typical U.S. diet, with its high share of animal products, requires twice as much water to produce as the nutritious but less meat-intensive diets common in some Asian and European nations. If U.S. consumers moved down the food chain, the same volume of water could produce enough food for two people instead of one, leaving more water in rivers and aquifers. But given the rates of groundwater depletion, there is no longer any reasonable alternative to tackling the problem directly. Aquifer management will be an essential part of any strategy for living within the limits imposed by a finite supply of fresh water.

The Groundwater Revolution

During the first century of the modern irrigation age—roughly from 1850 to 1950—efforts to develop water supplies focused mainly on rivers. Government agencies and private investors constructed dams to capture river water and canals to deliver that water to cities and farms. By the middle of this century, engineers had built impressive irrigation schemes in China, India, Pakistan, and the United States, and these nations became the world's top four irrigators. The Indus River system in South Asia, the Yellow and Yangtze Rivers in China, and the Colorado and Sacramento-San Joaquin river systems of the western United States were each irrigating sizable areas by 1950. The global irrigation base then stood at 100 million hectares, up from 40 million in 1900.

Between 1950 and 1995, world irrigated area increased to more than 250 million hectares. Even as the construction of large dams for hydroelectric power, water supply, and flood control picked up pace, a quiet revolution in water use unfolded during this period. Rural electrification, the spread of diesel pumps, and new well-drilling technologies allowed farmers to sink millions of wells into the aquifers beneath their land. For the first time in human history, farmers began to tap groundwater on a large scale.

Aquifers are in many ways an ideal source of water. Farmers can pump groundwater whenever they need it, and that kind of availability typically pays off in higher crop yields. Compare this with the standard scenario for irrigating with river water: river flow is erratic, so a reservoir is usually required to store flood water for use in the dry season. And reservoirs—especially arid-land reservoirs such as Lake Nasser behind Egypt's High Aswan Dam—can lose 10 percent or more of their water to evaporation. In addition, the large canal networks that move water out of reservoirs are often unreliable—they may not deliver enough water when farmers actually need it. Aquifers, on the other hand, have a fairly slow and steady flow that is usually available year-round and they don't lose water to evaporation. Finally, groundwater is generally less expensive to develop than river water. Data from 191 irrigation projects funded by the World Bank show that groundwater schemes cost a third less on average than surface schemes.

Not surprisingly, huge numbers of farmers and investors turned to groundwater as soon as they acquired the means to tap into it. In China, the number of irrigation wells shot up from 110,000 in 1961 to nearly 2.4 million by the mid-1980s. In India, government canal building nearly doubled the area under surface irrigation between 1950 and 1985, but the most impressive growth was in groundwater development: the area irrigated by tubewells ballooned from 100,000 hectares in 1961 to 11.3 million hectares in 1985—a 113-fold rise, most of it privately funded. (A tubewell is a narrow well that is drilled into an aquifer, as opposed to a larger-

Ancient Romans made this water-carrying pipe with cement and crushed rock. Courtesy George E. Bartuska, Winter Park, Florida.

diameter well that is excavated, either by hand or with machinery.) In neighboring Pakistan, groundwater was the fastest-growing form of irrigation from the mid-1960s through the 1980s. A public program of tubewell development failed miserably, but private groundwater investments climbed steeply. The total number of tubewells in that country rose from some 25,000 in 1964 to nearly 360,000 in 1993.

After World War II, the United States experienced a groundwater boom as well. Farmers in California stepped up their pumping of groundwater beneath the rich soils of the Central Valley, which was well on its way to becoming the nation's fruit and vegetable basket. But the greatest aquifer development was in the U.S. Great Plains, a region that straddles the 100th meridian, the nation's transition zone from rain-fed to irrigated agriculture. In a striking bit of good fortune, the drier western portion of the plains is underlain by a vast underground pool called the Ogallala. One of the planet's greatest aquifers, it spans portions of eight states, from South Dakota in the north to Texas in the south. The Ogallala extends for 453,000 square kilometers, and—prior to exploitation—held 3,700 cubic kilometers of water, a volume equal to the annual flow of more than 200 Colorado Rivers. In the years after World War II, a new generation of powerful centrifugal pumps allowed farmers to tap into this water on a large scale, first in northwest Texas and western Kansas, and then gradually farther north into Nebraska. Today, the Ogallala alone waters one-fifth of U.S. irrigated land.

Taking Stock

Like any renewable resource, groundwater can be tapped indefinitely as long as the rate of extraction does not exceed the rate of replenishment. In many regions, however, aquifers get so little natural recharge that they are essentially nonrenewable. These "fossil aquifers" are the remnants of ancient climates that were much wetter than current local conditions. Pumping from fossil aquifers depletes the supply, just as pumping from an oil reserve does. Even where aquifers do get replenished by rainfall, few governments have established rules and regulations to ensure that they are exploited at a sustainable rate. In most places, any farmer who can afford to sink a well and pump water can do so unrestrained. Ownership of land typically implies the right to the water below. The upshot is a classic "tragedy of the commons," in which individuals acting out of self-interest deplete a common resource.

In India, for example, the situation has become so severe that in September 1996 the Supreme Court directed one of the country's premier research centers to examine it. The National Environmental Engineering Research Institute, based in Nagpur, found that "overexploitation of ground water resources is widespread across the

The Ogallala Aquifer

Area enlarged below.

When Major Stephen Long struck out west, up the South Platte River in 1820, he named the "desolate waste" he encountered west of the 100th meridian the Great American Desert. Attempts to cultivate this arid land led to disasters such as the Dust Bowl. But in the 1950s, new pumps opened up the Ogallala aquifer, one of the world's largest underground reservoirs. Changing the desert into a breadbasket, the aquifer now waters one-fifth of U.S. irrigated land. But overpumping is draining the Ogallala much more quickly than it is recharged. Falling water tables and higher pumping costs have forced many farmers to abandon irrigation: while more than 5.2 million hectares were irrigated by the Ogallala in 1978, a decade later that number had dropped 20 percent, to 4.2 million. Without significant changes, the Ogallala oasis may turn out to be little more than a mirage.

country." Water tables in critical agricultural areas are sinking "at an alarming rate," due to rapid proliferation of irrigation wells, which now number at least 6 million, and the failure to regulate pumping adequately. Nine Indian states are now running major water deficits, which in the aggregate total just over 100 billion cubic meters (bcm) a year—and those deficits are growing (see table, "Water Deficits in Key Countries and Regions, Mid-1990's").

The situation is particularly serious in the northern states of Punjab and Haryana, India's principal breadbaskets. Village surveys found that water tables are dropping 0.6 to 0.7 meters per year in parts of Haryana and half a meter per year across large areas of Punjab. In the state of Gujarat, on the northwest coast, 87 out of 96 observation wells showed declining groundwater levels during the 1980s, and aquifers in the Mehsana district are now reportedly depleted. Overpumping in Gujarat has also allowed salt water to invade the aquifers, contaminating drinking water supplies. In the state of Tamil Nadu, in the extreme south, water tables have dropped by as much as 30 meters since the 1970s, and aquifers in the Coimbatore district are now dry.

Farmers usually run into problems before the water disappears entirely. At some point, the pumping costs get out of hand or the well yields drop too low, and they are forced to choose among several options. They can take irrigated land out of production, eliminate a harvest or two, switch to less water-intensive crops, or adopt more-efficient irrigation practices. Apart from shifting out of thirsty nonstaple crops like sugarcane or cotton, improving efficiency is the only option that can sustain food production while lowering water use. Yet in India, investments in efficiency are minuscule relative to the challenge at hand. David Seckler, Director General of the International Water Management Institute in Sri Lanka, estimates that a quarter of India's grain harvest could be in jeopardy from groundwater depletion.

Besides threatening food production, groundwater overpumping is widening the income gap between rich and poor in some areas. As water tables drop, farmers must drill deeper wells and buy more powerful pumps. In parts of Punjab and Haryana, for example, wealthier farmers have installed more expensive, deeper tubewells costing about 125,000 rupees ($2,890). But the poor cannot afford such equipment. So as the shallower wells dry up, some of the small-scale farmers end up renting their land to the wealthier farmers and becoming laborers on the larger farms.

Other countries are facing similar problems. In Pakistan's province of Punjab—the country's leading agricultural region, which is just across the border from the Indian state of the same name—groundwater is being pumped at a rate that exceeds recharge by an estimated 27 percent. In Bangladesh, groundwater use is about half the rate of natural replenishment on an annual basis. But during the dry season, when irrigation is most needed, heavy pumping causes many wells to go dry. On about a third of Bangladesh's irrigated area, water tables routinely

drop below the suction level of shallow tubewells during the dry months. Although monsoon rains recharge these aquifers and water tables rise again later in the year, farmers run out of water when they need it most. Again, the greatest hardships befall poor farmers, who cannot afford to deepen their wells or buy bigger pumps.

In China, which is roughly tied with India for the most irrigated land, groundwater conditions are equally unsettling. Northern China is running a chronic water deficit, with groundwater overpumping amounting to some 30 bcm a year. Of the three major river basins in the region, the Hai is always in deficit, the Yellow is almost always in deficit, and the Huai is occasionally. This northern and central plain produces roughly 40 percent of China's grain. Across a wide area, the water table has been dropping 1 to 1.5 meters a year, even as water demands continue to increase.

Modeling work by Dennis Engi of Sandia National Laboratories in New Mexico suggests that the water deficit in the Hai basin could grow by more than half between 1995 and 2025, even assuming that China completes at least part of a controversial plan to divert some Yangtze River water northward. Engi projects a 190 percent deficit increase for the Yellow River basin. Over the time frame of Engi's study, the combined deficit in these two basins could more than double, from 27 bcm to 55 bcm.

As in India, the unsustainable use of groundwater is creating a false sense of the nation's food production potential. The worsening groundwater deficits will eventually force Chinese farmers to either take land out of irrigation, switch to less thirsty crops, or irrigate more efficiently. How they respond will make a big difference to China's grain outlook: that projected 2025 deficit for the Hai and Yellow River basins is roughly equal to the volume of water needed to grow 55 million tons of grain—14 percent of the nation's current annual grain consumption and about a fourth of current global grain exports.

In the United States, farmers are overpumping aquifers in several important crop-producing regions. California is overdrafting groundwater at a rate of 1.6 bcm a year, equal to 15 percent of the state's annual groundwater use. Two-thirds of this depletion occurs in the Central Valley, which supplies about half of the nation's fruits and vegetables. By far the most serious case of depletion, however, is in the region watered by the Ogallala aquifer. Particularly in its southern reaches, the Ogallala gets very little replenishment from rainfall, so almost any pumping diminishes it. Currently the aquifer is being depleted at a rate of some 12 bcm a year. Total depletion to date amounts to some 325 bcm, a volume equal to the annual flow of 18 Colorado Rivers. More than two-thirds of this depletion has occurred in the Texas High Plains.

Driven by falling water tables, higher pumping costs, and historically low crop prices, many farmers who depend on the Ogallala have already abandoned irrigated agriculture. At its peak in 1978, the total area irrigated by the Ogallala in Colorado, Kansas, Nebraska, New Mexico, Oklahoma, and Texas reached 5.2 million hectares. Less than a decade later, this area had fallen by nearly 20 percent, to 4.2 million hectares. A long-range study of the region, done in the mid-1980s, suggested that more than 40 percent of the peak irrigated area would come out of irrigation by 2020; if this happens, another 1.2 million hectares will either revert to dryland farming or be abandoned over the next two decades.

Desert Fantasies

In North Africa and the Arabian Peninsula, where it rarely rains, a number of countries depend on fossil aquifers. Saudi Arabia, for instance, sits atop several deep aquifers containing some 1,919 cubic kilometers of water—just over half as much as the Ogallala. The Saudis started pumping water on a grand scale after the OPEC oil embargo of the 1970s. Fear of a retaliatory grain embargo prompted the government to launch a major initiative to make the nation self-sufficient in grain by encouraging large-scale wheat production in the desert. The government heavily subsidized land, equipment, and irrigation water. It also bought the wheat at several times the world market price. From a few thousand tons in the mid-1970s, the annual grain harvest grew to a peak of 5 million tons in 1994. Saudi water demand at this time totaled nearly 20 bcm a year, and 85 percent of it was met by mining nonrenewable groundwater. Saudi Arabia not only achieved self-sufficiency in wheat; for a time, it was among the world's wheat exporters.

But this self-sufficiency would not last. Crop production soon crashed when King Fahd's government was forced to rein in expenditures as the nation's revenues declined. Within two years, Saudi grain output fell by 60 percent, to 1.9 million tons in 1996. Today Saudi Arabia is harvesting slightly more grain than in 1984, the year it first became self-sufficient, but because its population has

grown from 12 million to more than 20 million since then, the nation has again joined the ranks of the grain importers.

Moreover, the Saudis' massive two-decade experiment with desert agriculture has left the nation much poorer in water. In its peak years of grain production, the nation ran a water deficit of 17 bcm a year, consuming more than 3,000 tons of water for each ton of grain produced in the hot, windy desert. (The standard ratio is 1,000 tons of water per ton of grain.) At that rate, groundwater reserves would have run out by 2040, and possibly sooner. In recent years, the annual depletion rate has dropped closer to the level of the mid-1980s, but the Saudis are still racking up a water deficit on the order of 6 bcm a year.

Africa's northern tier of countries—from Egypt to Morocco—also relies heavily on fossil aquifers, with estimated depletion running at 10 bcm a year. Nearly 40 percent of this depletion occurs in Libya, which is now pursuing a massive water scheme rivaled in size and complexity only by China's diversion of the Yangtze River. Known as the Great Man-Made River Project, the $25 billion scheme pumps water from desert aquifers in the south and transfers it 1,500 kilometers north through some 4,000 kilometers of concrete pipe.

The brainchild of Libyan leader Muammar Qaddafi, the artificial river was christened with great pomp and ceremony in late August 1991. As of early 1998, it was delivering 146 million cubic meters a year to the cities of Tripoli and Benghazi. If all stages are completed, the scheme will eventually transfer up to 2.2 bcm a year, with 80 percent of it destined for agriculture. As in Saudi Arabia, however, the greening of the desert will be short-lived: some water engineers say the wells may dry up in 40 to 60 years.

Some water experts have called the scheme "madness" and a "national fantasy." Foreign engineers involved in the project have even questioned Qaddafi's real motives. Some have pointed out that the pipelines are 4 meters in diameter, big enough to accommodate trucks or troops. Every 85 kilometers or so, engineers are building huge underground storage areas that apparently are more elaborate than needed for holding water. The master pipeline runs through a mountain where Qaddafi is reported to be building a biological and chemical weapons plant. But other engineers have scoffed at the possibility of any military motive, noting, for example, that the pipelines have no air vents.

From the fields of North Africa to those of northern China, the story is essentially the same: many of the world's most important grainlands are consuming groundwater at unsustainable rates. Collectively, annual water depletion in India, China, the United States, North Africa, and the Arabian Peninsula adds up to some 160 bcm a year—equal to the annual flow of two Nile Rivers. (See table, "Water deficits in Key Countries and Regions, Mid-1990's.) Factoring in Australia, Pakistan, and other areas for which this author did not have comparable data would likely raise this figure by an additional 10 to 25 percent.

Water Deficits in Key Countries and Regions, Mid-1990s

Country/Region	Estimated Annual Water Deficit (billion cubic meters per year)
India	104.0
China	30.0
United States	13.6
North Africa	10.0
Saudi Arabia	6.0
Other	unknown
Minimum Global Total	163.6

SOURCE: Global Water Policy Project and Worldwatch Institute.

The vast majority of this overplumped groundwater is used to irrigate grain, the staple of the human diet. Since it takes about 1,000 tons of water to produce one ton of grain (and a cubic meter of water weighs one metric ton), some 180 million tons of grain—roughly 10 percent of the global harvest—is being produced by depleting water supplies. This simple math raises a very unsettling question: If so much of irrigated agriculture is operating under water deficits now, where are farmers going to find the additional water that will be needed to feed the more than 2 billion people projected to join humanity's ranks by 2030?

Texas Ingenuity

The only way to sustain crop production in the face of dwindling water supplies is to use those supplies more efficiently—to get more crop per drop. Few farmers have a better combination of incentive to conserve and opportunity to innovate than those in nortwest Texas. As the Ogallala shrinks, water efficiency is increasingly the ticket to staying in business. And the response of these Texan farmers is grounds for hope: better irrigation technologies and practices can substantially delay the day of reckoning—buying valuable time to make an orderly transition to a more sustainable water economy.

During the 1980s, the steady drop in underground water levels prompted local water officials and researchers to put together a package of technologies and management options that has boosted the region's water productivity. Spearheaded by the High Plains Underground Water Conservation District in Lubbock, which overseas water management in 15 counties of northwest Texas, the effort has involved a major upgrade of the region's irrigation systems.

Many conventional gravity systems, in which water simply flows down parallel furrows, are less than 60 percent efficient: more than 40 percent of the water runs off the field or seeps through the soil without benefiting the crop. Farmers in the High Plains have been equipping their systems with surge valves that raise efficiency to about 80 percent. Just as the name implies, surge irrigation involves sending water down the furrows of a field in a series of pulses rather than in a continuous stream. The initial pulse somewhat seals the soil, letting subsequent surges flow more quickly and uniformly down the field. This evens out the distribution of water, allowing farmers to apply less at the head of their fields while still ensuring that enough water reaches crops at the tail-end. A time-controlled valve alternates the flow of water between rows, and its cycle and flow rates can be adjusted for different soils, furrow lengths, and other conditions. When combined with soil moisture monitoring and proper scheduling of irrigations, surge systems can cut water use by 10 to 40 percent compared with conventional furrow irrigation. Savings in the Texas High Plains have averaged about 25 percent. High Plains farmers have

typically recouped their investment in surge equipment—which ranges from $30 to $120 per hectare depending on whether piping is already in place—within two years.

Many farmers in the region are also using more efficient sprinklers. Conventional sprinklers are more efficient than furrow irrigation in most contexts, because they apply water more uniformly. But in dry, windy areas like the U.S. Great Plains, spraying water high into the air can cause large losses from evaporation and wind drift. The High Plains District is encouraging the use of two varieties of low-pressure sprinklers. One type delivers a light spray from nozzles about a meter above the soil surface, and typically registers efficiencies of 80 percent, about the same as surge irrigation (see table, "Efficiencies of Selected Irrigation Methods, Texas High Plains").

A second variety, however, does substantially better. Low-energy precision application (LEPA) sprinklers deliver water in small doses through nozzles positioned just above the soil surface. They nearly eliminate evaporation and wind drift, and can raise efficiency to 95 percent—often cutting water use by 15 to 40 percent over other methods. In the High Plains District, LEPA has also increased corn yields about 10 percent and cotton yields about 15 percent. The water savings plus the yield increases add up to substantial gains in water productivity. Farmers converting to LEPA typically recoup their investment in two to seven years, depending on whether they are upgrading an existing sprinkler or purchasing a new one. Virtually all the sprinklers in the High Plains District are now either the low-pressure spray or LEPA.

More recently, the district has begun experimenting with drip irrigation of cotton. Using a network of perforated plastic tubing installed on or below the surface, drip systems deliver water directly to the roots of plants. Drip irrigation has cut water use by 30 to 70 percent in countries as diverse as India, Israel, Jordan, Spain, and the United States. And because plants grow better with optimal moisture, drip systems often boost yields by 20 to 50 percent. Since drip systems cost on the order of $2,500 per hectare, they have typically been used just for high value crops like fruits and vegetables. But as water itself grows more expensive and as new, lower-cost systems hit developing-country markets, the technology will become more useful. Because cotton is such a thirsty and widely planted crop, using drip systems to irrigate it could save large quantities of water in Texas and elsewhere. Working with local farmers, the district is giving drip a tough test by comparing its performance to that of LEPA—the most water-efficient sprinkler design now on the market. After the first year of trials, drip produced 19 percent more cotton per hectare than the LEPA-irrigated fields.

The Texas High Plains program has also included substantial extension work to help farmers adopt water-saving practices. (Extension programs are outreach efforts by government agricultural agencies and some universities.) For example, extension agents spread the word about furrow diking—one of the most readily accessible water-saving measures. Furrow dikes are small earthen ridges built across furrows at regular intervals down the field. They form small basins that trap both rain and irrigation water, thereby reducing runoff and increasing soil absorption. Furrow dikes are key to obtaining the highest possible irrigation efficiency with LEPA, for example, and to storing as much pre-season rainfall in the soil as possible.

Constructing furrow dikes costs about $10 per hectare. James Jonish, an economist at Texas Tech University, points out that if furrow dikes capture an extra five centimeters of rainfall in the soil, they can boost cotton yields by up to 225 kilograms of lint per hectare, a potential economic gain of $400 per hectare, depending on cotton prices. In contrast, getting those higher yields by pumping an additional five centimeters of groundwater would cost $15 to $22 per hectare and would of course hasten the aquifer's depletion. Overall, the High Plains District program has allowed growers to boost the water productivity of cotton, which accounts for about half the cropland area, by 75 percent over the last two decades. Full irrigation of cotton used to require a well capable of producing at least 10 gallons a minute per acre (four-tenths of a hectare), but the district now considers 2 to 3 gallons a minute sufficient.

Despite these successes, High Plains farmers face an uphill battle. Drought conditions in 1998 forced them to pump more groundwater than usual. Water tables dropped an average of 0.64 meters between early 1998 and early 1999, twice the average annual drop over the last decade. The first half of 1999 was wetter than usual but given the general trend, further improvement is essential. The district is now ramping up a program in which computer systems use real-time weather data and more precise information on crop water needs to adjust irrigation regimes. This approach will, for example, allow a two-and-a-half-day cycle of LEPA irrigation, rather than the usual five- to seven-day cycle. Shorter cycles should make it possible to maintain

a nearly ideal moisture environment with even less water than the standard LEPA approach, since the very small volumes of water released can be carefully calibrated to match the crop's immediate demand. Preliminary results with corn and cotton show promising yield increases. Water district assistant manager Ken Carver expects the program to go into widespread use soon after its introduction this year. The potential of this approach is enormous: it offers a way to irrigate corn, wheat and other grains nearly as efficiently as drip systems irrigate fruits, vegetables, and cotton. In areas where groundwater is diminishing, these methods hold out hope that production declines can at least be delayed—and in some areas, perhaps, avoided altogether.

Setting New Rules

No government has made a concerted effort to solve the problem of groundwater overpumping. Indeed, most contribute to the problem by subsidizing groundwater use. Many farmers in India, for example, pay only a flat fee for electricity, which makes the marginal cost of pumping groundwater close to zero. Why invest in more-efficient irrigation technologies if it costs nearly the same to pump 10,000 cubic meters of groundwater as it does to pump 5,000?

Likewise, Texas irrigators get a break on their federal income taxes for depleting the Ogallala aquifer: they receive a "depletion allowance" much as oil companies do for depleting oil reserves. Each year, they measure how much their water table has dropped, calculate the value of that depleted water, and then claim an adjustment on their income tax. This subsidy may partially explain why some farmers use the water saved through efficiency improvements to grow thirstier crops rather than leaving it in the ground. From a social standpoint, it is far more sensible to tax groundwater depletion in order to make

Efficiencies of Selected Irrigation Methods, Texas High Plains

Irrigation Method	Typical Efficiency	Water Application Needed to Add 100 Millimeters to Root Zone	Water Savings Over Conventional Furrow[1]
	(percent)	(millimeters)	(percent)
Conventional Furrow	60	167	—
Furrow with Surge Valve	80	125	25
Low-Pressure Sprinkler	80	125	25
LEPA Sprinkler	90–95	105	37
Drip	95	105	37

[1]Data do not specify what portion of savings result from reduced evaporation versus runoff and seepage.
SOURCE: Based on High Plains Underground Water Conservation District (Lubbock, Texas), *The Cross Section*, various issues.

current users pay more of the real costs of their activities. Such a tax would allow products made with the depleted water—whether beef steaks or cotton shirts—to better reflect their true ecological costs.

Governments have also failed to tackle the task of regulating access to groundwater. To prevent a tragedy of the commons, it's necessary to limit the number of users of the common resource, to reduce the quantity of the resource that each user can take, or to pursue some combination of these two options. This regulating function can be performed by a self-governing communal group—in which rights and responsibilities are determined by the farmers themselves—or by a public agency with authority to impose rules for the social good on private individuals. In reality, however, groundwater conditions are rarely even monitored, much less regulated.

Only recently has the groundwater issue begun to appear on national agendas—and still only in a few countries. Officials in India circulated a "model groundwater bill" in 1992, but none of the Indian states has passed legislation along those lines. Some have made efforts to regulate groundwater use through licensing, credit, or electricity restrictions, or by setting minimum well-spacing requirements. But no serious efforts have been made to control the volume of water extracted. V. Narain, a researcher at the New Delhi-based Tata Energy Research Institute, puts it simply: "groundwater is viewed essentially as a chattel attached to land," and there is "no limit on how much water a landowner may draw."

Indian researchers and policymakers broadly agree that rights to land and water need to be separated. Some have argued for turning de facto private groundwater rights into legal common property rights conferred upon communities in a watershed. But instituting such a reform can be a political high-wire act. Wealthy farmers, who have the ear of politicians, do not want to lose their ability to pump groundwater on their property in any quantity they desire.

The United States has no official national groundwater policy either. As in India, it is up to the states to manage their own aquifers. So far, only Arizona has passed a comprehensive groundwater law that explicitly calls for balancing withdrawal with recharge. Arizona's strategy for meeting this goal by 2025 would take some of the strain off its overpumped groundwater by substituting Colorado River water imported through an expensive, federally-subsidized canal project. But few regions can rely on such an option, which in any case merely replaces one type of excessive water use with another.

An important first step in developing a realistic groundwater policy is for governments to commission credible and unbiased assessments of the long-term rate of recharge for every groundwater basin or aquifer. This would establish the limit of sustainable use. The second step is for all concerned parties—including scientists, farmer and community groups, and government agencies—to devise a plan for balancing pumping with recharge. If current pumping exceeds the sustainable limit, achieving this goal will involve some mix of pumping reductions and artificial recharge—the process of channeling rainfall or surplus river water into the underground aquifer, where this is possible.

Arriving at an equitable way of allocating groundwater rights such that total pumping remains within sustainable levels will not be easy. Legislatures or courts might need to invoke a legal principle that elevates the public interest over private rights. One possibility, for example, is the public trust doctrine, which asserts that governments hold certain rights in trust for the public and can take action to protect those rights from private interests.

Some scholars have recommended use of the public trust doctrine to deal with India's groundwater problem. Recent rulings in the United States show that this legal instrument is potentially very powerful. The California Supreme Court ordered Los Angeles to cut back its rightful diversions of water from tributaries that feed Mono Lake, declaring that the state holds the lake in trust for the people and is obligated to protect it. The applicability of the public trust or similar doctrines may vary somewhat from one legal system to the next, but where a broad interpretation is feasible, there could be sweeping effects since even existing rights can be revoked in order to prevent violation of the public trust.

Once a legal basis for limiting groundwater use is established, the next step is to devise a practical plan for actually making groundwater use sustainable. Mexico is one of the few countries that seem to be tackling this task head on. After enacting a new water law in 1992, Mexico created River Basic Councils, which are intended to be water authorities open to a high degree of public participation. For example, the council for the Lerma–Chapala River basin, an area that contains 12 percent of Mexico's irrigated land, is in the process of setting specific regulations for each aquifer in the region. Technical committees are responsible for devising plans to reduce overpumping. Because these committees are composed of a broad mix of players, including the groundwater users themselves, they lend legitimacy to both the process and the outcome.

Although the details of a workable plan will vary from place to place, it is now possible to draw a rough blueprint for sustainable groundwater use. But nearly everywhere, the first big hurdle is overcoming the out-of-sight, out-of-mind syndrome. When looking at, say, a field of golden wheat, it can be difficult to imagine why harvests like that can't just go on forever. But the future of that crop—and of humanity itself—will depend on how well we manage the water below.

Sandra Postel is director of the Global Water Policy Project in Amherst, Massachusetts, and a senior fellow at the Worldwatch Institute. She is the author of Pillar of Sand: Can the Irrigation Miracle Last? *(W. W. Norton & Company, 1999), from which this article is adapted.*

The deep green sea

The ocean used to seem infinite in its bounty. Now it needs care and maintenance, writes Edward Carr

A second fall

THE eviction of Adam and Eve from the garden of Eden marked the end of man as a hunter-gatherer. For most of history, mankind had survived on berries, nuts and wild animals, but as numbers grew and food became scarce, people were reduced to farming. As God told Adam, "The earth will be cursed. You will get your food from it only by labour all the days of your life." After the freedom of the forests and the plains, it was backbreaking work. The first farmers suffered from rotten teeth and stunted bones. Farming was the antithesis to the nomadic way of life, bringing with it a domesticated landscape, a settled existence, ownership, and laws to protect it.

Something similar is now happening to the ocean. Where once it seemed infinite in its bounty, it is suffering from overfishing and pollution. Wherever humanity meets the sea, the sea comes off worse. Two-thirds of the world's 5.5 billion people live within 50 miles (80km) of the coast, and much of the pollution from the land runs to the sea. Residents, tourists, commercial interests and wildlife are all fighting for their corner of the garden.

After decades of expansion, many of the world's fishing grounds are already overfished, and many more soon will be. The scale of the hunt is awesome. In a study published in the journal *Nature,* Daniel Pauly and Villi Christensen, then both working at the International Centre for Living Aquatic Resources Management (ICLARM), a non-profit research centre in Manila, tried to measure how much of the tiny marine plants, called phytoplankton, is needed to support the life that man extracts from the sea. They concluded that people take 25–35% of the output of the richest areas of the sea: the continental shelf and the places where currents saturated in nutrients well up from the deep. Although these areas are small, less than a tenth of the ocean surface, the finding is alarming. Mankind's share

of the output of the land, at 35–40%, is not that much higher—and look how irrevocably the land has been changed by this exploitation.

Then there is global warming with all its uncertainties. Tens of millions of people—most of them poor—who live only a few metres above the high-tide mark have much to fear from even a slight rise in the sea level. Hundreds of millions more who have settled on the coast will also suffer if today's Prosperos end up creating more or wilder storms.

"The sea is not landscape. It is the experience of eternity," wrote the German novelist Thomas Mann. Yet the fringes of eternity are polluted with nitrates and blooms of foetid algae. Immensity and fecundity were once the ocean's defining characteristics. Now the sea turns out to be just another environment under threat. What the British poet W.H. Auden called "the alpha of existence, the symbol of potentiality" seems tired and worn.

There was no more sea

The time has come for people to change the way they think about the sea. Hunter-gatherers were never banished from the salt water. Although coastal states control the waters to 200 miles off shore they find it hard to exert their authority there. Most of the deep sea is subject to the even frailer rule of international law. Scientific ignorance and the sea's lack of natural boundaries further frustrate the task of designing institutions to manage the marine environment. Little is known about the precise effects of, say, the changing climate on fish stocks or the remote consequences of estuarine pollution.

Despite being badly governed, the sea provides vast benefits. For some, these are measured in jobs—fishing, along with processing and marketing on land, for example,

Reprinted with permission from *The Economist,* May 23, 1998, Survey pp. 1-15. © 1998 by The Economist, Ltd. Distributed by The New York Times Special Features.

employs about 200m people. To many more the benefits are food, recreation and protection against storms. And everyone needs the sea for shipping and to wash away waste, recycle water, and provide a habitat for wildlife. In a recent paper, Robert Costanza of the University of Maryland put a value of $21 trillion on these services, compared with $12 trillion for what the land offers. The numbers are debatable, but the idea behind them makes sense. Environmentalists would like the sea to be a pristine environment; others treat it as a waste-dump: in fact it is a resource that must be preserved and harvested.

To enhance its uses, the water must become ever more like the land, with owners, laws and limits. Fishermen must behave more like ranchers than hunters. Polluters should pay something for the damage caused by their pollution. Planners will have to balance the natural habitat against development and prepare, if necessary, for a rapid rise in sea-level. Should the world's population double, mankind may have to treat the coastal waters like prime agricultural land.

It will not be easy to extend fallible laws and regulations to a realm that has stood for freedoms dating from before civilisation. Attempts to "manage" the sea are seen as somehow unnatural. Yet the laws and regulations are coming all the same. Byron was right in 1817 when he wrote: "Roll on thou deep and dark blue ocean—roll! Man marks the earth with ruin—his control stops with the shore." But he is right no longer.

This has been declared the year of the ocean: a time for glossy display, including an Expo that has just opened in Lisbon. Few want to think about the sea's fall from grace, its loss of infinity; and no one likes to pay for resources that had always been considered free. The second fall will no more feel like progress than did the first.

On the edge

WHY are people drawn to the sea? A recent book by Elaine Morgan, a British writer, argues that it is because part of the evolution of *Homo sapiens* took place on the seashore. The story is highly speculative: the aquatic ape protected himself from the water by becoming balder and fatter than his forest-bound relatives. Like seals, dolphins and other large aquatic mammals, man is equipped for immersion, thanks to a high concentration of haemoglobin and the rare ability to breathe at will (without which, incidentally, it would be impossible to talk). Perhaps the only ape on two legs waded before he walked.

Paleontologists scoff at such circumstantial evidence. But perhaps the hordes moving to the coast know something the academics do not; likewise the trippers squeezed into a ribbon of tarry, cigarette-strewn sand. Thirteen of the world's 16 cities with more than 10m people are on the coast. In America, almost half of all new residential development is near the ocean, and people are moving there at the rate of 3,600 a day.

The coast is the place where everything comes together. It is the marine environment from which people obtain the most benefit. But the demands made on the coast for different purposes—commercial, residential, recreational—often conflict. Efforts to allocate the right to pollute and exploit the coastline and coastal waters are fraught with complexity.

And confusion. People tend to think of oil pollution as the biggest threat, and to blame it on large spills. In fact, the amount of oil entering the ocean has been falling, and large well-publicised oil spills make up only a small part of the total. Industrial dumping—such as the fateful release of mercury from a factory in Minimata Bay in Japan in the 1950s, causing appalling disease—is now illegal in most countries, and is easily detected. Occasionally, nature itself is the polluter. According to a United Nations team*, volcanic eruptions on the sea bed account for far greater quantities of heavy metals and radioactivity than do man-made sources.

The real damage to the coast comes from a myriad small parts that add up to one big whole. Each day New York, a city of over 7m people, deposits 500 tonnes of treated sewage in the Atlantic. A city of 5m people would release some 42m litres (8.8m gallons) of petroleum products a year, roughly the quantity of oil spilled by the *Exxon Valdez*. James Baker, the head of America's National Oceanic and Atmospheric Administration (NOAA), gives warning that the chemistry of the water round the coast is gradually changing. He thinks coastal pollution is as serious a problem as climate change.

Too many people want too much from the coast

The most visible consequence of human habitation is rubbish. No coastline, however far-flung, is free from it. In the early 1990s, Tim Benton, a scientist visiting the Pitcairn Islands (four dots in the Pacific Ocean 5,000 miles east of Australia), was struck by the rubbish washed up on the beaches. One morning, on a small uninhabited atoll called Ducie Island, the remotest of the Pitcairns, he decided to record what he found. The 953 objects included a meat pie and six light bulbs (see table 1).

Ducie's rubbish, which probably came from boats, was ugly, but fairly harmless. Crowded coasts face a bigger threat from compounds containing nitrogen and phospho-

---

*"The State of the Marine Environment", by the Group of Experts on the Scientific Aspects of Marine Pollution. Blackwell, 1990

Beachcombed

Beach debris from Ducie Island

Item	Number
Unidentified (or broken) plastic pieces	268
Glass bottles	171
Bottle tops	74
Plastic bottles	71
Buoys: small	67
Buoys: pieces	66
Buoys: large	46
Pieces of rope	44
Segments of plastic pipe	29
Shoes	25
Jars	18
Crates	14
Copper sheeting from hulls of wrecks	8
Aerosol cans	7
Food or drink cans	7
Fluorescent tubes	6
Light bulbs	6
Jerry cans	4
Cigarette lighters	3
Pen tops	2
Dolls' heads	2
Gloves (1 pair)	2
Asthma inhaler	1
Construction-worker's hat	1
Football (punctured)	1
Glue syringe	1
Lorry-tyre	1
Plastic coat-hanger	1
Plastic foot-mat	1
Plastic skittle	1
Small gas cylinder	1
Tea strainer	1
Tinned meat pie	1
Toy soldier	1
Toy aeroplane	0.5

Source: T. Benton

rus. According to one book*, the North Sea now collects four times as much nitrate and eight times as much phosphate as it did 20 years ago. Some of the pollution comes from easily identifiable sources, mainly treated sewage. But most originates from the drainage of hundreds of thousands of farms and the exhaust of millions of petrol and diesel engines.

With these "non-point" sources, identifying the polluter is impossible. Some 40% of the land in the United States, including midwestern farm land, drains into the Gulf of Mexico. The nitrate-rich river water has spoiled an area of the sea bed the size of New Jersey. Nobody knows the cost of this damage—nor how much each farmer caused and what it would cost to prevent it. Even if they did, studies in other regions—admittedly less exposed to agricultural pollution—show that, typically, 40% of the nitrate in the sea originally came from the air.

To complicate the picture, while too much of the stuff is certainly a bad thing, some of it is probably better than none at all. Limited amounts of nitrate and phosphate—which go into making fertiliser—are almost certainly beneficial. When the High Aswan dam was built on the Nile in the 1960s, the reduction in nutrients washing into the Mediterranean cut the fish catch immediately offshore from 38 tonnes in 1962 to less than 6 tonnes in 1975. The Mediterranean as a whole has confounded scientists, who in the late 1970s had said that the sea was fully exploited. Since then the catch has almost doubled. John Caddy, of the Food and Agriculture Organisation (FAO) in Rome, suggests that this may be due to a greater concentration of nutrients.

Yet, as Mr Caddy would be the first to point out, too many nutrients are harmful. The gravest example is the Black Sea, into which rivers drain from a vast area of Europe and Asia. Since the 1950s, concentrations of nitrate and phosphate in the Danube, for example, have increased up to tenfold. Worse, the pollutants become concentrated in the Black Sea, because the only exit to the open ocean is through the Bosporus and the Sea of Marmara. This has caused algae to grow, making the waters turbid, which prevents light from penetrating much below the surface. Organic sediment containing dead algae settles on the sea floor, where it absorbs oxygen as it rots. That leaves insufficient oxygen for benthic (bottom-dwelling) species, many of which die. New species, such as jellyfish, have supplanted the sea's original inhabitants. Only six of the 26 original commercial fish are often still caught there, according to David Aubrey of the Woods Hole Oceanographic Institution in Massachusetts.

As an enclosed body of water, the Black Sea is exceptional, but other coasts have also been affected by pollution. One symptom is "harmful algal blooms"—sudden growths of a single type of alga which are usually unsightly, often foul-smelling and occasionally toxic. Such blooms have a long history. The first plague that Moses visited upon Egypt was a blood-red tide which killed fish and fouled the water. These days, places that never had blooms are seeing them for the first time, and places used to having them are suffering more often, and for longer.

Blooming algae

Along the Chinese coast, aquaculture has been struck by an organism called *Noctiluca scintillans,* which turns the water tomato-red and kills shrimp. A related species, called *Gymnodinium Mikimotoi,* also bloomed there recently, killing half the annual production of farmed fish in Hong Kong, where it had never been seen before. In Texas, in the Laguna Madre, a brown tide caused by an alga called *Aureoumbra lugunensis* lasted for seven years. A few scientists argue that more blooms are seen today because people are looking for them. But most think the increase is real, and that it has a number of causes—possibly including climate change—beside the extra nutrients running off from the land.

The main trouble with blooms is that they deprive other species of oxygen. Little is known about the lasting effects this might have. A few types of alga are clearly harmful. *Gymnodinium breve* leaves toxic residues in shellfish. After inhaling tiny droplets of the poison, people have difficulty breathing, and in Florida in 1996 it killed 150 manatees, an endangered sea mammal. Algae of the genus *Chaetoceros* kill fish by clogging their gills. Other organisms cause memory loss in people and suppress the immune system. One organism, *Pfiesteria piscicida,* discovered by scientists at North Carolina State University in 1992, achieved notoriety last year after it was detected in Chesapeake Bay, killing tens of thousands of fish. It may also have caused nausea, memory loss and stomach cramps

*"The Wealth of Oceans", by Michael Weber and Judith Gradwohl. Norton, 1995

in fishermen and others in close contact with the water. For all that, the direct damage caused by algal blooms is probably more aesthetic than economic. According to an unpublished study[†] of the cost of blooms off America in 1987–92, the total bill averages only about $40m a year.

One explanation for the recent flourishing of blooms is that new species of alga are being introduced in the ballast water of ships and in new species of farmed shellfish. This form of "pollution" has a long history, but it has worsened with the growth in shipping traffic. According to Sea Grant, part of NOAA, in 1850 one new species was introduced into America every 36 weeks. By 1985 the rate had increased to one every 12 weeks. Ronald Baird, of Sea Grant, complains that it is hard to find a native species in San Francisco Bay these days.

The new species can do great damage. At one point in 1992, smacks of comb-jellyfish, *Mnemiopsis leidyi*, accounted for 90% of the Black Sea's entire wet biomass, according to one Russian scientist. *Mnemiopsis* not only competes with fish for food, but eats fish eggs and larvae too. In the Mediterranean, where local sea plants have been weakened by pollution, an alga called *Caulerpa taxifolia* has taken root. It was discovered 14 years ago on the beach below the Monaco Oceanographic Museum. The museum, then run by the late Jacques Cousteau, was growing the weed in its tanks.

As well as producing waste, people use a lot of land. In Maryland, for example, half an acre is developed for each new resident. In the rich world, many of the remaining undeveloped sites are now protected by law.

Marine habitats are lost too. Estuaries and wetlands are important nurseries for juvenile fish and crustaceans. Ocean-going salmon returning to their river to spawn find their way blocked by dams. And even if they manage to climb the river, many of their smolt are chewed up by power-station turbines on the way back to the sea. Farmers have converted mangrove swamps into brackish ponds for shrimp and fish. In Thailand, about 30% of the mangroves have been lost to aquaculture, in the Philippines as many as half.

The most alarming loss of habitat, however, is on coral reefs. According to SeaWeb, a charity based in Washington, DC, that provides information about the marine environment, 10% of the world's reefs have been destroyed and another 30% will all but disappear within the next 20 years. And this is one of the more sober estimates.

The loss of reef has a host of causes. Sediment from forestry sluices into coastal waters, smothering coral. Tourism disrupts the habitat. In a single day the anchor of a cruise ship can destroy an area of coral reef half the size of a football pitch. The rubble left behind kills more reef later. Overfishing removes the fish that graze on algae. In

Jamaica, this led to a population explosion among algae-grazing sea urchins, and when those succumbed to a disease in the early 1980s, the algae overran the coral.

In Asia, fish are often caught by using bombs and cyanide. The explosive came first, left over from the second world war. But sodium cyanide is better for stunning the fish, and is less likely to injure the fisherman. Both techniques are used to capture live fish for aquaria and for restaurants in Hong Kong. Wealthy Chinese like to see their supper on the fin before they eat it.

These methods have a disastrous effect on fish. The most valuable species are few and far between and grow slowly. Carl Safina, an environmental activist, mentions[*] a Napoleon wrasse at Hong Kong's Ocean Park aquarium that took nearly 20 years to grow from 450 grammes (1lb) to 32kg; a large specimen on the reef can reach more than 180kg. The fishing also tears the coral apart or poisons it. Coral takes about 40 years to recover from blast fishing.

Blast and cyanide fishing are illegal in most countries; in the Philippines they have been banned since 1979. Yet they continue, despite the risks to the fishermen (it is not unusual to see a Filipino fisherman who has lost a hand). The reason is money. Studies of the effects of anchor damage, cyanide and blast fishing in the north-western Philippines, published last year by John McManus and Rodolfo Reyes of ICLARM and Cleto Nanola of the University of the Philippines suggest that a traditional Filipino fisherman can expect to earn around $1 a day, while a blast fisher might earn $15–40 from a single catch.

Even if they are reluctant to fish, many fishermen need to pay back money they have borrowed from the boats from Hong Kong. In any case, the Hong Kongers are prepared to pay a lot. One official at the World Bank was told about live groupers (big reef fish) selling in Hong Kong last year for HK$10,000 ($1,300) apiece.

Many people, rich and poor, want to live by the sea, and many of those who can't want to visit it. In developing countries coastal planners have trouble just coping with the local population. According to Stephen Lintner of the World Bank, they are swamped by the arrival of poor migrants from inland. In developed countries things are not so much better organised. Tom Collins, of the Scripps Institution of Oceanography in California, was part of a committee to manage San Diego Bay on which 30 groups were represented, including federal, state and city government, and various lobbies. It took five years to agree on the scientific data needed to understand the bay's ecosystems, and another five years to prepare a plan of action. But by that time some people had retired, there was a new agenda, and funding was hard to come by. After a decade's work, the programme looks like [it's] fizzling out.

[†]"Estimated Annual Economic Impacts Resulting from Harmful Algae Blooms in the United States", by D.M. Anderson, P. Hoagland, Y. Kaoru and A.W. White, 1998

[*]"Song for the Blue Ocean", by Carl Safina, Henry Holt, 1997

Going deep

To CALL the planet we cling to "earth" is to be grossly anthropocentric. "Ocean" would be more accurate. Almost 71% of our planet's surface is covered by sea (by an odd coincidence, precisely the proportion of the human body that is salt water). Similarly, when people talk about the ocean, they usually mean coastal waters, or possibly the seas over the continental shelf. In fact, the shelf covers only 6% of the planet's surface, and those people who venture into the open ocean usually skim whales, tuna and other large creatures from the surface, or rush to safety on the other side. Of the volume of the planet in which traces of life can be found, something over 90% is deep under water.

By virtue of its inaccessibility to man, the deep is as pristine an environment as can be (though scientists trawling 4km down complain of the coke cans and clinker they find everywhere). The deep is owned by nobody and governed by international treaty, unlike coastal waters, which are under the control of the states that border them. In this sense the deep-water environment is the ultimate commons—one that is all the harder to manage sensibly because so little is known about it.

Modest trawl-sampling of the deep began only in 1872 with the British ship HMS *Challenger*. On its four-year voyage, *Challenger* found 103 new species. They are still stored in tall glass jars in the basement of London's Natural History Museum, shoulder to shoulder with specimens collected by HMS *Beagle,* which had carried Darwin to the Galapagos Islands 37 years earlier.

The discovery of new species, which began with animals washed up on the shore in the 18th century, has shown no sign of slowing (see chart 2). Indeed, an animal as large as the megamouth shark, which is 4.5 metres (15 feet) long and weighs 750kg, was one of the horrors of the half-known deep that turned up only a few years ago. The shark, which lives only 300 metres down, has since been caught alive on several occasions. Deeper-living creatures rarely survive the journey to the surface. A deep-water scientist will almost never hold a living specimen of the creatures he spends a lifetime studying.

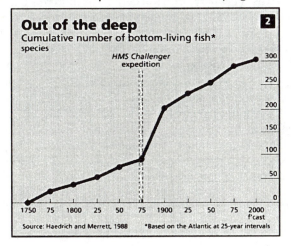

Out of the deep **2**
Cumulative number of bottom-living fish* species

Source: Haedrich and Merrett, 1988   *Based on the Atlantic at 25-year intervals*

Life below the surface ranges from gloomy to black. At only 10 metres down, most of the red light in the spectrum has been absorbed, which is why the underwater has a greeny-blue tint. At 50 metres, only 5% of the light is left. At 150 metres, photosynthesis stops. In even the clearest ocean, below 1,000 metres it is eternally night.

For the animals in the deep (there are no plants and, oddly perhaps, no insects, the most successful land animals), everything comes from the surface. The fish swimming freely in the body of the water column, known as pelagic fish, and those near the bottom, called demersal fish, each take their share of the surface crumbs as they fall to the sea floor. With increasing depth, there is less to be had. As a rule, only about 5% of the food at the surface is available to creatures lower down, and four-fifths of that is captured before it reaches the sea bed.

Davy Jones' locker is the ultimate commons: vast, ownerless and largely unknown

Because many deep-sea creatures make their own light, there is still a need for disguise in the dark deep. This is why many deep-living species, such as *Gonostoma bathyphilum*, a 10cm-long machete-shaped fish, are completely black. A few, such as the orange roughy and the 7cm-long deep shrimp, *Acanthephyra purpurea*, are bright scarlet—a colour that is invisible in the lunar glow from other creatures' luminescent organs. Some species, such as the angler fish, produce light to attract prey. In others living and feeding near the bottom, such as the grenadier, the light organs presumably warn off predators or signal to mates.

Because food is scarce, many animals grow slowly and live a long time. The Pacific slope-dwelling grenadier respires at one hundredth the rate of its distant relative, the Atlantic cod. The abyssal grenadier has a liver that can store enough food to keep it going for 186 days if needs be. Some species forage, whereas others probably live in suspended animation, waiting to be roused by a passing morsel. All the really deep species are adapted to the intense pressure: at the deepest parts of the ocean this can reach 1,100 atmospheres, the equivalent of 50 jumbo jets weighing down on a human.

In the open ocean, surface nutrients are limited and phytoplankton are scarce. In effect, the high seas are a blue desert. On the sea bed far below, therefore, most of the sediment is mineral, and accumulates at a rate of only 1mm every thousand years. Where there is more phytoplankton on the surface, nearer the continental shelf, a more nutritious silt washes down. These areas contain more of the life that is found everywhere on the sea floor, including worms, crabs, bivalves and the odd sea cucumber. Buried in the sediment are many sorts of tiny organisms. Some scientists think that the sea floor may contain up to 10m different species. But that is pure guesswork: according to Elisabeth Mann Borgese of Dalhousie University, in Canada, only 1.5% of the sea bed has been explored.

Here and there, this watery desert is dotted with islands of fire. Nine-tenths of this planet's volcanic activity takes place on the sea floor. Water that has seeped into the earth's crust is heated and driven out into the cold sea in mineral-charged jets called black smokers. It is dark here too, but there are colonies of bacteria that can metabolise the abundant hydrogen sulphide (a substance poisonous to most life). Some of the bacteria are free-living, others find a home in shrimps, clams and worms, which harvest them for food. An entire ecosystem, including crabs and snails, lives off the shrimps and clams.

Growth is faster here than on the rest of the sea floor. A 22cm giant clam could be just six-and-a-half years old, whereas shells from sediments in 3,800 metres of North Atlantic water were found to have grown to only 8mm in roughly a century. Other bacteria live in or near the chimneys of minerals that are deposited by the saturated water. According to Holger Jannasch, a scientist at Woods Hole and one of the first explorers of hot vents, some of these creatures can survive at 113°C, far beyond the temperature used for pasteurisation. The implications have not been lost on biotechnologists, who see a potential for exploiting the newly found enzymes.

Indeed, exploitation of the deep seems only a matter of time. At the end of last year an Australian firm, the Nautilus Mineral Corporation, won a licence to extract gold from the chimneys left by extinct hot vents at depths of 1.2-1.7km in the Bismarck Sea off the coast of Papua New Guinea. The reserves, richer than many on land, could be worth billions of dollars, says the firm. Further in the future, it may be possible to extract metals from the manganese nodules that collect like tennis balls on the sea floor (an idea that enjoyed a vogue in the 1970s, but proved uneconomic then). And at depths below 300 metres, methane is locked away in cages of water molecules. Off the coast of Central America huge deposits have been found that might one day become a source of natural gas.

Fisheries are also extending into deeper waters, with the Patagonian toothfish in the Southern Ocean, and the orange roughy, which is fished from depths of 400 metres to 1,800 metres off the coast of Australia and New Zealand and in the Atlantic. In a recent book*, Nigel Merrett of the Natural History Museum in London and Richard Haedrich of the Memorial University in Canada warn against this deep-water fishing. Because food is scarce, deep-living fish grow slowly, and some spawn only once in their long lives. There are few predators in the deep, probably because there is not much to prey on. A new predator armed with nets and a diesel engine might, literally, clean up—and leave nothing.

---

*"Deep-Sea Demersal Fish and Fisheries," by Nigel Merrett and Richard Haedrich. Chapman & Hall, 1997

A fisherman's tale

AT DAWN the boats across the Maricaban Strait dim their floodlights and haul in their nets. Light-fishing is illegal in the Philippines, but the law is routinely ignored. It is a better way of catching fish, and fish are increasingly hard to come by in the South China Sea.

The boats take their haul to market in Anilao, 20 minutes down the coast. Bonito are for sale at the water's edge, and stalls a few paces from the harbour offer rabbit fish, snappers, goat fish and a ropey-looking marlin. The market, which starts at around 6.30am, used to last until mid-morning, but this Saturday the tubs of fish are gone by 8am. Many fish are small, some below spawning age. Filipinos now serve guests species of fish that they barely considered edible a decade ago. One market trader has given up fish and taken to selling chicken instead.

The scarcity is the result of overfishing, and it affects both poor and rich countries, polluted and unpolluted. Although the rich world can afford to manage its fisheries, and commands the expertise of some of the world's best fisheries biologists, it has brought some spectacular failures on itself. In the Grand Banks, off the coast of New England and Canada, it has presided over the collapse of possibly the world's most valuable fishing grounds.

The banks' abundance was legendary. In his recent book on the cod, Mark Kurlansky recalls that when Cartier "discovered" the mouth of the St Lawrence river in 1534, he found a thousand Basque vessels already fishing there. Eventually, the banks attracted fishermen from all over the Atlantic. But by 1992, the biomass of spawning cod off Newfoundland and Labrador had fallen to only 22,000 tonnes, compared with 1.6m tonnes 30 years earlier. America halved its fishing effort in the New England groundfish fisheries. Canada closed the Grand Banks, announcing a five-year aid package worth C$1.5 billion ($1.05 billion). The collapse has cost 40,000 jobs in Newfoundland.

The effects of overfishing are masked by the overall statistics, which show that the world's supply of fish has continued to grow nicely as the fishing effort has intensi-

Overfishing is one part human nature, and two parts poor management.

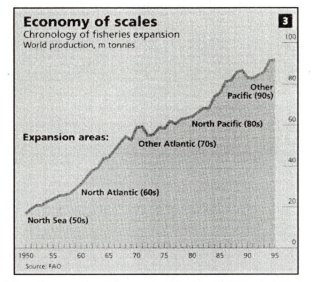

Economy of scales
Chronology of fisheries expansion
World production, m tonnes

3

Expansion areas:

Other
Pacific (90s)

North Pacific (80s)

Other Atlantic (70s)

North Atlantic (60s)

North Sea (50s)

Source: FAO

fied in one ocean after another (see chart 3). But the statistics aggregate hundreds of species, and in a practice reminiscent of a Soviet factory of former days, report the catch by weight rather than by value—a number that is hard to collect. Overfishing threatens to become ubiquitous, and on the whole has not been remedied even in fishing grounds such as the North Sea, where it was first identified as long ago as the beginning of this century.

The world catch of demersal fish (which include the best fish to eat, such as cod and haddock) has not grown since the early 1970s (see chart 4). Instead, the growth in landings has come from aquaculture and large volumes of pelagic fish, such as the Peruvian anchoveta, that are used mostly to make meal. One study suggests that there are now more low-value pelagic fish precisely because large numbers of their valuable predators have been taken. Indeed, as people "fish down the food chain" in this way, the available catch might increase disproportionately, since predators consume more than their own weight in prey. In some fisheries, therefore, the volume of the catch has grown even as its value has fallen.

The overfishing is spreading. The FAO, which does more than anyone to monitor the world's fisheries, says that 35% of the 200 main stocks are currently in decline and 25% at their peak. Almost all were underexploited a few decades ago. Stocks that have crashed are rarely given the chance to recover completely. Except for stocks in the south-east Pacific (where the newly discovered Japanese pilchard has boosted catches), the stocks classified by the FAO in 1992 as overexploited have been in decline for three decades. Over that period the catch of these stocks has fallen by 4m tonnes, or a third.

First catch your handout

The reason why overfishing can easily happen is that in most fisheries just about anyone has the right to have a go, and plenty have exercised that right. In past decades, the number of fishermen, as

well as fish farmers, has been growing across the developing world. According to Richard Grainger of the FAO, the total worldwide has more than doubled in the past 25 years.

"Open access" can lead to absurd races for fish. In Alaska in the early 1990s anyone could catch sable fish, although the overall total was controlled. As a result, a year's worth of sable fish were usually caught off the coast of Alaska in under a week. Not only are such scrambles dangerous for fishermen but, since most people will pay less for a frozen fish than a fresh one, they are wasteful too. In most fisheries there is no finishing line: the race goes on, week after week, month after month.

But overfishing is more than, in the language of economists, "a tragedy of the commons". Governments have used subsidies to encourage people to work and invest in fishing, especially after territorial waters were extended to 200 miles in the 1970s and foreign fleets were kicked out. A new study by the World Bank* estimates that these subsidies are worth a total of up to $16 billion a year. They come in many forms, including direct aid for building boats and state-financed fisheries management.

Even America, having scrapped programmes to expand the national fleet, still exempts fishing from fuel duty and lets fishermen defer income tax. Fishermen exploit a resource that belongs to everyone, without paying rent—unlike, say, companies that log government-owned land. If you count that as a subsidy too, the study says, the total aid to fishing worldwide amounts to as much as $21 billion. This is more than a quarter of fishing boats' total revenues, making fishing one of the most subsidised industries anywhere (though less so than farming).

The combination of open access and subsidy inevitably leads to overcapacity. FAO scientists estimate that 53% of the world's fishing fleet is superfluous. In 1996 the EU decided that its fleet should be cut by 40% over six years (although it later retreated from this goal). According to an American estimate, Russia should lose two-thirds of its fleet.

*"Subsidies in World Fisheries: a Re-examination", by Matteo Milazzo. World Bank, 1998

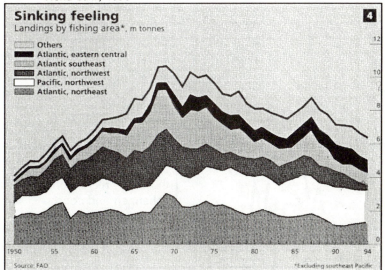

Sinking feeling
Landings by fishing area*, m tonnes

4

- Others
- Atlantic, eastern central
- Atlantic southeast
- Atlantic, northwest
- Pacific, northwest
- Atlantic, northeast

Source: FAO *Excluding southeast Pacific

Nevertheless, some countries are still expanding their fishing industries. The number of Chinese fishermen quadrupled between 1970 and 1990. The distant-water fleet has grown especially fast and Chinese officials say they want it to grow further. The EU has bought licences in such places as Africa as a way to deal with overcapacity at home. When Morocco and Namibia tried to end these agreements in the 1990s, the EU applied intense diplomatic pressure. The EU has sometimes paid its fishermen to give up their boats and exported the surplus hulls. The extra boats that arrived in Argentina helped destroy the hake fishery there.

All this points to another factor in overfishing: increasing technological sophistication. Distant-water fleets bring industrial fishing to countries such as Gabon or Guinea, which do not have big boats of their own. Technology has improved rapidly. The last American sailing boat was fishing on the Grand Banks as recently as 1963. What with new engines, satellite navigation, sonar, computerised gear, you name it, it is still improving all the time. Andy Smith, of the FAO, reckons that even if the fleet's tonnage remained the same, its fishing capacity would increase by 3% a year.

In the face of overfishing, governments have tried to control both the effort that goes into fishing and the catch. This has two shortcomings. The first is that not enough may be known about the fish. The collapse of the Pacific sardine fishery in the 1940s (see chart 5), which killed Cannery Row and provided a novel for John Steinbeck, was once regarded as a result of overfishing. Research on sediments by the Scripps Institution shows that the collapse was in fact a natural oscillation. In such circumstances, overfishing makes matters worse. Michael Mullin of Scripps says it delayed the return of the sardine by about 15 years.

The obvious answer is to manage fish stocks conservatively. But that is to ignore the other shortcoming of government controls: the bad blood between fishermen and fisheries managers. To a large extent this is a symptom of the overcapacity created by subsidies and open access, which keeps fishermen under constant financial pressure. "Scientists think fishermen overfish, and fishermen think scientists overprotect," laments James Baker of NOAA.

The institutions designed to manage fisheries often do not work. America has set up eight regional councils to recommend how to manage fisheries. They are meant to represent all interests, including those of recreational fishermen and conservationists, but some of them have been hijacked by commercial fishermen. Can-

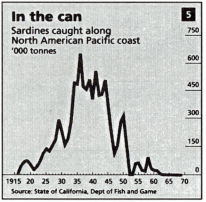

In the can
Sardines caught along North American Pacific coast
'000 tonnes

5

750
600
450
300
150
0

1915 20 25 30 35 40 45 50 55 60 65 70
Source: State of California, Dept of Fish and Game

ada's more autocratic system has proved even less effective. At the end of March the Canadian parliament recommended sacking the officials responsible for the Atlantic cod fishery. The EU's common fishery policy is widely loathed for failing either to conserve stocks or to keep fishermen happy. Developing countries often have no fisheries management at all. What laws there are tend to be ignored—sometimes by foreign fleets that have bribed their way in.

The damage from overfishing is mostly economic. According to Mr Grainger of the FAO, the world catch, worth more than $80 billion, could be 10–20% larger with good fisheries management. America estimates that the profits from its part of the Grand Banks could be $150m higher. In many poor countries an individual fisherman's catch has barely grown since 1981; sometimes it has dropped.

Fishing also seems to bring even supposedly friendly countries to blows. In 1995 Canada arrested the *Estai*, a Spanish boat from Vigo, which led to a row with the EU. The British have been getting worked up for years about Spanish "quota hoppers", boats that have, quite legally, bought the right to fish from British skippers. Canada and America fight a running battle over salmon on the northwestern coast. Last year a gang of Canadian fishermen blockaded an American ferry in British Columbia. Japan and South Korea have been sparring over the fishing around some rocks the Japanese call Take-shima and the Koreans Tok-to.

But there is a less-noticed toll, too. Some types of fishing lead to large amounts of "by-catch", made up of unwanted species. Nobody knows how much is killed this way, but the best estimate is 22m tonnes, roughly a quarter of the total wild catch.

On the whole, overfishing does not lead to the biological extinction of species. Left for a few years, the fish seem to recover. According to Pamela Mace, a distinguished fisheries biologist with NOAA, this has happened with herring in Norway and the Gulf of Maine, and striped bass on the Atlantic coast of America. But trawling can damage the sea bed. Some parts of the benthic habitat are scoured several times a year, which gives the animals and plants insufficient time to recover.

Yet fishing does have subtler genetic consequences. Rather than destroy, say, the herring species in its entirety, it may destroy particular groups of fish, such as spring-spawning herring. Surviving fish may also be changed by the relentless hunt. The cod on the Grand Banks now reach sexual maturity at two years of age, instead of four as they used to—presumably because early-maturing fish have a better chance of spawning. And there is no guarantee that ecosystems will re-establish themselves. The Grand Banks have become home to the Arctic cod, which competes with its Atlantic cousin for food.

Although most fish will not die out as a result of overfishing, a few species of marine animals are threatened with extinction. Most at risk are valuable animals that are stationary. Paul Dayton and Mia Tegner from Scripps have tracked the decline of the white abalone, a shellfish living in the kelp off the Californian coast that has been ruthlessly pursued. Fishermen took 65 tonnes of white abalone in 1972. Now the scientists think that only a few dozen specimens remain. Large, slow-growing creatures, such as whales, are also in danger, as are sharks and skates, which reach sexual maturity late and have few offspring. Sturgeon are included on the list of endangered species. So are sharks, which are killed for their fins.

Fish and ships

The future of fishing rests on two pillars. The first is better management. This is not a matter of coming up with some big idea, but of making lots of detailed improvements, often at [a] local level. Access can be limited by licensing. Fishermen can be rewarded for husbanding the stock. Satellites and electronic logs can help enforcement officers catch offenders at sea. New gear can reduce the by-catch and protect endangered species, such as turtles and sea birds.

The second pillar is aquaculture. This is growing rapidly, more than doubling in volume to 28m tonnes and almost trebling in value to $43 billion between 1986 and 1995, according to a new report by the FAO. About half of this takes place in freshwater ponds.

Aquaculture is usually pilloried for the pollution it causes. The culprits are shrimp and fin fish such as salmon. A study in 1994 found that 80kg of nitrogen compounds and 7.5kg of phosphates were produced for each tonne of farmed salmon, and that 70–80% of the antibiotics that were supposed to protect the fish went to waste. Shrimp cultivation can also pollute, but spectacular outbreaks of disease in Asia farms have been a great incentive for better management.

Pollution from fish farming can be avoided. It is hardly in the farmers' interest to waste medicine and feed. Moreover, carnivorous finfish and crustaceans make up a tenth of marine aquaculture by weight. A far larger proportion is seaweed and shellfish, which are filter-feeders and require no added food. Because they depend on clean water, their farmers are likely to seek a clean environment.

The real worry about aquaculture is genetic. New species, strains and breeds are being used in aquaculture, and being created by it. When fish are farmed, they become domesticated. Farm-bred rainbow trout come to the surface when people approach; their wild cousins hide. Farmed tilapia can be handled without struggling; the wild fish suffer. Such differences will grow as strains are bred in captivity. More importantly, there is a great temptation to breed improved varieties: salmon that will grow faster, taste better and keep fresher.

These fish may present a danger to wild strains. True, many are unfit to survive outside their cages. True again, breeders will be able to make almost all the hatchlings sterile, or dependent upon some man-made chemical. But these safeguards are not yet absolute, and experience has shown that farmed fish will escape to the wild. As things stand, an escaped gene is more of a threat in the boundless sea than it ever would be on land.

Come the storm-blast . . .

CANADIANS are used to snow. But last winter brought something worse: ice that paralysed Quebec, twisted electricity pylons like wire coat-hangers and deprived 3m people of power, some of them for weeks. The country's armed-services chief described Montreal's South Shore as "Sarajevo without the bullets".

The ice storm was caused by El Niño, a weather pattern produced by a change in the Pacific Ocean currents that in the past year has been blamed for almost every twitch of the North American barometer. The ice started as moisture, carried northwards on a current of warm air. In any normal winter it would have fallen as snow. But El Niño creates wetter and warmer weather on America's east coast. This year the extra water froze only when it fell into the cold Canadian airmass below. Proof, if any were needed, that changes in the ocean can have freak effects thousands of miles away.

There was a time when meteorologists looked on the ocean in two contradictory ways: as an infinite reservoir of heat and water, and as a passive recipient of changes in the atmosphere, cooling or warming in response. As John Woods of Imperial College in London explains, this is changing now, partly because more powerful computers can model what goes on in the water, but also because of worries about climate change. And there is a growing conviction that fluctuations in ocean currents are important in their own right—especially as oil and gas production moves into deeper waters.

. . . the ocean is equal partner to the air

The ocean matters to the climate in three ways. First, it acts as a store for water, heat and carbon. The ocean contains 96% of the planet's water, and 50 times as much carbon as the atmosphere. The top 3 metres of the ocean can store the same amount of heat as the entire atmosphere. The ocean also transports prodigious amounts of water, heat and carbon. The various currents that operate between 30° and 40° north, mainly the Gulf Stream in the Atlantic and the Kuroshio in the Pacific, between them carry 2 petawatts of heat northwards, the equivalent of 1,000 large power stations. The Gulf Stream shifts up to 150m cubic metres of water a second, over 100 times more than all the world's fresh-water rivers put together. Lastly, there are exchanges between the ocean and the atmosphere through warming and cooling, evaporation and rainfall, and photosynthesis. Some parts of the ocean lose more water vapour than they receive in rain, and vice versa. The Pacific, for example, is less saline and therefore less dense than the Atlantic, and stands almost half a metre higher.

The whole climatic machine is driven by the sun and the earth. In the tropics the sun strikes squarely from directly overhead. But in temperate and polar latitudes, the earth's surface curves away from the sun, so its beams strike only obliquely. The surplus energy arriving at the equator then spreads to the poles in currents of warm water and warm water-laden air. The ocean currents, called gyres, are swirled around by the earth's rotation and crimped by its land masses.

This is uncontroversial. So is forecasting tomorrow's weather, which will follow predictably from today's. However, an unknown lurks between the specificities of weather and the generalities of meteorology: nobody can say much that is useful about the climate next year.

And that is the big achievement of the scientists who successfully forecast El Niño several months in advance. The value of accurate El Niño forecasts to agriculture in the southern United States has been put at $260m by the Organisation for Economic Co-operation and Development. And those people who heeded official advice and mended their roofs before the "pineapple expresses" began to roll in from the Pacific saved themselves untold trouble.

As Daniel Cayan, of the Scripps Institution, points out, El Niño is probably the easiest such phenomenon to understand: it follows a regular cycle, and its effects are widespread. Recently, other systems have been found in the temperate latitudes of the Atlantic and the Pacific. Many others may be waiting to be discovered.

Mike McCartney and his colleagues at Woods Hole have studied a phenomenon called the North Atlantic Os-

cillation (NAO). When the NAO is high, that means a high-pressure region in the Azores and a low near Iceland. Westerly winds are warmed as they cross the Atlantic from North America to Europe, bringing mild weather with them. When the oscillation switches to a new phase, the Icelandic low moves to the south. The prevailing winds over Europe now contain cold, dry polar air, leading to harsher weather. They cross the ocean towards Canada, becoming warmer as they do so, and bringing mild weather to Labrador. The NAO flips from one state to the other many times a year. For a few decades one state is more common than the other, before its opposite again prevails. It is this longer-term pattern that particularly interests scientists.

The rapidly changing atmosphere is a flibbertigibbet without permanence. This has led Mr McCartney to conclude that the long-term pattern is caused by alternating packets of cold and warm water passing along the north Atlantic gyre. Because the packets of water take a few decades to work their way through the currents, the NAO has a "memory".

Another system that has been discovered is the Pacific Decadal Oscillation (PDO), in the north Pacific, which has been extensively studied by Tim Barnett of Scripps with scientists from the Max-Planck-Institut for meteorology in Hamburg. It, too, may depend upon the stately progression of warmer or colder water around the gyre.

The PDO and the NAO now hint at the possibility of proper long-term forecasts. But aside from such practical applications, understanding systems in which the ocean and the atmosphere interact is vital in gauging how the climate is changing naturally—and therefore how much of the warming seen in the past century is due to mankind.

Indeed, climate change has lent a sense of urgency to oceanography. Curiosities have taken on a new significance. One oddity, called the Younger Dryas, a short ice

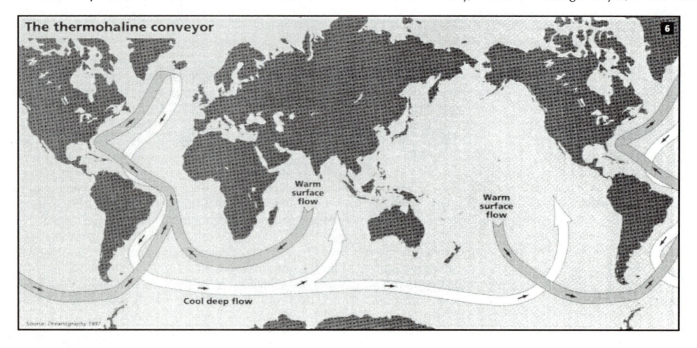

The thermohaline conveyor 6

Warm surface flow

Warm surface flow

Cool deep flow

Source: Oceanography 1997

age roughly 12,500 years ago, chilled the entire northern hemisphere during a period of warming. In a decade or so the temperature fell several degrees, staying low for some 1,300 years. The scientists of the Intergovernmental Panel on Climate Change (IPCC), who study global warming, have identified such sudden events as one of the surprises that today's climate might spring again.

Wallace Broecker of Columbia University in New York has suggested that the Younger Dryas was caused by a breakdown in the "thermohaline circulation", which carries heat in the ocean northwards from the equator. Normally, warm currents lose heat and water to the air on their way to the pole. Eventually, somewhere near Iceland, the cold and salty water becomes dense enough to sink to the ocean floor, where it begins a submarine trek back southwards (see map 6). Mr Broecker speculated that fresh water from a melting ice sheet could form a "cap" that stops the current sinking. Having blocked the circulation, it would prevent the arrival of equatorial heat at the poles.

Nobody knows whether such a mechanism is possible today. Although computer models can recreate the effect, some scientists doubt whether there is enough fresh water in the north Atlantic Ocean to cap the circulation. However, large pools of fresh water have been observed there. Robert Dickson, from the fisheries laboratory in Lowestoft on the east coast of Britain, followed a "great salinity anomaly" (a pool of water less saline than the surrounding sea) as it proceeded around the north Atlantic in the late 1960s to early 1980s. He is tracking a new salinity anomaly even now.

Sea surge

Climate change is surrounded by huge uncertainty. Assuming there is no Younger-Dryas-like ice age, one concern is a rise in the sea level. This has varied enormously in the past. Towards the end of the last ice age 18,000 years ago the sea was at least 100 metres lower than it is today. Conversely, 120,000 years ago, when the earth was slightly warmer than it is today, the sea was 5–6 metres higher than now.

Even the half-metre rise during the next century predicted by the IPCC is worrying for maritime countries, which may have to decide how to strengthen their coastal defences. For some it could be disastrous. Some 7% of the area of Bangladesh, with 6m inhabitants, is less than a metre above sea level. A rise of 3 metres would drive 30m Bangladeshis from their homes. Moreover, as people extract ground water for drinking, the country is sinking. By 2100 it could easily have dropped by 1.2 metres. And even if land is not permanently under water, it is vulnerable to storms, which in April 1991 killed 100,000 Bangladeshis.

The 1,190 islands in the Maldives and the Marshall Islands are an average of only 3 metres above sea level. According to Sir John Houghton, of the IPCC, a half-metre rise would take much of their land and turn up to half of their freshwater to brine.

A changing climate would affect sea life too. The current El Niño has reduced the plankton on the Californian coast by 70%. Salmon have deserted America and moved north to Canada and Alaska.

El Niños are a common event, and their effect is not likely to be lasting. Climate change would be different. Marea Hatziolos of the World Bank fears that coral, which are sensitive to temperature, will not be able to adapt, and will die. Keith Brander, of the International Council for the Exploration of the Sea, in Copenhagen, has shown how a warm period coincided with the appearance of cod off the coast of Greenland in the 1920s. Forty years later, when the weather turned cold again, they disappeared almost immediately. Andrew Bakun of the FAO speculates that there is a climatic link between the simultaneous variations in the stocks of pelagic fish seen on different sides of the world, such as pilchards off South Africa and anchoveta off Peru.

American officials complain that it has been impossible to negotiate with Canada over the northward-shifting salmon. Imagine the shift repeated, stock after stock, country after country. There might be fewer fish, and there would be no guarantee that those fish which migrate beyond the range of a particular fleet would be replaced. Some of those in the rich world who depend upon fishing for their livelihood would no longer have anything to catch. Some of those in poor countries who depend upon fish for their food would go hungry.

Bobbing bytes

COASTAL waters, fishing and climate change all require more attention from governments. The exception is shipping. There was a time when maritime strategists were busy discovering a route to the Indies, finding the longitude, and deciding whether dreadnoughts should burn coal or oil. Today, shipping gets its share of criticism for things like spilling oil and dumping rubbish at sea, but it is no longer the political issue it was. This is thanks partly to international laws and codes, many of which took decades to hammer out, and which now guarantee right of way and safe passage. But efficiency born of new technology and competition has also played its part.

Take, for example, containerisation, which amounted to building a logistical Internet decades before the real thing was invented. Like a packet of data, a container is just a box with an address. Like the World Wide Web, container routes have the economies of a network: the more users, the greater the benefit. As railways, shipping lines and haulage firms adapted their equipment to carry containers, the efficiencies mounted rapidly.

Containers are digital. Container ships no longer carry varied cargo, but standard boxes measured in one or two TEUS—20-foot-equivalent units. The point of containerisation is that the content of each box is irrelevant. It is the box itself that matters to the crane operators, shipping lines, railways and lorry drivers that handle them. Because every container is identical, it is simply another "packet" to be routed through the transport network.

The idea dates back to the 1950s, when vacuum tubes were still warm. It was the brainchild of Malcom McLean, a haulier from Cape Fear, North Carolina. The shipping lines and railway companies dismissed his scheme but Mr McLean, undeterred, bought a coastal tanker and converted it to carry lorry trailers. On April 26th 1956, the *Ideal X* carried its load from Port Newark, New York, to Houston in Texas. The voyage was a success, and within a decade shipping lines were convinced that international routes could also be served by container. Ten years after the *Ideal X*'s voyage, the *American Racer* sailed for Europe.

The unions quickly saw the threat of what became known as the "longshoreman's coffin". The shipping lines were not too enthusiastic either. In a dilemma that will be familiar to today's telephone companies, they were loth to spend money on a container network when they had already invested heavily in old-fashioned equipment.

Shipping shows a way to manage the use of the sea

Yet the savings have proved immense. Thanks to containers, sea transport these days represents only 1–1.5% of the total cost of a typical product, compared with 5–10% before their introduction. A ship spends 24 hours in port today, rather than three weeks under the old system of pallets. In total, 60% by value of sea-borne trade now goes by container.

Inevitably, there have been losers. The jobs of hundreds of thousands of dockers have disappeared. In 1956, 31,000 longshoremen were employed in the ports run by the New York Port Authority (NYPA); now barely a tenth of that number are left. The world's great harbours have suffered too. Container ships require a new sort of dockside crane and loading yard, so the NYPA built Port Elizabeth in New Jersey, the first harbour for container ships. The life went out of the old docks in such cities as Copenhagen and London. One of the bosses of a container line recently admitted to the *Journal of Commerce,* a sister publication of *The Economist,* that the business has lost its romance.

In the same way that globalisation has led to competition in

telecoms and the privatisation of the old state-owned monopolies, so the logic of containerisation has undermined the two governmental pillars of merchant shipping. The first is national ownership. Shipping was once so central to a nation's prosperity that it was treated as a protected industry. Governments wanted to be sure that a merchant navy was always at their disposal, and that hostile powers would not be able to cut off trade. Shipping lines were not for sale to foreigners.

But the 1990s have seen a series of international shipping mergers. Last year Neptune Orient Lines (NOL) of Singapore paid $825m for American President Lines (APL) of California, America's second-largest container line. Britain's P&O and Nedlloyd of the Netherlands have already merged their container businesses to create one of the world's largest shipping lines. South Korea's Hanjin has bought a majority share of DSR-Senator. There have been many smaller deals as well.

National boundaries have been further blurred by alliances in which shipping lines join forces to buy road, rail and port capacity. Mr McLean's SeaLand has an alliance with Maersk of Denmark. Hyundai Merchant Marine, Mitsui OSK Line and the new NOL/APL are in what they call the Global Alliance. And P&O Nedlloyd has joined four other lines in the "Grand Alliance".

These manoeuvrings are designed to lower costs in an industry that has been plagued by overcapacity. During the past decade, prices for most trades have been steady or falling (see chart 7). According to John Reeve, of A.T. Kearney, a management consultancy, volume has grown by an average of 9.4% a year since 1991, against only 4.1% for sales revenue.

Modes and nodes

Customers worry that the consolidation will reduce competition, and that fear is undermining the second principle of merchant shipping, immunity from antitrust prosecution. There was a logic to this when there were fewer ships and no communications. The first ship to market gets the best price for its commodity; late arrivals sell into a glut. In order to avoid booms and busts and ensure a steady supply for consumers, shipping lines were allowed to organise "conferences" for each trade. These set rates and helped establish timetables for sailings.

The shipping lines claim that the conferences are still beneficial. In general, there are enough lines outside the agreement to keep prices down, though the conference running the trade between Europe and America did manage to impose a notorious hike in prices at the start of the 1990s. However, the conferences restrict innovation in services and technology by limiting the ability of the lines to charge different prices. Partly because those outside the lines, such as China's Cosco and Taiwan's Evergreen, have thrived, the days of the conferences are probably numbered. In March, for example, the American senate passed a law which proposes that lines be able to strike exclusive deals with customers. This will, in ef-

Boxed in   **7**
Revenues, compound annual growth
1991-96, %
0   2   4   6   8
Global airlines
US trucking
Container shipping
Source: A.T. Kearney

fect, remove the largest customers from the conference system.

With the decline of conferences and of national ownership, merchant shipping is starting to look like just another business. When America shipped huge amounts of materials for the Gulf war, nobody seemed to mind that many of the ships it used were owned by foreign lines. According to Mr Reeve, the process will go further as shipping is subsumed by its homologue, the Internet. In an electronic world, the real power lies with the brain

that buys and sells space on lorries, trains and ships, not the brawn that shifts the goods. The sea will become just a node between routers. People will still share the destination of John Masefield, who "must go down to the seas again, to the lonely sea and the sky"; but few will share this British poet's quest. Nobody seeks a tall ship in the container age.

These days, shipping is governed by international law and the market. It is efficient and—generally—well organised. How can fishing and coastal waters best achieve a similar balance?

The deep green sea

THE politics of the sea suffers from three twists that also complicate the politics of other environments. First, nobody knows exactly how marine environments are affected by people, so policy will usually have to be devised before there is conclusive proof of, say, a rise in the sea level or the destruction of habitat.

Second, much that happens in and around the sea involves what economists call externalities—things that entail costs which the beneficiary does not fully bear. When a trawler damages the sea bed, it is the whole fleet that pays the price in lost fish. When a shrimp farmer fells mangroves, he does not pay for making the coast more prone to storm damage and erosion.

Third, just about any policy directed at the sea seems to involve a bewildering number of government bureaucracies—and possibly several countries as well. America's Environmental Protection Agency reports that shallow marine habitat in the mid-Atlantic region is regulated by 17 agencies (and this number does not include local jurisdictions). The FAO estimates that roughly a seventh of the fish caught at sea are part of stocks that straddle an international boundary.

Wavelength

Given these complications, how should the sea be treated? Marine environments vary enormously, but here are eight rules that apply to most:

• If you want to protect an environment, stop subsidising its destruction. There are already too many fishermen, so it does not make sense to spend public money to attract more. Ultimately, fishermen should pay a rent for the fish they catch.

• Limit access to resources. The oyster is a good example. In mid-19th-century Britain the poor used to get through around 500m oysters a year. "Poverty and oysters always seems to go together," as Sam Weller observed in Dickens's "Pickwick Papers". Common ownership of the foreshore and sewage, leading to overfishing and poisoning, put paid to that. Today the British slurp only a few million of the molluscs a year.

By contrast, 19th-century France controlled pollution and passed laws to limit oyster fishing. Later it restricted

concessions to specially trained people. Like the British, the French were big oyster eaters then, but unlike the British they never stopped. Today they scoff 2 billion of the things a year.

• Where possible, put resources into private hands. A number of countries have given individual fishermen a fixed share of the catch. These quotas are permanent and can be bought or sold, so they reflect the value of the fish that are still in the water. Quotas encourage fishermen to think about investing in conserving the stock instead of trying to catch the fish before someone else grabs them.

Transferable quota systems have been tried in a range of countries, including New Zealand, Australia, America, Chile, Iceland and the Netherlands. Others, such as Argentina, are thinking about them. Where they are in operation, the fishermen have begun to use words such as "product" and "customers". They complain that the joy has gone out of the life—but they are making money.

• Recognise that, except in emergencies, both central governments and international organisations make poor administrators. This is because coastal waters and fishing are complex, involving dozens of competing interests. Central authorities often lack the information they need to design a regime for the coast and fisheries, let alone enforce it.

The centre can, however, pass laws and offer advice. Governments can delegate powers to local authorities to manage their part of the coast and lay down procedures and budgets. The FAO has produced a useful "code of conduct for responsible fisheries", which includes details on coastal-zone management and aquaculture. There is also an international agreement on managing stocks that straddle international borders. The International Council for the Exploration of the Sea (ICES) helps to take the politics out of management by offering independent assessments of stocks.

• Get people to look after themselves. San Salvador Island, in the north of the Philippines, has been involved in a project to create "community management" of the coral reef. In the 1980s the villagers were using cyanide and explosives to fish the reef. Catches had fallen from more than 20kg of fish per trip in the 1960s to under 5kg by the end of the 1980s. In 1989, after encouragement from a local environmental group and a popular vote, San Salvador created a 137-hectare marine reserve, including a portion of the reef, in the best-preserved part of the shoreline. Fishing was banned, the villagers helped patrol the reserve and violators were punished. Within two years the villagers' catches outside the reserve had increased by about a third.

The strength of a community is that it can impose social norms, which are as important as legislation in guiding people's conduct. In industrialised countries, quota-owners may eventually start to behave like communities too. In New Zealand, quota-holders have begun to form associations to decide the policy for their stock. In Iceland it has become socially unacceptable for fishermen to cheat. Those who do face their friends' scorn long before they face prosecution.

• Set up reserves to preserve important habitat. The San Salvadorians were on to a good thing. Reserves are now seen as a way to protect fish stocks in developing and developed countries alike.

Three researchers based in Nouméa in New Caledonia, 800 miles off the east coast of Australia, recently published a study* on how reserves can protect coral reefs. They looked at the fish around five islands in New Caledonia's south-western lagoon before the reserves were created, and again five years later. They concluded that in the reserves the number of different species had grown by 67%, the number of fish by 160% and the biomass by 246%. Those islands where the reserves were most closely watched seemed to improve more than the others.

Reserves not only provide a sanctuary for fish, but a stock that can migrate to areas open to fishing. Moreover, they can provide a reference point against which scientists can measure the change in environments elsewhere. As Paul Dayton of Scripps observes, one of the difficulties of managing marine resources is that nobody any longer has a clear idea of what a normal habitat is like.

There is a movement in America to get 20% of the coastal waters set aside as reserves within the next 20 years. The campaign is a good idea, but the target is somewhat arbitrary. Nobody really knows how big reserves need to be or how to design them.

• The flip side of sanctuaries inside reserves is exploitation outside. As long as the marine environment is safeguarded by the sorts of rules outlined above, there is no reason not to use the sea to the full. The purpose of man-

*"Effects of Marine Reserves on Coral Reef Fish Communities from Five Islands in New Caledonia", by L. Wantiez, P. Thollot and M. Kulbicki. *Coral Reefs*, November 1997

aging coastal waters is not to keep them in a "natural" state. That would be impossible, largely because most coastlines have already been altered by such things as dams, pollution and aquaculture. Instead, management should make these areas more useful.

Fishermen might want to "fertilise" the water to help plankton to grow. Oil companies might want to dispose of rigs in deep water, where they might do less harm than if they were dismantled near the shore. Although they are unpleasant, algal blooms might not justify expensive remedial action.

• Lastly, governments should remember that there is more than one marine environment. John Steele of Woods Hole argues for different types of management in different places. The coast needs to be actively managed because so many people have competing claims to it. Policy cannot recreate a pristine coastal environment even if that were thought desirable. Deep waters, on the other hand, are vast and pristine, and have no need for management. The task there is conservation: to ensure that species are not destroyed, that the harmful effects of mining or dumping are limited. In-between lies the continental shelf, where fishing is intensive and most oil and gas is produced. Here people must strive to find a balance between management and conservation.

The great mirror
Baudelaire described the sea as the mirror of a free man. In superstitious times the sea reflected the fear of monsters and raiding parties. In the age of empire its glassy surface dispatched fleets and trade. For the romantics the sublime sea represented freedom from stuffy, money-obsessed convention. At the end of the 20th century, it seems, the brine is clouded with environmental pessimism.

More mouths, more money and more mess lead to an exploited sea, runs the refrain. In developing countries it is hard to manage resources for the long term, and even successful schemes are vulnerable to changes in the local hierarchy. Rich countries seem to get bogged down in politics.

The pity is that if people gave the sea a chance, it would repay them handsomely. Because it has few boundaries, it has always been subjected to constant change. Within limits, this has made marine life adaptable and resilient; but humanity has, in places, begun to test those limits. If people want both to preserve the sea and extract the full benefit from it, they must now moderate their demands, and structure them. They must put aside ideas of the sea's immensity and power, and instead take stewardship of the ocean, with all the privileges and responsibilities that implies.

The Great Climate Flip-flop

by WILLIAM H. CALVIN

ONE of the most shocking scientific realizations of all time has slowly been dawning on us: the earth's climate does great flip-flops every few thousand years, and with breathtaking speed. We could go back to ice-age temperatures within a decade—and judging from recent discoveries, an abrupt cooling could be triggered by our current global-warming trend. Europe's climate could become more like Siberia's. Because such a cooling would occur too quickly for us to make readjustments in agricultural productivity and supply, it would be a potentially civilization-shattering affair, likely to cause an unprecedented population crash. What paleoclimate and oceanography researchers know of the mechanisms underlying such a climate flip suggests that global warming could start one in several different ways.

For a quarter century global-warming theorists have predicted that climate creep is going to occur and that we need to prevent greenhouse gases from warming things up, thereby raising the sea level, destroying habitats, intensifying storms, and forcing agricultural rearrangements. Now we know—and from an entirely different group of scientists exploring separate lines of reasoning and data—that the most catastrophic result of global warming could be an abrupt cooling.

We are in a warm period now. Scientists have known for some time that the previous warm period started 130,000 years ago and ended 117,000 years ago, with the return of cold temperatures that led to an ice age. But the ice ages aren't what they used to be. They were formerly thought to be very gradual, with both air temperature and ice sheets changing in a slow, 100,000-year cycle tied to changes in the earth's orbit around the sun. But our current warm-up, which started about 15,000 years ago, began abruptly, with the temperature rising sharply while most of the ice was still present. We now know that there's nothing "glacially slow" about temperature change: superimposed on the gradual, long-term cycle have been dozens of abrupt warmings and coolings that lasted only centuries.

The back and forth of the ice started 2.5 million years ago, which is also when the ape-sized hominid brain began to develop into a fully human one, four times as large and reorganized for language, music, and chains of inference. Ours is now a brain able to anticipate outcomes well enough to practice ethical behavior, able to head off disasters in the making by extrapolating trends. Our civilizations began to emerge right after the continental ice sheets melted about 10,000 years ago. Civilizations accumulate knowledge, so we now know a lot about what has been going on, what

> "Climate change" is popularly understood to mean greenhouse warming, which, it is predicted, will cause flooding, severe windstorms, and killer heat waves. But warming could lead, paradoxically, to drastic cooling—a catastrophe that could threaten the survival of civilization

---

William H. Calvin is a theoretical neurophysiologist at the University of Washington at Seattle.

From *The Atlantic Monthly*, January 1998, pp. 47-50, 52-54. © 1998 by William H. Calvin. Reprinted by permission.

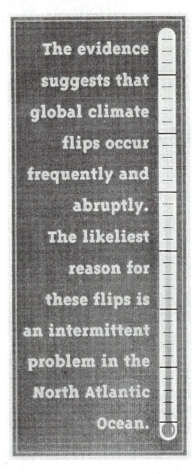

The evidence suggests that global climate flips occur frequently and abruptly. The likeliest reason for these flips is an intermittent problem in the North Atlantic Ocean.

has made us what we are. We puzzle over oddities, such as the climate of Europe.

Keeping Europe Warm

EUROPE is an anomaly. The populous parts of the United States and Canada are mostly between the latitudes of 30° and 45°, whereas the populous parts of Europe are ten to fifteen degrees farther north. "Southerly" Rome lies near the same latitude, 42°N, as "northerly" Chicago—and the most northerly major city in Asia is Beijing, near 40°N. London and Paris are close to the 49°N line that, west of the Great Lakes, separates the United States from Canada. Berlin is up at about 52°, Copenhagen and Moscow at about 56°. Oslo is nearly at 60°N, as are Stockholm, Helsinki, and St. Petersburg; continue due east and you'll encounter Anchorage.

Europe's climate, obviously, is not like that of North America or Asia at the same latitudes. For Europe to be as agriculturally productive as it is (it supports more than twice the population of the United States and Canada), all those cold, dry winds that blow eastward across the North Atlantic from Canada must somehow be warmed up. The job is done by warm water flowing north from the tropics, as the eastbound Gulf Stream merges into the North Atlantic Current. This warm water then flows up the Norwegian coast, with a westward branch warming Greenland's tip, 60°N. It keeps northern Europe about nine to eighteen degrees warmer in the winter than comparable latitudes elsewhere—except when it fails. Then not only Europe but also, to everyone's surprise, the rest of the world gets chilled. Tropical swamps decrease their production of methane at the same time that Europe cools, and the Gobi Desert whips much more dust into the air. When this happens, something big, with worldwide connections, must be switching into a new mode of operation.

The North Atlantic Current is certainly something big, with the flow of about a hundred Amazon Rivers.

And it sometimes changes its route dramatically, much as a bus route can be truncated into a shorter loop. Its effects are clearly global too, inasmuch as it is part of a long "salt conveyor" current that extends through the southern oceans into the Pacific.

I hope never to see a failure of the northernmost loop of the North Atlantic Current, because the result would be a population crash that would take much of civilization with it, all within a decade. Ways to postpone such a climatic shift are conceivable, however—old-fashioned dam-and-ditch construction in critical locations might even work. Although we can't do much about everyday weather, we may nonetheless be able to stabilize the climate enough to prevent an abrupt cooling.

Abrupt Temperature Jumps

THE discovery of abrupt climate changes has been spread out over the past fifteen years, and is well known to readers of major scientific journals such as *Science* and *Nature*. The abruptness data are convincing. Within the ice sheets of Greenland are annual layers that provide a record of the gases present in the atmosphere and indicate the changes in air temperature over the past 250,000 years—the period of the last two major ice ages. By 250,000 years ago *Homo erectus* had died out, after a run of almost two million years. By 125,000 years ago *Homo sapiens* had evolved from our ancestor species—so the whiplash climate changes of the last ice age affected people much like us.

In Greenland a given year's snowfall is compacted into ice during the ensuing years, trapping air bubbles, and so paleoclimate researchers have been able to glimpse ancient climates in some detail. Water falling as snow on Greenland carries an isotopic "fingerprint" of what the temperature was like en route. Counting those tree-ring-like layers in the ice cores shows that cooling came on as quickly as droughts. Indeed, were another climate flip to begin next year, we'd probably complain first about the drought, along with unusually cold winters in Europe. In the first few years the climate could cool as much as it did during the misnamed Little Ice Age (a gradual cooling that lasted from the early Renaissance until the end of the nineteenth century), with tenfold greater changes over the next decade or two.

The most recent big cooling started about 12,700 years ago, right in the midst of our last global warming. This cold period, known as the Younger Dryas, is named for the pollen of a tundra flower that turned up in a lake bed in Denmark when it shouldn't have. Things had been warming up, and half the ice sheets covering Europe and Canada had already melted. The return to ice-age temperatures lasted 1,300 years. Then, about 11,400 years ago, things suddenly warmed up again, and the earliest agricultural villages were established in the Middle East. An abrupt cooling got started 8,200 years ago, but it aborted within a century, and the temperature changes since then have been gradual in comparison. Indeed, we've had an unprecedented period of climate stability.

Coring old lake beds and examining the types of pollen trapped in sediment layers led to the discovery, early in the twentieth century, of the Younger Dryas. Pollen cores are still a primary means of seeing what regional climates were doing, even though they suffer from poorer resolution than ice cores (worms churn the sediment, obscuring records of all but the longest-lasting temperature changes). When the ice cores demonstrated the abrupt onset of the Younger Dryas, researchers wanted to know how widespread this event was. The U.S. Geological Survey took old lake-bed cores out of storage and re-examined them.

Ancient lakes near the Pacific coast of the United States, it turned out, show a shift to cold-weather plant species at roughly the time when the Younger Dryas was changing German pine forests into scrublands like those of modern Siberia. Subarctic ocean currents were reaching the southern California coastline, and Santa Barbara must have been as cold as Juneau is now. (But the regional record is poorly understood, and I know at least one reason why. These days when one goes to hear a talk on ancient climates of North America, one is likely to learn that the speaker was forced into early retirement from the U.S. Geological Survey by budget cuts. Rather than a vigorous program of studying regional climatic change, we see the shortsighted preaching of cheaper government at any cost.)

In 1984, when I first heard about the startling news from the ice cores, the implications were unclear—there seemed to be other ways of interpreting the data from Greenland. It was initially hoped that the abrupt warmings and coolings were just an oddity of Greenland's weather—but they have now been detected on a worldwide scale, and at about the same time. Then it was hoped that the abrupt flips were somehow caused by continental ice sheets, and thus would be unlikely to recur, because we now lack huge ice sheets over Canada and Northern Europe. Though some abrupt coolings are likely to have been associated with events in the Canadian ice sheet, the abrupt cooling in the previous warm

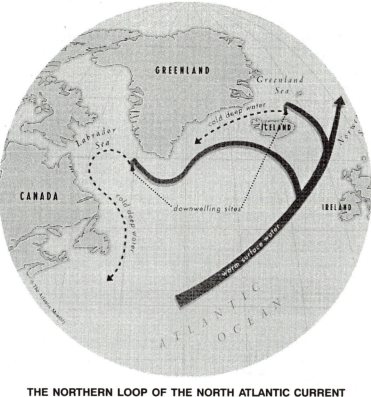

THE NORTHERN LOOP OF THE NORTH ATLANTIC CURRENT

period, 122,000 years ago, which has now been detected even in the tropics, shows that flips are not restricted to icy periods; they can also interrupt warm periods like the present one.

There seems to be no way of escaping the conclusion that global climate flips occur frequently and abruptly. An abrupt cooling could happen now, and the world might not warm up again for a long time: it looks as if the last warm period, having lasted 13,000 years, came to an end with an abrupt, prolonged cooling. That's how our warm period might end too.

Sudden onset, sudden recovery—this is why I use the word "flip-flop" to describe these climate changes. They are utterly unlike the changes that one would expect from accumulating carbon dioxide or the setting adrift of ice shelves from Antarctica. Change arising from some sources, such as volcanic eruptions, can be abrupt—but the climate doesn't flip back just as quickly centuries later.

Temperature records suggest that there is some grand mechanism underlying all of this, and that it has two major states. Again, the difference between them amounts to nine to eighteen degrees—a range that may depend on how much ice there is to slow the responses. I call the colder one the "low state." In discussing the ice ages there is a tendency to think of warm as good—and therefore of warming as better. Alas, further warming might well kick us out of the "high state." It's the high state that's good, and we may need to help prevent any sudden transition to the cold low state.

Although the sun's energy output does flicker slightly, the likeliest reason for these abrupt flips is an intermittent problem in the North Atlantic Ocean, one that seems to trigger a major rearrangement of atmospheric circulation. North-south ocean currents help to redistribute equatorial heat into the temperate zones, supplementing the heat transfer by winds. When the warm currents penetrate farther than usual into the northern seas, they help to melt the sea ice that is reflecting a lot of sunlight back into space, and so the earth becomes warmer. Eventually that helps to melt ice sheets elsewhere.

The high state of climate seems to involve ocean currents that deliver an extraordinary amount of heat to the vicinity of Iceland and Norway. Like bus routes or conveyor belts, ocean currents must have a return loop. Unlike most ocean currents, the North Atlantic Current has a return loop that runs deep beneath the ocean surface. Huge amounts of seawater sink at known downwelling sites every winter, with the water heading south when it reaches the bottom. When that annual flushing fails for some years, the conveyor belt stops moving and so heat stops flowing so far north—and apparently we're popped back into the low state.

Flushing Cold Surface Water

SURFACE waters are flushed regularly, even in lakes. Twice a year they sink, carrying their load of atmospheric gases downward. That's because water density changes with temperature. Water is densest at about 39°F (a typical refrigerator setting—anything that you take out of the refrigerator, whether you place it on the kitchen counter or move it to the freezer, is going to expand a little). A lake surface cooling down in the autumn will eventually sink into the less-dense-because-warmer waters below, mixing things up. Seawater is more complicated, because salt content also helps to determine whether water floats or sinks. Water that evaporates leaves its salt behind; the resulting saltier water is heavier and thus sinks.

The fact that excess salt is flushed from surface waters has global implications, some of them recognized two centuries ago. Salt circulates, because evaporation up north causes it to sink and be carried south by deep currents. This was posited in 1797 by the Anglo-American physicist Sir Benjamin Thompson (later known, after he moved to Bavaria, as Count Rumford of the Holy Roman Empire), who also posited that, if merely to compensate, there would have to be a warmer northbound current as well. By 1961 the oceanographer Henry Stommel, of the Woods Hole Oceanographic Institution, in Massachusetts, was beginning to worry that these warming currents might stop flowing if too much fresh water was added to the surface of the northern seas. By 1987 the geochemist Wallace Broecker, of Columbia University, was piecing together the

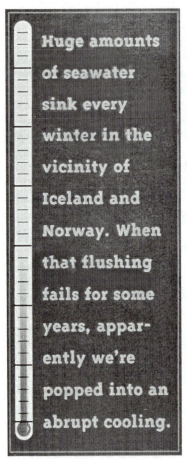

Huge amounts of seawater sink every winter in the vicinity of Iceland and Norway. When that flushing fails for some years, apparently we're popped into an abrupt cooling.

paleoclimatic flip-flops with the salt-circulation story and warning that small nudges to our climate might produce "unpleasant surprises in the greenhouse."

Oceans are not well mixed at any time. Like a half-beaten cake mix, with strands of egg still visible, the ocean has a lot of blobs and streams within it. When there has been a lot of evaporation, surface waters are saltier than usual. Sometimes they sink to considerable depths without mixing. The Mediterranean waters flowing out of the bottom of the Strait of Gibraltar into the Atlantic Ocean are about 10 percent saltier than the ocean's average, and so they sink into the depths of the Atlantic. A nice little Amazon-sized waterfall flows over the ridge that connects Spain with Morocco, 800 feet below the surface of the strait.

Another underwater ridge line stretches from Greenland to Iceland and on to the Faeroe Islands and Scotland. It, too, has a salty waterfall, which pours the hypersaline bottom waters of the Nordic Seas (the Greenland Sea and the Norwegian Sea) south into the lower levels of the North Atlantic Ocean. This salty waterfall is more like thirty Amazon Rivers combined. Why does it exist? The cold, dry winds blowing eastward off Canada evaporate the surface waters of the North Atlantic Current, and leave behind all their salt. In late winter the heavy surface waters sink en masse. These blobs, pushed down by annual repetitions of these late-winter events, flow south, down near the bottom of the Atlantic. The same thing happens in the Labrador Sea between Canada and the southern tip of Greenland.

Salt sinking on such a grand scale in the Nordic Seas causes warm water to flow much farther north than it might otherwise do. This produces a heat bonus of perhaps 30 percent beyond the heat provided by direct sunlight to these seas, accounting for the mild winters downwind, in northern Europe. It has been called the Nordic Seas heat pump.

Nothing like this happens in the Pacific Ocean, but the Pacific is nonetheless affected, because the sink in the Nordic Seas is part of a vast worldwide salt-conveyor belt. Such a conveyor is needed because the Atlantic is saltier than the Pacific (the Pacific has twice as much water with which to dilute the salt carried in from rivers). The Atlantic would be even saltier if it didn't mix with the Pacific, in long, loopy currents. These carry the North Atlantic's excess salt southward from the bottom of the Atlantic, around the tip of Africa, through the Indian Ocean, and up around the Pacific Ocean.

There used to be a tropical shortcut, an express route from Atlantic to Pacific, but continental drift connected North America to South America about three million years ago, damming up the easy route for disposing of excess salt. The dam, known as the Isthmus of Panama, may have been what caused the ice ages to begin a short time later, simply because of the forced detour. This major change in ocean circulation, along with a climate that had already been slowly cooling for millions of years, led not only to ice accumulation most of the time but also to climatic instability, with flips every few thousand years or so.

Failures of Flushing

FLYING above the clouds often presents an interesting picture when there are mountains below. Out of the sea of undulating white clouds mountain peaks stick up like islands.

Greenland looks like that, even on a cloudless day—but the great white mass between the occasional punctuations is an ice sheet. In places this frozen fresh water descends from the highlands in a wavy staircase.

Twenty thousand years ago a similar ice sheet lay atop the Baltic Sea and the land surrounding it. Another sat on Hudson's Bay, and reached as far west as the foothills of the Rocky Mountains—where it pushed, head to head, against ice coming down from the Rockies. These northern ice sheets were as high as Greenland's mountains, obstacles sufficient to force the jet stream to make a detour.

Now only Greenland's ice remains, but the abrupt cooling in the last warm period shows that a flip can occur in situations much like the present one. What could possibly halt the salt-conveyor belt that brings tropical heat so much farther north and limits the formation of ice sheets? Oceanographers are busy studying present-day failures of annual flushing, which give some perspective on the catastrophic failures of the past.

In the Labrador Sea, flushing failed during the 1970s, was strong again by 1990, and is now declining. In the Greenland Sea over the 1980s salt sinking declined by 80 percent. Obviously, local failures can occur without catastrophe—it's a question of how often and how widespread the failures are—but the present state of decline is not very reassuring. Large-scale flushing at both those sites is certainly a highly variable process, and perhaps a somewhat fragile one as well. And in the absence of a flushing mechanism to sink cooled surface waters and send them southward in the Atlantic, additional warm waters do not flow as far north to replenish the supply.

There are a few obvious precursors to flushing failure. One is diminished wind chill, when winds aren't as strong as usual, or as cold, or as dry—as is the case in the Labrador Sea during the North Atlantic Oscillation. This El Niño-like shift in the atmospheric-circulation pattern over the North Atlantic, from the Azores to Greenland, often lasts a decade. At the same time that the Labrador Sea gets a lessening of the strong winds that aid salt sinking, Europe gets particularly cold winters. It's happening right now: a North Atlantic Oscillation started in 1996.

Another precursor is more floating ice than usual, which reduces the amount of ocean surface exposed to the winds, in turn reducing evaporation. Retained heat

eventually melts the ice, in a cycle that recurs about every five years.

Yet another precursor, as Henry Stommel suggested in 1961, would be the addition of fresh water to the ocean surface, diluting the salt-heavy surface waters before they became unstable enough to start sinking. More rain falling in the northern oceans—exactly what is predicted as a result of global warming—could stop salt flushing. So could ice carried south out of the Arctic Ocean.

There is also a great deal of unsalted water in Greenland's glaciers, just uphill from the major salt sinks. The last time an abrupt cooling occurred was in the midst of global warming. Many ice sheets had already half melted, dumping a lot of fresh water into the ocean.

A brief, large flood of fresh water might nudge us toward an abrupt cooling even if the dilution were insignificant when averaged over time. The fjords of Greenland offer some dramatic examples of the possibilities for freshwater floods. Fjords are long, narrow canyons, little arms of the sea reaching many miles inland; they were carved by great glaciers when the sea level was lower. Greenland's east coast has a profusion of fjords between 70°N and 80°N, including one that is the world's biggest. If blocked by ice dams, fjords make perfect reservoirs for meltwater.

Glaciers pushing out into the ocean usually break off in chunks. Whole sections of a glacier, lifted up by the tides, may snap off at the "hinge" and become icebergs. But sometimes a glacial surge will act like an avalanche that blocks a road, as happened when Alaska's Hubbard glacier surged into the Russell fjord in May of 1986. Its snout ran into the opposite side, blocking the fjord with an ice dam. Any meltwater coming in behind the dam stayed there. A lake formed, rising higher and higher—up to the height of an eight-story building.

Eventually such ice dams break, with spectacular results. Once the dam is breached, the rushing waters erode an ever wider and deeper path. Thus the entire lake can empty quickly. Five months after the ice dam at the Russell fjord formed, it broke, dumping a cubic mile of fresh water in only twenty-four hours.

The Great Salinity Anomaly, a pool of semi-salty water derived from about 500 times as much unsalted water as that released by Russell Lake, was tracked from 1968 to 1982 as it moved south from Greenland's east coast. In 1970 it arrived in the Labrador Sea, where it prevented the usual salt sinking. By 1971–1972 the semi-salty blob was off Newfoundland. It then crossed the Atlantic and passed near the Shetland Islands around 1976. From there it was carried northward by the warm Norwegian Current, whereupon some of it swung west again to arrive off Greenland's east coast—where it had started its inch-per-second journey. So freshwater blobs drift, sometimes causing major trouble, and Greenland floods thus have the potential to stop the enormous heat transfer that keeps the North Atlantic Current going strong.

The Greenhouse Connection

OF this much we're sure: global climate flip-flops have frequently happened in the past, and they're likely to happen again. It's also clear that sufficient global warming could trigger an abrupt cooling in at least two ways—by increasing high-latitude rainfall or by melting Greenland's ice, both of which could put enough fresh water into the ocean surface to suppress flushing.

Further investigation might lead to revisions in such mechanistic explanations, but the result of adding fresh water to the ocean surface is pretty standard physics. In almost four decades of subsequent research Henry Stommel's theory has only been enhanced, not seriously challenged.

Up to this point in the story none of the broad conclusions is particularly speculative. But to address how all these nonlinear mechanisms fit together—and what we might do to stabilize the climate—will require some speculation.

Even the tropics cool down by about nine degrees during an abrupt cooling, and it is hard to imagine what in the past could have disturbed the whole earth's climate on this scale. We must look at arriving sunlight and departing light and heat, not merely regional shifts on earth, to account for changes in the temperature balance. Increasing amounts of sea ice and clouds could reflect more sunlight back into space, but the geochemist Wallace Broecker suggests that a major greenhouse gas is disturbed by the failure of the salt conveyor, and that this affects the amount of heat retained.

In Broecker's view, failures of salt flushing cause a worldwide rearrangement of ocean currents, resulting in—and this is the speculative part—less evaporation from the tropics. That, in turn, makes the air drier. Because water vapor is the most powerful greenhouse gas, this decrease in average humidity would cool things globally. Broecker has written, "If you wanted to cool the planet by 5°C [9°F] and could magically alter the water-vapor content of the atmosphere, a 30 percent decrease would do the job."

Just as an El Niño produces a hotter Equator in the Pacific Ocean and generates more atmospheric convection, so there might be a subnormal mode that decreases heat, convection, and evaporation. For example, I can imagine that ocean currents carrying more warm surface waters north or south from the equatorial regions might, in consequence, cool the Equator somewhat. That might result in less evaporation, creating lower-than-normal levels of greenhouse gases and thus a global cooling.

To see how ocean circulation might affect greenhouse gases, we must try to account quantitatively for important nonlinearities, ones in which little nudges provoke great responses. The modern world is full of objects and systems that exhibit "bistable" modes, with thresholds for flipping. Light switches abruptly change mode when nudged hard enough. Door latches suddenly give way. A gentle pull on a trigger may be ineffective, but there comes a pressure that will suddenly fire the gun. Thermostats tend to activate heating or cooling mechanisms abruptly—also an example of a system that pushes back.

We must be careful not to think of an abrupt cooling in response to global warming as just another self-regulatory device, a control system for cooling things down when it gets too hot. The scale of the response will be far beyond the bounds of regulation—more like when excess warming triggers fire extinguishers in the ceiling, ruining the contents of the room while cooling them down.

Preventing Climate Flips

THOUGH combating global warming is obviously on the agenda for preventing a cold flip, we could easily be blindsided by stability problems if we allow global warming per se to remain the main focus of our climate-change efforts. To stabilize our flip-flopping climate we'll need to identify all the important feedbacks that control climate and ocean currents—evaporation, the reflection of sunlight back into space, and so on—and then estimate their relative strengths and interactions in computer models.

Feedbacks are what determine thresholds, where one mode flips into another. Near a threshold one can sometimes observe abortive responses, rather like the act of stepping back onto a curb several times before finally running across a busy street. Abortive responses and rapid chattering between modes are common problems in nonlinear systems with not quite enough oomph—the reason that old fluorescent lights flicker. To keep a bi-stable system firmly in one state or the other, it should be kept away from the transition threshold.

We need to make sure that no business-as-usual climate variation, such as an El Niño or the North Atlantic Oscillation, can push our climate onto the slippery slope and into an abrupt cooling. Of particular importance are combinations of climate variations—this winter, for example, we are experiencing both an El Niño and a North Atlantic Oscillation—because such combinations can add up to much more than the sum of their parts.

We are near the end of a warm period in any event; ice ages return even without human influences on climate. The last warm period abruptly terminated 13,000 years after the abrupt warming that initiated it, and we've already gone 15,000 years from a similar starting point. But we may be able to do something to delay an abrupt cooling.

Do something? This tends to stagger the imagination, immediately conjuring up visions of terraforming on a science-fiction scale—and so we shake our heads and say, "Better to fight global warming by consuming less," and so forth.

Surprisingly, it may prove possible to prevent flip-flops in the climate—even by means of low-tech schemes. Keeping the present climate from falling back into the low state will in any case be a lot easier than trying to reverse such a change after it has occurred. Were fjord floods causing flushing to fail, because the downwelling sites were fairly close to the fjords, it is obvious that we could solve the problem. All we would need to do is open a channel through the ice dam with explosives before dangerous levels of water built up.

Timing could be everything, given the delayed effects from inch-per-second circulation patterns, but that, too, potentially has a low-tech solution: build dams across the major fjord systems and hold back the meltwater at critical times. Or divert eastern-Greenland meltwater to the less sensitive north and west coasts.

Fortunately, big parallel computers have proved useful for both global climate modeling and detailed modeling of ocean circulation. They even show the flips. Computer models might not yet be able to predict what will happen if we tamper with downwelling sites, but this problem doesn't seem insoluble. We need more well-trained people, bigger computers, more coring of the ocean floor and silted-up lakes, more ships to drag instrument packages through the depths, more instrumented buoys to study critical sites in detail, more satellites measuring regional variations in the sea surface, and perhaps some small-scale trial runs of interventions.

It would be especially nice to see another dozen major groups of scientists doing climate simulations, discovering the intervention mistakes as quickly as possible and learning from them. Medieval cathedral builders learned from their design mistakes over the centuries, and their undertakings were a far larger drain on the economic resources and people power of their day than anything yet discussed for stabilizing the climate in the twenty-first century. We may not have centuries to spare, but any economy in which two percent of the population produces all the food, as is the case in the United States today, has lots of resources and many options for reordering priorities.

Three Scenarios

FUTURISTS have learned to bracket the future with alternative scenarios, each of which captures important features that cluster together, each of which is compact enough to be seen as a narrative on a human scale. Three scenarios for the next climatic phase might be called population crash, cheap fix, and muddling through.

The population-crash scenario is surely the most appalling. Plummeting crop yields would cause some powerful countries to try to take over their neighbors or distant lands—if only because their armies, unpaid and lacking food, would go marauding, both at home and across the borders. The better-organized countries would attempt to use their armies, before they fell apart entirely, to take over countries with significant remaining resources, driving out or starving their inhabitants if not

using modern weapons to accomplish the same end: eliminating competitors for the remaining food.

This would be a worldwide problem—and could lead to a Third World War—but Europe's vulnerability is particularly easy to analyze. The last abrupt cooling, the Younger Dryas, drastically altered Europe's climate as far east as Ukraine. Present-day Europe has more than 50 million people. It has excellent soils, and largely grows its own food. It could no longer do so if it lost the extra warming from the North Atlantic.

There is another part of the world with the same good soil, within the same latitudinal band, which we can use for a quick comparison. Canada lacks Europe's winter warmth and rainfall, because it has no equivalent of the North Atlantic Current to preheat its eastbound weather systems. Canada's agriculture supports about 28 million people. If Europe had weather like Canada's, it could feed only one out of twenty-three present-day Europeans.

Any abrupt switch in climate would also disrupt food supply routes. The only reason that two percent of our population can feed the other 98 percent is that we have a well-developed system of transportation and middlemen—but it is not very robust. The system allows for large urban populations in the best of times, but not in the case of widespread disruptions.

Natural disasters such as hurricanes and earthquakes are less troubling than abrupt coolings for two reasons: they're short (the recovery period starts the next day) and they're local or regional (unaffected citizens can help the overwhelmed). There is, increasingly, international cooperation in response to catastrophe—but no country is going to be able to rely on a stored agricultural surplus for even a year, and any country will be reluctant to give away part of its surplus.

In an abrupt cooling the problem would get worse for decades, and much of the earth would be affected. A meteor strike that killed most of the population in a month would not be as serious as an abrupt cooling that eventually killed just as many. With the population crash spread out over a decade, there would be ample opportunity for civilization's institutions to be torn apart and for hatreds to build, as armies tried to grab remaining resources simply to feed the people in their own countries. The effects of an abrupt cold last for centuries. They might not be the end of *Homo sapiens*—written knowledge and elementary education might well endure—but the world after such a population crash would certainly be full of despotic governments that hated their neighbors because of recent atrocities. Recovery would be very slow.

A slightly exaggerated version of our present know-something-do-nothing state of affairs is know-nothing-do-nothing: a reduction in science as usual, further limiting our chances of discovering a way out. History is full of withdrawals from knowledge-seeking, whether for reasons of fundamentalism, fatalism, or "government lite" economics. This scenario does not require that the shortsighted be in charge, only that they have enough influence to put the relevant science agencies on starvation budgets and to send recommendations back for yet another commission report due five years hence.

A cheap-fix scenario, such as building or bombing a dam, presumes that we know enough to prevent trouble, or to nip a developing problem in the bud. But just as vaccines and antibiotics presume much knowledge about diseases, their climatic equivalents presume much knowledge about oceans, atmospheres, and past climates. Suppose we had reports that winter salt flushing was confined to certain areas, that abrupt shifts in the past were associated with localized flushing failures, *and* that one computer model after another suggested a solution that was likely to work even under a wide range of weather extremes. A quick fix, such as bombing an ice dam, might then be possible. Although I don't consider this scenario to be the most likely one, it is possible that solutions could turn out to be cheap and easy, and that another abrupt cooling isn't inevitable. Fatalism, in other words, might well be foolish.

A muddle-through scenario assumes that we would mobilize our scientific and technological resources well in advance of any abrupt cooling problem, but that the solution wouldn't be simple. Instead we would try one thing after another, creating a patchwork of solutions that might hold for another few decades, allowing the search for a better stabilizing mechanism to continue.

We might, for example, anchor bargeloads of evaporation-enhancing surfactants (used in the southwest corner of the Dead Sea to speed potash production) upwind from critical downwelling sites, letting winds spread them over the ocean surface all winter, just to ensure later flushing. We might create a rain shadow, seeding clouds so that they dropped their unsalted water well upwind of a given year's critical flushing sites—a strategy that might be particularly important in view of the increased rainfall expected from global warming. We might undertake to regulate the Mediterranean's salty outflow, which is also thought to disrupt the North Atlantic Current.

Perhaps computer simulations will tell us that the only robust solutions are those that re-create the ocean currents of three million years ago, before the Isthmus of Panama closed off the express route for excess-salt disposal. Thus we might dig a wide sea-level Panama Canal in stages, carefully managing the changeover.

Staying in the "Comfort Zone"

STABILIZING our flip-flopping climate is not a simple matter. We need heat in the right places, such as the Greenland Sea, and not in others right next door, such as Greenland itself. Man-made global warming is likely to achieve exactly the opposite—warming Greenland and cooling the Greenland Sea.

A remarkable amount of specious reasoning is often encountered when we contemplate reducing carbon-dioxide emissions. That increased quantities of greenhouse gases will lead to global warming is as solid a scientific prediction as can be found, but other things influence climate too, and some people try to escape confronting the consequences of our pumping more and more greenhouse gases into the atmosphere by supposing that something will come along miraculously to counteract them. Volcanos spew sulfates, as do our own smokestacks, and these reflect some sunlight back into space, particularly over the North Atlantic and Europe. But we can't assume that anything like this will counteract our longer-term flurry of carbon-dioxide emissions. Only the most naive gamblers bet against physics, and only the most irresponsible bet with their grandchildren's resources.

To the long list of predicted consequences of global warming—stronger storms, methane release, habitat changes, ice-sheet melting, rising seas, stronger El Niños, killer heat waves—we must now add an abrupt, catastrophic cooling. Whereas the familiar consequences of global warming will force expensive but gradual adjustments, the abrupt cooling promoted by man-made warming looks like a particularly efficient means of committing mass suicide.

We cannot avoid trouble by merely cutting down on our present warming trend, though that's an excellent place to start. Paleoclimatic records reveal that any notion we may once have had that the climate will remain the same unless pollution changes it is wishful thinking. Judging from the duration of the last warm period, we are probably near the end of the current one. Our goal must be to stabilize the climate in its favorable mode and ensure that enough equatorial heat continues to flow into the waters around Greenland and Norway. A stabilized climate must have a wide "comfort zone," and be able to survive the El Niños of the short term. We can design for that in computer models of climate, just as architects design earthquake-resistant skyscrapers. Implementing it might cost no more, in relative terms, than building a medieval cathedral. But we may not have centuries for acquiring wisdom, and it would be wise to compress our learning into the years immediately ahead. We have to discover what has made the climate of the past 8,000 years relatively stable, and then figure out how to prop it up.

Those who will not reason
Perish in the act:
Those who will not act
Perish for that reason.

—W. H. Auden

WHILE CLIMATE TREATY NEGOTIATORS DANCE ON WITH THEIR SLOW GIVE-AND-TAKE, THE CLIMATE ITSELF IS RUNNING AMOK.

LAST TANGO IN BUENOS AIRES

When the Kyoto Protocol was signed a year ago, hopes ran high that the world was finally on the way to reducing carbon dioxide emissions and getting the global climate back under control. But since then, complicated new provisions (critics call them loopholes) have sharply divided key governments. The making of the treaty has become a black box—a process largely invisible and incomprehensible to the public. Meanwhile, the apparent effects of global warming are beginning to break out in ways that call for far more decisive action than the past ten years of negotiation have produced. Unless the November meeting of climate treaty negotiators in Buenos Aires demonstrates real progress, it may be time to take a whole new approach to the problem.

by Christopher Flavin

THE WORLD'S CLIMATE RARELY SENDS CLEAR SIGNALS. THE INteractions of hundreds of variables—of sunlight, ocean currents, precipitation, fire, volcanic eruptions, topography, and the respiration of living things—produce a complex system that scientists are just beginning to understand, and that defies precise forecasts. In any given year, some regions are warmer than normal while others are cooler. Almost any short-term climatic phenomenon, even an extreme one, can be explained as something that falls within the enormous range of natural climatic variability. Until this year.

Even before 1998 comes to a close, it is clear that this year is one for the meteorological record books. Although annual temperature records have become routine recently—all 14 of the warmest years since 1860 have occurred in the past two decades—the record is usually broken by a couple of hundredths of a degree. But the average temperature for January–August 1998 was a full four tenths of a degree warmer than the average for 1997, the previous record-setting year (see figure). In fact, six of the first eight months of 1998 set an all-time temperature record for the month—exceeding the monthly figures recorded in the 139 years that global average temperatures have been tracked.

At first, scientists were inclined to attribute these surprising readings to El Niño, a periodic warming of the eastern Pacific that began in 1997 and extended through the first half of 1998. But as they looked back at the historical trend, it became clear that previous El Niño-related warmings had been far more modest. As month after month of record-breaking data spewed from their computers, the atmospheric scientists expressed growing awe. James Baker, administrator of the U.S. National Oceanic and Atmospheric Administration said, "There is no time in recorded data history that we have seen this sequence of record-setting months."

In earlier years, some scientists' concerns about global warming were assuaged by the fact that satellite-based microwave measurements of temperatures high in the atmosphere since 1979 did not appear to reflect the warming trend from ground-based readings. But this slender straw was swept away in August by a report by scientists Frank Wentz and Matthias Schabel that appeared in the British journal *Nature*. It demonstrated that the widely reported satellite data were skewed by the failure to account for the predictable gravity-induced decay in the orbits of the satellites. Once corrected for, the satellite data demonstrate the same broad warming trend as the ground-level thermometers—including the dramatic spike in 1998.

Scientists have known for some time that the climate is a "non-linear system" that may respond marginally or not at all to initial changes—but then leap suddenly to a new equilibrium, if pushed a little further. Although it is too early to know for sure, the global climate may have just crossed such a threshold. Since the beginning of the twentieth century, human activities have added 925 billion tons of carbon dioxide (CO_2) to the atmosphere, taking concentrations of this heat-trapping gas to the highest levels in 160,000 years. The climate record shows that when CO_2 concentrations reached even close to such levels in the past—during the Eemian interglacial period, for example, beginning 135,000 years ago—they were accompanied by a rapid rise in temperatures.

Though it is impossible to connect any single weather event to global climate change, the past year has been marked by a worldwide pattern of unusually severe weather. China was swept by its worst floods in three decades last summer, with 56 million people reported to be at least temporarily displaced from their homes in the Yangtze basin alone. The $36 billion in estimated damages matches or exceeds the total weather-related losses for the world in every year prior to 1995. Meanwhile, two-thirds of Bangladesh was under water for most of the summer, as torrential monsoon rains cascaded down from the Himalaya and storm surges came up from the sea, covering much of the capital, Dhaka, and destroying the country's rice crop.

At least 54 other countries were hit by severe floods in 1998, and at least 45 were stricken by droughts, many of which led to runaway wildfires. Tropical forests normally do not burn, but unusually harsh droughts contributed to a series of unprecedented fires in southeast Asia starting in late 1997 and in the Amazon through most of 1998. Last spring, much of southern and central Mexico was aflame, leading to air quality alerts in Texas and noticeably smoky air as far north as Chicago. By early summer, scores of fires were sweeping the sub-tropical forests of Florida, leading to the evacuation of an entire country.

RARELY HAVE THE RHYTHMS OF THE NATURAL WORLD BEEN SO out of synch with those of the political world. Even as the climate sent ever-stronger signals of disruption in 1998, efforts to deal with the problem bogged down in glacial and contentious negotiations over the terms of the Kyoto Protocol on climate change.

The effort to build a global climate agreement is in fact already a decade-long saga that began with a major scientific conference on the issue in Toronto in 1988. The scientists there called for a 20 percent cut in carbon dioxide emissions by 2005, which then led to extended efforts on the part of scientists, industrial interest groups, non-governmental organizations, and politicians to forge an international agreement to move in that direction. By the time of the 1992 Earth Summit in Rio de Janeiro, the "Framework" Convention on Climate Change had been forged, but due to the strong objections of the Bush Administration in the United States, still did not include legally binding limits.

After Rio, governments worked for several years to strengthen the climate treaty by adding specific limits on the amounts of greenhouse gases that could be emitted by each industrial country. This process was expected to

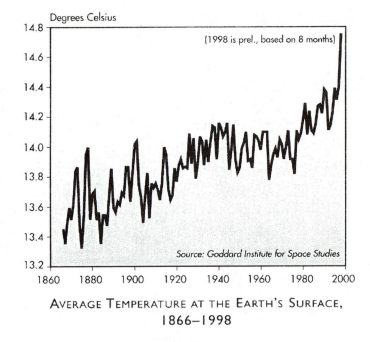

AVERAGE TEMPERATURE AT THE EARTH'S SURFACE, 1866–1998

culminate in the signing of a protocol to the convention that included legally binding emissions limits, in Kyoto, Japan last December. But agreement proved elusive. As the Kyoto conference began, governments were still widely divided on key elements of the agreement, including the overall level to which emissions would be limited. The United States, for example, only wanted to cut emissions back to the 1990 level, while the European Union wanted to cut them to 15 percent below that level.

By the beginning of its final week, the Kyoto conference had become "an emotional roller-coaster for delegates who watched the treaty's fortunes rise, fall, and rise again," according to a *Washington Post* correspondent. Core elements of the treaty remained unresolved, ranging from the level of emission cuts to be mandated to whether planting or protecting trees could be counted against those emission commitments.

With the negotiations bogged down, U.S. Vice President Al Gore, who had devoted much of his 1992 book *Earth in the Balance* to the problem of climate change, was dispatched to Kyoto. Soon after his arrival, the U.S. delegation shifted its position on emission limits and agreed to reduce its emissions 7 percent from 1990 levels—roughly half way between the U.S. and European positions. But on the evening of December 10, as the deadline for concluding the historic conference came and went, other unresolved issues remained—some of which would determine the significance of the numbers that had been agreed to. Raul Estrada Oyuela, the Argentine Chair of the conference, who had been working behind the scenes for months to forge essential compromises, refused to give up. He ordered the "committee of the whole," composed of all 159 national delegations, to re-convene at 1 am, and meet until a conclusion was reached.

Through the wee hours of December 11, Estrada methodically moved the assembled delegates through the remaining passages of disputed text: whether trading of emissions commitments would be permitted among industrial countries, and whether developing countries would be encouraged to adopt voluntary commitments.

As discussions seesawed back and forth, oil producers like Kuwait did their best to derail the agreement, while European and small island countries worked to strengthen it. But the main axis of the battle soon formed around China and the United States, the two largest emitters, who were deeply divided both on trading and on the question of developing country commitments. As positions hardened, hope of an agreement began to fade.

The U.S. delegation, which had brought Under-secretary of State Stuart Eizenstat in from Washington to be its "closer," became so panicky at one point that delegates were standing on their table, waving for Estrada's attention in the huge hall. Given the vice president's close identification with the issue, the Clinton-Gore Administration could not afford to be found holding the noose if the Kyoto agreement was strangled.

As dawn approached, the Kyoto conference hall was beginning to resemble a week-old battlefield. Bleary-eyed reporters and NGO observers wandered the facility searching for remnants of food or coffee, while inside the plenary hall government delegates held their ground on various items, waiting for the other side to back down in the face of mounting sleep deprivation. Many delegates had passed out, one with his head resting in an ashtray. Chinese and Russian speaking interpreters pulled off their headphones and left, and the Japanese conference center staff threatened to cut off the electricity if the conference was not shut down.

But Estrada, an old hand in chairing contentious negotiations, took advantage of the exhaustion. Seizing on a few half-compromises, he began gaveling closed key portions of the agreement. With the spotlight of the world's media upon them, delegates decided they had more to fear from a failed agreement than one with which they only partially agreed, and stood aside as Estrada pushed relentlessly through the text.

At 10:15 am, Estrada called for adoption of the protocol by consensus, and despite remaining reservations, no government was prepared to stand in the way. The deed was done. Hundreds of delegates rushed out to press conferences, declared victory, and headed for the Osaka International Airport.

During the next 24 hours, headlines around the world proclaimed a great success at Kyoto. Chairman Estrada stated that he was "deeply satisfied" with the outcome, and the World Resources Institute called it "an historic step in the history of humanity." Clouds remained on the horizon—particularly the threats of U.S. Senators not to ratify the agreement—but most observers, including this author, were hopeful that the remaining holes could be patched by the Fourth Conference of the Parties in Buenos Aires this November.

Sadly, the past 12 months have turned the Kyoto conference into a kind of high-water mark, from which the climate negotiations have steadily retreated in the past year. Divisions among national governments have only widened since Kyoto, and the holes in the agreement are beginning to seem more substantial than the protocol itself. Indeed, by creatively papering over wide differences between various nations, the Kyoto negotiators may have crafted an agreement that is barely workable in the best of circumstances, and in the current political climate could lead to paralysis.

At its core, the Kyoto Protocol has four major weaknesses that will need to be remedied if it is to be effective in slowing climate change before irreversible damage is done.

❶ **WEAK COMMITMENTS:** Since the 1988 Toronto Conference, the cornerstone of climate negotiations has been the setting of binding limits on the emissions of greenhouse gases by industrial countries—the countries that have accounted for the bulk of the emissions so far. The 1992 Framework Convention includes a voluntary goal of holding those emissions to the 1990 level in 2000. Some European countries are already meeting this goal, thanks mainly to cuts in coal subsidies. But Australia, Canada, the United States, and other industrial nations are not, due in part to their low fuel prices, and to their failure to enact aggressive energy conservation measures. The main goal for the Kyoto agreement was to establish a new legally binding target for the year 2010.

The negotiators in Kyoto settled on nation-by-nation limits that add up to a reduction in greenhouse gas emissions of 5.2 percent below the 1990 level for all industrial nations. Little noticed outside climate policy circles, however, was the curious fact that total CO_2 emissions by industrial countries was—and is—already below 1990 levels, due to steep declines in the former Soviet Union. As a result, the protocols target, were it to cover just CO_2, translates to a mere 2.5 percent cut from the 1997 level.

Within that goal, industrial countries agreed to a range of specific targets—cuts of 8 percent in the European Union, 7 percent in the United States, and 6 percent in Japan—along with an 8 percent increase in Australia. These numbers represent backroom political deals more than they do analyses of the economic potential to reduce emissions in a given country. Australia, for example, has a government dominated by mining interests that wish to boost their export of energy-intensive products to Asian nations—a development that will of course worsen the greenhouse problem.

The anemia of the Kyoto figures can be seen when they are contrasted with what is eventually needed to stabilize CO_2 concentrations. According to the International Panel on Climate Change, the official scientific body that advises the Conference of the Parties, the amount of reduction that eventually will be required is not 5.2 percent, but 60 to 80 percent below the 1990 levels. Yet, when emissions of developing countries are added to those of the industrial countries covered by the protocol, the global total is projected to increase to some 30 percent *above* the 1990 level by 2010.

The most hopeful thing that can be said of the Kyoto Protocol is that it echoes Lao Tse's comment that a journey of a thousand miles begins with single step. The protocol could, perhaps, set the stage for more ambitious agreements later, as has occurred with earlier environmental treaties. But if—as now seems likely—it takes years to ratify the protocol, and years more to enact the national policies needed to achieve its weakened goals, the encounter in Buenos Aires could turn out to be little more than an elaborate tango—a few impressive steps that end up going nowhere.

❷ SEARCHING FOR "FLEXIBILITY": As climate negotiations grew tense late last year, the Clinton Administration was increasingly desperate to find a way of bridging the huge gulf in emissions goals that separated the United States from the European Union. The key, U.S. officials felt, was to come up with a series of provisions—critics called them loopholes—that would make it less expensive to meet the protocol's goals, and that would avoid the need to take a big bite out of domestic CO_2 emissions. The levels the European were asking for, they believed, would require politically impossible measures that were already being aggressively fought by a multimillion dollar TV and newspaper ad campaign sponsored by the coal, oil, and automobile industries.

Australia, Canada, and New Zealand had similar concerns, and strongly supported the search for "flexibility." European governments were not nearly so worried about tough targets since, unlike the United States, they had not substantially increased their emissions during the 1990s. But even many of their leaders privately welcomed the notion of flexibility that would allow them to delay enacting any new energy taxes or other constraints on politically powerful industries.

During the Kyoto negotiations, the focus turned to a target that would cover a "basket" of six greenhouse gases rather than focusing on each one individually. This "comprehensive" approach seemed logical enough, since it covered all the important greenhouse gases, including methane and HFCs, not just CO_2. But it also happened to be a great convenience to U.S. delegates who were looking for ways to avoid sharp CO_2 reductions that would arouse a hornet's nest of industry outrage. Experts had identified a potential for easy reductions in some of the more minor greenhouse gases, which might offset some of the projected increase in the nation's carbon dioxide emissions.

But this approach seems likely to lead to an accounting nightmare, in part because there is no reliable emissions inventory for some of these gases, and each has a distinct (and in some cases uncertain) lifetime in the atmosphere. As a result, this "comprehensive" approach is likely to reduce the clarity of the protocol, and could well encour-

age cheating. (One of the keys to the pioneering 1987 Montreal Protocol on Substances That Deplete the Ozone Layer is that it dealt with each of the offending gases individually and specifically, so that countries knew exactly what was needed—and would be exposed if they did not.)

At the insistence of the United States, as well as Canada and New Zealand, the Kyoto Protocol also allows countries to count carbon absorption by forests (and perhaps later by peat bogs and other carbon "sinks") as offsets against emissions. Under the agreement, carbon flow resulting from both additions to and subtractions from sinks is to be included in national inventories. A coal-burning power company in Ohio, for example, could receive offset credits for financing a tree-planting project in Oregon.

In principle, this idea makes sense—tree planting should be encouraged. But the proposed scheme for doing this is exceedingly complex, combining an accounting maze with uncertain science. Biologists point out that there is not yet enough data on natural carbon cycling to establish full accounting and verification procedures for carbon sinks. And like the provision on the "other" gases, this one complicates monitoring and enforcement, and encourages governments to fiddle with the figures. In response to these concerns, the provision on sinks has been sent back for scientific review, which is to be completed by 2000.

❸ HOT AIR TRADING: Another form of "flexibility" in the Kyoto Protocol is the concept of emission-allowance trading, an idea pioneered and highly touted by U.S. government regulators, private companies, and even some environmental groups. It is modeled on provisions in the U.S. Clean Air Act that allow power companies to "trade" their sulfur dioxide reduction obligations, in the theory that this will encourage cuts to be made wherever it is least expensive to do so. In the context of global climate change, nations would have the option of buying greenhouse gas emission allowances from other countries that have more than met their own requirements.

The concept has met with considerable skepticism in Europe, as well as in developing countries, which worry that it will dilute the commitments and encourage some governments to avoid difficult domestic policy decisions. Still, a growing number of governments have warmed to the idea in recent months, recognizing that it could improve the economic efficiency of the agreement by channeling capital to economies where it can make the most difference. After a tense standoff, the U.S.-sponsored article on emission allowance trading was accepted, though with obvious reluctance. In a gesture that carried symbolic, if not legal, weight, Estrada cut the trading provision to a few lines and pushed it to the back of the protocol.

It was not until after the weary delegates had arrived home from Kyoto that many of them realized that the United States had pulled a fast one. Under the protocol, Russia and Ukraine must only hold their emissions to the

1990 level, which would allow them to increase emissions 50 and 120 percent respectively from their current depressed levels. Experts do not expect either nation to come close to such increase, even if their economies rebound robustly, so these emission allowances would be available for purchase by countries like the United States, which expect to fall well short of the targets in the protocol. In short, the United States and Russia could make a trade that allowed the United States to take credit for emission reductions that stemmed from the Russian economic collapse of the early 1990s—without reducing future greenhouse gas output by even a molecule.

Although the U.S. government has been vague about its emissions trading intentions, the official plan produced by the White House in July would achieve up to 75 percent of the U.S. reduction requirement by purchasing allowances from the Russians and Ukrainians. While such a deal might result in the United States adding $10–$20 billion a year to Russia's empty treasury, it is hard to see how the climate would benefit. The idea has been widely denounced by everyone from Greenpeace to the U.S. National Coal Association, so it is not clear that it has much of a constituency. Indeed, this kind of trading threatens to undermine more legitimate trading proposals that are tied to specific projects, such as the article on "joint implementation" which is intended to encourage rich industrial countries to invest in climate projects in the former Eastern Bloc. European governments have suggested putting a percentage limit on trading—to encourage adoption of domestic policies—but even this might not be enough to correct a provision that undermines both the effectiveness and legitimacy of the protocol.

❹ **THE RATIFICATION TRAP:** While all of these problems are thorny ones, they should in theory be surmountable. But many of the all-important details—including how emissions trading will work—were not included in the Kyoto Protocol, and will have to be added to it if the protocol is to be effective. At negotiating sessions in Bonn, Germany, in June—the last before Buenos Aires—vituperation outweighed progress. In the European and developing country views, the United States has riddled the protocol with sneaky loopholes, while U.S. officials believe that the Europeans are trying to wriggle out of an agreement that was made in good faith in Kyoto.

Complicating the process further is the issue of ratification. The Kyoto Protocol will only go into force if ratified by enough industrial countries to represent at least 55 percent of industrial country emissions. In theory, the protocol could go into force without U.S. assent, as may occur with the land mines treaty negotiated last year. But due to concerns over competitiveness as well as fairness, neither the Europeans nor the Japanese wish to move forward with an agreement that excludes the world's largest greenhouse gas emitter.

Leading U.S. Senators, meanwhile, say they will not move forward with ratification without "new specific scheduled commitments to limit or reduce greenhouse gas emissions" by developing countries—a position with which the Clinton Administration has felt compelled to go along. U.S. officials have been vague as to what such a commitment might consist of, and developing countries are rightly wary of being asked to reduce their emissions, which already average less than one-tenth the U.S. per capita level. A year and a half of arm-twisting has yielded little progress, and the impasse gives the United States an effective veto over the protocol.

As 1998 drags to a close amidst financial crisis and political scandal, the climate negotiations are bogged down by a dangerous combination of impotence and ineptitude. And with the coal, oil, and automobile lobbies again stepping up their climate ad campaigns, it is unclear that the key countries have the political will needed to forge the compromises that are needed. The negotiating process itself seems to have become a kind of diplomatic black hole—sucking in endless quantities of legal, economic, and scientific capital. The thousands of government officials, NGO lobbyists, and observers who follow the process closely continue to circle the globe, attending dozens of meetings on sinks, emissions trading, and other climate issues *du jour*. The climate cognoscenti now speak their own acronym-filled language—interlaced with references to AGBM, QUELRO, SBSTA, and LUCF—and are prone to describing labyrinthine sideways movements as "progress." But the negotiations are increasingly disembodied from the real world threats—from massive floods to rampant disease—that a changing climate represents.

Meanwhile, the process of implementing national policies that will actually reduce emissions—which had gained substantial momentum prior to Kyoto—has stalled since then. President Clinton, for example, who talked extensively about climate change when he was in China this summer, has been unable to persuade the U.S. Congress to adopt even a modest package of new climate policies. Europe has seen a similar lack of progress, as it has bickered over "burden-sharing" its goals and debating emissions trading with the United States. And the new Japanese plan, released in August, is based largely on building 20 nuclear plants—a step that government officials privately acknowledge will never be permitted by the Japanese public.

ONE OF THE IRONIES OF THE YEAR SINCE KYOTO IS THAT WHILE the national and international political processes have stagnated, opportunities for economically cutting emissions have blossomed. Motivated in part by the prospect of legally binding emissions limits, companies, cities, and individuals have pursued a host of new approaches. From those emerging possibilities, a less legalistic, more productive approach to the climate problem may emerge.

◆ British Petroleum President John Browne surprised the oil industry when he announced last year that after extended internal deliberations, his company had concluded that climate change is a serious threat that will inevitably reshape the energy industry. Browne later announced BP's intention to reduce its emissions 10 percent and to step up investment in solar energy. The American Petroleum Institute denounced BP for "leaving the church," but Enron Corp, North America's largest gas company, and Royal Dutch Shell, the world's biggest petroleum firm, have joined BP in acknowledging the severity of the climate problem and beginning to shift their own investment strategies.

◆ During the very month of the Kyoto Conference, Toyota stunned the auto world with the delivery to its showrooms of the world's first hybrid electric car, the Prius—with twice the fuel economy and half the CO_2 emissions of conventional cars. Marketed as a "green" sedan, the Prius sold so quickly in Japan this year that Toyota had to open a second assembly plant. The shock waves were evident at the massive Detroit Motor Show in January, where each of the U.S. Big Three companies announced plans for new generations of hybrid and fuel cell cars. In a 1998 speech that might be compared to Mao expressing second thoughts about communism, General Motors president John Smith said, "No car company will be able to survive in the 21st century by relying on the internal-combustion engine alone."

◆ As national governments dither over the Kyoto Protocol, a surprising number of city governments are moving forward with active efforts to reduce their emissions. Over 100 cities, representing 10 percent of global emissions, have joined the Cities for Climate Protection program to reduce those emissions by investing in public transportation, tightening up public buildings, planting trees, and installing solar collectors. Toronto, which was the first city to announce a climate plan—in honor of its role in hosting the first major climate meeting a decade ago—is working to reduce its emissions by 20 percent. And Saarbrucken, a medium-sized city in a coal-mining region of southern Germany, has already cut its emissions by 15 percent, in part via effective energy management and public education campaigns.

◆ A few national governments are also showing the way. After a decade of effort, Denmark now generates 8 percent of its electricity from wind power, and another fraction from the combustion of agricultural wastes. Already, the Danish wind industry employs 20,000 people, and wind turbines are the country's second largest export. And thanks to Denmark's efforts, wind power, at 25 percent per year, has been the world's fastest growing energy source since 1990.

Taken together, these efforts suggest that it will be easier and less expensive to reduce carbon dioxide emissions than it appeared a few years ago. As has been the case with almost every other environmental problem in the past

three decades, once we get serious about slowing climate change, we will likely find a host of innovative and inexpensive ways to do so. Thanks in part to the signal sent by the climate convention, as well as to those coming from the climate itself, that process is under way. The question now is how to speed it up.

◆ ◆ ◆

tango\tan-go\n: a ballroom dance of Latin-American origin in $2/4$ time with a basic pattern of step-step-step-step-close and characterized by long pauses and stylized body positions; also: the music for this dance

After a decade of stylized steps—and long pauses—doubts are growing as to whether this climate dance will ever be successfully completed. The brief glow of optimism that surged from Kyoto last fall has faded. Well-meaning diplomats have become handcuffed by an increasingly complex and unruly process. While it is essential to take the long view with a problem such as climate change, even that perspective provides little comfort today: The commitments agreed to in Kyoto are less clear, and arguably less stringent—once all of the "flexibility mechanisms" are included—than the voluntary emission goals established in Rio in 1992.

The glacial pace of climate negotiations in the past decade can be attributed in part to a powerful combination of forces: the intergenerational scale of the problem; only modest public alarm; broad and well-organized industry opposition; and the complex, multi-faceted nature of the problem being addressed. Together, these four factors make the climate-policy process an order of magnitude more challenging than any others so far. Solving this problem will truly put human institutions and ingenuity to the test.

If they are to get the protocol back on track, the negotiators who meet in Buenos Aires this November would do well to remember a distinction made by environmental negotiations expert David Victor of the Council on Foreign Relations in a 1998 book: when it comes to international environmental treaties, compliance and effectiveness are two different things. Unless it leads to major governmental policy changes that in turn lead to lower emissions of the most important greenhouse gas, carbon dioxide, the Kyoto Protocol will have fallen into the trap of debilitating compromise and complication that has plagued several other environmental agreements.

The climate negotiations have been guided in part by the lessons of one of the most successful of those agreements, the 1987 Montreal Protocol to protect the ozone layer. That agreement, in which many of the Buenos Aires negotiators were involved, led to an 80 percent reduction, within a decade of its adoption, in production of the gases that most damage the ozone layer. It did so by relying on three simple principles: Politics must follow science; environmental goals should be clear and simple; and industry consensus is essential to drive the process forward.

> **When other environmental treaties have run into similar problems, a leadership group of more committed governments has sometimes formed.**

But the challenge of Kyoto is far greater, in large measure because where the ozone problem could be solved with the effective participation of just a few dozen companies, the climate problem is driven by millions of actors, indeed by society as a whole. Although the new business created by the move away from fossil fuels is likely to roughly equal the business lost, the potential losers are far better organized.

As with the Montreal Protocol, the central focus of the Framework Convention on Climate Change is national emissions limits, leaving individual nations to decide how to achieve them. While the principle seems like a solid one, since it allows for national differences and permits flexibility, it has not worked in the climate arena, where carbon dioxide, unlike chlorofluorocarbons, is a virtual currency of modern energy economies that can be reduced only by addressing structural economic issues.

Even among industrial countries, the differences in emissions levels, economic structures, and political philosophies are so wide that no single goal has universal logic. One of the problems in Kyoto was the fact that countries such as the United States, which had substantially increased their emissions since 1990, were panicked by the challenge of meeting goals that seemed reasonable to other countries that had already reduced theirs. But once governments began differentiating the goals in Kyoto, the negotiations became a political free-for-all that undermined the credibility of the entire process. In addition, by bundling together six gases, and adding the highly complicated issues of sinks and trading to the protocol, the negotiators have created an agreement that will be nearly impossible to review or enforce, and that at best sends an ambiguous signal to governments and industries.

The challenge now is to renovate the baroque structure that the Kyoto plan has become—or else scrap it and get ready to start over. The negotiators who have labored so hard over the past decade to get the foundation of the protocol in place deserve one more try in Buenos Aires. But if—as now seems likely—that try produces no serious prospect of ratifying the protocol and implementing it, new approaches may be needed.

David Victor points out that when other environmental treaties have run into similar problems, a leadership group of more committed governments has sometimes formed—adopting a more stringent set of voluntary goals, which they then move immediately to implement. In the 1980s, European negotiations to reduce North Sea pollution and nitrogen oxide emissions each ran aground due to vehement opposition of major governments. But other countries moved ahead with voluntary commitments—complementing more modest, legally binding agreements that were also agreed to. Similarly, the international landmines treaty of 1997 was spearheaded by NGOs and by a small group of like-minded governments. They formulated an agreement that quickly won the support of most—though not all—governments. Holdouts like the United States are expected to join eventually.

This approach might well work for climate policy, building on the leadership roles of several European countries, and building support outward from there. Taking the idea a step further, it might even be feasible to bring regional and city governments and companies into such an agreement. They would pledge to each other not just to meet certain levels of emissions reductions, but to identify and adopt specific policy changes and investments—such as incentives for purchasing more efficient cars or rejuvenating public transportation—that will expeditiously achieve these reductions. They might also agree to experiment with emissions trading and CO_2 taxes.

The guiding principle of this new initiative would be to make climate stabilization an economic opportunity as well as an environmental necessity. As John Topping of the Climate Institute puts it, "A strategy that works is going to have to be one that has its own very positive economic feedbacks, one that extends opportunity rather than slowing it down." Like the Kyoto Protocol itself, this approach would still require political support—but on a local, regional, or national level.

Such an initiative would start with a relatively small group of committed institutions, drawing in a larger circle of participants over time, and gradually marginalizing those who are so mired in the status quo that they refuse to go along. The psychology of marginalization—and of shame—could turn out to be a powerful spur to action. If history is a guide, it might eventually lead to a second generation protocol—one that really works.

The key to any approach, of course, is strong public support for action on climate—support that is substantial enough to overcome the unavoidable tendency of many industries to fight change. Environmental groups need to do a better job than they have so far in mobilizing public action—but in the end, it may come down to the weather. Catastrophes have been the driving forces behind many previous environmental agreements. Tragically, the probability of such crisis is rising with the temperature.

Christopher Flavin is senior vice president of the Worldwatch Institute.

Unit Selections

Key Points to Consider

❖ How does an industrial system oriented to high rates of materials consumption contribute more to pollution than one based on sustainable practices? Are there ways to make the transition from material to sustainable industrial societies?

❖ What is meant by "biological invasion" and how can it be considered as pollution? Are there specific steps that might be taken to reduce the dangers of biological contamination of ecosystems?

❖ Explain the benefits and dangers of recycling human wastes in agricultural systems. Are there lessons that modern industrial societies can learn from older traditional societies in terms of managing the recycling problem?

❖ How can agricultural chemicals contribute to water pollution and what role does the food chain play in concentrating pollutants? How can severely polluted lakes be regenerated?

❖ What are greenhouse gases and how do they play a role in contributing to a potential warming of Earth's climate? How do current projections of future global temperatures compare with temperature changes in the past?

Links www.dushkin.com/online/

These sites are annotated on pages 4 and 5.

Of all the massive technological changes that have combined to create our modern industrial society, perhaps none has been as significant for the environment as the chemical revolution. The largest single threat to environmental stability is the proliferation of chemical compounds for a nearly infinite variety of purposes, including the universal use of organic chemicals (fossil fuels) as the prime source of the world's energy systems. The problem is not just that thousands of new chemical compounds are being discovered or created each year, but that their long-term environmental effects are often not known until an environmental disaster involving humans or other living organisms occurs. The problem is exacerbated by the time lag that exists between the recognition of potentially harmful chemical contamination and the cleanup activities that are ultimately required.

A critical part of the process of dealing with chemical pollutants is the identification of toxic and hazardous materials, a problem that is intensified by the myriad ways in which a vast number of such materials, natural and man-made, can enter environmental systems. Governmental legislation and controls are important in correcting the damages produced by toxic and hazardous materials such as DDT or PCBs or CFCs, in limiting fossil fuel burning, or in preventing the spread of living organic hazards such as pests and disease-causing agents. Unfortunately, as evidenced by most of the articles in this unit, we are losing the battle against harmful substances regardless of legislation, and chemical pollution of the environment is probably getting worse rather than better.

The first article in this unit deals with the ultimate causes of the chemical pollution problem: the high rate of consumption in industrial countries. In "Making Things Last: Reinventing Our Material Culture," Gary Gardner and Payal Sampat of the Worldwatch Institute suggest that an overdependence upon material consumption has led to many pollution problems arising from the disposal of solid waste. The solution to these problems and other pollution problems will be found only in the transition to a rational, sustainable materials society. A pollution problem of another kind is the subject of the second selection in the unit. In "Crawling Out of the Pipe," author Chris Bright of the Worldwatch Institute explores the realm of biological pollution, the creation of hazardous waste that reproduces itself. Bright's examination ranges from biotic spills to intentionally introduced exotic or alien species that spread far beyond their intended ranges and exert wide-ranging impact on native species and entire ecosystems.

Similar emphasis on organic or biological pollution is offered in the third article in this last

unit, which focuses on humanity's oldest environmental problem—how to deal with our own waste. In "Recycling Human Waste: Fertile Ground or Toxic Legacy?" Gary Gardner of the Worldwatch Institute deals with the risks and benefits of sewage reuse. Recycling human waste, Gardner notes, has a long and noble history, particularly in the Orient where "night soil" has long been an integral part of the agricultural system. Unfortunately, in the modern world, the use of human wastes often carries unacceptable dangers. Still, if the problem of toxic materials can be resolved, alternative waste technologies hold great promise since they recycle in a regenerative loop, in the same ways as nature.

The section's fourth selection continues with the theme of chemical pollution and the interrelationship between chemical additives and biological systems. In "Lessons from Lake Apopka," Ted Williams, one of America's foremost environmental writers, examines the case of a Florida lake fouled by agricultural chemicals. Here, the contaminated runoff from pesticide-laden farmlands was metabolized in the lake's waters by fish that were then consumed by fish-eating birds. The birds began to die in large numbers, evidence of the toxicity of their very food supply. Finally, in the concluding article in the section, the most topical of today's pollution issues is discussed: the buildup of greenhouse gases. In "Earth's Last Gasp?" Daniel Lashof addresses the accumulation of greenhouse gases in the atmosphere. The potential for global warming has increased concern that if atmospheric pollution is not controlled, the next century will face a greater rate of warming than at any period in the last 10,000 years.

The pollution problem might appear nearly impossible to solve. Yet solutions exist: massive cleanup campaigns to remove existing harmful chemicals from the environment and to severely restrict their future use; strict regulation of the production, distribution, use, and disposal of potentially hazardous chemicals; the development of sound biological techniques to replace existing uses of chemicals for such purposes as pest control; the adoption of energy and material resource conservation policies; and more conservative and protective agricultural and construction practices. We now possess the knowledge and the tools to ensure that environmental cleanup is carried through. (It will not be an easy task, and it will be terribly expensive. It will also demand a new way of thinking about humankind's role in the environmental systems upon which all life forms depend.) If we do not complete the task, the support capacity of the environment may be damaged or diminished beyond our capacities to repair it. The consequences would be fatal for all who inhabit this planet.

Making Things Last: Reinventing Our Material Culture.

High rates of consumption threaten the environment. Here are ways we can live well without trashing the world.

By Gary Gardner and Payal Sampat

PHOTOS: © PHOTODISC, INC.

A bulldozer at work in a giant landfill. Twentieth-century manufacturing has wasted unprecedented amounts of raw materials, but new policies can help create sustainable business practices, according to researchers at the Worldwatch Institute.

An extraterrestrial observer of the earth might conclude that the conversion of raw materials to waste is a major purpose of human economic activity.

In fact, the scale of materials used by Americans, Europeans, Japanese, and other industrial-country citizens in the twentieth century dwarfs that of any previous era. Consumption of metal, glass, wood, cement, and chemicals in industrial countries since 1900 is unprecedented, having grown 18-fold in the United States alone, according to the U.S. Geological Survey.

Modern manufacturing has transformed a global river of materials into a stunning array of new products, from skyscrapers and space-craft to plastic bags, compact discs, contact lenses, and ball-point pens. The unparalleled waste that characterizes this materially unique century has also wrought extraordinary damage on human and environmental health.

This abuse of the environment is the product of a "frontier" mindset that views materials, and the earth's capacity to absorb wastes, as practically limitless. The frontier perspective may have seemed appropriate in the nineteenth century, when global population had not yet reached 2 billion, but it has led to an increasingly disruptive industrial system that equates progress with materials consumption. A different mindset will be needed in order to prevent industrial economies from further damaging the natural landscape.

Promoting Service Providers

Perhaps the most revolutionary shift toward sustainable materials use is the conversion of manufacturing firms to service-providing firms. Service providers earn their profits not by selling goods, such as wash-

Originally published in the May 1999 issue of *The Futurist*, pp. 24-28. © 1999 by The World Future Society, 7910 Woodmont Ave., Bethesda, MD 20814; http://www.wfs.org/wfs. Reprinted by permission.

ing machines or cars, but by providing the services that goods currently deliver—convenient cleaning of clothes, for example, or transportation. Providers could also be responsible for all of the materials and products used to provide their service, maintaining those goods and retrieving them when they wear out. Service firms would thus have a strong incentive to make products that last and can be easily repaired, upgraded, reused, or recycled.

Many service-provider firms would lease their products rather than sell them. The Xerox Corporation, for example, now leases most of its office copy machines as part of a redefined mission to provide document services, rather than to sell photocopiers. The new arrangement gives Xerox a strong incentive to maximize the life of its machines: Between 1992 and 1997, the company doubled its share of remanufactured copiers to 28%, keeping 30,000 tons of waste out of landfills in 1997 alone. Each remanufactured machine meets the same standards, and carries the same warranty, as a newly minted one. In addition, Xerox introduced a product-return program for spent copy and printer cartridges in 1991, and it now recaptures 65% of used cartridges.

Consumers could help save on materials by eliminating goods that spend most of their time idle. For example, using laundry services rather than home washing machines could dramatically cut materials use per wash, because semi-commercial machines are used more intensively than home washers. Home washers are also 10 to 80 times more materials intensive—depending on how they are disposed of—than the machines used in a laundromat. If dismantled and recycled, a home washer uses 10 times as much material per wash as a semi-commercial machine that is disposed of in the same way.

Washing may be a function that consumers would prefer to retain in their homes, but even home washing could be accommodated by a service firm that leases the machines. This option would save less material than the use of a laundromat, but much more than if machines are bought by individuals. In sum, whether service is provided directly (by hiring someone to mow your lawn, for example) or indirectly (by leasing a lawn-mower), replacing infrequently used goods with services can save tons of material.

In some cases, service providers can replace materials with intelligence or labor. As the computer revolution continues to unfold, digital technology—basically embodied intelligence—can be used to breathe new life into products that rapidly become obsolete, such as cameras and televisions. If product capabilities are upgraded through the replacement of a computer chip, then perfectly good casings, lenses, and picture tubes can avoid a premature trip to the landfill. Similarly, labor can be used to extend the useful life of products: Service providers need workers to disassemble, repair, and rebuild their leaseable goods, saving materials and increasing employment at the same time.

Copy machines could be part of a revolutionary shift toward sustainable use in which businesses provide services rather than selling machines. The Xerox Corporation already leases most of its office copiers and maintains old machines longer, keeping them out of landfills.

A Boost in Recycling

The gains from a revolutionized service economy can be augmented by an equally ambitious overhaul of recycling practices. Some products are already designed with recycling in mind. German automakers now bar-code car components to show scrap dealers the mix of materials contained in each piece. And some producers of cars, television sets, and washing machines build their products for easy disassembly at the end of the product's life.

Easy disassembly can bring substantial gains. Xerox's ambitious plan to boost its share of remanufactured machines from the current 28% to 85%, for example, is feasible because of the company's 1997 shift to redesigned, easily disassembled copy machines. Widespread adoption of these "design-for-environment" initiatives could boost recycling rates throughout the economy. And there is much room for improvement: Today, just 17% of durable goods are recycled in the United States.

With the right incentives, much greater materials reductions from recycling are possible. For example, Germany implemented a revolutionary package-waste ordinance in 1993 that holds producers accountable for nearly all of the packaging material they generate. The new law increased the amount of packaging recycled from 12% in 1992 to 86% in 1997. The law also gave producers a strong incentive to cut their use of packaging, which dropped 17% for households and small businesses between 1991 and 1997. The use of secondary packaging—outer containers like the box around a tube of toothpaste—has also declined in Germany. Now several other countries, including Austria, France, and Belgium, have adopted similar recycling legislation.

Making the Most of Materials

As with service firms and recycling, materials efficiency can be imaginatively rethought and powerfully up-graded. If the efficiency of a product were measured not just at the factory gate—in terms of the materials required to produce it—but across its entire life, characteristics such as durability and capacity for reuse would suddenly become more important.

Reducing logging and mining would save gargantuan amounts of energy.

For example, doubling the useful life of a car may involve no improvement in materials efficiency at the factory, but it cuts in half both the resources used and the waste generated per trip over the car's life—a clear increase in total resource efficiency. Recognizing these benefits, many companies are emphasizing the durability of the products they use. Toyota, for example, shifted to entirely reusable shipping containers in 1991, each with a potential lifetime of 20 years. Advances like these, expanded to the entire economy, would sharply reduce container and packaging waste—which account for 30% of inflows to U.S. landfills.

Product life is also extended through the remanufacture, repair, and reuse of spent goods. The environmental impact of beverage consumption in Denmark has fallen considerably since the country switched from aluminum cans to glass containers that can be reused 50 to 100 times. Widespread adoption of these measures would in some ways be a step back to the fu-ture. Most grandparents in industrial countries can remember an economy in which milk bottles and other beverage containers were washed and reused, shoes were re-soled, clothes were mended, and machines were rebuilt. Some may remember that all but two of the U.S. ships sunk at Pearl Harbor were recovered, overhauled, and recommissioned, in part because of the savings in time and material that this option offered. That such practices seem strange to new generations of consumers is a reflection of how far industrial economies have drifted from the careful use of materials resources.

A logger takes down another tree. The government should end subsidies for the logging and mining industries that make virgin materials seem cheap, the authors say. This policy would encourage greater use of recycled materials.

People recycle more when disposal is taxed. Waste taxes based on the amount of garbage generated are most effective when combined with curbside recycling, according to the authors.

Extending product life offers an array of advantages over the habitual use of virgin materials and the manufacturing of new products. For starters, fewer wastes are generated when products spend more time circulating through an economy. But less apparent gains are at least as important. Reducing logging and mining would save gargantuan amounts of energy: Materials extraction and processing account for an estimated 75% of the energy used by industry in some industrial countries.

Shifting Gears

Overhauling materials practices will require policies that steer economies away from forests, mines, and petroleum stocks as the primary source of materials and away from landfills and incinerators as cheap disposal options. Businesses and consumers need to be encouraged to use far less virgin material and to tap the rich flow of currently wasted resources through product reuse, remanufacturing, or sharing, or through materials recycling.

A key step in this direction is to abandon the government subsidies

Materials Efficiency: A Balance Sheet

Product	Efficiency Gains	Factors that Undercut Efficiency Gains
Plastics in Cars	Use of plastics in U.S. cars increased by 26% between 1980 and 1994, replacing steel in many uses and reducing car weight by 6%.	Cars contain 25 chemically incompatible plastics that, unlike steel, cannot be easily recycled. Most plastic in cars winds up in landfills.
Bottles and Cans	Aluminum cans weigh 30% less today than they did 20 years ago.	Cans replaced an environmentally superior product—refillable bottles; 95% of soda containers were refillable in the United States in 1960.
Lead Batteries	A typical automobile battery used 30 pounds of lead in 1974, but only 20 pounds in 1994—with improved performance.	U.S. domestic battery shipments increased by 76% in the same period, more than offsetting the efficiency gains.
Radial Tires	Radial tires are 25% lighter and last twice as long as bias-ply tires.	Radial tires are more difficult to retread. Sales of passenger car retreads fell by 52% in the United States between 1977 and 1997.
Mobile Phones	Weight of mobile phones was reduced 10-fold between 1991 and 1996.	Subscribers to cellular telephone service jumped more than eightfold in the same period, nearly offsetting the gains from making phones lighter. Moreover, the mobile phones did not typically replace older telephones, but were additions to a household's phone inventory.

Source: *Mind Over Matter*

that make virgin materials seem cheap. Whether in the form of direct payments or as resource giveaways, assistance to mining and logging firms makes virgin materials artificially attractive to manufacturers. The 1872 Mining Law in the United States, for example, continues to give mining firms access to public lands for just $12 per hectare, without requiring payment of royalties or even the cleanup of mining sites. The effect of this virtual giveaway is to encourage virgin materials use at the expense of alternatives such as recycling.

By closing the subsidy spigot for extractive industries, policy makers can earn double dividends. The environmental gains would be substantial because most materials-driven environmental damage occurs at the extractive stage. And the public treasury would be fattened through the elimination of tax breaks or other treasury-draining subsidies, and possibly through payments from the mining and logging operations that remain open. What's more, these benefits would be achieved at little social cost: Mining and logging, for example, provide relatively few jobs. In the United States, metals mining employed 52,000 workers in 1996, just 0.04% of the total U.S. work force that year.

Waste generation can also be substantially curtailed, even to the point of near-zero waste in some industries and cities. A handful of firms report achieving near-zero waste levels at some facilities. The city of Canberra, Australia, is pursuing a "No-Waste-by-2010" strategy, while the Netherlands has set a national waste-reduction goal of 70% to 90%. A key way to meet such ambitious targets is to tax waste in all its forms, from smokestack emissions to landfilled solids. Pollution taxes in the Netherlands, for example, were primarily responsible for a 72% to 99% reduction in heavy metals discharges into waterways between 1976 and the mid-1990s. High landfill taxes in Denmark have boosted construction debris reuse from 12% to 82% in eight years—far above the 4% rates of most industrial countries. Such a tax could bring huge materials savings in the United States, where construction-materials use between 2000 and 2020 is projected to exceed total use in the twentieth century.

At the consumer level, a waste tax can take the form of fees that are based on the amount of garbage generated. Cities that have shifted to such a system have seen a substantial reduction in waste generation. "Pay-as-you-throw" programs, in which people are charged by the bag or by volume of trash, illustrate the direct effect of taxes on waste. For example, Dover, New Hampshire, and Crockett, Texas, reduced household waste by about 25% in five years once such programs were introduced. These initiatives are most effective when coupled with curbside recycling programs: As disposal is taxed, people recycle more. Eleven of 17 U.S. communities with record-setting recycling rates use pay-as-you-throw systems.

A modified version of a waste tax is the refundable deposit—essentially a temporary tax that is returned to the payer when the taxed material is brought back. High deposits for refillable glass bottles in Denmark have yielded 98% to 99% return rates.

Recognizing the problems caused by our dependence on materials is a first step in making the leap to a rational, sustainable materials economy. Once we grasp this idea, the opportunities to dematerialize our economies are well within reach. Societies that shed their attachment to things and focus instead on delivering what people actually need might be remembered 100 years from now as the creators of the most durable civilization in history.

About the Authors

Gary Gardner is a senior researcher at the Worldwatch Institute, 1776 Massachusetts Avenue, N.W., Washington, D.C. 20036. Telephone 1-202-452-1999; Web site www.worldwatch.org.

Payal Sampat is a Worldwatch staff researcher who studies human development issues and sustainable materials use.

This article is adapted from their report *Mind Over Matter: Recasting the Role of Materials in Our Lives*. Worldwatch Institute. 1998. 60 pages. Paperback. $5 plus shipping. The report may also be downloaded from the Worldwatch Institute Web site for $5.

CRAWLING OUT OF THE PIPE

The hazardous waste that makes more of itself

by Chris Bright

Bioinvasion, the spread of non-native "exotic" species, may be the least visible and least predictable of all the major dimensions of ecological decline. It is also one of the most dangerous, because exotics often create pressures for which there is no local evolutionary precedent: native species simply may not be adapted to live with the invaders. The result, increasingly, is widespread suppression of natives and sometimes extinction. As a threat to global biological diversity, bioinvasion may now be surpassed only by the broadest category of environmental decline, habitat loss.

Some exotics are released intentionally—trees for plantations, for example, or fish for aquaculture. But many of the worst invasions have been accidents. Industry and trade are continually leaking weeds, forest pests, aggressive crabs, predatory jellyfish, and all sorts of other invasive organisms out into the world's natural spaces. Sometimes even the intentional releases go wild, and spread far beyond their appointed ranges.

The convulsions have ebbed away but left a low-grade infection, incurable and subject to flare-up. This is the victim: the Black Sea, where Ovid passed his exile, where the Byzantine Empire rose and gave way to the Crusaders, the Golden Horde, and the Ottoman Turks. These are the waters stained by the terrible pogroms of Stalin and Hitler, caressed by generations of Russian elite on holiday.

And all that time, along the Atlantic coast of the Americas, constellations of little luminescent blobs were drifting along, here and there, out beyond the roar of the surf. This is the pathogen: the Leidy's comb jelly (*Mnemiopsis leidyi*), a widespread species but nothing special. Until one day in the early 1980s, when a ship enroute from—who knows?—New York, maybe, or Caracas, sailed up the Bosporus, into the Black Sea, and squirted the jelly out of its ballast water tanks.

Leidy's comb jelly eats the myriad tiny animals known collectively as zooplankton. And since nothing in the Black Sea would eat the jelly, it launched one of the most intense biological invasions ever recorded in a marine ecosystem. By late 1988, a single cubic meter of Black Sea water could contain as many as 500 jellies, most of them probably smaller than your thumb. If all of the jellies could have been hauled out of the sea that fall and weighed, the take would have come to between 900 million and 1 billion tons—at least 10 times the total world fishery catch for that year. But the anchovies and other fish that make up the sea's traditional catch had largely disappeared. The Black Sea had been poisoned by ballast water, one of the most common forms of marine pollution today—and one of the most dangerous.

Despite its apparent stability, a big ship doesn't sail simply by virtue of its design, any more than an airplane flies simply because it has wings. Keeping a ship upright takes ballast water—lots of it. Moving that water in and out of the cavernous tanks designed to hold it is as critical a part of the nautical routine as managing the rudder or the engines. Ballast water must be taken on when cargo is unloaded, or as fuel is consumed, or to provide extra stability in heavy weather, or sometimes to make the ship ride low enough to pass under a bridge. And for every reason that it's pumped aboard, there's a corresponding reason for pumping it out—taking aboard cargo, making the ship ride high enough to move into a shallow harbor, and so on. The ballast capacity of a big tanker can exceed 200,000 cubic meters—enough to fill 2,000 Olympic-sized swimming pools—and its pumps can move that water at rates as high as 20,000 cubic meters an hour. That's not gentle suction. Most ballasting is done around harbors, in shallow water, and ships sometimes scour the bottom as they're ballasting up. In the resultant turmoil, the slurry gushing into the tanks may contain hundreds of cubic meters of sediment—along with any small creatures that happen to be in the water, the mud, or on nearly harbor pilings.

The tanks of a large ship may come to support a chaotic but more-or-less permanent living community. A large ballast tank can only be emptied completely by opening it up, and that is only done during dry-dock overhaul, which on a well-maintained vessel might occur every three to five years. Routine use always leaves plenty of room for biological activity. In one recent survey of large ships reporting no ballast on board, the burden of unpumpable water and sediment in their "empty" tanks averaged 157.7 metric tons—enough to fill perhaps a dozen dump trucks.

Ballast water is a soup stocked from harbors all over the world. The holes in ballast intake grates are usually about a centimeter wide. That's probably plenty of room for most marine organisms in larval form—most fish larvae, for instance, are small enough to pass through. Sometimes the grates fall off, allowing much larger creatures to enter. In April 1995, for example, the tanks of a ship that had come into Baltimore harbor from the eastern Mediterranean were found to contain more than 50 healthy mullet from 30 to 36 centimeters long.

But some of the most significant stowaways are microscopic: in 1991, ballast discharge from ships arriving in Peruvian ports from South Asia is thought to have unleashed the first cholera epidemic that the Western Hemisphere had seen for more than a century. The outbreak may have infected several million people and killed 10,000 of them. Ships outbound from Latin America were found to have cholera-laden ballast upon arrival in ports in Australia and the United States. In 1992, as the epidemic gained momentum in South America, more cases of imported cholera were observed in the United States than in any year since surveillance for that disease began.

There are more than 28,700 vessels in the world's major merchant fleets and they make up by far the largest part of the world's trading infrastructure. About 80 percent of the world's commodities travel by ship for at least part of the journey to their consumers; and the volume of seaborne trade is climbing steadily upward. From 1970 to 1996, the trade nearly doubled (it climbed from 10,654 billion ton-miles, the standard industry measure, to 20,545 btm). Through its ballast systems, the world merchant fleet has in effect superimposed a second set of currents on the world's oceans, and these meta-currents are far more efficient at transporting life over long distances than are the natural ones. On any day, the meta-currents are moving perhaps 3,000 different species of every conceivable ecological function: green plant, pathogen, parasite, herbivore, carnivore, scavenger. And in harbor after harbor, the same species are appearing over and over again—the same crabs and clams, the same worms, sometimes even the same fish. The world trading system is creating an extra-geographical marine biota. (See table "Caught Up in the Meta-Currents.")

In the Black Sea, the process was so traumatic partly because the native biota was already so sick. Over the previous several decades, the sea had grown steadily more polluted from fertilizer run-off and the raw sewage of some 170 million people. This nutrient-rich pollution was feeding clouds of algae, which were robbing the water of light and burning up oxygen as they decayed. The Black Sea is naturally anoxic (oxygen-poor) to begin with. For millennia, rafts of plant material would sweep in from the Danube and the other tributary rivers, consuming the oxygen as they rotted, and leaving only a film of aerated water riding a vast anoxic pool—the largest such pool on earth. The algae had begun to suffocate that upper layer of life. The algae were also shading out the huge shallow-water seagrass beds that had once functioned as the sea's "lungs"—and as prime habitat for fish, crustaceans, sponges, and many other creatures. But zooplankton eat algae—and zooplankton were just about all that remained of the sea's battered immune system. Then the jelly ate virtually all the zooplankton. Algae and jelly were almost the only living things in the water. At its peak, the jelly alone accounted for 95 percent of the sea's entire wet weight biomass.

By the mid-1990s, the jelly was showing signs of having exhausted its larder. Its Black Sea population has declined, but by 1992 it had invaded the Sea of Marmara, below the Bosporus, and it has turned up farther south, in the Aegean as well. Eventually, it might infest much of the Mediterranean coastline. Shipping could also take it north, up the great European rivers that run into the Black Sea, and into the Baltic. Neither the Mediterranean nor the Baltic are in robust health and we have no way of knowing how either would cope with an *M. leidyi* infection. In the meantime, several jellyfish native to the Black Sea have established themselves in the Chesapeake Bay on the U.S. East Coast, and in San Francisco Bay on the West Coast.

Despite their capacity for havoc, most ballast-water invaders don't get much press. To the news media and probably to the public in general, marine pollution usually means oil spill. The 1989 Exxon Valdez spill in Alaska's Prince William Sound, for example, attracted major media coverage for months. But what about the spill that is spreading through the Sound today? In December 1997, the U.S. Fish and Wildlife Service announced that it had discovered four new species of zooplankton in the Sound, where they had been released from tanker ballast. The plankton appear to have come from East Asia via San Francisco Bay. Scientists are concerned that the invaders may develop a taste for the same foods that are needed by the Dungeness crab, an important fishery species. As more and more Alaskan oil is pumped, some scientists fear that ballast releases like these could become a general threat to the state's fisheries. The biotic spills, in other words, could become a far greater danger to Alaskan coasts than the oil spills. After all, oil spills may be a grave environmental insult, but they eventually go away. Biotic spills do not.

Biotic spills have been a major ecological side-effect of commerce for centuries, but ballast water is a fairly recent variation on the theme. Keeping a ship afloat by pumping some of the ocean into it was an innovation made possible by motorized pumps and metal hulls. By the turn of the century both of these technologies were well established and ballast tanks had become common. The first known ballast water invasion dates from the same era: a Chinese species of plankton, *Biddulphia sinensis,* appeared in the North Sea.

Earlier generations of sailors shoveled ballast into their ships: rocks, earth, scrap metal, any other heavy portside debris—along with the resident beetles, earthworms, sandfleas, and seeds. Ballast was supposed to be dumped and collected at specific sites around harbors. By the last century, botanists knew that these "ballast points" were good places to prospect for exotic flora. Some of those plants have since gone prospecting on their own. Alligator weed (*Alternanthera philoxeroides*), an aggressive South Ameri-

can plant that flourishes both in water and on land—and that is naturally resistant to herbicides—grew out of the ballast heaps near Newcastle, Australia, about 50 years ago. It is now choking irrigation ditches and natural waterways all along the coast of New South Wales, and unless it is controlled, experts fear it could spread around the country. Animals emerged from the heaps as well. One of the most common snails on the Northeast coast of the United States may have arrived on the shores of the New World in shovelfuls of ballast: the European periwinkle (*Littorina littorea*). In the late 19th century it exploded, zebra-mussel fashion, along the intertidal zone and rearranged (in ways no longer entirely clear) shoreline and marsh ecology from Newfoundland to New Jersey.

The wooden hulls of sailing vessels also had enormous biological potential. Seaweeds and barnacles colonized the surface, creating mobile habitat for fish, shrimp, crabs, and other little animals. The resultant fouling communities, teeming with all sorts of life, could be more than a meter thick. Specialized boring molluscs called shipworms

CAUGHT UP IN THE META-CURRENTS

Almost every kind of marine organism is riding the shipping routes in ballast tanks . . .

Outbound from Europe	The zebra mussel, a **shellfish** native to the Caspian Sea region, is rearranging the ecology of many North American waterways.
	The ruffe, a European **fish**, is established in the Great Lakes and is beginning to outcompete the yellow perch and walleye—native fish with an economic value of $90 million annually.
	A Mediterranean **fan worm** now forms a kind of living carpet over parts of the floor of Port Phillip Bay, on the southeastern coast of Australia, to the detriment of the local scallop fishery.
. . . from the Americas	The Leidy's comb jelly, a **jellyfish** native to the western Atlantic coast, devastated the Black Sea fisheries.
	The American razor clam, a **shellfish** native to the North American Atlantic coast, has established itself along the western and northern European coasts.
	A **bristle worm** from the North American Atlantic coast now constitutes 97 percent of the biomass of the large bottom-dwelling species in the Vistula lagoon, on the Polish coast.
. . . from East Asia	The Chinese mitten **crab** and an Asian **clam** have invaded San Francisco Bay.
	At least eight East Asian **copepods** are living on the Pacific coast of the Americas.
	A **starfish** from the Northwestern Pacific has invaded the Tasmanian coast; it is threatening local shellfish industries and endangering the native spotted handfish—which could become the first known marine fish to go extinct during the historic era (although there have likely been undocumented extinctions).
	Poisonous dinoflagellate "red tide" **plankton**, native to the waters off Japan, occasionally shut down oyster farms along the southeast coast of Australia.
	Various **seaweeds** native to the Japanese coast are established in the waters off Tasmania and along both coasts of the United States.
. . . from South Asia	The Indian bream, a **fish**, is established in western Australia.
	Another **fish**, the Indo-Pacific goby, is established in Nigeria, Cameroon, and the Panama Canal.
	A **crab** native to the Indo-Pacific and established in the eastern Mediterranean has now appeared in the waters off Cuba, Venezuela, Colombia, and Florida.
. . . from Australia	An Australian **barnacle** is outcompeting native barnacles over stretches of European coast.

For sources, see chapter 7 of Life Out of Bounds.

took up residence inside the hulls, and their continual gnawing opened up little caverns that also became home to other travelers. As early as the 16th century, shipworms were regarded as so serious a problem that the British Admiralty ordered English ships to stay clear of those South American waters deemed most heavily infested with them.

Today, solid ballast is a thing of the past and hull fouling communities are much sparser, thanks to toxic antifouling paints, high sailing speeds, and port times often measured in hours instead of months. But this ancient pathway of invasion has not been closed entirely. A modern hull can offer well over a hectare of surface (easily 3 acres) below the water line, so even a light encrustation could be substantial enough to innoculate a harbor. And some species of seaweed are now resistant to the copper-based toxins in the antifouling paints. Recent fouling introductions include the Mediterranean mussel (*Mytilus galloprovincialis*), which was discovered in Hong Kong in 1983, and the Asian brown seaweed *Undaria pinnatifida,* which is apparently spreading along the Pacific coast of South America, the Atlantic coast of Europe, and the Australian coast by riding on ships' hulls.

Probably the richest fouling communities these days are riding on a kind of vessel that didn't exist during the days of sail: semisubmersible oil drilling platforms, which are towed from one seabed oil field to another. Our thirst for oil is dispersing various species of fish, sea anemonies, crabs, barnacles, and algae—but not necessarily the same ones that rode the tall ships. Oil drilling is usually done off shore, so the platforms are moving open-ocean species, rather than the estuary and near-shore creatures most frequently found on ships.

The ship itself remains a complicated nexus of invasion routes, both ancient and modern. Apart from hull surface and ballast tank, exotic species stowaway in bilges (the ship's "storm sewers"), sea chests (the ports leading to the ballast tanks), nets, chain lockers—and in some places an ancient mariner would never dream of. In the U.S. Pacific Northwest, a series of portside infestations of the Asian strain of the gypsy moth (*Lymantria dispar*) were detected in 1991 and apparently eliminated over the course of the ensuing year. (The gypsy moth, a widespread Eurasian insect, is a serious exotic pest of broadleaf forest in eastern North America. Thus far, only the European strain of the moth has established itself in North America; the Asian strain is much more mobile and therefore much more dangerous.) The pathway of invasion, it turned out, was the lighting aboard grain carriers coming in from East Asia. The ships' lamps produced light of a wavelength that strongly attracted the moths, and the fast crossing times— so important in reducing hull fouling—helped insure the moths' safe arrival. No doubt, there are other shipboard pathways that haven't yet been discovered because we haven't yet traced an invader back through them.

The trading network is injecting exotics deep within the continents as well. A major leap in invasion potential involves containers, those big metal boxes that have revolutionized the freight industry over the past couple of decades. Containers are nearly ubiquitous. They move by ship, train, and truck—in fact, the trailers of many trucks *are* containers. They can be stacked for weeks or even months in ports or railyards, allowing plenty of time for pests to enter. They offer a safe haven to anything that manages to get inside, since they are very difficult to inspect. They are rarely cleaned between shipments, and they may not be unpacked until they are hundreds of kilometers from their ports of entry. Containers have integrated sea and land transit. They have ruptured the ancient pattern of ship-borne invasion, in which exotics simply made their way inland from ports.

The overwhelming share of world shipping volume is in bulk commodities, like grain or oil. Materials of this sort can't be containerized, but almost everything else can be. And increasingly, it is. In 1995, the most recent year for which figures are available, world container traffic had reached 135 million TEUs ("twenty-foot equivalent units"—because containers come in several sizes, total volume is measured by an abstract unit rather than by the absolute number of containers). As a share of total shipping volume, container traffic is growing steadily; it has risen from a mere 1.6 percent in 1980 to 6.4 percent by the end of 1996—a fourfold increase. And the container is becoming a major means of linking developing world economies with their industrialized trading partners: by 1996, slightly over half of world container volume was passing through the ports of developing countries.

Containers have been identified as significant pathways for insects, weed seeds, slugs, and snails. One of the most dangerous exotics known to be using this pathway is the Asian tiger mosquito (*Aedes albopictus*), an extremely aggressive biting pest. In Asia, this mosquito is a major vector of dengue fever, an excruciating disease that gets its common name from the pain it inflicts: "break-bone fever." Dengue infects about 560,000 people each year and kills 23,000. The mosquito can carry at least 17 other viral diseases, including various forms of encephalitis and yellow fever.

For decades, the Asian tiger mosquito had been a common pest throughout much of the Indo-Pacific region, from Madagascar all the way to Hawaii. Then in the mid-1980s, it embarked on its version of world conquest. It is currently known to have established itself in the southeastern United States, Brazil, southern Europe, South Africa, Nigeria, New Zealand, and Australia. It may have been a factor in the 1986 yellow fever epidemic in Rio de Janeiro, in which about 1 million people were infected. In 1991, it was discovered in the midst of a yellow fever outbreak in Nigeria. Around the same time, it was a suspected vector in several encephalitis epidemics in Florida. Researchers fear that the continued spread of the mosquito could substantially increase the disease burden of both the developed and developing worlds. Even where the diseases it carries are already well established, its arrival could be trouble. In the Caribbean, for example, dengue fever is primarily a disease of the cities because the virus still lacks an efficient rural vector—a role this mosquito could readily play.

The vector of this vector, it turns out, is the containerized used tire. Millions of used tires are traded internationally every year—some to make recycled rubber products or asphalt, but most as fuel for powerplants, cement kilns, and so forth. A tire with a little water in it is ideal mosquito habitat—and have you ever tried to empty a wet tire completely? Unless you puncture it, you can't. Within the peculiar contours of one of the world's most common objects, fluid dynamics and gravity will defeat your every maneuver.

A more recent container-borne invader is the Asian longhorn beetle (*Anoplophora glabripennis*). Since 1996, this wood-boring insect from China has turned up in more than 30 warehouses all over the United States and has succeeded in launching small infestations around Chicago and New York City. The beetle will attack a wide range of broadleaf trees, injuring or killing them by boring through their sapwood. Counter-attack is very difficult, since the beetle spends most of its life inside the tree, where it cannot be reached by pesticides and may often go undetected until the damage is done. At present the only method of control consists of cutting, chipping, and burning every tree known or suspected of being infested. U.S. foresters have no way of knowing what the beetle would do if it were to establish itself in the country permanently, but it is conceivable that some native American maples could join the list of trees currently threatened or rendered functionally extinct by exotic pests. (See table "Infected Forests.") The beetle travels in untreated wood pallets and packing material. Over China's strenuous objections, the U.S. government has now imposed emergency restrictions on this type of packing—a move that could affect up to one-half of China's $63 billion worth of annual exports to the United States.

I t is apparently a universal dimension of culture, the essential human enterprise, to be riddled with hundreds of these accidental thoroughfares, which have conveyed other organisms far beyond their natural ranges. This biotic mixing has exercised a profound influence on landscape and seascape, yet the results have often gone unnoticed. During the last century, for example, wooden-hulled ships apparently brought a tiny, wood-boring crustacean (the isopod *Sphaeroma terebrans*) to the Atlantic coasts of the Americas from the Pacific. *S. terebrans* has spread throughout the Atlantic mangrove communities—the fringe of stilt-rooted trees common along tropical and warm temperate shores. It attacks and kills mangrove root tips, thereby controlling the trees seaward spread. According to James Carlton, a professor at Williams College in Connecticut and the world's preeminent authority on marine exotics, *S. terebrans* has "virtually 'reset' the seaward history" of the western Atlantic's mangrove ecosystems.

In the coastal communities they dominate, mangroves knit sea and shore together. They buffer the coasts from surf. Their roots shelter rich communities of fish, crabs, and many other marine organisms. Birds, mammals, and reptiles live in the branches above. *S. terebrans* doesn't seem to have doomed the western Atlantic mangrove communities, but as with the European periwinkle farther north, the little isopod's invasion is a change at once enormous and very subtle. What difference does it make? As far as the ecology is concerned, there may never be a definitive answer—it all depends on the era in which the question is asked, and what else is happening in the mangroves. But think about *S. terebrans* as a cultural phenomenon: our forebears inadvertently rescripted the functioning of a vast (if very narrow) ecosystem, and we have lived with the invasion for a century or so. Yet apparently, the change remained completely invisible until Carlton discovered it.

Many biotic spills have spread a similar stain—vast but very hard to read. In Europe, for example, a fungal pathogen of North American crayfish was accidentally released into Italian waters around 1860 and is inexorably erasing the native crayfish from that continent. Probably very few Europeans know that the crayfish in their streams are largely exotic North American species, introduced because they are resistant to the fungus. This remedy, incidentally, is a further injury to the patient: without the North American crayfish, the epidemic might have reduced the native crayfish to remnant populations and then run out of steam for lack of victims. But the plague now has a permanent host in the North American crayfish, and the beleaguered native species must now face exotic competitors as well as the exotic disease.

Canals have been highly efficient corridors of invasion, when they connected bodies of water that had previously been distinct. The barriers thus breached may not even be noticed by terrestrial, canal-building vertebrates, but the view looks very different from the water. In the U.S. Northeast, the Erie canal, completed in 1823, broke through the hump of land geographers call the Allegheny Divide. For over 10,000 years, since the retreat of the glaciers, the divide had separated what is now the Great Lakes Basin from coastal rivers like the Hudson. More than a score of exotic fish and molluscs have arrived in the Hudson drainage through the canal. The Suez Canal, a conduit for 20 percent of world maritime traffic, rejoined the Red Sea to the Mediterranean in 1869, after some 20 million years of separation. Thus far, nearly 300 exotics are thought to have found their way into the Mediterranean through the Suez, including the Red Sea jellyfish (*Rhopilema nomadica*), which now produces mass summertime swarms along the sea's eastern coast. A harbinger, perhaps, of what the Leidy's comb jelly may do if it makes its way down from the north.

If you know what to look for, you can read the results of past ambitions, conflicts, and blunders large and small in the landscape around you. Around some European cit-

INFECTED FORESTS

A sampler of North American trees and the exotics that are threatening them.

1892   The white pine blister rust (*Cronartium ribicola*) is introduced from Europe in infected nursery stock. The rust has eliminated some stands of whitebark pine (*Pinus albicaulis*), which is native to the Rocky Mountains. The pine is vulnerable to the rust over its entire range.

1904   The chestnut blight (*Cryphonectria parasitica*) arrives in shipments of Asian chestnut nursery stock. The blight has completely suppressed the American chestnut (*Castanea dentata*), formerly a keystone species in most of the deciduous forests east of the Mississippi. The chestnut is now "functionally extinct."

1923   The fungus now known as the Port-Orford-cedar root disease (*Phytophthora lateralis*) arrives in shipments of Asian conifer nursery stock. The disease is killing the Port-Orford cedar (*Chamaecyparis lawsoniana*), which is native only to northern California and southern Oregon. The cedar may be vulnerable over its entire range, at least at lower elevations.

1920s   The hemlock woolly adelgid (*Adelges tsugae*) is discovered on the West Coast. This Asian insect infests and kills Canadian hemlock (*Tsuga canadensis*), a major component of the eastern coniferous forests. The die-back is especially severe in the U.S. Northeast but the hemlock may be vulnerable over its entire range. (A recently-discovered Japanese ladybug, which appears to prey exclusively on the adelgid, may eventually ease the threat. The ladybug is being released as a bio-control agent.)

1920s?   The beech scale complex, consisting of a scale insect (*Cryptococcus fagisuga*) and one or two fungi (*Nectria* spp.), is introduced on European beech nursery stock. The disease has killed over half the trees in some northeastern stands of American beech (*Fagus grandifolia*); the full extent of the threat is not known.

1930   The Dutch elm disease, a complex consisting of a European bark beetle (*Scolytus multistriatus*) and the fungus *Ophiostoma ulmi*, probably from Asia, arrives in shipments of veneer logs from Europe. The disease has caused the functional extinction of the American elm (*Ulmus americana*), native to the East and Midwest.

1967   The butternut canker (*Sirococcus clavigignenti-juglandacearum*), a fungus of unknown origin but almost certainly exotic, is discovered in Wisconsin. The fungus has completely eliminated some populations of butternut (*Juglans cinerea*), a sparsely-distributed tree native to the East and Midwest. The tree is threatened throughout its range.

1976   The dogwood anthracnose (*Discula destructiva*), a fungus of unknown origin but probably exotic, is discovered in Washington state. The disease is killing off the Pacific dogwood (*Cornus nuttallii*), native to the West Coast, and the eastern dogwood (*C. florida*), native to the East and Midwest. The course of the epidemic cannot be predicted, but in the Southeast, at least, the fungus' sensitivity to heat limits its effects on the eastern dogwood.

Primary source: Faith Thompson Campbell and Scott E. Schlarbaum, *Fading Forests: North American Trees and the Threat of Exotic Pests* (New York: Natural Resources Defense Council, 1994).

ies, for instance, you can still find the remnants of various "siege flora"—the growing remains of the meals, bedding, and forage of besieging armies of the past. Military movements have triggered more spectacular invasions too: the brown tree snake (*Boiga irregularis*) is thought to have arrived on the Pacific island of Guam in U.S. military transports around 1950. The brown tree snake has eaten 12 of the island's 14 land bird species into extinction in the wild, and several lizard and bat species as well.

Many industries—some of them still with us, some largely forgotten—have left an enormous biotic legacy in the form of invasion. Some 500 exotic plant species growing around the French city of Montpellier, for instance, have been attributed to wool imports; for centuries, wool scouring was an important local industry. It was the oyster industry, about a century ago, that inadvertently released the North American Atlantic cordgrass onto the coast of the Pacific Northwest, in shipments of oyster "seed." In its new range, the cordgrass has converted extensive tracts of tidal mudflats—essential for many bird and fish species—into much less productive marsh. A failed soap-making industry helped the highly invasive Chinese tallow tree into the forests and wetlands of the U.S. Southeast. (The tree's seeds can be made into soap; unfortunately, since the tree is also beautiful, there is another pathway through which it moves: horticulture.) The failed enterprise that has probably left the greatest biotic scar was the tragic attempt to produce silk in Massachusetts by importing the gypsy moth.

Today, the invasion potential of trade and industry is expanding radically in several dimensions at once. In terms of volume, speed, trade routes, and the variety of organisms involved, the modern trading system dwarfs anything previous eras have seen. Take volume first: at the turn of the century, a substantial ship might have a capacity of 3,000 tons; by World War II, 10,000-ton ships were common; today, ships are often 150,000 to 250,000 tons and the largest vessels exceed 600,000 tons. The sheer increase in size may help explain why ballast water invasions seem to have gone from a dribble to a torrent somewhere in the 1970s or early 1980s.

For many types of organisms, greater speed may be more important than greater volume, since the shorter the time in transit, the higher the odds of survival. For ships, the quantum leap in speed actually occurred in the latter half of the last century. In 1851, the William T. Coleman California Line was billing its *Syren*—"The A 1 Extreme Clipper Ship"—as capable of sailing from San Francisco to Boston (via Cape Horn) in 100 days, and from Calcutta to Boston in 96 days. It would have taken the *Syren* four to six weeks to cross the Atlantic. The transition from sail to steam cut that time in half: by the turn of the century, steamers were crossing the Atlantic in only two weeks. Land transportation underwent a revolution at about the same time. By the 1870s, North America had been girded by rail and it was possible to travel from one coast to the other in a couple of days. The rail system included ubiq-uitous water towers—an essential part of transportation infrastructure in the steam age. Rail and water offered an unprecedented opportunity to fisheries authorities, who were eager to flood the continent's waters with their favorite fish. Stock could be moved rapidly over great distances and the fish tanks topped up whenever locomotive boilers were refilled. Soon drainages all over the United States were feeling the plunge of exotic fingerlings.

Air traffic, of course, represents another quantum leap in speed, and air cargo is a rapidly expanding sector in the trade network. Air cargo traffic is growing at about 7 percent a year (in terms of ton-kilometers). In 1989, only three airports received more than a million tons of cargo; by 1996, that number had risen to 13. Many organisms that would die or be detected during a shipboard crossing can travel easily by air, including human pathogens. Anyone infected with cholera who boarded the *Syren* in Calcutta would have been very sick long before reaching Boston. But cholera and many other diseases are bound to travel undetected on dozens of air routes.

 Because the world trading system is so large and complex, the pathways within it are in a continual state of flux. Like vessels in some sort of global capillary network, they are constantly growing and constantly withering away, only to rebuild themselves elsewhere. As developing countries trade increasingly among themselves, it is likely that whole new sets of pathways will open up—between India and Africa, for example, or Latin America and Southeast Asia. The geographical shifting, along with the complexity of the pathways themselves, give the "ecology" of the world trading system a kind of demented complexity, like a Rube Goldberg drawing. Who would have thought, prior to the early 1980s, that rubber recycling would be instrumental in spreading a mosquito? Or that manufacturers of a certain kind of light were unwittingly increasing the pest risks to North American coniferous forest?

What is true of the trading system in general is also true of many industries in particular. The forest products industry is a prime example of the trend. The movement of forest products has always entailed serious ecological risk—a shipment of veneer logs, for example, brought the Dutch elm disease to North America. (See table, "Infected Forests".) But those risks have increased enormously as the trade in raw wood products continues to grow, both in volume and in the number of trade routes involved. From 1970 to 1994, the most recent year for which figures are available, export volumes of raw logs increased 21 percent (to 113.4 million cubic meters). Trade in sawnwood nearly doubled (to 108 million cubic meters). Among the countries that have substantially increased their raw log exports in recent years are China, Ghana, Papua New Guinea, the Solomon Islands, Russia, New Zealand, and Chile. Bigger importers include China, Korea, Taiwan, and a number of African countries.

What the logs contain besides wood is anybody's guess. At a conference on the dangers of raw wood imports in 1996, a former Oregon Department of Agriculture inspector recalled opening up the hatches of a wood chip carrier that had just arrived from Brazil and watching "a cloud of insects" escape. According to many experts, North America would risk a disaster of epochal proportions if lumber companies in the U.S. Pacific Northwest succeed in weakening federal regulations on importing raw logs. Relaxing the regulations would make it easier to feed the region's over-capacity sawmills, but it would also greatly increase the odds of hundreds of new forest pests eventually making their way into western North America.

Some mill owners, for instance, have been promoting the idea of importing Siberian logs. (Strictly speaking, it is already legal to do this, but no company has found an economical way to handle the required treatment procedures, which involve debarking, heating, then storing the logs in sanitary conditions until shipment.) A U.S. Forest Service inventory of organisms associated with Siberian larch, a major timber species in eastern Russia, turned up 175 species of arthropods (insects and their relatives), nematodes, and fungi, including a Eurasian spruce bark beetle (Ips typographus) that occasionally explodes in outbreaks lethal to millions of trees in its native range. Thus far, U.S. inspectors have found this beetle nearly 200 times in incoming shipments of European and Asian goods. In 1993, an infestation was detected around Erie, Pennsylvania and eradicated. Weakened regulations would presumably increase the likelihood of the beetle establishing itself in North America. And the results, according to the Forest Service, could be "as disastrous for North American spruce as the Dutch elm disease was to elms."

But not all biologically dirty industries are as large as the forestry sector. Some small industries are playing outsized roles as biopolluters—horticulture, for example. (See table, "Garden Variety Monsters.") About 60 percent of the worst plant invaders of North American natural areas are still being grown and sold by the North American nursery industry. One global survey of woody plant invasions found that in the 624 cases in which the origin of the invasion could be ascertained, 59 percent came from botanical gardens, landscaping, or other amenity purposes. In addition to escaped garden plants, horticulture releases a large number of weeds, insects, slugs, and pathogens. Historic nursery trade contributions to North America include the chestnut blight, the white pine blister rust, and the beech bark disease complex. (See table, "Infected Forests".)

The pet trade, the animal equivalent of horticulture, is another major conduit of invasion. The domestic cat, for example, is a formidable and now a nearly universal predator. Cats—many of them gone wild—appear to be a serious stress on bird populations in Europe and North America and on small mammal populations in Australia. There are plenty of other ex-pets out there as well. Consider the booming reptile trade. In Flor- ida, the trade has introduced about 20 species of exotic lizards, some of which prey on native lizards. Florida may eventually become home to breeding populations of exotic pythons; since no big constrictors are native to the state, local birds and other potential prey species may not be adapted to cope with them. In Hawaii, escaped chameleons are competing with native birds for insects. And perhaps the most popular reptile in the U.S. pet trade, a native North American turtle called the common slider (Trachemys scripta), has attracted the attention of animal breeders in various developing countries; common sliders are now sliding into the rivers of Panama, Malaysia, and Thailand.

But by far the most ecologically disruptive sectors of the pet industry is the aquarium trade. In increasing numbers, aquatic plants, snails, shrimp, fish, and various other denizens of hobby aquariums are finding their way into natural waters. Some escape from breeding facilities; others are offered their freedom by soft-hearted but misguided owners who have tired of their charges. The results have really put the industry on the map. Hydrilla, a popular aquarium plant from South Asia, escaped from a culture facility in Florida in the early 1950s and is now a premier aquatic weed throughout the Southeast, as well as on much of the West Coast. Hydrilla is clogging more than 40 percent of Florida's rivers and lakes.

Various species of aquarium fish—and the collection includes a substantial share of the world's tropical freshwater fish—are rapidly approaching cosmopolitan status. Such standard ornamentals as guppies and swordtails, both native to Central America, can now be found in tropical ponds and streams all over the world, especially near cities. Some highly disturbed but relatively clean habitats, like the canal systems of central Florida or the streams on the Hawaiian island of Oahu, have in effect become giant natural aquaria; aquarium species now dominate.

Healthy aquarium fish command a good price and efficient transport makes it possible to sell to distant markets, so breeders have set up shop throughout the warm regions of the world. If it's beautiful and breeds easily, it has a good chance of making a new life in the southeastern United States, Thailand, Malaysia, India, and various places in between. In the United States, 65 percent of the exotic fish species that are completely foreign to the country arrived through the aquarium trade. And new ones are establishing themselves all the time. At the time of writing, the latest addition is an Asian eel that has taken up residence in ponds near the Chattahoochee River, a major southeastern river. Like the Asian walking catfish that has invaded Florida, the eel is an efficient predator that can breathe both air and water, and it's capable of moving overland from one pool to another.

The aquarium trade is spreading fish pathogens as well. For example, at least 42 diseases have been identified in aquarium fish awaiting shipment into Australia. In that country and in other parts of the world, some of these pathogens have escaped into the wild; a few apparently owe a nearly worldwide distribution to this industry. Some ecologists speculate that escaped aquarium pathogens may be a factor in global amphibian decline.

New industries will doubtless create new pathways, or expand old ones. In Europe and North America, for example, the resurgence of interest in herbal medicine is likely to result in more medicinal plant invasions. Herbal medicine was probably one of the pathways that spread purple loosestrife. (See table, "Garden Variety Monsters.") A plant in more recent vogue is Saint John's wort (*Hypericum perforatum*); herbalists credit it as an antidepressant; natural areas managers know it as a serious weed.

A set of new pathways may emerge from bioremediation, the increasingly common practice of using living things to clean up contaminated sites. In its most common form, bioremediation involves the release of bacteria to break down large organic chemicals (such as petroleum derivatives) into smaller, more benign compounds that will

dissipate more readily into the environment. (The bacteria used are not pathogens—they don't cause diseases.) This kind of bioremediation is effective and cheap; it's expected to reduce clean-up costs on sites contaminated primarily by organic chemicals by a factor of 10. The U.S. Environmental Protection Agency has concluded, for example, that if bioremediation had been used to clean up the Exxon Valdez spill, the cost would have come in under $250 million, instead of the actual $2.5 billion. Most bacteria used in bioremediation belong to very widespread groups, but our understanding of bacterial distribution is not highly developed, and in the process of cleaning up oil spills, we may create some bacterial spills.

Spills of a very different sort are likely to result from phytoremediation, a form of bioremediation that uses certain plants to draw up soil contaminants. The process involves sowing a suitable plant on a contaminated area, allowing the "crop" to mature, and then cutting or up-

GARDEN VARIETY MONSTERS

Rubber Vine	Introduced from Madagascar as an ornamental and possible rubber source into northern Australia at the turn of the century. This plant now infests some 350,000 square kilometers of tropical Queensland, where it chokes out native grassland and forest, smothering trees up to 30 meters high.
Clematis vitalba	This ornamental vine from northern Europe had escaped from gardens in New Zealand by the 1930s. It is doing to that country's forests what rubber vine is doing to northern Australia. When a stand of smothered trees collapses, clematis blankets the resulting tangle, forming mats over a meter thick and preventing any regeneration.
Water Hyacinth	A South American aquatic plant introduced during the 19th century into the southern United States, Africa, and southern Asia. Its original use was often as a pool ornament; subsequent uses have included fodder, green manure, biogas production, and wastewater treatment. But given the number of lakes and rivers that have disappeared beneath it, many water managers would be glad to get rid of it without using it at all.
Purple Loosestrife	This European wetland plant probably first reached North America at the end of the 18th century in wool imports and solid ship ballast; during the 19th century it was imported for ornamental and probably for medicinal purposes. It has now overrun more than 600,000 hectares of North American temperate and boreal wetland, where it has eliminated native vegetation and ruined the waterfowl forage base.
Knotweeds	Bamboo-like plants from east Asia introduced into Europe and North America during the 19th century as ornamentals and, in Europe, for game forage. On both continents, knotweeds are outcompeting native riverside vegetation and choking off water courses.
Saltcedars or Tamarisks	Scrubby, Asian trees introduced into the western United States beginning in the early 19th century, primarily as ornamentals but also for erosion control along rivers. Today they infest more than 600,000 hectares along rivers and streams, forming dense thickets of little wildlife value and often eliminating surface water. In the U.S. Southwest, saltcedars may now absorb a greater quantity of water than is used by all the cities of southern California combined.
Miconia	A beautiful tree from the American tropics, miconia is a favorite in tropical botanical gardens all over the world. But the tree casts dense shade that excludes other vegetation. Its seedlings reach sexual maturity in only a few years, then produce millions of seeds of their own. In French Polynesia, miconia is smothering virtually all of the territory's major islands. On Tahiti, where it is known as "the green cancer," miconia has displaced more than two-thirds of the native forest, and is threatening 25 percent of the island's native wildlife species.

For sources, see chapter 6 of *Life Out of Bounds*.

rooting it. The contaminant-laden plants can then be treated as toxic waste. Phytoremediation is used primarily to clean up metals such as lead, zinc, or chromium. Sometimes it's even possible to recover usable amounts of metals from the contaminated harvest. The process has been used to clean up radioactive contamination too. The oil-seed crop, Indian mustard (*Brassica juncea*), for example, is being used in Ukraine to pull strontium and cesium out of soils contaminated by the Chernobyl disaster.

There are apparently a large number of plants that can "hyperaccumulate" metals, especially in the tropics. In the flora of Cuba alone, for example, one botanist has identified 80 species that concentrate nickel. Some geneticists, not content with these naturally-occurring forms, are searching hyperaccumulating bacteria for metal-hungry genes, which they can then splice into plants. One group has created a transgenic form of *Arabidopsis thaliana* (a plant commonly used in genetic experiments) that absorbs mercury and exhales a faint mercurial plume into the air. Transgenic or not, a metal-laden plant could make a formidable invader. Hyperaccumulation has survival value: it tends to make plant tissues toxic or unpalatable to insects and pathogens. In the continual war with the insects, plants with this internal "armor" could well have an edge over more edible native competitors.

In terms of immediate social effect, the most important set of pathways involves the growing movement of humanity itself, which is increasingly stirring the world's human pathogens into a single, integrated, microbial system. No previous era has experienced such an uproar of human movement. Every week, about 1 million people move between the developed and the developing worlds; every day, about 2 million people cross an international border. Travel and tourism is now the world's biggest industry, in terms of its annual receipts, which amount to more than $3.4 trillion. World air passenger traffic—the best single indicator of long distance travel—is increasing at about 6 percent per year. By 2000, the civilian world air fleet will be moving more than 1.7 billion passengers annually, 522 million of them on international flights.

People infected with serious communicable diseases are presumably moving through this system all the time. Doubtless, many of them have no idea they're infected. In the United States, for example, there are about 1,000 new cases of malaria every year, and nearly all of the victims apparently pick up the disease while traveling. The infectious potential of an airplane is not simply a matter of quick transit—it's also the result of close confinement within the plane, especially for respiratory infections. Consider this: every hour, the average pair of human beings takes in roughly 833 liters of air, or 83 percent of a cubic meter. A really big plane, like a 747, can carry about 400 people, who would have a collective respiration rate of around 333 cubic meters per hour. The maximum cabin volume of a 747 is 876 cubic meters (but that's empty volume—before people come on board). Airplane ventilation systems admit small amounts of fresh air at fairly rapid intervals, but it may take 30 minutes or so to flush cabin air completely. Given the amount of breathing that is going on in the cabin, that leaves plenty of time for little clouds of microbes to move from one set of lungs to another. So an airplane that takes off with one infected passenger may well arrive with several. And if a crew member is infected, then several plane-loads of people could be exposed before the disease is discovered. In 1993, an investigation by the U.S. Centers for Disease Control and Prevention uncovered a case in which tuberculosis had been transmitted through one flight attendant to 23 other crew members in this fashion.

Permanent migration, like tourism, has reached unprecedented levels. Every year, some 110 million people immigrate to another country. In addition to these "standard" immigrants, the stream of international refugees and internally displaced persons has increased almost every year since the end of World War II. Since the beginning of this decade alone, their number has grown by more than 60 percent, from about 30 to 48 million. Many of these people end up in camps or shantytowns that are among the world's most miserable and disease-ridden places.

In general, the world we are traveling through seems to be getting sicker. Over the past two decades, some 30 "new" diseases have emerged—diseases like AIDS, Ebola, and the "flesh-eating" streptococcus. At the same time, several of humanity's oldest and deadliest scourges—malaria, cholera, and tuberculosis, for example—may be gathering strength. This resurgence of infectious disease is driven by a complex of environmental and social forces. Water-borne diseases like cholera lurk in the open, untreated sewers used by some 1.7 billion people, mostly in the rapidly growing slums of Third World cities. Other pathogens are spreading because their vectors are on the move—creatures like the Asian tiger mosquito. And a growing number of pathogens—all three of the ancient diseases just mentioned, for example—have evolved drug resistant strains. (Another reason for the resurgence, however, may be the fact that some 2.5 billion people, about 40 percent of the global population, don't have access to essential drugs at all.) Infectious diseases kill about 16.4 million people every year; that's about a third of all human mortality.

Human movement is the common denominator within much of this complex: it makes every local misery a global concern. Take the mosquito-vectored disease, yellow fever, for example. Yellow fever has two strongholds: the forests of Latin America and the west African countryside. In 1992, for the first time in a quarter-century, the African reservoir of the disease reached east, into Kenya. Many experts fear that the Kenya epidemic is the beginning of a new conquest. Kenya is a favorite destination for Indian emigrants; there is, consequently, a considerable amount of air traffic between the two countries. Yellow fever is not yet present in Asia and the Indian population is wholly unvaccinated against it. Some experts regard an Indian epidemic as all but inevitable—especially since another favorite destination of Indian emigrants is . . . Latin America.

Travel not only spreads diseases, it can intensify them. It used to be, for example, that on any particular Caribbean island, there was only one type of dengue fever, but travel and trade are mixing the forms of the disease. Infection with multiple strains of dengue produces dengue hemorrhagic fever (DHF), a condition that is far more likely to be fatal than ordinary dengue. Globally, the incidence of DHF has increased nearly tenfold, to 260,000 cases per year, since 1986. Such overlapping infections may open up whole new dimensions of public ill-health. One reason AIDS kills much faster in Africa than it does in other parts of the world may be that so many of its victims are also infected with malaria. Malaria (another mosquito-borne disease) is already infecting 225 million people a year and killing 2 million of them. Perhaps one side-effect of its resurgence will be an increase in the death toll from AIDS.

Medieval Arabian scholars were able to map the path of the Black Death. From its origin in the central Asian steppes, it followed the trade routes overland to the Crimean peninsula of the Black Sea, then sailed to Byzantium and on to the great cities of the eastern Mediterranean. Those chroniclers were watching a particularly horrible form of biotic mixing on a continental level. At the end of the 15th century, as the Age of Discovery opened, the biotic turmoil began to unfold on a global level, as the European biota spilled out over much of the earth. Gradually, over the ensuring centuries, various creatures from other regions were pulled into the flux—South American potatoes, Australian eucalypts, North American salmonids. Today, we have inaugurated a new era of ecological chaos. There is no longer any single predominating current, nor is there any type of organism that we can say with assurance is exempt from movement. Just about anything could be transported anywhere. Who will be able to map the plagues of the next millennium?

Chris Bright is senior editor of WORLD WATCH *and a research associate at the Worldwatch Institute.* Life Out of Bounds: Bioinvasion in a Borderless World *was published by W. W. Norton & Company in October 1998 for the Worldwatch Environmental Alert Series. It can be ordered through the Institute web site, www.worldwatch.org, or by calling (800) 555-2028.*

RECYCLING HUMAN WASTE:

Fertile Ground or Toxic Legacy?

Recycling human waste isn't like recycling newspapers. The use of "night soil" on cropland is ancient, but modern sewage and farming systems have greatly complicated the risks of using our most obvious fertilizer.

by Gary Gardner

In 1997 the U.S. Environmental Protection Agency (EPA) approved a plan that takes sewage recycling to new and bizarre levels. Wastewater from cleanup of the Lowry Landfill near Denver—a Superfund site contaminated with chemicals and heavy metals, including nuclear waste—was to be dumped into local sewers and treated at the local sewage treatment plant. The plant would mix the toxic brew with ordinary sewage, process it, and release the resulting products: water to the South Platte River, and sludge to nearby farms for use as fertilizer. The program was part of the agency's attempt to recycle a greater share of U.S. sludge to "beneficial uses."

The plan, which drew howls of local protest, is an extreme example of a growing trend: the use of human waste to fertilize farms, in spite of unresolved questions about the practice's risks. As greater quantities of human waste are produced, and as traditional dumping areas are placed off-limits or become increasingly costly, policymakers have resorted to this ancient strategy to dispose of the nutrient-rich material. But because modern waste flows are dirtier than those of centuries past, capturing the benefits of reuse with minimal risk is a growing challenge.

The experience of modern sludge reuse has the qualities of a fable, with valuable lessons for the larger question of recycling. Global materials use is far greater than the planet can sustain; Mathis Wackernagel and William Rees of the University of British Columbia have shown that today's economies already consume one third more resources and ecoservices than nature can deliver sustainably. Reducing our "ecological footprint" will therefore require a far greater level of materials *reuse*. But as

recycling moves well beyond newspapers and aluminum cans, it is important to distinguish between beneficial recycling—the return of materials to advantageous and environmentally benign uses—and careless reuse, which is sometimes little more than dumping under a green label. The lessons of this fable are important for industrialized nations active in recycling human waste. They are even more timely for the many developing country cities that are busy planning and designing sanitation systems for the next century.

An Ancient Practice

Recycling human waste has a long and noble history. Chinese agriculture, for example, was sustained for thousands of years by the "night soil" collected from cities and rural villages. In his classic study *Farmers of Forty Centuries*, agricultural historian F.H. King reports that farmers would build roadside outhouses and post advertising to entice travelers to use them, so desired was the excrement as a supplemental source of nutrients and organic matter. The city of Shanghai commonly sold the right to collect the city's night soil for sale in the countryside, a concession that in 1908 brought the equivalent of $31,000 in gold to municipal coffers.

Organic recycling was less common outside of Asia, but eventually became more widely practiced as burgeoning cities scrambled to get rid of their waste. By the mid-nineteenth century, as some European cities passed the one million mark in population, sewage was collected by scavengers and delivered to nearby "sewage farms" for

From *World Watch*, January/February 1998, pp. 28-34. © 1998 by the Worldwatch Institute. Reprinted by permission.

use as fertilizer. The practice soon spread to cities in the United States, Australia, and Mexico. Indeed, by the early twentieth century, with sewers commonly in use in more developed countries, land application of sewage was the sole method of disposal in many metropolitan areas.

In this pre-modern era, and in many developing countries today, the chief health risk from sewage came from its pathogen content. Untreated sewage is alive with bacteria, viruses, and parasites, which can spread to people through water supplies, food fertilized with waste, or direct contact. Open-air sewage flows facilitate the spread of sickness, prompting outbreaks of cholera and other infectious diseases, as occurred in urbanized countries in centuries past, and continues to occur in developing countries today. The spouse of a Worldwatch researcher recalls the terrible choice faced by villagers in her native South Korea in the 1960's: use raw human waste in rice paddies to ensure higher production—but at the cost of widespread sickness, as parasites from feces became intestinal worms in nearly all villagers—or protect the village from the health threat of human waste and accept lower yields. Pathogens are a serious and even deadly threat, but they

are relatively short-lived, eventually breaking down in the soils to which they are applied.

In this century, underground sewers became increasingly common, and some were eventually connected to treatment plants. Used together, the two technologies greatly reduced the pathogen menace. But new contaminants surfaced in many cities. As industries hooked up to public sewers, their waste flows—often containing toxic chemicals and heavy metals—mixed with human waste. Sewage treatment processes, while somewhat effective at killing pathogens, did not eliminate these other contaminants; instead, the pollutants simply accumulated in the sludge. But because most sludge was destined for disposal at a landfill, in an incinerator, or even on the ocean bottom, authorities saw little reason to worry about these substances.

Over the past quarter century, however, several developments have renewed interest in recycling human waste to land. Urban growth and an increasingly sewered population have concentrated more and more human waste in urban areas. Indeed, U.S. sewage sludge has doubled in quantity since 1972, even though population has grown

NEIGHBORHOOD SEWAGE TREATMENT FACILITY

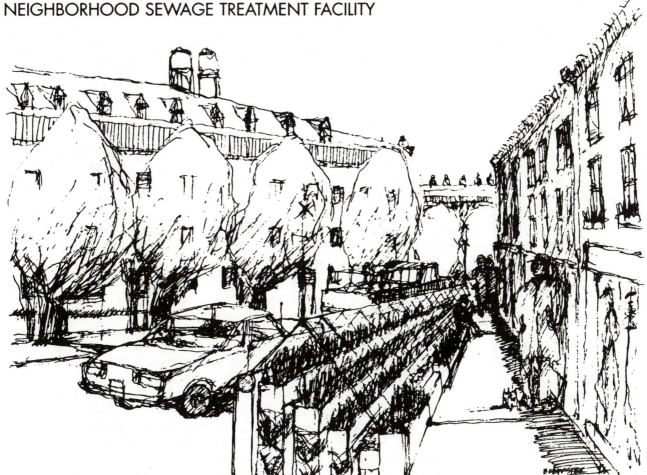

A creative approach to sewage recycling, conceived by Living Technologies of Vermont, would place a small-scale treatment facility right in a neighborhood. Sewage could be treated locally and inexpensively, in a small, contained loop that would produce clean water for use on neighborhood gardens.

by only 25 percent, largely because of the 1972 Clean Water Act, which funded a boom in sewer construction. At the same time, waste disposal sites are less available, or more expensive. Ocean dumping of sewage sludge was outlawed in the United States in 1992, and will be illegal in Europe after 1998. Incineration is costly, and landfills leak greenhouse gases—globally, landfills account for some ten percent of the world's human-origin emissions of methane, an exceptionally potent greenhouse gas.

Meanwhile, many arid nations have begun to tap wastewater for irrigation as they struggle to deal with chronic water scarcity. And the use of manufactured fertilizers—the technology that has largely undercut the prac-

Nearly all of the tens of thousands of chemicals and metals flowing through modern economies—including PCBs, pesticides, dioxins, heavy metals, asbestos, petroleum products and industrial solvents—are potentially a part of sewage flows.

tice of reapplying wastes to soils—has been blamed for a variety of pollution ills, from unhealthy nitrate levels in drinking water to algae blooms that rob fish and other aquatic species of oxygen.

All of these problems are related to the snipping open of the "organic loop," which ended the circular flow of human waste from people to farms, then back to people in the form of food. The natural response to resolving these problems was to re-connect the loop by once again recycling human (and other organic) waste. By the early 1990s, fully a third of the sewage sludge generated in Europe, and more than a quarter of that produced in the United States, was being applied to farmland. And a joint World Bank-U.N. Development Programme study estimated in 1985 that some 80 percent of the wastewater in developing countries was used for permanent or seasonal irrigation. Most of this irrigation flow would have been raw sewage, as even today less than 10 percent of sewered cities in developing countries are connected to treatment plants.

Read the Label

Reconnecting a materials loop can happen in many ways, some more harmful than others. Ideally, recycling would imitate nature's cycling process, which is more efficient and benign than any process created by humans, with all materials productively reused. But recycling can

be difficult in modern industrial economies, which mix materials in combinations and concentrations not normally found in nature. Wood pulp, for example, can be processed into paper using a solution of caustic soda and sodium sulfide, with sulfate remaining in the final paper product. Paper may then be dyed or coated or may have adhesive material attached to it. By the end of its useful life, paper may contain several foreign materials that complicate its return to the soils that nourish tree roots.

Even for simple flows of organic material like that of human waste, industrial economies have complicated the prospects for reuse. On the journey from toilet to treatment plant, excreta mixes with toxic chemicals and heavy metals, which are poured down household drains and leached from household plumbing, or dumped into sewers by industry. Indeed, nearly all of the tens of thousands of chemicals and metals flowing through modern economies—including PCBs, pesticides, dioxins, heavy metals, asbestos, petroleum products and industrial solvents—are potentially a part of sewage flows. Some of these materials degrade quickly with no harm to the environment, while others persist for decades or even centuries; some soils in Italy, for example, still contain lead leached from the pipes of ancient Rome. Natural cycling tends to keep potentially polluting materials spread thin. Human economies, however, often distill and concentrate harmful pollutants in our waste streams. Depending on the levels of concentration, returning these wastes to farmland can be more dangerous than beneficial.

How much waste is too much is hotly debated in industrialized countries, especially the United States. Controversy there centers on rules set down in 1993 by the EPA, known as the "Part 503" sludge standards for their place in the Code of Federal Regulations. Years in the making, and the product of an extensive risk assessment process, the rules are nevertheless criticized by citizens groups and at least one academic institute for being insufficiently cautious. The ongoing debate over the standards highlights several issues that are important for recycling in general.

First, it is crucial to document the levels of potentially harmful extraneous matter in material destined for recycling, and the quantities in which they are present. The average makeup of sewage sludge in the United States is generally known, thanks to a National Sewage Sludge Survey undertaken by the EPA in 1988. But because sludge contents differ from place to place—or even from day to day in the same place—the makeup of a particular batch of land-applied sludge is too often unknown. For example, the survey found toxic chemicals were present at such low levels nationally that the EPA decided not to regulate them. Despite the low national average, high levels of toxic chemicals have been found in the sludge of towns with industries that use those particular chemicals. The 503 rules would not prevent such highly contaminated sludge from being used on cropland.

Nor do the rules set standards for radioactivity, or require testing for it—which explains how nuclear waste-tainted sludge from the Lowry landfill could pass muster for use on cropland. A 1994 report by the U.S. General Accounting Office (GAO) found that between 1983 and 1991, nine cases of radioactive contamination of sewage treatment plants were found—even without a systematic inspection regime in place. Indeed, only 15 of 1100 hospitals, manufacturers, and other sites that discharge radioactive material to sewers had been inspected by the Nuclear Regulatory Commission (NRC), at the time of the GAO report. And of the treatment plants surveyed, most had no idea that radioactive material could be part of their inflow, and did not test for it. Neither the EPA nor the NRC know how much material is thrown into sewers, nor how great a threat this material poses to contamination of sewage sludge.

The EPA is quick to point out that the presence of contaminants in U.S. sewage flows is lower than it was two decades ago, because many industries now "pretreat" their waste to reduce the levels of contaminants that enter sewers. Seven eastern U.S. cities, for example, saw metals contamination of sewage drop by an average 35 percent between 1988 and 1996. And those who dump large amounts of contaminants can likely be identified, according to the EPA, once authorities are alerted to the problem and place monitors in sewers. Nevertheless, the rules would do little to prevent dangerous one-time dumping, or to detect it when it occurs.

Second, it is important to understand the hazards posed by contaminants in recycled material. The EPA asserts that the risk assessment used to develop the 503 rules was sufficiently conservative to protect the public. But Cornell University's Waste Management Institute charges that the assessment was not cautious enough, and that the full effects of sludge on the environment and on humans are not understood. Cornell researcher Murray McBride says that too little is known about the long-term behavior of metals in sludge-applied soils, for example, and that heavy metals could eventually be freed up and absorbed by crops. This "time bomb" theory postulates that as organic matter in sludge breaks down over time, the bonds that keep metals from travelling—either down into groundwater or up into crops—will be weakened. Metals that are largely immobile in the short run, he asserts, could well be found in our food and our drinking water in the long run. Other scientists, including long-time sludge researcher Dr. Rufus Chaney of the U.S. Department of Agriculture, argue that enough long-term studies on sludge have been done to show that no sludge "time bomb" exists. But given the stakes involved—human health and increasingly precious cropland—the burden of proof lies with those who assert that the risk is acceptable.

Likewise, our understanding of the threat posed by toxic chemicals—which are entirely unregulated under 503—is not well understood. Chemicals that persist in the environment, including the pcbs and dioxins found in sewage sludge, are now suspected of mimicking hormones and causing reproductive abnormalities in humans and wildlife, even when their presence is so minute it must be measured in parts per *trillion*. EPA Administrator Carol Browner warned in September 1997 that rising rates of several cancers in children—testicular cancer is up 70 percent in the past two decades—may be connected to the omnipresence of chemicals in the U.S. economy since mid-century. Prudence would counsel against allowing such chemicals to become part of the nation's drinking water or food supply.

Finally, even if all parties were to agree on recycling standards and their coverage, the consensus would mean little if the rules go unenforced. On this question, even many defenders of the 503 regulations acknowledge the need for improvement. The 503 rules were written to be "self-implementing," meaning that treatment plant operators are responsible for testing sludge for regulated pollutants, and farmers keep track of low-grade sludge applications ("high quality" sludge requires no tracking whatsoever). Testing of sludge is required monthly where the largest quantities are produced, and as seldom as once a year for the smallest quantities. Such infrequent monitoring is a poor defense against indiscriminate dumping into sewers. And stored material is not regulated, even though pathogens can re-generate in sludges that are held aside for the winter, or until after a field is harvested.

While the standards and regulations are still hotly debated, and because the stakes are high, caution should be the watchword. Until the risks are better understood, sludge might best be land applied only to non-agricultural land. The material has been successfully used, for example, to "bio-remediate" and restore degraded lands, including Superfund sites and strip-mined areas. It can also be used to green highway meridians and golf courses. Beyond limiting its use, enforcement needs to be stepped up to ensure that today's standards are being honored. And stricter pretreatment programs should be instituted to cover a broader range of polluters, and to enforce a lower level of dumping. The cleaner the sludge, the more likely its organic richness could eventually be applied to cropland.

The Wrong Tool for the Job

Debating acceptable levels of contaminants, however, begs the fundamental question of whether pollutants should be in sludge at all. The question is largely avoided in Europe and the United States—where the focus is on finding acceptable pollution standards—because industrial nations are wedded to technologies designed for *disposal*, rather than *recycling*. On several counts, today's system of flush toilets, sewers, and treatment plants are inferior technologies for recycling human waste.

Sewers, as noted, commonly serve residences and industry together, a practice that often contaminates organic matter with heavy metals or toxic chemicals. While many of these impurities could in theory be removed at the treatment plant, the process would be very expensive. From a recycling perspective, it would be far better to prevent human waste from mixing with other wastes in the first place. Segregation of waste streams could be achieved by using separate sewers for human and other wastes, by treatment of industrial waste at the factory, or by treatment of human waste in residences or office buildings.

In addition, treatment plants are designed to recycle water, but not sludge. Treatment essentially involves removing a concoction of benign elements (organic matter and nutrients) and nasty ones (pathogens, toxic chemicals, and heavy metals) from the water that carries them. The process yields relatively clean (but non-potable) water, and sludge, a muck that is thick with elements removed from the water. Thus, the cleaner the water produced, the dirtier the sludge. As long as sludge was destined for burial or incineration, contaminant levels were ignored. But when applied to land, of course, the pollution content matters a great deal.

Moreover, treatment plants often eliminate some of the material that should be recycled. The digestion process—the "stomach" of a treatment plant where bacteria break down organic matter and kill most pathogens—converts part of the sewage's nitrogen content to a gaseous form, which is then lost to the atmosphere. Nitrogen is the single most important nutrient for plant growth; eliminating any of it makes little sense from a recycling perspective. Indeed, using a digester to recycle sewage is akin to firing up an incinerator to recycle newspapers.

Finally, conventional treatment methods (with the exception of disinfection, a high level of treatment that is unaffordable in many developing countries) reduce pathogens by too little for safe reuse in agriculture. A conventional treatment plant can reduce the number of fecal coliforms in a milliliter of water from 100 million to 1 million, a 99 percent reduction—but not enough for use on crops. For unrestricted irrigation use, the World Health Organization recommends a fecal coliform level a thousand

INSIDE A SOLAR SEWAGE WALL

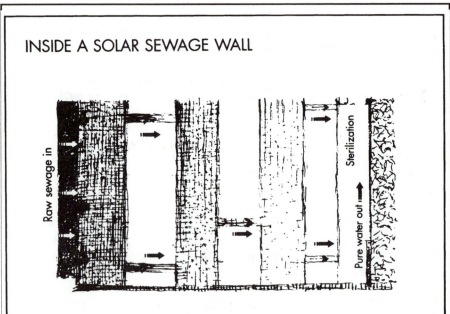

The neighborhood sewage wall, an alternative idea for sewage treatment, would channel sewage through a series of terraced planters that progressively filter and purify the waste. Each terrace would contain the plants and bacteria best suited for the various stages of treatment. The resulting effluent could be used on local gardens, and the plants could be harvested and composted.

ALL ARTICLE ILLUSTRATIONS ARE BY ELISE BREWSTER, FROM *FROM ECO-CITIES TO LIVING MACHINES: PRINCIPALS OF ECO-LOGICAL DESIGN* BY NANCY JACK TODD AND JOHN TODD. © 1994 BY NANCY JACK TODD AND JOHN TODD. USED BY ARRANGEMENT WITH NORTH ATLANTIC BOOKS, BERKELEY, CA.

times lower—no greater than 1,000 per milliliter.

Some technologies modify conventional sewage treatment to produce a product that gets closer to a safe recyclable. One such process is called advance alkaline stabilization, and is used by an Ohio-based company called N-VIRO. The company mixes roughly equal parts of sewage sludge and alkaline material such as cement kiln dust to produce a sludge product called "N-VIRO soil." The alkaline dust raises the pH level, which prevents most of the sludge's metals from leaching or being taken up by plants. In addition, the dust pasteurizes the sludge, killing pathogens so thoroughly that it eliminates the need for digestion. And skipping the nutrient-hungry and methane-belching digestion process yields more recycled material with fewer emissions of greenhouse gases. Moreover, because digestion is typically capital-intensive, its removal makes sewage treatment more affordable. Middlesex County in New Jersey, for example, opted for the N-VIRO process over a conventional plant and saved 2 million dollars annually in operating costs.

While the N-VIRO process aims to reconnect the organic loop safely, it is still used in conjunction with some disposal technologies, such as sewers that mix domestic and industrial wastes. To this degree, "N-VIRO soil" is riskier than waste processed entirely with recycling technologies. The N-VIRO process does not eliminate or neutralize toxic chemicals, for example, and some scientists worry that immobilized metals could be freed in soils with extremely high pH levels, although such conditions are rare. The process is most promising, therefore, where contaminant levels are very low, both in the sludge and in the kiln dust that is mixed with it.

Rethinking Recycling

The emerging recycling lesson is this: the more that reuse of human waste relies on conventional *disposal* technologies, the less likely that such reuse will be benign recycling. This is bad news for cities with heavy investments in disposal systems; they may require extensive adjustments to achieve environmentally benign recycling. It is good news, however, for cities that have not yet committed to a particular system of sanitation, and for cities that face extensive rehabilitation of old systems. These later-developing cities have a chance to "leapfrog" ahead to alternative technologies designed for recycling—and to save scarce investment funds in the process.

Common to many alternative systems is the separation of human waste from other contaminants. One way of doing this is to treat industrial wastes at the source, so that they never enter the public sewer system. To some degree, this is already done at many factories and plants through the "pretreatment" processes that partially remove pollutants from waste flows. But complete treatment is possible as well, as demonstrated through the systems developed by Living Technologies of Vermont. Modeled on nature's cleansing processes, the systems use plants, microorganisms, and fish, in combination with solar energy, to progressively treat industrial wastes in a series of pools and constructed wetlands. The firm has found a robust market for these facilities, with 20 projects built or under construction since 1992 at businesses and institutions as diverse as the M&M/Mars Company in Brazil and Oberlin College in Ohio. The systems require space, of course, which may be in short supply at some facilities. They also need maintenance by a trained technician.

The people at Living Technologies have other plans for waste treatment, including neighborhood-level "sewage walls" that would run the length of a residential block, separating street from sidewalk. (See illustrations.) The wide, low walls slope toward the sidewalk and contain four terraces filled with plants and capped with glass. Wastewater from the street's houses is filtered progressively through the terraces until treated and ready for use on gardens or other areas. Not yet in operation, the design nevertheless offers a vision of how human waste might be recycled cleanly and locally.

Another separation strategy is to treat domestic wastes at the source. Household treatment has the advantage of isolating human waste from home-grown chemicals and metals: detergents, soaps, and cleaning solvents, for example, and copper and other metals that leach from plumbing. Composting toilets are one viable on-site recycling technology. They look like standard flush models (without the water tank, as most use no water) and can hold up to several years' worth of excreta. They require some maintenance, including occasional additions of bulking material such as popcorn (to create the air pockets needed to support microbes) and periodic inspection of the compost itself, but the burden is minimal. These systems create a fertilizing product that can be applied to home gardens or, where economically feasible, collected and sold to farmers. They are not yet widely used in homes because plumbing codes often discriminate against them, and because they are expensive ($1000 to $6000 in the United States). They are also culturally unattractive in many societies accustomed to flush toilets. Still, the municipality of Tanum, Sweden is successfully converting homes to composting technology as part of its bid to become free of flush toilets.

In developing countries, a new and promising option for processing domestic waste is a series of simple technologies developed in Mexico and known collectively by their Spanish acronym, SIRDO. SIRDO systems use "double-vault" waste treatment; one chamber collects current wastes while the other is closed for several months as previously deposited material composts. Solar heating and bacteria transform wastes and other carbon matter into a safe and odorless "biofertilizer" that is sold to nearby farms.

SIRDO technology is used in diverse ways. Some designs are "dry," requiring no water—and no sewage infrastructure—for their operation. Dry units are self-contained structures that are detached from a house and serve one or two families. They compost household organic matter together with human waste, thereby easing pressure on both landfills and sewage treatment plants. "Wet" SIRDO units are neighborhood-level miniplants that biologically process the wastes of up to 1,000 people, operating in conjunction with existing flush toilets and local sewer lines. "Wet" systems separate greywater from solids and percolate it through a bed of sand and gravel until it is purified enough to reuse on gardens, or to irrigate nonfood crops.

These alternative technologies also have substantial side benefits. To the extent that they recycle water, or do not require it, they are especially attractive for arid areas as a source of water savings. Flush toilets have been shown to account for 20–40 percent of the residential water use in industrial countries; the proportion would undoubtedly be higher in developing countries. With the population of "water-stressed" countries expected to more than triple by 2025, any technology that can reduce water demand merits serious consideration.

Moreover, many of these systems require less investment—only one seventh as much, and perhaps substantially less—than is needed for conventional sewer and treatment plant infrastructure. The World Bank estimates that developing countries will need 600 *billion* dollars' worth of water and sewer investments in the coming decades; inexpensive and ecologically sound alternatives could greatly reduce this budgetary burden. The burden might even be avoided entirely, because some of these technologies actually pay for themselves. A cost-benefit analysis of the SIRDO technology undertaken by the U.S.-based National Wildlife Federation (NWF) found that the start-up costs can be recovered within 2 to 20 years, depending on the model, through the sale of the fertilizer they generated. Indeed, fertilizer sales are sufficient to boost incomes as well: families earn some $30 to 60 dollars annually from their toilets, a modest but meaningful income supplement for people living on the economic margin.

A Material World

The appeal of these alternative waste technologies is that they recycle in a regenerative loop as nature does. Natural cycling systems tend to eliminate harmful materials that could pollute their own loops, as a wetland does when it removes nutrients from overenriched waters. Even a conventional engineer, if charged with designing from scratch a recycling system for human waste, would hardly choose to introduce extraneous metals or toxic chemicals to the mix. The verity that "nature knows no waste" is true not only because all materials are recycled, but also because they are cycled usefully.

Nature-centered recycling is a compelling option for the reuse of materials—from human waste to sawdust—as societies struggle to eliminate the flow of resources straight to the dump. The struggle is herculean: the Organisation for Economic Cooperation and Development recently adopted as a long-range goal a ten-fold reduction in materials flows in industrialized countries. This vision will certainly require high rates of recycling, especially for material like human waste for which the "reduce" and "reuse" options (in the troika of "reduce, reuse, recycle") are not viable strategies. As communities choose recycling—and as they choose to make that recycling a clean replica of nature—they will move a large step closer to sustainable management of our planet's resources.

Gary Gardner is a research associate at the Worldwatch Institute. He is the author of Worldwatch Paper 135, Recycling Organic Waste: From Urban Pollutant to Farm Resource.

BY TED WILLIAMS On December 20, 1998, members of the Florida Audubon Society observed 173 species of birds on Lake Apopka, a record for the past 99 years. By March hundreds of fish-eating birds were dying, some convulsing and bleeding from the eyes and beak, symptoms of pesticide poisoning. What no one knew was that for 50 years the lakebed had been distilling a toxic cocktail whose fatal ingredients included DDT.

PHOTOGRAPHY BY ARTHUR MORRIS

[LESSONS FROM LAKE APOPKA]

THE FISH EATERS STARTED DYING EARLY LAST OCTOber—white pelicans, great egrets, great blue herons, ring-billed gulls, wood storks. They were still dying on March 25, when I walked along the dike that separates 13,000 acres of central-Florida farmland from the 31,000-acre Lake Apopka. Already I'd seen two buzzard-picked pelican carcasses and a great blue that hadn't been dead 24 hours. The meat eaters were dying, too. A great horned owl had expired the day before, and a peregrine falcon would go down the following week—ominous signs, because they suggest secondary poisoning from eating dead or moribund birds. Making the die-off all the more poignant was the beauty and fertility of the place. Tree swallows in great, dark clouds swirled over young grass. Yellow-rumped and pal warblers wafted through the lush that line the lake's north shore. Ospreys, clutching pesticide-laced tilapia (invasive fish from Africa), hunched on moss-draped snags. Great blue herons billowed out of irrigation ditches, shaking their tails and tucking in their pterodactyl necks. Northern harriers dipped low over newly fallow fields, wings wobbling in the wind. Coots and common moorhens picked their way over water hyacinths and dollar weed. And in the big canal that collects water from the lake, alligators and Florida red-bellied turtles surveyed me with shrewd, half-closed eyes.

As natural wetlands have been drained and filled, flooded agricultural lands have become increasingly vital to shorebirds as feeding and staging areas. On December 20, 1998, when these fields had been intentionally flooded in winter for the first time, members of the Florida Audubon Society and the Florida Ornithological Society gathered here for the Christmas Bird Count, a nationwide census organized by the National Audubon Society. They observed 173 species, apparently more than had been recorded at any other non-coastal site in the 99 years that these counts have been held. There was even talk of nominating the area as "a site of international significance" (more than 100,000 shorebirds seen

annually). What made the 1998 count even more remarkable, however, was that for the first time ever there were lots of the larger, fish-eating birds, mostly white pelicans.

One of the fish eaters I encountered—a great blue heron—wasn't hunting or even flying. It was just standing bowlegged on the bare dike. I'd been asked by Harold Weatherman—a heavy-equipment operator who works for the local farmers and who somehow wound up in charge of the rescue operation—to bring in any ailing birds I could catch. As I eased toward the heron, it walked toward the canal like an old man with gout. From a distance of three feet I made a lunge for its neck, came up with only a handful of unfurled wing, then fell in the mud. The bird mustered barely enough strength to flap to the other side of the canal. Just as well that it die with dignity.

Rehabilitation hasn't been working. Of the roughly 160 fish-eating birds Weatherman has turned over to the Florida Audubon Society Center for Birds of Prey, all have died, save two white pelicans. "I can still close my eyes and see fields full of pelicans kicking and twitching," he told me. "I felt so sorry for them. Sometimes I'd have one under each arm, and they'd be be dead before I got back to the truck. It was heartbreaking." Later he showed me a video he'd taken of hundreds of pelicans in a ditch, glutting themselves on tilapia. The ditch was so full of birds that hundreds of others had to wait their turn on the adjacent road.

According to the U.S. Fish and Wildlife Service, the birds contain organochlorine pesticides in concentrations that are off the charts—specifically, DDT (and its breakdown product DDE), toxaphene, dieldrin, and chlordane, banned in 1972, 1982, 1987, and 1988 respectively. For example, one great blue heron's fatty tissue had 23,041 parts per million of DDE alone. That's *2.3 percent*. Because shorebirds are lower on the food chain, feeding on organisms that collect far fewer pesticides than fish, they haven't been dying.

From *Audubon*, July/August 1999, pp. 64-72. © 1999 by Ted Williams. Reprinted by permission.

Many of the herons and pelicans Weatherman picked up were convulsing and bleeding from the eyes and beak, symptoms of organochlorine poisoning. Was someone still using these poisons? Was there an illegal dump that no one knew about? Almost everyone I talked to, including the Florida Audubon Society's chief ornithologist, Gian Basili, said they couldn't imagine how there could suddenly be enough residual pesticides in the soil to kill all these birds. "Two thousand acres of farm fields were flooded every summer and fall for the past 50 years, and although birds and birders flocked to the area for 40 years, no one ever reported any significant bird mortality," said Basili.

At this writing the body count stands at more than 1,200 (about half picked up on-site)—mostly white pelicans but including at least 47 wood storks, an endangered species. That's probably a tiny fraction of the actual death toll, because most poisoned birds are never found. (In an exercise I participated in three years ago at the Patuxent Wildlife Research Center, in Laurel, Maryland, Fish and Wildlife Service instructors scattered 100 bird carcasses over six acres of closely mown field. Three days later—because of scavenging by birds and mammals and because dead birds are just hard to see—15 searchers could find only 11.)

A scarlet sun was sinking into Lake Apopka when I spotted three human figures backlit on the dike. They were the criminal-investigation team from the Fish and Wildlife Service—special agents Frank Kuncir, Bruce Corley, and Jack Baker. Kuncir, who was in charge of the operation, had hovered a Bell Jet Ranger helicopter over what he estimated to be 1,500 wood storks (about 14 percent of the US nesting population) and 6,000 white pelicans (about half of those that winter in Florida). "They didn't even flush," he told me. "Later, I walked right up to them and tapped them on the beaks."

"What's going to happen to them?" I asked.

"They're going to die," he said. "Dead pelicans have been showing up as far away as Mississippi and Louisiana. This didn't have to happen. It's the worse human-caused disaster affecting migratory birds and endangered species that I've seen in 27 years of wildlife law enforcement."

Worried about possible human exposure, Kuncir had pulled his people off the fields four days earlier. But the Mexican farmworkers, many unemployed because the farms are out of production, show no such concern—even though the fields have been posted, gated, and plastered with signs that read, in Spanish and English, "WARNING: THE FISH IN THIS CANAL MAY BE CONTAMINATED. DO NOT HANDLE OR EAT." The workers, many with large families, keep sneaking in to catch the superabundant tilapia. On the morning of March 26, Weatherman found a throw net in a canal, apparently abandoned the night before by someone we had scared off. Special Agent Corley, who wanted fish for pesticide sampling, asked Weatherman to net some. With one throw he caught so many he couldn't lift the net.

Speaking of the danger more eloquently than any warning sign was a sick great blue heron not 10 feet from the throw net. Weatherman stood across the canal from me, toting a long fiberglass pole with a wide-strap noose at the end. "Can you see that bird?" he called. When I directed him to the cutbank under which the heron was hiding, he slipped the noose over its neck, then hauled it squawking and flapping to high ground.

STIR UP LAKE APOPKA WITH AN OUTBOARD MOTOR, and the methane from the bottom sludge can get so strong you need a surgical mask to breathe. A generation ago the lake was sweet and clear, offering what some said was the best bass fishing on the planet. It supported 29 fishing camps and attracted anglers from all over the world.

But, in 1941, came the beginning of the end. For the war effort the Florida Legislature created the Zellwood Drainage and Water Control District, by which vegetable farmers could dike off and drain the part of the lake that was saw grass marshland, and which acted as its kidneys. This process shrank the lake from 50,000 to 31,000 acres. Now instead of saw grass Lake Apopka grew sweet corn, carrots, lettuce, radishes, celery, and parsley. The thick, peaty soil of the resulting "muck" farms, as

JOHN PEMBERTON/*THE FLORIDA TIMES-UNION*

they came to be called, was some of the most fertile in the world, often allowing three crops a year. When exposed to air, the soil decayed, releasing enormous amounts of phosphorus. To this organic broth, on advice of the fertilizer industry, the farms added even more phosphorus in commercial concoctions. For half a century they blitzed the former lakebed with fertilizers and pesticides, irrigating with lake water, flooding in summer for weed and nematode control, and continually pumping polluted water back into Lake Apopka. Further fouling the lake was orange pulp from the citrus industry and sewage from the city of Winter Garden, both on the south shore.

The guru of American sweet-corn growers—veteran muck farmer and crop duster Carroll Potter, not yet retired at 83—explained to me that he'd finally figured out by trial and error that the fertilizer companies had been full of, well, their own product, and that the soil didn't need manmade phosphorus. It did need pesticides, though, he allowed. When organochlorines were legal he used all the ones recommended by the experts, especially DDT. But he said he couldn't imagine how there could be enough residual pesticides in the soil to kill this many birds. It had been difficult for me to imagine, too. But as he talked it got easier.

Potter recounted how the superfertile bottom of Lake Apopka had become the sweet-corn capital of the world. When his friend Pearl Stutzman first planted sweet corn here, in 1946, his neighbors told him you couldn't grow it in Florida because the corn earworms and fall armyworms would "eat it up." When Stutzman started dusting every three days with DDT, they told him there was no way you could put that much pesticide on any crop and make a profit. But 75 percent of his ears turned out to be worm free, and when he sent them to New York City, he got $5.75 a crate. "That was unheard of," said Potter. "When Stutzman dusted every other day he got 85 percent control. Finally, he dusted every day and got 98 percent. Didn't even have to grade it. Pretty soon everyone had a patch of sweet corn." Potter is the only original muck farmer who still drives a tractor and the only original crop duster who can still pass a flight test. "It was all the DDT I inhaled when I was young that makes me healthy," he told me. "I believe it. Yes, sir."

The pesticides had never caused any major bird kills in Lake Apopka. But the massive loads of phosphorus from the decaying soil and commercial fertilizers nourished carpets of alien water hyacinths that inconvenienced the fishing camps. At their request, the US Army Corps of Engineers clicked the nutrient-recycling process into fast-forward by spraying the plants with herbicide, causing them to rot and release the phosphors they'd taken up from the polluted water. Suddenly free of shade, and with even more phosphorus available, algae took over. This, in turn, set off an explosion of algae-eating gizzard shad, which the state attempted to control with poison. But instead of removing the dead fish, it left 30 million pounds of them to fester in the lake, fur-

The recipe for death began in the 1940s, when "muck" farmers reclaimed parts of the lakebed and doused crops with DDT. Contaminated runoff collected in irrigation ditches, where it was metabolized by tilapia, an invasive fish. The muck (bottom) released huge doses of phosphorus, some of which was later removed by applying alum (in vats). Not until fish-eating birds migrated here last fall and began dying did Harold Weatherman (opposite) and others realize how toxic the tilapia had become.

ther speeding nutrient recycling. In the 1970s the Clean Water Act shut down the flow of sewage and orange pulp, but agriculture, designated a "non-point source," was exempt. Muck-farm waste increased until, by the late 1980s, 5 million gallons of effluent were being pumped from the fields into the lake every day.

In 1985 the Florida Legislature created the Lake Apopka Restoration Council, which experimented with nutrient removal by planting water hyacinths—letting them take up phosphorus and then removing them—and by netting out gizzard shad, each of which is almost 1 percent phosphorus. It also ordered a state agency called the St. Johns River Water Management District to develop a plan to restore the lake. Two years later the legislature directed St. Johns to finish the council's work. Hyacinth planting and removal proved inefficient, but shad netting showed promise. Today the St. Johns district pays commercial fishermen about $250,000 to remove 2 million pounds of shad a year.

Naturally, it made no sense to be hauling out nutrients while the muck farmers were pumping them back in. So in 1988 the water-management district asked the farmers to put in settling ponds. One muck farm operation, A. Duda & Sons, complied voluntarily, spending more than $2 million to make ponds on 350 of its acres and reducing its phosphorus discharge by roughly 75 percent. But the 12 farms that made up the 9,000-acre Zellwood district came up with all sorts of reasons why cleanup couldn't be done, even though the state and the St. Johns district were going to foot two-thirds of the bill. When St. Johns ordered the cleanup, Zellwood hired lawyers, and in 1995 it got the effluent standards overturned on the technicality that St. Johns lacked authority to give such orders. Subsequently, Florida lawmakers granted that authority. They also appropriated funds for St. Johns to buy out the muck farmers and restore the land to lake and marsh. The state could have used eminent domain, but these days government seizure of family farms doesn't pay well in court or in the press. So the farmers got fair market value—$91 million for 12,500 of the 13,000 acres and all their equipment, $18.5 million of it from the US Department of Agriculture's Wetland Reserve Program. The St. Johns district hopes to acquire the remaining 500 acres for $11 million.

As part of its wetland-restoration effort, St. Johns flooded 5,000 acres of the Zellwood district last summer and fall. So, for the first time ever, water remained on the fields last winter, attracting the migratory white pelicans that spend the cold months in Florida. Most likely that's why no one had seen dead fish-eating birds before. A risk assessment, commissioned by St. Johns before the land was flooded, had found some danger to birds, but only a chronic threat to the viability of eggs. This, the agency concluded, was outweighed by the long-term benefits to wildlife of wetland restoration—and it thought it had dealt with the threat of direct mortality by identifying such hot spots as pesticide storage and loading areas and making the muck farmers clean them up as a condition of sale. Project manager David Stites claims his agency had no way of predicting the bird kill, and he's probably right.

ON THE OTHER HAND, THERE HAD BEEN A FEW HINTS. For example, in the mid-1980s the lake's alligator population had crashed. Only 4 percent of the eggs were hatching, as opposed to 75 to 90 percent in healthy lakes. The few alligators that did hatch had malformed reproductive organs and gross hormonal imbalances. Researchers at the University of Florida suspected endocrine disruption by organochlorine pesticides, especially after high levels of DDT and DDE turned up in alligator tissue. When the researchers painted these poisons on healthy alligator eggs, they replicated the hatching failure and deformities.

And in 1992 and 1994, St. Johns flooded muck farms around Lake Griffin, into which Apopka—one source of the north-flowing St. Johns River—eventually discharges. Hatch rates of alligator eggs then dropped to 4 percent, and largemouth bass became sterile.

To review its risk assessment for the current wetland restoration around Lake Apopka, the state had hired Tim Gross, a toxics expert with the University of Florida, who had been studying reproductive failure of fish and alligators in Lake Griffin. "There's no hurry to restore the wetlands. Just stop farming, let plants grow, flood the land gradually," said Gross. "How they [St. Johns] screwed up is that they did not monitor what was going on."

Says Stites, "We had intended to monitor for risk. But things kind of got ahead of us. We needed the farmers to leave their land in a clean condition, not covered with weeds, so we had them flood their fields. We had intended to draw the water back down, but one thing led to another—and then the birds started dying."

Six months before the die-off, St. Johns's own biologist, Roxanne Conrow, had issued this warning: "While the muck farm areas around Lake Apopka may be a convenient site to view a variety of wintering shorebirds, this birding enthusiasm [for flooding] should be tempered with the knowledge that year-round use of pesticides on these sites may have a very negative impact on many varieties of birds. . . . Restoration of those sites will no doubt result in a dramatic change in the species and numbers of birds using the area. We likely will see an increase in birds adapted to deeper marsh habitats . . . such as the American white pelican."

But the state had been under pressure to show taxpayers something for their $91 million investment. Even the Florida Audubon Society had urged that the fields be flooded in 1999. In a report published two weeks before the birds started dying, the society had downplayed the residual-pesticide danger and criticized Conrow for presenting "no data or references to support these statements." Commented Florida Audubon's Basili, "The data we had did not suggest grave risk to birds, but now we know otherwise."

Less understandable than this kind of public impatience and government acquiescence is the fact that no state or federal agency is managing the site to minimize exposure of fish-eating birds that are still drawn to ditches rippling with toxic tilapia. With water always seeping into the ditches, they can't be completely drained, but why have they been allowed to serve as feeding stations for wading birds for more than half a year?

A S I WANDERED THROUGH THE ZELLWOOD DISTRICT, watching all the birds and wondering which were going to die or produce nonviable eggs, I contemplated the different ways we attempt to remediate pollution. When industry makes a mess, we call in the Superfund cops, take away the land, and make industry pay for the cleanup; when agriculture makes a mess, we call in the appraisers, pay fair market value for the land, and clean up after the farmers.

"We did everything the way the people who manufactured the pesticides recommended," says lifelong Zellwood muck farmer Jan Potter, Carroll's son. "We should not be held liable. It was the manufacturers; it was the government." Maybe so. And yet there's no denying that the muck farmers have done pretty well for themselves. First they were allowed to drain the public's marshland, thereby reducing Florida's second biggest lake to its fourth. Then their farming practices destroyed the rest of the lake and poisoned its former bottom. Last year, having profited from the public's lakebed for more than 50 years, they sold it to the public at the appraised value of pristine farmland. When St. Johns required them to clean up their pesticide hot spots as a condition of sale, they set a limit on how much they'd spend—usually 5 percent of the purchase price. And now St. Johns is building a 3,500-acre marsh "flow-away"—an artificial kidney to replace the one the farmers destroyed—that will clean up the lake the farmers polluted. Lake water will be pumped through the marsh, where algae and sediments will settle out, then discharged back into the lake. That has already cost the public $20 million, and it will cost $10 to $14 million more.

It's easy to learn the wrong lessons from all this. *The Orlando Sentinel*, for example, has tirelessly editorialized against public purchase of the muck-farms—even the 500 acres that remain—calling it a "polluters' relief bill." It certainly is, but the newspaper's claim that the purchase was ill-advised does not follow. Real restoration of Lake Apopka couldn't happen when the muck farmers were polluting it. And even if it were possible, making them clean up would have cost more in legal fees than the buyout. "Bite the bullet; pay for it; fix it," advises Jim Swann, who just stepped down from the St. Johns board after serving 10 years. "You don't make agriculture do anything. You pay for doing it for them. It is their congressionally given right to do wrong."

Now that the public owns its lakebed again, Apopka's kidneys can be regenerated. Perhaps St. Johns will have to encourage vegetation unattractive to fish-eating birds—cattails, for instance. Perhaps, for the safety of shore-birds, America's prime inland shorebird-watching site will have to be deepened and thereby done away with. As hard as the folding of the muck farms has been and will be on wildlife, my conversations with Stites and his colleagues gave me the impression that water managers and wetland restorers have learned some important lessons.

Yet if the public learns the wrong lesson—that state and federal farmland-to-wetland programs are bad deals for taxpayers and wildlife—the tragedy of Lake Apopka will have only just started. Agencies like St. Johns cannot wait to acquire land until scientists say they've studied potential problems "sufficiently," because such studies never end. Research can come later—though before flooding.

On my last day in Florida I found myself standing with Dave Stites beside the nascent marsh flow-away. There was less wildlife here, just a few redwings riding cattails and shouting into the wind, and anhingas and cormorants, black wings open, standing like priests on the banks of the canal that carries Apopka's vile water to Lake Griffin and the St. Johns River. To our right were hills of bulldozed, sun-cracked peat and the new pipes that would move water through the flowway. When the system is completed in 2005, the lake's entire water volume will get filtered twice a year. Barring loss of political will, the children of today's grade-schoolers will be swimming and catching trophy bass in Lake Apopka.

Stites and his outfit may have called some important shots wrong, but I had a hunch he was right about one thing. "This bird die-off," he said, "is a bump in the road, not the end of the road."

In the mid-1980s, alligators in Lake Apopka began to show gross deformities, and their hatch rates crashed. Researchers suspected endocrine disruption caused by pesticides.

Ted Williams vows to catch a 10-pound bass in Lake Apopka.

EARTH'S LAST GASP?

" . . . Entrenched special interests, such as the coal and oil industries, can be expected to use every tool at their disposal to fight sensible climate policies, regardless of the broad-scale benefits for the economy and the environment."

by Daniel A. Lashof

WHEN COAL, oil, and natural gas are burned to generate electricity, drive automobiles, run factories, and heat homes, the atmosphere is polluted with carbon dioxide, a gas that traps heat like the glass panes of a greenhouse. Scientists have been observing the buildup of carbon dioxide and other so-called greenhouse gases in the atmosphere for decades with increasing interest and concern. Yet, the problem of human-induced global climate change, or global warming, didn't emerge onto the public agenda until 1988, when a string of unusually hot weather, coupled with the Congressional testimony of NASA scientist Jim Hansen proclaiming a "high degree of confidence" that humans already were changing the Earth's climate, garnered headlines around the country.

During the following four years, a string of record temperatures and high-profile reports kept global warming in the headlines. This intense period of publicity and diplomatic activity culminated in the Earth Summit at Rio de Janeiro in June, 1992, where 150 nations signed the Rio Climate Treaty, committing themselves to preventing "dangerous" interference with the climate system.

A combination of factors conspired to move global warming off the front pages following the Earth Summit. Media coverage and Congressional concern seem to be driven more by how hot it was last summer in the eastern U.S. (less than one percent of the planet's surface) than by long-term global warming trends and considered scientific

Dr. Lashof is a senior scientist specializing in climate change, Natural Resources Defense Council, Washington, D.C.

opinion. When particles injected into the stratosphere by the Mt. Pinatubo volcanic eruption in the Philippines in June, 1991, temporarily cooled global temperatures by about 0.5°C, this apparently took the heat off policymakers as well.

Recently, though, the climate issue has made a comeback. By the end of 1994, the Pinatubo plume almost completely had settled, and global temperatures returned to record levels in 1995, just as climate models had predicted at the time of the eruption. Meanwhile, an international panel involving around 2,500 scientists from 130 countries quietly had been preparing an updated assessment of climate change. When the Intergovernmental Panel on Climate Change (IPCC) adopted its final report in the fall of 1995, it made headlines around the world for the conclusion that "the balance of evidence suggests a discernible human influence on global climate." Thus, the consensus of the international scientific community confirms Hansen's testimony, which had helped to launch climate change as a public issue seven years earlier. The panel report also included the following:

Rapid climate change. The average rate of warming over the next century probably will be greater than any seen in the last 10,000 years if global warming pollution is not controlled. Extrapolating from a wide range of scenarios for future pollutant emissions and the scientists' range of uncertainty about how the climate will respond to a given change in greenhouse gas concentrations, global mean temperature is projected to rise by 1.8 to 6.3°F between 1990 and 2100.

Death and disease. More than 500 deaths were caused by an intense heat wave that struck the midwestern U.S. in the summer of 1995. Although it is not possible to attribute this (or any other) particular event to global climate change, that is the type of event projected to become more frequent due to global warming. A study of Dallas, Tex., by researchers at the University of Delaware projects that the number of heat-related deaths would rise from an average of 20 per year currently to 620–1,360 per year in the middle of the next century. More outbreaks of infectious diseases, such as malaria and dengue fever, are foreseen as well. A Dutch study estimates that, by the middle of the 21st century, climate change could induce more than 1,000,000 additional malaria deaths per year.

Battered coasts. Global sea levels are expected to rise by one and a half feet during the next century. This will erode beaches, wipe out many wetlands, and allow storm surges to penetrate farther inland. In cities such as New Orleans, La., and Galveston, Tex., an increase in sea level will mean shoring up seawalls and dikes in order to prevent flooding. In many areas, protection will not be practical and retreat from the shoreline will be the only viable option.

Floods and droughts. As a result of global warming, more precipitation would come from intense storms and less from gentle drizzles, increasing the risk of storm damage and flooding. At the same time, warmer temperatures would reduce the amount of water stored in mountain snowpacks and dry soils more rapidly, making drought more likely, especially in the mountain West and mid-continental areas.

From *USA Today Magazine*, May 1997, pp. 50-53. © 1997 by the Society for the Advancement of Education. Reprinted by permission.

Insurance crisis. The string of hurricanes, storms, and floods over the last few years has caused billions of dollars in property damage, depleting insurance industry reserves and threatening major companies with bankruptcy. Before 1980, there had been no individual events that caused insured losses over $1,000,000,000; since then, there have been more than a dozen weather-induced billion-dollar catastrophes. Although burgeoning property values in vulnerable areas are a major factor in the heightened losses, claims have risen as a percentage of insured values. There is great concern in the insurance industry that the frequency of extreme weather events could be increasing. Hurricane Andrew, with $20,000,000,000 in insured losses, combined with other recent catastrophes to put nine U.S. insurance companies out of business. It easily could have been much worse—had Andrew struck just 20 miles to the north, damages would have been $75,000,000,000. The insurance industry has taken note of these risks and is beginning to call for pollution cuts.

Ecological havoc. The ecological implications of climate change will be more subtle than a hurricane, but may be no less significant. According to the World Wildlife Fund, numerous endangered species currently confined to reserves or small pockets of intact habitat could be pushed over the edge to extinctions as suitable climate zones shift out from under protected areas. Migration of alpine species upslope has been reported, and some of these species soon could be pushed off mountaintops. Widespread forest dieback—a condition in woody plants whereby peripheral parts are killed—could occur as projected rates of global warming shift climate zones toward the poles as much as 10 times faster than trees can disperse. In the ocean, measurements of zooplankton abundance off the coast of California show an 80% decline over the last 40 years associated with warmer surface water temperatures and reduced transport of nutrients from deeper layers of the ocean.

None of this is to suggest that the exact consequences of unabated climate change can be predicted. Nor would it be responsible to assert that the Chicago heat wave, Texas drought, Alaska forest fires, or any other individual extreme event definitely could be the result of greenhouse gas emissions. Nevertheless, the dimensions of the global warming threat are clear, and it would be equally irresponsible to ignore the risk that there is a connection. While we can hope that the climate problem turns out to be less severe than current projections indicate, if we choose not to respond, it is equally likely that things will be worse.

Stabilizing concentrations

In principle, at least, the world has agreed that an indefinite buildup of greenhouse gases in the atmosphere poses unacceptable risks and that action must be taken to stabilize the concentrations of these gases at a "safe" level. Nevertheless, governments have not yet come to terms with what actually must be done to achieve the laudable goals of the Rio Climate Treaty. Under the terms of that agreement, industrialized nations were supposed to have established national plans designed to reduce their emissions to 1990 levels by the year 2000. While most of these countries have complied with their procedural obligations by writing plans, few of those schemes appear likely to achieve the agreed pollution reduction target.

Furthermore, even if industrialized country pollution emissions were stabilized at current levels, this would not stabilize greenhouse gas concentrations. Because excess CO_2 remains in the atmosphere for decades to centuries before it is removed into the deep ocean, the atmosphere will continue to accumulate carbon until global emissions are cut substantially. Parties to the treaty recognized this, again in principle, when they agreed in a 1995 conference in Berlin to negotiate legally binding emission reduction targets for the period beyond the year 2000.

The next step in these negotiations should be for governments to use the results of the science panel report to conclude formally that allowing the concentration of greenhouse gases to reach the equivalent of twice pre-industrial carbon dioxide levels would be dangerous and must be avoided under the terms of the Rio Climate Treaty. An appropriate long-term goal would be to stabilize greenhouse concentrations below the equivalent of 450 parts per million by volume (ppmv) of carbon dioxide. (Pre-industrial CO_2 concentrations were 280 ppmv; current CO_2 concentrations are 360 ppmv; and CO_2-equiv-alent greenhouse gas concentrations are about 420 ppmv.) This long-term science-based objective should be used to set shorter-term emission reduction obligations through the protocol that is being negotiated.

Options under consideration range from voluntary targets to a binding emission reduction of 20% below 1990 levels by 2005 for industrialized countries. The disappointing results of the voluntary target adopted at Rio should make it clear that this approach is unacceptable—it merely will perpetuate the situation, in which most governments use inaction in other countries as an excuse to delay action at home. Similarly, merely stabilizing emissions at 1990 levels, a widely discussed approach, would not begin to put the world on a path to stabilizing concentrations at a safe level. Only industrialized country emission reductions on the order of 20% over the next 10–15 years, as has been proposed by Germany and the Alliance of Small Island States, would keep global emissions within a "safe landing corridor," leading to stabilization of greenhouse gas concentrations at a level well below an equivalent doubling of CO_2.

Ultimately, global emission reductions will be needed, based on an enforceable system of emission allowances assigned to each country. Before such a global regime can be contemplated, though, industrialized countries, and in particular the U.S., as the world's richest nation and largest polluter, must provide political and technological leadership. This will require more than good speeches; it will necessitate action that genuinely reduces U.S. greenhouse gas pollution.

Coal and oil interests are quick to argue that such pollution reductions seriously would damage the U.S. economy. Still, the U.S. could cut greenhouse gas pollution to 20% below 1990 levels by 2010 while increasing long-run economic growth, according to a preliminary government analysis presented at a workshop hosted by five Federal agencies. While the U.S. has not endorsed any specific targets and timetables for greenhouse gas pollution after the year 2000, this and other analyses presented at the workshop show that the barriers to substantial emission reductions are political, not economic.

Even the generally favorable results obtained in recent economic modeling exercises are likely to overestimate short-run adjustment costs. Industry and government consistently have overestimated the cost and underestimated the feasibility of pollution reductions. Macroeconomic models fail to account for the potential of dynamic technological, institutional, and organizational change to achieve emission reductions at dramatically lower costs or a net profit.

For example, in 1989, industry estimated that it would run $1,500 per ton to reduce sulfur dioxide emissions, but emission allowances are trading for about 20 times less (well under $100 per ton, including futures contracts out to 2003). An analysis presented by John Hoffman of the Environmental Protection Agency found that dramatic technological and organizational innovations are possible that could reduce U.S. emissions to 20% below 1990 levels by 2010 at a net profit, even without considering the macroeconomic benefits of using emission allowance auction revenues to reduce taxes. Similar results, based on regional or sectoral studies, have been obtained by many other analysts.

Benefits

Action to cut greenhouse gas emissions will have additional benefits as well. Consider electric power plants and automobiles, for instance. These two sources alone are responsible for more than half of U.S. carbon dioxide emissions and are expected to account for about three-quarters of the emission increases in the absence of new policies.

Any strategy for cutting U.S. greenhouse gas emissions will result by necessity in reduced consumption of coal and oil by power plants and cars. This, in turn, will reduce local and regional air pollution, as well as Americans' economically damaging dependence on imported oil.

Power plants are responsible for 70% of sulfur oxide emissions, 33% of nitrogen oxides, and 23% of mercury emissions. Coal-fired power plants are the largest single source of fine particles that have been shown to be responsible for tens of thousands of premature cardiopulmonary deaths in U.S. cities. Thus, reducing demand for electricity by using it more efficiently—replacing resistance heating with ground-source heat pumps that are more than three times as efficient, for example—and substituting cleaner fuels, such as natural gas and renewable energy sources, will reduce acid rain, smog, fine particle concentrations, and toxic loadings while cutting carbon dioxide emissions. The Natural Resources Defense Council has employed advanced technology and design concepts to create lighting systems in its offices that provide enhanced visual performance while cutting electricity requirements by 75%.

Similarly, automobiles are responsible for 22% of nitrogen oxide emissions and 27% of volatile organic compound emissions, and are the driving force behind our growing dependence on imported oil. The U.S. Energy Information Administration projects net oil imports will rise from 45% of domestic consumption in 1995 to 58% in 2005. Americans' import dependence already is higher than it was in 1973 and 1979, when OPEC price increases were a major factor in pushing the U.S. economy into a recession.

A study by the Oak Ridge National Laboratory shows that, by 2005, OPEC will reach the same market share with which it triggered the two previous oil price spikes. The report notes that a profit-maximizing OPEC would raise oil prices about threefold for as long as it could maintain them—about two years. Over this period, it would have extracted $500,000,000,000—$2,000 for every man, woman, and child—from the American economy. Thus, reducing oil consumption by making cars that go farther on each gallon of gasoline will have enormous economic as well as environmental benefits.

The economic good news, however, should not be read to imply that reducing emissions will be easy. Institutional and organizational change always is hard, even when it has clear long-term benefits. The political task of enacting emission reductions remains enormous, as entrenched special interests, such as the coal and oil industries, can be expected to use every tool at their disposal to fight sensible climate policies, regardless of the broad-scale benefits for the economy and the environment.

ON FINDING OUT MORE

There is probably more printed information on environmental issues, regulations, and concerns than on any other major topic. So much is available from such a wide and diverse group of sources, that the first effort at finding information seems an intimidating and even impossible task. Attempting to ferret out what agencies are responsible for what concerns, what organizations to contact for specific environmental information, and who is in charge of what becomes increasingly more difficult.

To list all of the governmental agencies private and public organizations, and journals devoted primarily to environmental issues is, of course, beyond the scope of this current volume. However, we feel that a short primer on environmental information retrieval should be included in order to serve as a springboard for further involvement; for it is through informed involvement that issues, such as those presented, will eventually be corrected.

I. SELECTED OFFICES WITHIN FEDERAL AGENCIES AND FEDERAL-STATE AGENCIES FOR ENVIRONMENTAL INFORMATION RETRIEVAL

Appalachian Regional Commission
1666 Connecticut Avenue, NW, Washington, DC 20235 (202) 884-7799 *http://www.arc.gov*

Council on Environmental Quality
Old Executive Office Bldg., Room 360, Washington, DC 20502 (202) 456-6224
http://www.whitehouse.gov/CEQ/

Delaware River Basin Commission
P.O. Box 7360, West Trenton, NJ 08628-0360 (609) 883-9500 *http://www.state.nj.us/drbc/drbc.htm*

Department of Agriculture
14th and Independence Avenue, SW, Washington, DC 20250 (202) 720-2791 *http://www.usda.gov*

Department of the Army (Corps of Engineers)
20 Massachusetts Ave., NW, Washington, DC 20314-1000 (202) 761-0660 *http://www.usace.army.mil*

Department of Commerce
14th and Constitution Ave. NW, Washington, DC 20230 (202) 482-2000 *http://www.doc.gov*

Department of Defense
Public Affairs, 1400 Defense Pentagon, Room 1E757, Washington, DC 20301-1400 (703) 697-5737
http://www.defenselink.mil/index.html

Department of Health and Human Services
200 Independence Avenue, SW, Washington, DC 20201 (202) 619-0257 *http://www.os.dhhs.gov*

Department of the Interior
1849 C Street, NW, Washington, DC 20240-0001 (202) 208-3100 *http://www.doi.gov*
- Bureau of Indian Affairs (202) 208-3711
- Bureau of Land Management (202) 452-5125
- National Park Service (202) 208-6843
- United States Fish and Wildlife Service (202) 208-4131

Department of State, Bureau of Oceans and International Environmental and Scientific Affairs
2201 C Street, NW, Washington, DC 20520 (202) 647-2492
http://www.state.gov/www/global/oes/index.html

Department of the Treasury, U.S. Customs Service
1300 Pennsylvania Avenue, NW, Washington, DC 20229 (202) 927-1000 *http://www.customs.ustreas.gov*

Environmental Protection Agency (EPA)
401 M Street, SW, Washington, DC 20460 (202) 260-2090
- Region 1, One Congress Street, John F. Kennedy Building, 11th Floor, Boston, MA 02203-0001 (617) 565-3420 (888) 373-7341 http://www.epa.gov/region01/ (Connecticut, Maine, Massachusetts, New Hampshire, Rhode Island, Vermont)
- Region 2, 290 Broadway, New York, NY 10007-1866 (212) 637-3000 http://www.epa.gov/region02/ (New Jersey, New York, Puerto Rico, Virgin Islands)
- Region 3, 1650 Arch Street, Philadelphia, PA 19100-2029 (215) 814-5000 (800) 438-2474 http://www.epa.gov/region03/ (Delaware, District of Columbia, Maryland, Pennsylvania, Virginia, West Virginia)
- Region 4, 4 Forsyth Street, SW, Atlanta, GA 30303-3104 (404) 562-9900 http://www.epa.gov/region04/ (Alabama, Florida, Georgia, Kentucky, Mississippi, North Carolina, South Carolina, Tennessee)
- Region 5, 77 West Jackson Blvd., Chicago, IL 60604-3507 (312) 353-2000 http://www.epa.gov/region5/ (Illinois, Indiana, Michigan, Minnesota, Ohio, Wisconsin)
- Region 6, 1445 Ross Avenue, Suite 1200, Dallas, TX 75202 (214) 665-2200 (800) 887-6063 http://www.epa.gov/region06/ (Arkansas, Louisiana, New Mexico, Oklahoma, Texas)
- Region 7, 726 Minnesota Avenue, Kansas City, KS 66101 (913) 551-7003 (800) 223-0425 http://www.epa.gov/region07/ (Iowa, Kansas, Missouri, Nebraska)
- Region 8, 999 18th Street, Suite 500, Denver, CO 80202-2466 (303) 312-6312 (800) 227-8917 http://www.epa.gov/region08/ (Colorado, Montana, North Dakota, South Dakota, Utah, Wyoming)
- Region 9, 75 Hawthorne Street, San Francisco, CA 94105 (415) 744-1500 http://www.epa.gov/region09/ (Arizona, California, Hawaii, Nevada, American Samoa, Guam, Trust Territories of Pacific Islands, Wake Island)
- Region 10, 1200 Sixth Avenue, Seattle, WA 98101 (206) 553-1200 (800) 424-4372 http://www.epa.gov/region10/ (Alaska, Idaho, Oregon, Washington)

Federal Energy Regulatory Commission
825 North Capitol Street, NE, Washington, DC 20426 (202) 208-0000 *http://www.ferc.fed.us*

Interstate Commission on Potomac River Basin
6110 Executive Boulevard, Suite 300, Rockville, MD 20852-3903 (301) 984-1908
http://www.potomacriver.org

Nuclear Regulatory Commission
One White Flint North, 11555 Rockville Pike, Rockville, MD 20852-2738 (301) 415-7000 *http://www.nrc.gov*

Susquehanna River Basin Commission
1721 North Front Street, Harrisburg, PA 17102 (717) 238-0422 *http://www.srbc.net*

Tennessee Valley Authority
400 West Summit Hill Drive, Knoxville, TN 37902 (423) 632-2101 *http://www.tva.gov*

II. SELECTED STATE, TERRITORIAL, AND CITIZENS' ORGANIZATIONS FOR ENVIRONMENTAL INFORMATION RETRIEVAL

A. *Government Agencies*

Alabama:
Department of Conservation and Natural Resources, P.O. Box 301450, Montgomery, AL 36130-1450 (334) 242-3486
http://www.dcnr.state.al.us

Alaska:
Department of Environmental Conservation, 410 Willoughby Avenue, Suite 105, Juneau, AL 99801-1795 (907) 465-5060
http://www.state.ak.us

Arizona:
Department of Water Resources, 500 North 3rd Street, Phoenix, AZ 85004-3226 (602) 417-2400
http://www.adwr.state.az.us

Natural Resources Division, 1616 West Adams Street, Phoenix, AZ 85007 (602) 542-4625

Arkansas:
Department of Pollution Control and Ecology, 8001 National Drive, Little Rock, AR 72209 (501) 682-0744

http://www.adeq.state.ar.us

Energy Office, 1 State Capitol Mall, Little Rock, AR 72201-1012 (501) 682-7325
California:
Conservation Department Resources Agency, 801 K Street, MS24-01, Sacramento, CA 95814 (916) 322-1080
http://www.consrv.ca.gov

Environmental Protection Agency, 555 Capital Mall, Suite 525, Sacramento, CA 95814 (916) 445-3846
http://www.calepa.ca.gov
Colorado:
Department of Natural Resources, 1313 Sherman Street, Room 718, Denver, CO 80203-2239 (303) 866-3311
http://www.dnr.state.co.us
Connecticut:
Department of Environmental Protection, State Office Building, 79 Elm Street, Hartford, CT 06106-5127 (860) 424-3000
http://www.dep.state.ct.us
Delaware:
Natural Resources and Environmental Control Department, 89 Kings Highway, Dover, DE 19903 (302) 739-5823
http://www.dnrec.state.de.us
District of Columbia:
Environmental Regulation Administration, 2100 Martin Luther King Jr. Avenue, SE, Suite 203, Washington, DC 20020 (202) 404-1167
http://clean.rti.org/state/washdc.htm
Florida:
Department of Environmental Protection, 3900 Commonwealth Blvd., M.S.10, Tallahassee, FL 32399-3000 (850) 488-1554
http://www.dep.state.fl.us
Georgia:
Department of Natural Resources, 205 Butler Street, SE, Atlanta, GA 30334-4100 (404) 656-3500
http://www.ganet.org/dnr/
Guam:
Environmental Protection Agency, IT&E Harmon Plaza, Complex Unit D-107, 130 Rojas St., Harmon, Guam 96911 (617) 646-9402
Hawaii:
Department of Land and Natural Resources, P.O. Box 621, Honolulu, HI 96809 (808) 587-0400
http://www.hawaii.gov/dlnr/Welcome.html
Idaho:
Department of Lands, P.O. Box 83720, Boise, ID 83720-0050 (208) 334-0200
http://www2.state.id.us/lands/index.htm

Department of Water Resources, 1301 North Orchard Street, Boise, ID 83706 (208) 327-7900
http://www.idwr.state.id.us
Illinois:
Department of Natural Resources, 524 South 2nd Street, Springfield, IL 62701 (217) 785-0075
http://dnr.state.il.us
Indiana:
Department of Natural Resources, 402 W. Washington St., Indianapolis, IN 46204-2212 (317) 232-4020
http://www.state.in.us/dnr/
Iowa:
Department of Natural Resources, Wallace State Office Bldg., Des Moines, IA 50319 (515) 281-4367
http://www.state.ia.us/dnr/
Kansas:
Department of Health and Environment, Landon State Office Bldg., Topeka, KS 66612 (785) 296-1522
http://www.state.ks.us/public/kdhe/
Kentucky:
Natural Resources and Environmental Protection Cabinet

Capital Plaza, Frankfort, KY 40601 (502) 564-3350
http://www.nr.state.ky.us/nrhome.htm
Louisiana:
Department of Environmental Quality, 7290 Bluebonnet Blvd., Baton Rouge, LA 70810 70817-4401 (225) 765-0741
http://www.deq.state.la.us

Department of Natural Resources, 625 North 4th Street, Baton Rouge, LA 70804-9396 (504) 342-2707
http://www.dnr.state.la.us/index.ssi
Maine:
Department of Environmental Protection, 17 State House Station, Augusta, ME 04333-0017 (207) 287-7688 (800) 452-1942
http://www.state.me.us/dep/
Maryland:
Department of Natural Resources, 580 Taylor Avenue, Tawes State Office Bldg., Annapolis, MD 21401 (410) 260-8400
http://www.dnr.state.md.us
Massachusetts:
Department of Environmental Management, 100 Cambridge Street, 19th Floor, Boston, MA 02202 (617) 727-3163
http://www.state.ma.us/dem/dem.htm
Michigan:
Department of Natural Resources, Box 30028, Lansing, MI 48909 (517) 373-2329
http://www.dnr.state.mi.us
Minnesota:
Department of Natural Resources, 500 Lafayette Road, St. Paul, MN 55155-4046 (612) 296-2549
http://www.dnr.state.mn.us
Mississippi:
Department of Environmental Quality, P.O. Box 20305, Jackson, MS 39289 (601) 961-5171
http://www.deq.state.ms.us/domino/deqweb.nsf
Missouri:
Department of Natural Resources, P.O. Box 176, Jefferson City, MO 65102 (800) 334-6946
http://www.dnr.state.mo.us/homednr.htm
Montana:
Department of Natural Resources and Conservation, 1625 11th Avenue, P.O. Box 201601, Helena, MT 59620-1601 (406) 444-2074
http://www.dnrc.mt.gov
Nebraska:
Department of Environmental Quality, P.O. Box 98922, Lincoln, NE 68509 (402) 471-2186
http://www.deq.state.ne.us
Nevada:
Department of Conservation and Natural Resources, Capitol Complex, Carson City, NV 89710 (702) 687-5000
http://www.state.nv.us/cnr/
New Hampshire:
Department of Environmental Services, 6 Hazen Drive, P.O. Box 95, Concord, NH 03302-0095 (603) 271-3503
http://www.state.nh.us/des/

Department of Resources and Economic Development, P.O. Box 1856, Concord, NH 03302-1856 (603) 271-2411
http://www.dred.state.nh.us
New Jersey:
Department of Environmental Protection, 401 E. State Street, P.O. Box 402, Trenton, NJ 08625-0402 (609) 292-2885
http://www.state.nj.us/dep/
New Mexico:
Environmental Department, 1190 Saint Francis Drive, Santa Fe, NM 87505 (505) 827-2855 (800) 879-3421
http://www.nmenv.state.nm.us

New York:
  Department of Environmental Conservation, 50 Wolf Road, Albany, NY 12233 (518) 485-8940
  http://www.dec.state.ny.us
North Carolina:
  Department of Environment and Natural Resources, P.O. Box 27687, Raleigh, NC 27611 (919) 733-4984
  http://www.ehnr.state.nc.us/EHNR/
North Dakota:
  Game & Fish Department, 100 North Bismarck Expressway, Bismarck, ND 58501 (701) 328-6300
  http://www.state.nd.us/gnf/
Ohio:
  Department of Natural Resources, 1952 Belcher Drive, Building C-1, Columbus, OH 43224 (614) 265-6565
  http://www.dnr.state.oh.us

  Environmental Protection Agency, P.O. Box 1049, Columbus, OH 43216-1049 (614) 644-3020
  http://www.epa.state.oh.us
Oklahoma:
  Conservation Commission, 2800 North Lincoln Boulevard, Suite 160, Oklahoma City, OK 73105-4210 (405) 521-2384
  http://www.oklaosf.state.ok.us/~comscom/

  Department of Environmental Quality, 707 North Robinson, Oklahoma City, OK 73702 (405) 702-6100
  http://www.deq.state.ok.us
Oregon:
  Department of Environmental Quality, 811 S.W. 6th Avenue, Portland, OR 97204-1390 (503) 229-5696
  http://www.deq.state.or.us
Pennsylvania:
  Department of Environmental Resources, 400 Market Street, Harrisburg, PA 17105 (717) 787-2814
  http://www.dep.state.pa.us
Puerto Rico:
  Department of Natural Resources, P.O. Box 5887, San Juan, PR 00906 (787) 723-3090
Rhode Island:
  Department of Environmental Management, 235 Promenade Street, Providence, RI 02908 (401) 222-2771
  http://www.state.ri.us
South Carolina:
  Department of Health and Environmental Control, 2600 Bull Street, Columbia, SC 29201 (803) 734-5000
  http://www.state.sc.us/dhec/

  Department of Natural Resources, 1000 Assembly Street, Columbia 29201 (803) 734-3888
  http://water.dnr.state.sc.us
South Dakota:
  Department of Environment and Natural Resources, Joe Foss Bldg., 523 East Capitol, Pierre, SD 57501 (605) 773-3151
  http://www.state.sd.us/state/executive/ denr/denr.html
Tennessee:
  Department of Environment and Conservation, 401 Church St., 21st Floor, Nashville, TN 37243 (888) 891-8332
  http://www.state.tn.us/environment/
Texas:
  Natural Resources Conservation Commission, P.O. Box 13087, Austin, TX 78711 (512) 239-1000
  http://www.three.state.tx.us
Utah:
  Department of Natural Resources, 1594 West North Temple, Suite 3710, Salt Lake City, UT 84114 (801) 538-7200
  http://www.nr.state.ut.us
Vermont:
  Agency of Natural Resources, 103 South Main Street, Waterbury, VT 05671-0301 (802) 241-3614
  http://www.anr.state.vt.us

Virgin Islands:
  Department of Planning & Natural Resources, 396-1 Annas Retreat, Foster Bldg., Charlotte Amalie, U.S. Virgin Islands 00802 (340) 774-3320
  http://www.gov.vi/pnr/
Virginia:
  Secretary of Natural Resources, P.O. Box 1475, Richmond, VA 23212 (804) 786-0044
  http://snr.vipnet.org
Washington:
  Department of Ecology, P.O. Box 47600, Olympia, WA 98504-7600 (360) 407-6000
  http://www.wa.gov/ecology/

  Department of Natural Resources, P.O. Box 47000, Olympia, WA 98504-7000 (360) 902-1000
  http://www.wa.gov/dnr/
West Virginia:
  Division of Natural Resources, 1900 Kanawha Blvd. East, Charleston, WV 25305 (304) 558-2771
  http://www.dnr.state.wv.us
Wisconsin:
  Department of Natural Resources, Box 7921, Madison, WI 53707 (608) 267-7517
  http://www.dnr.state.wi.us
Wyoming:
  Department of Environmental Quality, 122 West 25th Street, Herschler Bldg., Cheyenne, WY 82002 (307) 777-7758
  http://deq.state.wy.us

B. Citizens' Organizations

Advancement of Earth & Environmental Sciences, International Association for, Northeastern Illinois University, Geography and Environmental Studies Department 5500 North St. Louis Avenue, Chicago, Illinois 60625 (312) 794-2628

Air Pollution Control Association 1 Gateway Center, 3rd Floor, Pittsburgh, PA 15222 (412) 232-3444

American Association for the Advancement of Science, 1200 New York Avenue, NW, Washington, DC 20005 (202) 326-6400
http://www.aaas.org

American Chemical Society, 1155 16th Street, NW, Washington, DC 20036 (202) 872-4600
http://acs.org

American Farm Bureau Federation, 225 Touhy Avenue, Park Ridge, IL 60068 (847) 685-8600
http://www.fb.com

American Fisheries Society, 5410 Grosvenor Lane, Suite 110, Bethesda, MD 20014-2199 (301) 897-8616
http://www.fisheries.org

American Forest & Paper Association, 1111 19th Street, NW, Suite 800, Washington, DC 20036 (202) 463-2438
http://www.afandpa.org

American Forests, P.O. Box 2000, Washington, DC 20013 (202) 955-4500
http://www.amfor.org

American Institute of Biological Sciences, 1444 Eye Street NW, Washington, DC 20005 (202) 628-1500
http://www.aibs.org

American Museum of Natural History, Central Park West at 79th Street, New York, NY 10024-5192 (212) 769-5100
http://www.amnh.org

American Petroleum Institute, 1220 L Street, NW, Washington, DC 20005-4070 (202) 682-8000
http://www.api.org

American Rivers, 1025 Vermont Avenue NW, Suite 720, Washington, DC 20005 (202) 347-7550
http://www.amrivers.org

Association for Conservation Information, P.O. Box 12559, Charleston, SC 29412 (803) 762-5032

Boone and Crockett Club, 250 Station Dr., Missoula, MT 59801 (406) 542-1888
http://www.boone-crockett.org

Center for Marine Conservation, 1725 DeSales Street, NW, Suite 600, Washington, DC 20036 (202) 429-5609
http://www.cmc-ocean.org

Citizens for a Better Environment, 3255 Hennepin Avenue South, Minneapolis, MN 55331 (612) 824-8637
http://www.cbemw.org

Coastal Conservation Association, 4801 Woodway, Suite 220W, Houston, TX 77056 (713) 626-4222
http://www.ccatexas.org

Conservation Foundation, 1250 24th Street, NW, Suite 400, Washington, DC 20037 (202) 293-4800

Conservation Fund, 1800 North Kent Street, Suite 1120, Arlington, VA 22209-2156 (703) 525-6300
http://www.conservationfund.org

Conservation International, 2501 M Street, NW, Suite 200, Washington, DC 20037 (202) 429-5660 (800) 429-5660
http://www.conservation.org

Defenders of Wildlife, 1101 14th Street, NW, #1400, Washington, DC, 20005 (202) 682-9400
http://www.defenders.org

Ducks Unlimited, Inc., One Waterfowl Way, Memphis, TN (901) 785-3825
http://www.ducks.org

Earthwatch Institute International, 680 Mt. Auburn Street, Watertown, MA 02471 (800) 776-0188
http://www.earthwatch.org

Environmental Action Foundation, Inc., 6930 Carroll Ave., Suite 600, Takoma Park, MD 20912 (301) 891-1100

Food and Agriculture Organization of the United Nations (FAO), Via delle Terme di Caracalla, 00100, Rome, Italy (396) 57051 *http://www.fao.org*

Friends of the Earth, 1025 Vermont Avenue, NW, Suite 300, Washington, DC 20005 (202) 783-7400
http://foe.co.uk

Greenpeace U.S.A., 1436 U Street, NW, Washington, DC 20009 (202) 462-1177
http://greenpeaceusa.org

International Association of Fish and Wildlife Agencies, 444 North Capitol Street, NW, Suite 544, Washington, DC 20001 (202) 624-7890
http://www.teaming.com/iafwa.htm

International Fund for Agricultural Development (IFAD), 107, Via del Serafico, 00142, Rome, Italy (3906) 54591
http://www.ifad.org

Keep America Beautiful, Inc., 1010 Washington Blvd., Stamford, CT 06901 (203) 323-8987
http://www.kab.org

National Association of Conservation Districts, 509 Capitol Court, NE, Washington, DC 20002 (202) 547-6223
http://www.nacdnet.org

National Audubon Society, 700 Broadway, New York, NY 10003 (212) 979-3000
http://www.audubon.org

National Environmental Health Association, 720 South Colorado Boulevard, 970 South Tower, Denver, CO 80246 (303) 756-9090
http://www.neha.org

National Fisheries Institute, 1901 N. Fort Myer Dr., Suite 700, Arlington, VA 22209 (703) 524-8880
http://www.nfi.org/main.html

National Geographic Society, 1145 17th Street, NW, Washington, DC 20036 (202) 857-7000
http://www.nationalgeographic.com

National Parks and Conservation Association, 1717 Massachusetts Avenue, NW, Washington, DC 20036 (202) 223-6722 (800) 628-7275
http://www.npca.org

National Wildlife Federation, 8925 Leesburg Pike, Vienna, VA 22184 (703) 790-4000
http://www.nwf.org

Natural Resources Council of America, 801 Pennsylvania Avenue, SE, No. 410, Washington, DC 20003 (202) 333-0411

Nature Conservancy, 1815 North Lynn Street, Arlington, VA 22209 (703) 841-5300
http://www.tnc.org

Population Association of America, 721 Ellsworth Drive, Suite 303, Silver Spring, MD 20910 (301) 565-6710
http://www.jstor.org

Rainforest Alliance, 650 Bleecker Street, New York, NY 10012 (212) 677-1900
http://www.rainforest-alliance.org

Save-the-Redwoods League, 114 Sansome Street, Room 605, San Francisco, CA 94104 (415) 362-2352
http://www.savetheredwoods.org

Sierra Club, 85 Second Street, 2nd Floor, San Francisco, CA 94105 (415) 977-5500
http://www.sierraclub.org

Smithsonian Institution, 1000 Jefferson Drive, S.W., Washington, DC 20560 (202) 357-2700
http://smithsonian.org

Society of American Foresters, 5400 Grosvenor Lane, Bethesda, MD 20814-2198 (301) 897-8720
http://www.safnet.org

Sport Fishing Institute, 1010 Massachusetts Avenue, NW, Suite 320, Washington, DC 20001 (202) 898-0770

United Nations Educational, Scientific, and Cultural Organization (UNESCO), UNESCO House, 7, Place de Fontenoy, 75352 Paris 07 SP France, (331) 45 68 10 00
http://www.unesco.org

United Nations Environment Programme/Industry & Environment Centre, Tour Mirabeau 39-43, quai André Citröen 75739 Paris, cedex 15, France (331) 44 37 14 50
http://www. unepie.org

Wilderness Society, 900 17th Street, NW, Washington, DC 20006-2596 (202) 833-2300
http://www.wilderness.org

World Wildlife Fund, 1250 24th Street, NW, Washington, DC 20077 (202) 293-4800
http://www.wwf.org

Zero Population Growth, Inc., 1400 16th Street, NW, Suite 320, Washington, DC 20036 (202) 332-2200
http://www.zpg.org

III. CANADIAN AGENCIES AND CITIZENS' ORGANIZATIONS
A: Government Agencies
Alberta:
Alberta Environmental Protection, 323 Legislature Bldg., 10800 97th Avenue, Edmonton, AB T5K 2B6 (403) 427-2391 *http://www.gov.ab.ca/env.html*

British Columbia:
Ministry of Environment, Lands, and Parks, 337, Parliament Bldgs., Victoria, BC V8V 1X4 (250) 387-1187
http://www.env.gov.bc.ca

Manitoba:
Manitoba Environment, 344 Legislative Bldg., Winnipeg, MB R3C 0V8 (204) 945-3522
http://www.gov.mb.ca/environ/index.html

Manitoba Natural Resources, Box 22, 200 Saulteaux Crescent, Winnipeg, MB R3J 3W3 (204) 945-6784
http://www.gov.mb.ca/natres/index.html

New Brunswick:
Department of Environment, 364 Argyle St., Fredericton, NB E3B 1T9 (506) 453-2558
http://www.gov.nb.ca/environm/

Department of Natural Resources and Energy, P.O. Box 6000, Fredericton, NB E3B 5H1 (506) 453-2614
http://www.gov.nb.ca/dnre/

Newfoundland and Labrador:
Department of Environment and Labour, Confederation Bldg., PO Box 8700, St. John's, NF A1B 4J6 (709) 729-2664
http://www.govt.nf.ca/env/labour/OHS/default.asp

Northwest Territories:
: Department of Resources, Wildlife, and Economic Development, #600 Scotia Centre, Bldg. Box 21, 5102-50 Avenue, Yellowknife, NT X1A 3S8 (867) 669-2366 http://www.rwed.gov.nt.ca

Nova Scotia:
: Department of Natural Resources, P.O. Box 698, Halifax, NS B3J 2T9 (902) 424-5935 http://www.gov.ns.ca/natr/

Department of the Environment, P.O. Box 2107, Halifax, NS B3J 3B7 (902) 424-5300 http://www.gov.ns.ca/envi/

Ontario:
: Ministry of Natural Resources, 300 Water Street, P.O. Box 7000, Peterborough, ON K9J 8M5 (705) 755-2000 (416) 314-2000 http://www.mnr.gov. on.ca/mnr/

Prince Edward Island:
: Department of Technology and Environment, Jones Bldg., 11 Kent Street, 4th Floor, P.O. Box 2000, Charlottetown, PEI C1A 7N8 (902) 892-5000 http://www.gov.pe.ca/te/index.asp

Quebec:
: Ministère de l'Environnement et de la Faune, Edifice Marie-Guyart, 675, boulevard René-Lévesque, Est, Québec, PC G1R 5V7 (418) 521-3830 (800) 561-1616 http://www.mef.gouv.qc.ca

Ministère des Ressources Naturelles, #B-302, 5700, 4 Avenue Ouest, Charlesbourg, PQ G1H 6R1 (418) 627-8600 http://www.mrn.gouv.qc.ca

Saskatchewan:
: Saskatchewan Environment and Resource Management, 3211 Albert Street, Regina, SK S4S 5W6 (306) 787-2700 http://www.gov.sk.ca/govt/environ/

Yukon Territory:
: Council on the Economy & the Environment, A-8E, P.O. Box 2703, Whitehorse, YT Y1A 2C6 (867) 667-5811 http://www.gov.yk.ca

Department of Renewable Resources, Box 2703, Whitehorse, YT Y1A 2C6 (867) 667-5811 http://www.gov.yk.ca

B. Citizens' Groups

Alberta Wilderness Association
: Box 6398, Station D, Calgary, AB T2P 2E1 (403) 283-2025 http://www.web.net/~awa/

BC Environmental Network (BCEN) 1672 East 10th Avenue, Vancouver, BC V5N 1X5 (604) 879-2272 http://www.bcen.bc.ca

Canadian EarthCare Society
: 1476 Water Street, Kelowna, BC V1Y 8P2 (604) 861-4788 http://www.earthcare.org

Ducks Unlimited Canada
: Oak Hammock Marsh, Stonewall, P.O. Box 1160, Oak Hammock Marsh, MB R0C 2Z0 (204) 467-3000 (800) 665-3825 http://www.ducks.ca

Federation of Ontario Naturalists
: 355 Lesmill Road, Don Mills, ON M3B 2W8 (416) 444-8419 http://www.ontarionature.org

L'Association des Entrepreneurs de Service en Environnement du Quebec (AESEQ)
: 911 Jean-Talon, Est 220, Montreal, PQ H2R 1V5 (514) 270-7110

New Brunswick Environment Industry Association
: P.O. Box 637, Stn. A, Fredericton, NB E3B 5B3 (506) 455-0212 http://www.nbeia.nb.ca/index.html

Prince Edward Island Environmental Network (PEIEN)
: 126 Richmond Street, Charleston, PEI C1A 1H9 (902) 566-4170 http://www.isn.net/~network/index.html

Yukon Conservation Society (YCS)
: P.O. Box 4163, Whitehorse, YT Y1A 3T3 (403) 668-6637

IV. SELECTED JOURNALS AND PERIODICALS OF ENVIRONMENTAL INTEREST

American Forests

American Forests
: 910 17th Street NW, Suite 600, Washington, DC 20006 (202) 955-4500 (800) 368-5748 http://www.amfor.org

American Scientist
: Scientific Research Society, P.O. Box 13975, Research Triangle Park, NC 27709-3975 (919) 549-0097 http://www.amsci.org/amsci/amsci.html

Annual Report of the Council on Environmental Quality
: Superintendent of Documents, U.S. Government Printing Office, Washington, DC 20401 (202) 512-1800 http://ceq.ch.doc.gov/nepa/reports/reports.htm

Audubon
: National Audubon Society, 700 Broadway, New York, NY 10003 (212) 979-3000 http://magazine.audubon.org

BioScience
: American Institute of Biological Sciences, 1444 Eye St. NW, Suite 200, Washington, DC 20005 (202) 628-1500 http://www.aibs.org

California Environmental Directory
: California Institute of Public Affairs, Box 189040, Sacramento, CA 95818 (916) 442-2472 http://www.igc.org/cipa/cipa.html#about

The Canadian Field-Naturalist
: Box 35069 Westgate, Ottawa, ON, Canada K1Z 1A2 (613) 722-3050 http://www.achilles.net/ofnc/cfn.htm

Conservation Directory
: National Wildlife Federation, 8925 Leesburg Pike, Vienna, VA 22184 (703) 790-4000 http://www.nwf.org/nwf/pubs/considir/index.html

Earth First! Journal
: P.O. Box 1415, Eugene, OR 97440-1415 (541) 344-8004 http://host.envirolink.org/ef/

E: The Environmental Magazine
: Earth Action Network, P.O. Box 5098, Westport, CT 06881 (203) 854-5559 http://www.emagazine.com

Environment
: Heldref Publications, 1319 18th Street, NW, Washington, DC 20036-1802 (202) 296-6267 http://www.heldref.org

Environment Reporter
: Bureau of National Affairs, Inc. 1231 25th Street, NW, Washington, DC 2037 (202) 452-4200 http://www.bna.com/prodcatalog/desc/ER.html

Environmental Action Magazine
: Environment Action, Inc. 6930 Carroll Ave., Suite 600, Takoma Park, MD 20912-4414 (301) 891-1106

Environmental Science and Technology
: American Chemical Society Publications Support Services, 1155 16th Street, NW, Washington, DC 20036 (202) 872-4554 (800) 227-5558 http://pubs.acs.org/journals/esthag/

Focus (bimonthly newsletter)
: World Wildlife Fund, 1250 24th Street, NW, Washington, DC 20037 (202) 293-4800 http://www.wwf.org

The Futurist
: World Future Society, 7910 Woodmont Avenue, Suite 450, Bethesda, MD 20814 (301) 656-8274 (800) 989-8274 http://www.wfs.org/wfs/

Greenpeace Magazine
  Greenpeace USA, 1436 U Street, NW, Washington, DC 20009 (202) 462-1177 (800) 326-0959
  http://www.greenpeaceusa.org
Journal of Soil and Water Conservation
  Soil and Water Conservation Society, 7515 Northeast Ankeny Road, Ankeny, IA 50021-9764 (515) 289-2331
  http://www.swcs.org
Journal of Wildlife Management
  The Wildlife Society, 5410 Grosvenor Lane, Suite 200, Bethesda, MD 20814-2197 (301) 897-9770
  http://www.wildlife.org/journal.html
Mother Earth News
  Sussex Publishers Inc., 49 E. 21st Street, 11th Floor, New York, NY 10010 (212) 260-7210
  http://www.MotherEarthNews.Com
National Wildlife
  National Wildlife Federation, 8925 Leesburg Pike, Vienna, VA 22184 (703) 790-4510
  http://www.nwf.org/nwf/natwild/
Natural Resources Journal
  University of New Mexico, School of Law, 1117 Stanford, NE, Albuquerque, NM 87131 (505) 277-4820
  http://www.unm.edu/~natresj/NRJ/NRJ.html
Nature
  Macmillan Publishers Ltd., Porter South, Grinan Street, London N1 9XW, England (44) 0171 833-4000
  http://www.nature.com
Nature Canada
  Canadian Nature Federation, One Nicholas Street, Suite 606, Ottawa, ON, Canada K1N 787 (613) 562-3447 (800) 267-40880
  http://www. cnf.ca/nc_main.html
Nature Conservancy Magazine
  1815 North Lynn Street, Arlington, VA 22209-2003 (703) 841-5300 (800) 267-4088
  http://www.tnc.org
Omni
  Omni Publications International Ltd., 277 Park Ave., New York, NY 10172 (212) 702-6000
  http://www.omnimag.com

Pollution Abstracts
  Cambridge Scientific Abstracts, 7200 Wisconsin Avenue, Suite 601, Bethesda, MD 20814-4823 (301) 961-6700 (800) 843-7751
  http://www.csa.com
Science
  American Association for the Advancement of Science, 1200 New York Avenue NW, Washington, DC 20005 (202) 326-6501
  http://www.sciencemag.org
Sierra Magazine
  Sierra Club, 85 2nd Street, 2nd Floor, San Francisco, CA 94105-3441 (415) 977-5750
  http://www.sierraclub.org/sierra/
Smithsonian
  900 Jefferson Drive, Washington, DC 20560 (202) 786-2900
  http://smithsonianmag.com
Technology Review
  201 Vassar Street, Cambridge, MA 02139 (617) 253-8250
  http://www.techreview.com
U.S. News and World Report
  2400 N Street, NW, Washington, DC 20037-1196 (202) 955-2000
  http://www.usnews.com/usnews/home.htm
The World & I
  New World Communications,3600 New York Avenue, NE, Washington, DC 20002 (800) 822-2822 (202) 635-4000
  http://www.worldandi.com

SOURCES used to compile this list: *Canadian Almanac Directory* 1997; *Carroll's Federal Directory*, April 1997; *Carroll's State Directory*, February 1997; *Congressional Quarterly's Washington Information Directory* 1997–1998; *Encyclopedia of Associations*, 32nd Edition, 1997; *Gale Directory of Publications and Broadcast Media*, 131st edition; *The World Almanac*, 199, Web search engines: Google, Metacrawler.

This glossary of environmental terms is included to provide you with a convenient and ready reference as you encounter general terms in your study of environment that are unfamiliar or require a review. It is not intended to be comprehensive, but taken together with the many definitions included in the articles themselves, it should prove to be quite useful.

Abiotic Without life; any system characterized by a lack of living organisms.

Absorption Incorporation of a substance into a solid or liquid body.

Acid Any compound capable of reacting with a base to form a salt; a substance containing a high hydrogen ion concentration (low pH).

Acid Rain Precipitation containing a high concentration of acid.

Adaptation Adjustment of an organism to the conditions of its environment, enabling reproduction and survival.

Additive A substance added to another in order to impart or improve desirable properties or suppress undesirable ones.

Adsorption Surface retention of solid, liquid, or gas molecules, atoms, or ions by a solid or liquid.

Aerobic Environmental conditions where oxygen is present; aerobic organisms require oxygen in order to survive.

Aerosols Tiny mineral particles in the atmosphere onto which water droplets, crystals, and other chemical compounds may adhere.

Air Quality Standard A prescribed level of a pollutant in the air that should not be exceeded.

Alcohol Fuels The processing of sugary or starchy products (such as sugar cane, corn, or potatoes) into fuel.

Allergens Substances that activate the immune system and cause an allergic response.

Alpha Particle A positively charged particle given off from the nucleus of some radioactive substances; it is identical to a helium atom that has lost its electrons.

Ammonia A colorless gas comprised of one atom of nitrogen and three atoms of hydrogen; liquefied ammonia is used as a fertilizer.

Anthropocentric Considering humans to be the central or most important part of the universe.

Aquaculture Propagation and/or rearing of any aquatic organism in artificial "wetlands" and/or ponds.

Aquifers Porous, water-saturated layers of sand, gravel, or bedrock that can yield significant amounts of water economically.

Atom The smallest particle of an element, composed of electrons moving around an inner core (nucleus) of protons and neutrons. Atoms of elements combine to form molecules and chemical compounds.

Atomic Reactor A structure fueled by radioactive materials that generates energy usually in the form of electricity; reactors are also utilized for medical and biological research.

Autotrophs Organisms capable of using chemical elements in the synthesis of larger compounds; green plants are autotrophs.

Background Radiation The normal radioactivity present; coming principally from outer space and naturally occurring radioactive substances on Earth.

Bacteria One-celled microscopic organisms found in the air, water, and soil. Bacteria cause many diseases of plants and animals; they also are beneficial in agriculture, decay of dead matter, and food and chemical industries.

Benthos Organisms living on the bottom of bodies of water.

Biocentrism Belief that all creatures have rights and values and that humans are not superior to other species.

Biochemical Oxygen Demand (BOD) The oxygen utilized in meeting the metabolic needs of aquatic organisms.

Biodegradable Capable of being reduced to simple compounds through the action of biological processes.

Biodiversity Biological diversity in an environment as indicated by numbers of different species of plants and animals.

Biogeochemical Cycles The cyclical series of transformations of an element through the organisms in a community and their physical environment.

Biological Control The suppression of reproduction of a pest organism utilizing other organisms rather than chemical means.

Biomass The weight of all living tissue in a sample.

Biome A major climax community type covering a specific area on Earth.

Biosphere The overall ecosystem of Earth. It consists of parts of the atmosphere (troposphere), hydrosphere (surface and ground water), and lithosphere (soil, surface rocks, ocean sediments, and other bodies of water).

Biota The flora and fauna in a given region.

Biotic Biological; relating to living elements of an ecosystem.

Biotic Potential Maximum possible growth rate of living systems under ideal conditions.

Birthrate Number of live births in one year per 1,000 midyear population.

Breeder Reactor A nuclear reactor in which the production of fissionable material occurs.

Cancer Invasive, out-of-control cell growth that results in malignant tumors.

Carbon Cycle Process by which carbon is incorporated into living systems, released to the atmosphere, and returned to living organisms.

Carbon Monoxide (CO) A gas, poisonous to most living systems, formed when incomplete combustion of fuel occurs.

Carcinogens Substances capable of producing cancer.

Carrying Capacity The population that an area will support without deteriorating.

Chlorinated Hydrocarbon Insecticide Synthetic organic poisons containing hydrogen, carbon, and chlorine. Because they are fat-soluble, they tend to be recycled through food chains, eventually affecting nontarget systems. Damage is normally done to the organism's nervous system. Examples include DDT, Aldrin, Deildrin, and Chlordane.

Chlorofluorocarbons (CFCs) Any of several simple gaseous compounds that contain carbon, chlorine, fluorine, and sometimes hydrogen; they are suspected of being a major cause of stratospheric ozone depletion.

Circle of Poisons Importation of food contaminated with pesticides banned for use in this country but made here and sold abroad.

Clear-Cutting The practice of removing all trees in a specific area.

Climate Description of the long-term pattern of weather in any particular area.

Climax Community Terminal state of ecological succession in an area; the redwoods are a climax community.

Coal Gasification Process of converting coal to gas; the resultant gas, if used for fuel, sharply reduces sulfur oxide emissions and particulates that result from coal burning.

Commensalism Symbiotic relationship between two different species in which one benefits while the other is neither harmed nor benefited.

Community Ecology Study of interactions of all organisms existing in a specific region.

Competitive Exclusion Resulting from competition; one species forced out of part of an available habitat by a more efficient species.

Conservation The planned management of a natural resource to prevent overexploitation, destruction, or neglect.

Conventional Pollutants Seven substances (sulfur dioxide, carbon monoxide, particulates, hydrocarbons, nitrogen oxides, photochemical oxidants, and lead) that make up the largest volume of air quality degradation, as identified by the Clean Air Act.

Core Dense, intensely hot molten metal mass, thousands of kilometers in diameter, at Earth's center.

Cornucopian Theory The belief that nature is limitless in its abundance and that perpetual growth is both possible and essential.

Corridor Connecting strip of natural habitat that allows migration of organisms from one place to another.

Critical Factor The environmental factor closest to a tolerance limit for a species at a specific time.

Cultural Eutrophication Increase in biological productivity and ecosystem succession resulting from human activities.

Crankcase Smog Devices (PCV System) A system, used principally in automobiles, designed to prevent discharge of combustion emissions into the external environment.

Death Rate Number of deaths in one year per 1,000 mid-year population.

Decomposer Any organism that causes the decay of organic matter; bacteria and fungi are two examples.

Deforestation The action or process of clearing forests without adequate replanting.

Degradation (of water resource) Deterioration in water quality caused by contamination or pollution that makes water unsuitable for many purposes.

Demography The statistical study of principally human populations.

Desert An arid biome characterized by little rainfall, high daily temperatures, and low diversity of animal and plant life.

Desertification Converting arid or semiarid lands into deserts by inappropriate farming practices or overgrazing.

Detergent A synthetic soap-like material that emulsifies fats and oils and holds dirt in suspension; some detergents have caused pollution problems because of certain chemicals used in their formulation.

Detrivores Organisms that consume organic litter, debris, and dung.

Diversity Number of species present in a community (species richness), as well as the relative abundance of each species.

DNA (Deoxyribonucleic Acid) One of two principal nucleic acids, the other being RNA (Ribonucleic Acid). DNA contains information used for the control of a living cell. Specific segments of DNA are now recognized as genes, those agents controlling evolutionary and hereditary processes.

Dominant Species Any species of plant or animal that is particularly abundant or controls a major portion of the energy flow in a community.

Drip Irrigation Pipe or perforated tubing used to deliver water a drop at a time directly to soil around each plant. Conserves water and reduces soil waterlogging and salinization.

Ecological Density The number of a singular species in a geographical area, including the highest concentration points within the defined boundaries.

Ecological Succession Process in which organisms occupy a site and gradually change environmental conditions so that other species can replace the original inhabitants.

Ecology Study of the interrelationships between organisms and their environments.

Ecosystem The organisms of a specific area, together with their functionally related environments; considered as a definitive unit.

Ecotourism Wildlife tourism that could damage ecosystems and disrupt species if strict guidelines governing tours to sensitive areas are not enforced.

Edge Effects Change in ecological factors at the boundary between two ecosystems. Some organisms flourish here; others are harmed.

Effluent A liquid discharged as waste.

El Niño Climatic change marked by shifting of a large warm water pool from the western Pacific Ocean toward the East.

Electron Small, negatively charged particle; normally found in orbit around the nucleus of an atom.

Eminent Domain Superior dominion exerted by a governmental state over all property within its boundaries that authorizes it to appropriate all or any part thereof to a necessary public use, with reasonable compensation being made.

Endangered Species Species considered to be in imminent danger of extinction.

Endemic Species Plants or animals that belong or are native to a particular ecosystem.

Environment Physical and biological aspects of a specific area.

Environmental Impact Statement (EIS) A study of the probable environmental impact of a development project before federal funding is provided (required by the National Environmental Policy Act of 1968).

Environmental Protection Agency (EPA) Federal agency responsible for control of air and water pollution, radiation and pesticide problems, ecological research, and solid waste disposal.

Erosion Progressive destruction or impairment of a geographical area; wind and water are the principal agents involved.

Estuary Water passage where an ocean tide meets a river current.

Eutrophic Well nourished; refers to aquatic areas rich in dissolved nutrients.

Evolution A change in the gene frequency within a population, sometimes involving a visible change in the population's characteristics.

Exhaustible Resources Earth's geologic endowment of minerals, nonmineral resources, fossil fuels, and other materials present in fixed amounts.

Extinction Irrevocable elimination of species due to either normal processes of the natural world or through changing environmental conditions.

Fallow Cropland that is plowed but not replanted and is left idle in order to restore productivity mainly through water accumulation, weed control, and buildup of soil nutrients.

Fauna The animal life of a specified area.

Feral Refers to animals or plants that have reverted to a non-cultivated or wild state.

Fission The splitting of an atom into smaller parts.

Floodplain Level land that may be submerged by floodwaters; a plain built up by stream deposition.

Flora The plant life of an area.

Flyway Geographic migration route for birds that includes the breeding and wintering areas that it connects.

Food Additive Substance added to food usually to improve color, flavor, or shelf life.

Food Chain The sequence of organisms in a community, each of which uses the lower source as its energy supply. Green plants are the ultimate basis for the entire sequence.

Fossil Fuels Coal, oil, natural gas, and/or lignite; those fuels derived from former living systems; usually called nonrenewable fuels.

Fuel Cell Manufactured chemical systems capable of producing electrical energy; they usually derive their capabilities via complex reactions involving the sun as the driving energy source.

Fusion The formation of a heavier atomic complex brought about by the addition of atomic nuclei; during the process there is an attendant release of energy.

Gaia Hypothesis Theory that Earth's biosphere is a living system whose complex interactions between its living organisms and nonliving processes regulate environmental conditions over millions of years so that life continues.

Gamma Ray A ray given off by the nucleus of some radioactive elements. A form of energy similar to X rays.

Gene Unit of heredity; segment of DNA nucleus of the cell containing information for the synthesis of a specific protein.

Gene Banks Storage of seed varieties for future breeding experiments.

Genetic Diversity Infinite variation of possible genetic combinations among individuals; what enables a species to adapt to ecological change.

Germ Plasm Genetic material that may be preserved for future use (plant seeds, animal eggs, sperm, and embryos).

Green Revolution The great increase in production of food grains (as in rice and wheat) due to the introduction of high-yielding varieties, to the use of pesticides, and to better management techniques.

Greenhouse Effect The effect noticed in greenhouses when shortwave solar radiation penetrates glass, is converted to longer wavelengths, and is blocked from escaping by the windows. It results in a temperature increase. Earth's atmosphere acts in a similar manner.

Gross National Product (GNP) The total value of the goods and services produced by the residents of a nation during a specified period (such as a year).

Groundwater Water found in porous rock and soil below the soil moisture zone and, generally, below the root zone of plants. Groundwater that saturates rock is separated from an unsaturated zone by the water table.

Habitat The natural environment of a plant or animal.

Hazardous Waste Waste that poses a risk to human or ecological health and thus requires special disposal techniques.

Herbicide Any substance used to kill plants.

Heterotroph Organism that cannot synthesize its own food and must feed on organic compounds produced by other organisms.

Hydrocarbons Organic compounds containing hydrogen, oxygen, and carbon. Commonly found in petroleum, natural gas, and coal.

Hydrogen Lightest-known gas; major element found in all living systems.

Hydrogen Sulfide Compound of hydrogen and sulfur; a toxic air contaminant that smells like rotten eggs.

Hydropower Electrical energy produced by flowing or falling water.

Infiltration Process of water percolation into soil and pores and hollows of permeable rocks.

Intangible Resources Open space, beauty, serenity, genius, information, diversity, and satisfaction are a few of these abstract commodities.

Integrated Pest Management (IPM) Designed to avoid economic loss from pests, this program's methods of pest control strive to minimize the use of environmentally hazardous, synthetic chemicals.

Invasive Refers to those species that have moved into an area and reproduced so aggressively that they have replaced some of the native species.

Ion An atom or group of atoms, possessing a charge; brought about by the loss or gain of electrons.

Ionizing Radiation Energy in the form of rays or particles that have the capacity to dislodge electrons and/or other atomic particles from matter that is irradiated.

Irradiation Exposure to any form of radiation.

Isotopes Two or more forms of an element having the same number of protons in the nucleus of each atom but different numbers of neutrons.

Keystone Species Species that are essential to the functioning of many other organisms in an ecosystem.

Kilowatt Unit of power equal to 1,000 watts.

Leaching Dissolving out of soluble materials by water percolating through soil.

Limnologist Individual who studies the physical, chemical, and biological conditions of aquatic systems.

Malnutrition Faulty or inadequate nutrition.

Malthusian Theory The theory that populations tend to increase by geometric progression (1, 2, 4, 8, 16, etc.) while food supplies increase by arithmetic means (1, 2, 3, 4, 5, etc.).

Metabolism The chemical processes in living tissue through which energy is provided for continuation of the system.

Methane Often called marsh gas (CH_4); an odorless, flammable gas that is the major constituent of natural gas. In nature it develops from decomposing organic matter.

Migration Periodic departure and return of organisms to and from a population area.

Monoculture Cultivation of a single crop, such as wheat or corn, to the exclusion of other land uses.

Mutation Change in genetic material (gene) that determines species characteristics; can be caused by a number of agents, including radiation and chemicals, called mutagens.

Natural Selection The agent of evolutionary change by which organisms possessing advantageous adaptations leave more offspring than those lacking such adaptations.

Niche The unique occupation or way of life of a plant or animal species; where it lives and what it does in the community.

Nitrate A salt of nitric acid. Nitrates are the major source of nitrogen for higher plants. Sodium nitrate and potassium nitrate are used as fertilizers.

Nitrite Highly toxic compound; salt of nitrous acid.

Nitrogen Oxides Common air pollutants. Formed by the combination of nitrogen and oxygen; often the products of petroleum combustion in automobiles.

Nonrenewable Resource Any natural resource that cannot be replaced, regenerated, or brought back to its original state once it has been extracted, for example, coal or crude oil.

Nutrient Any nutritive substance that an organism must take in from its environment because it cannot produce it as fast as it needs it or, more likely, at all.

Oil Shale Rock impregnated with oil. Regarded as a potential source of future petroleum products.

Oligotrophic Most often refers to those lakes with a low concentration of organic matter. Usually contain considerable oxygen; Lakes Tahoe and Baikal are examples.

Organic Matter Plant, animal, or microorganism matter, either living or dead.

Organophosphates A large group of nonpersistent synthetic poisons used in the pesticide industry; include parathion and malathion.

Ozone Molecule of oxygen containing three oxygen atoms; shields much of Earth from ultraviolet radiation.

Particulate Existing in the form of small separate particles; various atmospheric pollutants are industrially produced particulates.

Peroxyacyl Nitrate (PAN) Compound making up part of photochemical smog and the major plant toxicant of smog-type injury; levels as low as 0.01 ppm can injure sensitive plants. Also causes eye irritation in people.

Pesticide Any material used to kill rats, mice, bacteria, fungi, or other pests of humans.

Pesticide Treadmill A situation in which the cost of using pesticides increases while the effectiveness decreases (because pest species develop genetic resistance to the pesticides).

Petrochemicals Chemicals derived from petroleum bases.

pH Scale used to designate the degree of acidity or alkalinity; ranges from 1 to 14; a neutral solution has a pH of 7; low pHs are acid in nature, while pHs above 7 are alkaline.

Phosphate A phosphorous compound; used in medicine and as fertilizers.

Photochemical Smog Type of air pollution; results from sunlight acting with hydrocarbons and oxides of nitrogen in the atmosphere.

Photosynthesis Formation of carbohydrates from carbon dioxide and hydrogen in plants exposed to sunlight; involves a release of oxygen through the decomposition of water.

Photovoltaic Cells An energy-conversion device that captures solar energy and directly converts it to electrical current.

Physical Half-Life Time required for half of the atoms of a radioactive substance present at some beginning to become disintegrated and transformed.

Pioneer Species Hardy species that are the first to colonize a site in the beginning stage of ecological succession.

Plankton Microscopic organisms that occupy the upper water layers in both freshwater and marine ecosystems.

Plutonium Highly toxic, heavy, radioactive, manmade, metallic element. Possesses a very long physical half-life.

Pollution The process of contaminating air, water, or soil with materials that reduce the quality of the medium.

Polychlorinated Biphenyls (PCBs) Poisonous compounds similar in chemical structure to DDT. PCBs are found in a wide variety of products ranging from lubricants, waxes, asphalt, and transformers to inks and insecticides. Known to cause liver, spleen, kidney, and heart damage.

Population All members of a particular species occupying a specific area.

Predator Any organism that consumes all or part of another system; usually responsible for death of the prey.

Primary Production The energy accumulated and stored by plants through photosynthesis.

Rad (Radiation Absorbed Dose) Measurement unit relative to the amount of radiation absorbed by a particular target, biotic or abiotic.

Radioactive Waste Any radioactive by-product of nuclear reactors or nuclear processes.

Radioactivity The emission of electrons, protons (atomic nuclei), and/or rays from elements capable of emitting radiation.

Rain Forest Forest with high humidity, small temperature range, and abundant precipitation; can be tropical or temperate.

Recycle To reuse; usually involves manufactured items, such as aluminum cans, being restructured after use and utilized again.

Red Tide Population explosion or bloom of minute single-celled marine organisms (dinoflagellates), which can accumulate in protected bays and poison other marine life.

Renewable Resources Resources normally replaced or replenished by natural processes; not depleted by moderate use.

Riparian Water Right Legal right of an owner of land bordering a natural lake or stream to remove water from that aquatic system.

Salinization An accumulation of salts in the soil that could eventually make the soil too salty for the growth of plants.

Sanitary Landfill Land waste disposal site in which solid waste is spread, compacted, and covered.

Scrubber Antipollution system that uses liquid sprays in removing particulate pollutants from an airstream.

Sediment Soil particles moved from land into aquatic systems as a result of human activities or natural events, such as material deposited by water or wind.

Seepage Movement of water through soil.

Selection The process, either natural or artificial, of selecting or removing the best or less desirable members of a population.

Selective Breeding Process of selecting and breeding organisms containing traits considered most desirable.

Selective Harvesting Process of taking specific individuals from a population; the removal of trees in a specific age class would be an example.

Sewage Any waste material coming from domestic and industrial origins.

Smog A mixture of smoke and air; now applies to any type of air pollution.

Soil Erosion Detachment and movement of soil by the action of wind and moving water.

Solid Waste Unwanted solid materials usually resulting from industrial processes.

Species A population of morphologically similar organisms, capable of interbreeding and producing viable offspring.

Species Diversity A ratio between the number of species in a community and the number of individuals in each species. Generally, the greater the species diversity composing a community, the more stable is the community.

Strip Mining Mining in which Earth's surface is removed in order to obtain subsurface materials.

Strontium-90 Radioactive isotope of strontium; it results from nuclear explosions and is dangerous, especially for vertebrates, because it is taken up in the construction of bone.

Succession Change in the structure and function of an ecosystem; replacement of one system with another through time.

Sulfur Dioxide (SO₂) Gas produced by burning coal and as a by-product of smelting and other industrial processes. Very toxic to plants.

Sulfur Oxides (SOₓ) Oxides of sulfur produced by the burning of oils and coal that contain small amounts of sulfur. Common air pollutants.

Sulfuric Acid (H₂ SO₄) Very corrosive acid produced from sulfur dioxide and found as a component of acid rain.

Sustainability Ability of an ecosystem to maintain ecological processes, functions, biodiversity, and productivity over time.

Sustainable Agriculture Agriculture that maintains the integrity of soil and water resources so that it can continue indefinitely.

Technology Applied science; the application of knowledge for practical use.

Tetraethyl Lead Major source of lead found in living tissue; it is produced to reduce engine knock in automobiles.

Thermal Inversion A layer of dense, cool air that is trapped under a layer of less dense warm air (prevents upward-flowing air currents from developing).

Thermal Pollution Unwanted heat, the result of ejection of heat from various sources into the environment.

Thermocline The layer of water in a body of water that separates an upper warm layer from a deeper, colder zone.

Threshold Effect The situation in which no effect is noticed, physiologically or psychologically, until a certain level or concentration is reached.

Tolerance Limit The point at which resistance to a poison or drug breaks down.

Total Fertility Rate (TFR) An estimate of the average number of children that would be born alive to a woman during her reproductive years.

Toxic Poisonous; capable of producing harm to a living system.

Tragedy of the Commons Degradation or depletion of a resource to which people have free and unmanaged access.

Trophic Relating to nutrition; often expressed in trophic pyramids in which organisms feeding on other systems are said to be at a higher trophic level; an example would be carnivores feeding on herbivores, which, in turn, feed on vegetation.

Turbidity Usually refers to the amount of sediment suspended in an aquatic system.

Uranium 235 An isotope of uranium that when bombarded with neutrons undergoes fission, resulting in radiation and energy. Used in atomic reactors for electrical generation.

Zero Population Growth The condition of a population in which birthrates equal death rates; it results in no growth of the population.

AE Article Review Form

We encourage you to photocopy and use this page as a tool to assess how the articles in **Annual Editions** expand on the information in your textbook. By reflecting on the articles you will gain enhanced text information. You can also access this useful form on a product's book support Web site at **http://www.dushkin.com/ online/.**

NAME: _____ DATE: _____

TITLE AND NUMBER OF ARTICLE: _____

BRIEFLY STATE THE MAIN IDEA OF THIS ARTICLE: _____

LIST THREE IMPORTANT FACTS THAT THE AUTHOR USES TO SUPPORT THE MAIN IDEA:

_____

WHAT INFORMATION OR IDEAS DISCUSSED IN THIS ARTICLE ARE ALSO DISCUSSED IN YOUR TEXTBOOK OR OTHER READINGS THAT YOU HAVE DONE? LIST THE TEXTBOOK CHAPTERS AND PAGE NUMBERS:

_____

LIST ANY EXAMPLES OF BIAS OR FAULTY REASONING THAT YOU FOUND IN THE ARTICLE:

_____

LIST ANY NEW TERMS/CONCEPTS THAT WERE DISCUSSED IN THE ARTICLE, AND WRITE A SHORT DEFINITION:

_____

ANNUAL EDITIONS revisions depend on two major opinion sources: one is our Advisory Board, listed in the front of this volume, which works with us in scanning the thousands of articles published in the public press each year; the other is you—the person actually using the book. Please help us and the users of the next edition by completing the prepaid article rating form on this page and returning it to us. Thank you for your help!

ANNUAL EDITIONS: Environment 00/01

ARTICLE RATING FORM

Here is an opportunity for you to have direct input into the next revision of this volume. We would like you to rate each of the 30 articles listed below, using the following scale:

1. Excellent: should definitely be retained
2. Above average: should probably be retained
3. Below average: should probably be deleted
4. Poor: should definitely be deleted

Your ratings will play a vital part in the next revision. So please mail this prepaid form to us just as soon as you complete it. Thanks for your help!

RATING

ARTICLE

1. The Global Challenge
2. The Nemesis Effect
3. Windows on the Future: Global Scenarios & Sustainability
4. Crossing the Threshold: Early Signs of an Environmental Awakening
5. The Population Surprise
6. The Emperor's New Crops
7. The Technology of Hope: Tools to Empower the World's Poorest Peoples
8. Food Scarcity: An Environmental Wakeup Call
9. King Coal's Weakening Grip on Power
10. The End of Cheap Oil
11. Sunlight Brightens Our Energy Future
12. Bull Market in Wind Energy
13. Planet of Weeds
14. Old Growth for Sale
15. Alien Invasion

RATING

ARTICLE

16. The Organic Revolution
17. Not in My Backyard
18. The Ultimate Survivor
19. The Tragedy of the Commons: 30 Years Later
20. Lessons from the Land Institute
21. Winning the War for the West
22. When the World's Wells Run Dry
23. The Deep Green Sea
24. The Great Climate Flip-Flop
25. Last Tango in Buenos Aires
26. Making Things Last: Reinventing Our Material Culture
27. Crawling Out of the Pipe
28. Recycling Human Waste: Fertile Ground or Toxic Legacy?
29. Lessons from Lake Apopka
30. Earth's Last Gasp?

(Continued on next page)

BUSINESS REPLY MAIL
FIRST-CLASS MAIL PERMIT NO. 84 GUILFORD CT

POSTAGE WILL BE PAID BY ADDRESSEE

**Dushkin/McGraw-Hill
Sluice Dock
Guilford, CT 06437-9989**

ABOUT YOU

Name _____   Date _____

Are you a teacher? ☐   A student? ☐
Your school's name _____

Department _____

Address _____   City _____   State ____   Zip ____

School telephone # _____

YOUR COMMENTS ARE IMPORTANT TO US!

Please fill in the following information:
For which course did you use this book?
_____

Did you use a text with this *ANNUAL EDITION*? ☐ yes ☐ no
What was the title of the text?
_____

What are your general reactions to the *Annual Editions* concept?
_____

Have you read any particular articles recently that you think should be included in the next edition?
_____

Are there any articles you feel should be replaced in the next edition? Why?
_____

Are there any World Wide Web sites you feel should be included in the next edition? Please annotate.
_____

May we contact you for editorial input? ☐ yes ☐ no
May we quote your comments? ☐ yes ☐ no